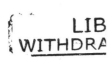

D1135306

METAMAN

GREGORY STOCK
METAMAN

BANTAM PRESS

LONDON · NEW YORK · TORONTO · SYDNEY · AUCKLAND

TRANSWORLD PUBLISHERS LTD
61-63 Uxbridge Road, London W5 5SA

TRANSWORLD PUBLISHERS (AUSTRALIA) PTY LTD
15-25 Helles Avenue, Moorebank, NSW 2170

TRANSWORLD PUBLISHERS (NZ) LTD
3 William Pickering Drive, Albany, Auckland

Published 1993 by Bantam Press
a division of Transworld Publishers Ltd
Copyright © 1993 by Gregory Stock

A catalogue record for this book is available from the British Library

0593 020758

Typeset in Century Old Style by Falcon Graphic Art Ltd
Wallington, Surrey
Printed by Butler & Tanner, Frome, Somerset

To Jeff, my brother and friend.

For encouraging and helping me at critical moments in my life, and for that walk long ago when we, as graduate students, first discussed the concept of a global super-organism.

ACKNOWLEDGEMENTS

WRITING A BOOK, ESPECIALLY one as eclectic as *Metaman*, draws upon the thoughts and efforts of hundreds of people, who each, in turn, draw upon many others. Fittingly, the process of preparing this book about the collaborative nature of the human endeavor has driven home to me, as nothing else could have, the absolute reality of this truth. Not only have the writings and research of others brought me countless insights, but many times I have picked up the telephone and – after a few referrals – reached some distant stranger who has clarified a confusing point for me, deepened an idea I was developing, or informed me of something important I did not know. I cannot now thank these many people individually, so I offer this general thanks in the hope that a few of them will chance upon it and recognize that it is meant for them. Also, I want to thank those in the Wednesday evening seminars of UCLA's Center for the Study of Evolution and the Origin of Life (CSEOL) for creating a free-wheeling environment where I could discuss and present some of the ideas in this book.

As to specific individuals, for their critical comments on various early drafts of my manuscript, I thank Melinda Ballou, Dick Campbell, Heather Campbell, Ann Cole, Charles Corso, Matthew Garrigue, Charles Ide, Kelly Jones, Kim Jones, Angelica Kusar, Debby McCurdy, Gary Novick, Marina Skumanich, Jane Stock, Lois Swanson, Fred Weber and Fareed Zakaria. For their library research, I thank Colleen Campbell and Sonya Weaver, and for preparing various figures, Norm Nason.. For research, comments on the manuscript, and help in tracking down various photographs, I thank Katherine Stock.

For their help, their encouragement, their enthusiasm, their suggestions, and their consistent willingness to talk about the manuscript and figures, I thank Donald Ponturo and Lori Fish. For their many excellent ideas and insights as well as consistently stimulating and challenging discussions, I thank Jeffry Stock, Gene Stock and John Campbell, who also hosted my extended visit to the University of California at Los Angeles while I was working on this book.

Finally, for the unique editorial assistance each provided, I thank Bob Bender, whose suggestions on the balance and focus of the book helped me improve its structure; Joe Spieler, whose in-depth critiques of various versions of my manuscript have forced me to sharpen my ideas; and Lilian McKinstry, whose perceptive comments on the tone and flow of the nearly finished manuscript helped me craft it into its finished form.

The rapid progress true science now makes occasions my regretting sometimes that I was born so soon. It is impossible to imagine the heights to which may be carried, in a thousand years, the power of man over matter.

Benjamin Franklin in a letter to the chemist Joseph Priestley,
8 February 1780.

CONTENTS

A NEW VISION

ILLUSTRATIONS

PREFACE

THIS IS A BOOK ABOUT the nature of life, the evolutionary significance of human civilization, and, most of all, the future of humankind. The book's scope is vast,* but its most important conclusion is extremely simple: humankind, far from being at the brink of cataclysm, is moving towards a bright future. Though humanity faces many problems, a broad historical perspective reveals them to be relatively minor perturbations in the larger trajectory of human civilization. There is little probability that any of today's difficulties will be more than footnotes to the end of this millennium and the beginning of the next. This era is likely to be remembered in the distant future not for its problems but for having pioneered computer intelligence, genetic engineering, and the exploration of space.

We live in extraordinary times filled with undeniable promise, yet pessimism about the human condition abounds even in the developed world. Such feelings arise both from our difficulty in comprehending the rapid, chaotic changes taking place around us, and from the lofty expectations we now have about the quality of human life. Such expectations, however, are a very recent phenomenon; that these high standards exist at all is solid evidence of how far human society has now progressed. Despite today's problems, most of humanity – by measures such as life expectancy, education, personal freedom, individual opportunity, and the satisfaction of basic needs – has never

* *Extensive notes follow the main body of text. These provide references, suggest further readings, explore interesting tangential topics, and expand upon points in the text.*

fared as well. What is truly remarkable is *not* that humanity still tolerates famine and abject poverty, but that for the first time ever it has the tools to eliminate them.

In the past few decades, our understanding of molecular biology, life's evolutionary history, and the potentials of technology has begun to yield a more complete biological interpretation of human society. Civilization is not something separate from nature but an intimate part of it, a living structure that is in many ways life's highest expression. This human-centered entity – purposeful in its behavior and rapidly developing – is beginning to alter the natural environment significantly. But global transformation is not new; the living world has always been dynamic and filled with progressive, large-scale change. The essential challenge today is to understand where this change is leading and how it can be influenced. Accomplishing this requires a fundamentally new concept of ourselves and our environment as well as a willingness to explore the implications of seeing human society in explicitly biological terms.

The metaphor that human civilization is an immense living being has been with us since the time of the ancient Greeks, its form changing as scientific and philosophic vocabularies have shifted.[1] In the twelfth century John of Salisbury, inspired by Aristotle's writings,[2] likened society to a creature in which each class played its God-given role: the king was the head, the Church the soul, judges and governors the eyes and ears, soldiers the hands, and peasants the feet.[3] In the late 1800s, Herbert Spencer in his influential *Principles of Sociology* drew a more detailed analogy between biological organisms and society by describing a 'social organism'.[4] In the early 1900s, Pierre Teilhard de Chardin, a biologist and Jesuit priest, linked evolutionary ideas to the concept of a global social organism and discussed the growing union of humankind in both biological and spiritual terms as an evolutionary transition towards a divine state.[5] He described something he labeled the 'noosphere', which was essentially an evolving collective mind. The great biologist Theodosius Dobzhansky extended Teilhard de Chardin's biological ideas in the 1960s, separating them from their theological framework.[6] These thinkers and others were reaching for a way of understanding the extraordinary phenomenon of human society – its power, its integration, its dynamism. Today, that understanding may be within our grasp.

To avoid any confusion, I want to clarify at this point that the concept of society as a living entity, one in which humans play a part analogous to the cells in an animal's body, is very different from the idea that all life is part of a single living organism – Gaia. The Gaia hypothesis[7] expresses the connectedness of all living things in our planetary ecosystem[8] and provides a poetic image of the earth to stimulate thought about the processes regulating our biosphere.[9] But for all this, the idea can bring little insight about *our* future because it views human civilization as largely irrelevant,[10] certainly not, as proposed here, a momentous step in the evolution of life.

My focus is on humanity: on trying to understand who *we* are and how *we* fit into the larger scheme of life. Comprehending the biological nature and significance of modern civilization is the key to understanding the future of humankind and leads to important new perspectives on the environmental and social concerns of today.[11]

THE NATURE OF METAMAN

. . . by integrations, direct and indirect, there have in course of time been produced social aggregates a million times in size the aggregates which alone existed in the remote past. Here, then, is a growth reminding us, by its degree, of growth in living bodies.

Herbert Spencer, 1875.[12]

1

PLANETARY SUPER-ORGANISM
Glimpses of a Promising Future

WALK THROUGH A LARGE modern city with its towering buildings honeycombed with countless passageways and offices, its asphalt and concrete roadways bustling with hordes of humans, and its subterranean tunnels accommodating power cables, sewers and water mains. Gaze down from your airplane window at the seemingly endless patchwork of fields spread over what was once wilderness. Relax in your living room as images from across the world parade before you on the evening news. Something strange and unlike anything in life's long history on earth is occurring. For more than 3.5 billion years the planet has teemed with life, and now, in a virtual instant, a part of that life has suddenly organized itself into a dense net of activity that is spreading over the globe and consciously reshaping large regions of its surface. We know this structure as human civilization. Certainly what we are witnessing is not biology as usual . . . or is it?

Imagine looking down from the moon at the night side of the earth, pitch dark and invisible except for a brightly lit network of human constructions – luminous cities, highways, canals, telephone and power lines. A faint, speckled web of light would seem to float in space. Some regions of this lacework would form intricate geometric patterns, others would seem random and disconnected. Far from inert, this distant pattern of light would change and grow over the decades, its shimmering fibers forming, extending, and joining in an almost vegetative fashion.

This resemblance to life is not mere happenstance; the thin planetary patina of humanity and its creations is actually a living entity.

It is a 'super-organism',[13] that is, a community of organisms so fully tied together as to be a single living being itself. Instead of referring to this entity using a term already filled with associations, let's start fresh and simply call it 'Metaman', meaning 'beyond, and transcending humans'. This name both acknowledges humanity's key role in the entity's formation and stresses that, though human-centered, it is more than just humanity. Metaman is also the crops, livestock, machines, buildings, communication transmissions and other non-human elements and structures that are part of the human enterprise.

Only a hundred years ago, humanity was still fragmented and living in relatively independent and isolated regions, but, increasingly, humankind is being bound together by a dense network of communication links and trade systems. Today, we are joined not only by

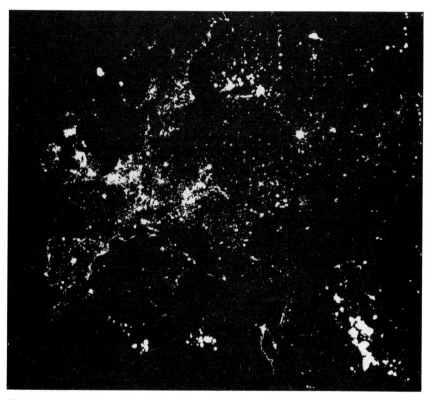

This image of the earth at night includes Europe, Northern Africa and the Middle East. The continents are not obscured by clouds because the image is a mosaic pieced together from different night-time satellite photos. The bright spots in the Middle East are overexposed images of the flames at large natural gas vents. Copyright Woodruff Sullivan, University of Washington, 1985.

obvious physical pathways such as highways, railway and phone lines, but by a myriad hidden connections as well. Without noticing, we walk above pipes and cables, beneath airplane flight corridors and satellite broadcasts, through radio and television transmissions. Indeed, if all communication suddenly became visible because any information or material moving from one place to another left behind a conspicuous threadlike trail, then soon everything and everyone would be ensnared in a dense tangle of fibers.

Modern technology is now drawing humanity into a cohesive entity in which activities are highly interdependent. Many businesses must virtually close down when the phone system fails. People wear clothing made on the other side of the world and eat food grown on distant farms. Agriculture now depends more on heavy equipment, fuels, and fertilizers than the labors of individual farmers. The whole structure of modern society, like an animal's tissues, is continually maintained and renewed through unceasing activity. Left untended, our vast farmlands would soon be parched or overrun by weeds; our highways, buildings and machines would gradually disintegrate.[14] We are accustomed to viewing the world at a human scale, so we tend to see such things as air travel, telecommunications, and even rubbish collection, in terms of how they serve people. But just as the activities of an animal's individual cells mesh to serve the needs of the animal as a whole, human activity has organized itself into large functional patterns that join to sustain the entirety of Metaman.

Metaman has many of the same basic needs an animal has: finding and consuming food, circulating energy and nutrients, replacing damaged and worn out parts, regulating its internal environment, and sensing and responding to changes in its surroundings. Needing nourishment, Metaman extends itself over the planet's surface, consumes what it finds, and circulates these vital materials using transportation systems akin to our own human arteries and veins. At a thousand sites Metaman gnaws the land to devour iron and other minerals, digs down miles to gulp oil, drinks rivers dry, and scoops up animals and plants. Metaman may be unlike any other living thing, but none the less it is feeding, moving, growing and rapidly evolving. Metaman is even likely to reproduce one day – by moving beyond the earth, out into space.

The concept of Metaman explains the fundamental dynamics shaping human society. Some social changes are the inevitable consequence of these larger forces and are essentially beyond our control, others are the product of alterable human influences and are subject to modification. Distinguishing between these two conditions is critical both in defining government priorities and in making decisions about the directions of our own lives.

Today, for example, many countries are being forced to consider whether it is possible for them to thrive over the long term if they isolate themselves economically. Examining the dynamics of Metaman suggests that this is not possible, and that any economic policies which do not allow for expanding international trade are seriously flawed because worldwide economic integration is inevitable. The concept of Metaman further implies that humankind has before it a long and vital future in a world where the natural environment will be managed, where the nation state will lose its dominance in world affairs, where technology will penetrate into virtually all aspects of human life, where human reproduction and biology will be managed, and where local cultural traditions will merge to form a rich global culture.

These developments are inevitable, but the presence of Metaman does not suggest that the detailed shape of society is predetermined. We and our leaders will ultimately decide whether humanity will provide for its children, care for its aged, increase opportunity and justice, and protect the beauty of the natural environment. These are *our* challenges, and understanding the dynamics of Metaman is essential in helping us meet them.

ORGANISMS AND SUPER-ORGANISMS

Although unique in form and substance, Metaman is none the less an extension of the animal kingdom. As a product of human activity, civilization is part of the so-called 'natural' world, not separate from it. The concept of Metaman suggests that the major evolutionary significance of humanity lies in the vast integrated entity it is creating rather than in the power of human beings as individuals. As individuals, humans are not far removed from chimpanzees, but *collectively* we are tremendously distant. Chipping stone into tools and painting images on cave walls were amazing accomplishments growing out of hundreds of millions of years of biological and social evolution. Yet now, in what amounts to but an instant of evolutionary time, we – through Metaman – have left those caves to walk on the moon. What and where will we be after another such instant?

What is most evident about the evolution of life thus far is that living things have become ever more complex. The advance from early bacteria to present plants and animals has not been smooth, however;

it has come about through a succession of distinct transitions, each to a fundamentally new type of living being formed from a union of existing creatures. As a consequence, the living world is a hierarchy of distinct levels. Organisms at each level are not only significantly more complex than ones at previous levels, they are actually composed of living forms from those lower levels.

Transitions to new levels of complexity have been exceedingly rare, having happened only three times in the entire history of the earth. The first was the tight association of biochemicals into primitive

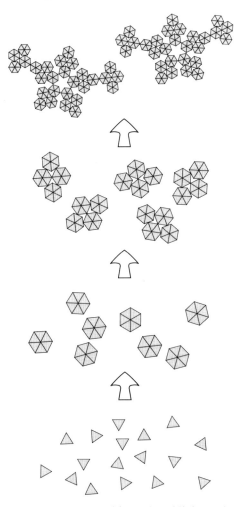

Biological evolution has generated a hierarchy of living things, with organisms at each higher level of complexity originating as a symbiotic union of those from the previous levels. In this schematic of the process, only one type of 'organism' is shown at each level.

bacteria-like cells, the second the combination of these bacteria into complex animal cells, and the third the organization of these larger cells into multicellular organisms.

This hierarchy of evolutionary change is the key to comprehending the extraordinary significance of human civilization, because life is now in the midst of yet a *fourth* evolutionary transition. Certain higher organisms, in particular, humans, are grouping into a social super-organism bound together by technology – Metaman. And there are strong indications that this breakthrough will be every bit as momentous as the previous three have been.

At first glance, it may not be obvious why these four particular evolutionary leaps completely overshadow other changes such as the progression from fish to land animals, or from reptiles to birds. But look more closely. The first leap, which took place more than 3.5 billion years ago, is that from the diverse biochemical reactions of the early earth to bacterial cells.[15] This is the fundamental transition: the passage from the non-living at its most complex to the living at its simplest. It produced the first organisms.[16] A bacterium is simple in form – essentially, just a slurry of biochemicals and aggregates of macromolecules in a membrane sack,[17] but it is alive.

The second transition, some 2.1 billion years ago,[18] was the evolution of higher cells, called eukaryotes. These exist today both as single-celled creatures and as the constituent cells of all plants and animals. Eukaryotic cells, which arose from a symbiotic union of bacteria,[19] are more complex than bacteria and as much as ten thousand times larger. These higher cells reproduce in a more sophisticated way than bacteria, have many separate internal compartments and specialized structures, and house their genetic material within a distinct nucleus.[20]

The next transition, the move to multicellularity some 700 million years ago,[21] opened extraordinary new possibilities by enabling cells to move beyond their individual capacities.[22] In this third phase of life's evolution, cells could begin to specialize and collaborate, thus building and refining much larger forms – *bodies*. How well they succeeded. A tree spreads its leaves to capture the sunlight, a clam filters food from the ocean waters, a frog flicks its tongue at a fly. As diverse as these complex creatures are, though, their fundamental anatomies are still only refinements of that single theme: multicellularity. The distinction between starfish, lizard and human comes from differing arrangements of cells, not from differences in the fundamental properties of cells.

A key to the fourth evolutionary transition – the formation of Metaman – was the evolution of a brain that would enable rich and

The evolution of multicellularity was the biological breakthrough that made possible all the higher life forms of today. Shown here are spherical colonies of a single-celled photosynthetic organism called volvox. Within the loose spheres of cooperating cells are 'daughter' colonies that will eventually break through the wall of their parent colony, swim free, and produce their own daughter colonies, some of which can already be seen.

diverse collaborations among individual humans. Such collaboration has made possible the complex communication and behavior that have been so crucial to the accelerating cultural process that has transformed human life. Now, with the arrival of modern technology, particularly electronic communications, human society is becoming an organic whole with internal dynamics, such as expanding communication and trade, that are the dominant factors in shaping civilization.

Because Metaman appears more 'technological' than 'biological', this fourth evolutionary leap may seem completely different from the previous three. But technology and biology are more closely related than they might at first seem. Consider shells and teeth; although not alive or even made of organic materials, they are part of an animal's body because they were deposited by its cells and are integrated into its form. The same can be said of the machines and other human creations that cement civilization together and are so integral to Metaman's existence; they too are part of Metaman.

Seeing Metaman in a larger evolutionary context suggests that civilization is not some strange aberration likely to self-destruct, but instead a natural continuation of the long evolutionary process. And as with previous major evolutionary breakthroughs, the potential of this newly formed super-organism, which has ushered in a new phase in the history of life, is immense.

Metaman is that part of humanity, its creations[23] and activities that are interdependent – joined together by trade, communications and travel. At the moment, the super-organism is primarily the world's industrialized countries and the urban areas in developing lands, but it is growing and spreading rapidly into the rural regions of the third world that are as yet peripheral to it. Power lines, roads and communication links are pushing into remote areas and joining them to the global network. International trade and investment are linking all countries to the global economy. Television and cinema are sowing their messages ever more widely and reinforcing the emerging global culture. The pattern of Metaman transforms all it touches, and even backcountry villages largely isolated from the workings of this super-organism feel its influences. Although Tanzania is still at the margin of Metaman, a girl born there today has a life expectancy of fifty-three years,[24] three years more than a baby born in the developed world in 1900.[25]

Metaman is presently crystallizing out of the totality of human endeavor that has been building and deepening for millennia throughout the world. And now this super-organism is rapidly transforming the larger human enterprise that bore it. Metaman is spreading by a process reminiscent of moisture freezing on a cold windowpane; countless tiny daggers shoot forward, branching, growing and building on previous crystals as they extend their organized pattern. Metaman, however, has a more complex boundary than the sharp one between water and ice: a continuum of intermediates lies between wild virgin forest and manicured golf green, between an Amazon tribesman with his blowgun and a corporate executive with his pocket cellular phone. Immense in size, discontinuous in form, Metaman is surrounded by communities at all possible stages in the process of joining to it.

 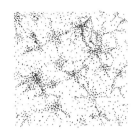 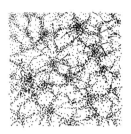

Schematic of the formation of Metaman: scattered human communities arose and became increasingly complex, but remained largely isolated from one another. As these societies grew larger and more complicated, the trade and communication between them proliferated and larger associations of human activity – cities, kingdoms, empires – began to form. With the advent of modern technology, our various connections with one another have become so pervasive that modern societies are no longer functionally distinct, but part of a larger integrated whole – Metaman. Illustration by Lori Fish.

CROSSING THE THRESHOLD

Several centuries ago, the special significance of humankind seemed clear to Western thinkers: the earth was the center of the universe and man was created in God's image. This reassuring belief not only provided people with a sense of their own unique importance, it told them how they fitted into the scheme of the cosmos. In the early 1600s, the Copernican revolution shattered this view by showing that the earth revolved around the sun. Abruptly, humanity was wrenched from its exalted station at the center of the universe[26] and left on a peripheral planet circling one of many stars.

An even greater adjustment awaited humanity when, in 1859, Darwin published his masterpiece on natural selection and evolution, *The Origin of Species*, and provided a believable alternative to the doctrine of divine creation. If humans could evolve by natural processes from animals, then where was the hand of God? And without God's hand, where could human specialness lie?

It is current fashion in some scientific circles to view humans as no more significant than any other life on earth. These voices dismiss, as an illusion inspired by self-serving human pride, the view that we are the crown of evolution. But human specialness is *no illusion*. Although individually we are not a final nor even a very large step in life's continuing evolution, humans are a critical step. Through us, life is making a momentous transition and crossing the threshold to a powerful new level of being.

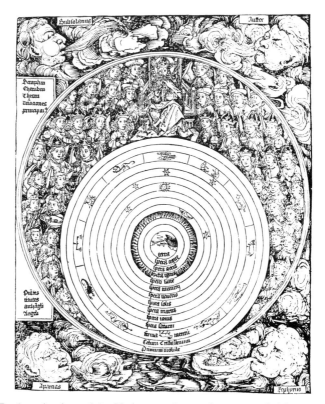

In this Ptolemaic view of the Universe, the earth surrounded by water, air and fire is circled by the moon, sun, planets and stars. All is being watched by a multitude of angels and God on his throne. There is no question about our central place in the cosmos depicted by early Christian schemas. Woodcut from the Nuremburg Chronicle, 1492. Courtesy Bettmann Archive.

Without contradicting our modern understanding of the universe, Metaman's existence affirms humanity's unique and special place among living things. The concept of a human-centered super-organism thus offers a connection between the spiritual issues that are commonly the province of religion and philosophy, and the scientific description of the natural world that so pervades everyday life.

Being part of a super-organism at first might seem somehow incompatible with human individuality, personal freedom and the basic concept of self. But consider the red blood cells in the human body: there is no other place these cells could more successfully bind and release oxygen than suspended in the blood stream, nourished by other organs, and defended by other cells. Without a doubt, red blood cells are in the ideal place to do what they do best and thereby fulfil the natural potential of their individual lives. Their service to the body is a manifestation of their very nature, not an imposed burden, and they are amply repaid because a healthy body, by *its* very nature, provides for their well-being.

In a similar fashion, Metaman provides human beings with an environment that increasingly is enabling us to pursue our chosen activities. As countries become more developed and affluent, personal fulfillment receives ever greater emphasis. Living inside Metaman does not enslave or diminish us as individuals; by sheltering us from the natural environment, bringing us food and water, and technologically extending our powers, Metaman enables us to express our individuality more fully. What Metaman today offers an average person in the developed world would have been the envy of royalty in previous eras. We visit distant lands, listen to the best musicians in the world, watch performances of great actors, talk to people thousands of miles away, and eat fresh fruit in summer and winter alike.

In much of the modern world, today's burden is not one of too little but too much choice.[27] Now, even when we buy food we have to make decisions: forty years ago a typical supermarket in the US had 2,000 items for sale, today it has 18,000.[28] As never before, we each have to set our own goals, choose our own lifestyles, determine our own professions, and find our own beliefs. None of these decisions is easy.

As our possible choices have multiplied, however, our behavior also has become more regulated. We may vacation on some far-away tropical island, but we must none the less pay taxes, build our houses to construction codes, obey traffic signals, and perhaps turn down our music late at night. How significantly, though, do such constraints reduce our freedom? We are now so used to traffic signals that unless we are hurrying we are nearly oblivious to them. They enable us to drive without carefully attending to other vehicles at every intersection, and, in a modern city, life without them – or any of a host of other regulatory devices – would be an ordeal.

Most of the constraints brought by Metaman resemble those imposed on us by our own biology. We do not resent that we can neither breathe underwater nor stare directly at the sun; these restrictions are part of being human and individuals have always known and accepted them. The constraints imposed by Metaman are equally natural mechanisms for ensuring human well-being, in this case within the social realm. Now they too are becoming simply an accepted part of life. A century ago it might have seemed intolerable for a merchant not to be allowed to sell some special patent medicine, or for a teacher not to be able to strike a student who was misbehaving. Today such restrictions seem quite normal. The social milieu of Metaman is becoming the natural environment for humanity, and as Metaman grows and evolves, human life is undergoing a metamorphosis.

SOCIETY TRANSFORMED

With human activity coalescing and quickening, the pace of social change is accelerating. Where is this leading? One thing is virtually certain: the future is going to be far stranger than is generally imagined. When writers look at the future they frequently conjecture fantastic, often improbable, new technologies and superimpose them on social frameworks not very different from those of today. *Star Trek* episodes are filled with 'transporter beams', 'warp speeds', 'intergalactic starships', and 'phasor' weapons, but the human relationships, motivations and interactions of the crew are familiar. Remove the high-technology devices, make the settings terrestrial, and the adventures could be contemporary. Such visions do not capture the radical transformation of human life in store for us. In the next few centuries, human form and experience will change too much for society to remain anything like it is today. Already, the time of routine visual telecommunication, clean and cheap power, bio-engineered plants and animals, computer-synthesized realities, and even human-machine hybrids is beginning.

Change surrounds us; to see it you need only compare your neighborhood to what it used to be, or watch a few old movies and television shows. These changes, however, hold a special significance because they are part of a much larger transformation. We are active participants in a major evolutionary transition that will alter human society more completely than anything previous. The emergence of Metaman signals the beginning of a new and fundamentally different era.

If Benjamin Franklin could return to life now, some two centuries after his death, he would be amazed by today's technology, but he would find society quite comprehensible. Not only do merchants and politicians today have concerns similar to those of his era; people themselves have remained essentially the same: we still get ill, we still marry and have children, we still grow old and die. The underlying fabric of society is largely unchanged. If Franklin moved forward another two centuries, however, society would no longer be so recognizable. By then, the basic anchors of human experience – aging, the senses, the body, childbirth – will be greatly altered. It is likely that machines will be intelligent participants in a closely knit global environment in which people's mental and physical capacities are enhanced by bio-machine interfaces, fetuses are nurtured in hospital incubation tanks, and humans are enjoying greatly extended life-spans.

Such possibilities sound fantastical, but they are practically inevitable extrapolations of the scientific and technological advances of recent decades. What is human society going to be like a hundred, a thousand, or ten thousand years from now? What are humans themselves going to be like? Consider, for example, human–machine hybrids. This powerful manifestation of the deepening union of humanity and technology is science fiction no longer; it is here, now. Already, tiny electrodes that can receive radio signals from a small external sound analyzer are being surgically implanted in the inner ears of more than a thousand patients a year.[29] These listening devices are so effective that some implant recipients who were previously deaf have learned to understand some 90 per cent of the words they hear; far from deaf, they can converse over the telephone. Nor is this example isolated, the miniaturization of electronics is revolutionizing medical prostheses broadly. Today, electronic and mechanical devices are used to treat physical impairments; tomorrow they may enhance normal functioning.

The changing character of technological advance accompanying the emergence of Metaman is even better illustrated by biotechnology, a field born only a few decades ago. Progress has been extraordinary: the structure of DNA was determined only forty years ago[30] and a gene first decoded only in 1977;[31] yet biologists are already engineering plants and animals that are 'transgenic', which means that functional genes from other species have been spliced into their genomes. There are now mice that are quite literally part human. Because they contain human genes, such animals are becoming enormously important for the study of human diseases; indeed, it is the prospect of medical progress that is likely to overcome public resistance to genetic engineering. But fighting disease is just a first step; molecular biology is moving so rapidly that engineering the human form, conquering aging, and designing new animals are no longer absurdities. Increasingly, the question is 'when', not 'if'.

Progress is equally as rapid in many other technologies: computers that can talk, understand simple spoken sentences, and even mimic intelligent human interaction will soon be here. How different the world will feel when humans and machines routinely communicate verbally: when a television set knows what its viewers like to watch

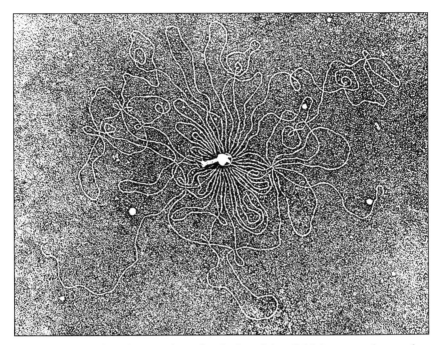

A thread of DNA – the genetic molecule found in all higher organisms – has spilled from the T2 virus at the center of this 40,000-magnification electron-microscope image. This DNA, which is some one hundred times the length of the virus itself, is a few dozen microns long – about a quarter the width of a human hair. Courtesy of Albrecht Kleinschmidt, University of Ulm.

and tells them about programs they might find appealing; when an electronic organizer verbally reminds a person of an appointment; when a computerized medical advisor kept in the home can listen to a person's medical questions and draw upon an accumulated medical history in answering them. Such things are dramatically going to change us, society, the human relationship with nature, and even basic human values. The possibilities for human reproduction, for example, are already beginning to expand. We are now living in a world where a woman using *in vitro* fertilization can bear a child after menopause or even give birth to her own granddaughter,[32] where a couple can have a baby to provide a bone-marrow transplant for another of their children,[33] and where a three-month-premature baby weighing only a pound can be kept alive.[34]

OUR PASSAGE TO A NEW ERA

Humanity's future is filled with amazing possibilities, but many people feel only a grim foreboding about what lies ahead. Visions of uncontrolled global warming, exhausted natural resources, a blighted environment, overpopulation and famine, burgeoning cancer from toxic wastes, and even nuclear war make them wonder how humankind will survive at all, let alone prosper. There is no question that real issues lie behind these fears, but just how seriously will such present-day concerns affect the future?

Some of them, population growth for instance, promise to have a great impact on society; others, however, are unlikely to have more than a minor effect on humanity. For example, though cancer causes great individual suffering, the cancer threat posed by pollutants and pesticides is a relatively minor *social* problem, particularly when considered in historical perspective. Actuarial calculations show that entirely eliminating all cancer caused by exposure to environmental pollutants, food additives, *and* nuclear materials would increase average human life expectancy by less than twelve weeks,[35] a minuscule fraction of the twenty-five-year rise in life expectancy since 1900 in the developed world.[36] Considering that cancer caused by cigarette smoking reduces average life expectancy by a full year,[37] clearly the most important cancer problem today is not from involuntary exposure to man-made carcinogens. These barely raise overall human mortality above 'natural' levels.

It is clear that human activity is now significantly perturbing the planetary environment, but again, it is important to put the magnitude of these influences in perspective. They may well affect the quality of life we and our children enjoy, but the environmental and climatic changes of today are not a global catastrophe and do not threaten humanity's survival. This is not a mere quibble; there is an enormous difference between changes that might sweep away humankind and ones that threaten only to make life unnecessarily difficult for the next few generations. When looking at an issue such as global warming, we should keep in mind that only 18,000 years ago Canada and northern Europe lay beneath glaciers more than a mile thick. With the arrival of these harsh conditions, primitive humans did not perish; they retreated. Our planetary environment is not an unchanging one that Metaman is wrenching away from some idealized 'natural' state; the earth has repeatedly undergone great and sometimes very rapid change.[38] What is different now, however, is Metaman's ability to buffer humankind from these changes, both

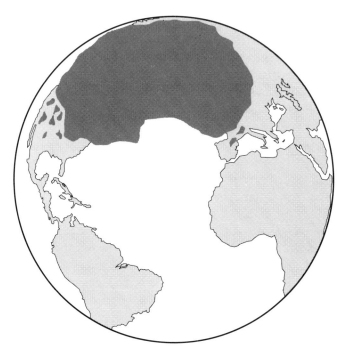

Maximum Extent of Glaciers
in Last Ice Age

Climatic changes today are small compared to recent periods of glaciation, when massive ice sheets reached into the American Midwest, and Chicago was covered by a mile of ice. Shown here is the maximum southern extension of the glaciers of the last Ice Age. Peak glaciation lasted from 22,000 to 14,000 years ago; by 10,000 years ago glaciers had retreated to near present levels.[39]

'natural' ones and those that are of its own making.

Ultimately, the most solid justification for environmental action is provided not by grim prophesies of impending global catastrophe but by basic concern about deterioration in the *quality* of human life. At this time of Metaman's formation, numerous problems threaten to degrade the lives of the next few generations substantially and need to be addressed effectively. Must humankind exhaust the earth's reserves of fossil fuels, erode its rich topsoil, empty its precious aquifers, cut down its beautiful forests, and otherwise despoil our environment?

At the root of these and other problems is excessive population growth, a phenomenon that many people view as nearly intractable because it seems to hinge on the basic human drive to reproduce. This pessimistic appraisal of the possibilities for family planning are wide of the mark; human reproduction patterns are already in the process of changing dramatically. In the developed world, birth rates have fallen enough in the past century nearly to halt population growth,[40] and in less-developed lands, birth rates have dropped by about a third since 1950.[41] The fall in death rates brought by introducing public health measures and modern medicine to these regions, however, has been even more precipitous, so population has burgeoned.[42]

There is no question that humanity will eventually reduce its population growth; birth rates are already dropping. What is at issue is whether strong family-planning efforts will occur now, or only after worsening overpopulation has made the issue more concrete by bringing widespread famine and pestilence that thrust the problem into sharper political focus. With international assistance for family-planning programs as yet very low,[43] and unmet demand for these programs in less-developed lands very high,[44] bringing human birth rates down sharply may be surprisingly easy once population growth becomes a high international priority. Precisely when this will happen, however, remains uncertain, so stabilizing human population may yet prove a difficult and painful passage for humankind. None the less, within several generations the transition is virtually certain to be completed.

The new thinking demanded by Metaman's emergence is particularly well illustrated in the environmental arena. Metaman is a potent, vital entity that is growing rapidly and playing an increasingly influential role in the planetary ecosystem. It is of paramount importance for us to understand that Metaman *will* remake the biosphere; we have no choice about this. Do what we will, within a few centuries as many as half of today's species are likely to be extinct,[45] and the planetary distribution of those remaining will be dramatically changed. It may be some consolation that most of these vanishing species are insects with small ranges restricted to the tropics, but none the less the list of endangered species for which we feel a deeper affinity is large and growing – the black rhino, African elephant, whooping crane, mountain gorilla.

It may be difficult to face, but what still remains of the wild and pristine natural world will be transformed,[46] and *we*, as part of Metaman, will be the architects. The choice now before humanity is simple: will we be deliberate in reshaping our environment, or careless? Attempting to minimize human influences will not be enough to enable us to avoid the dilemmas that come with our new powers. Such an approach to change can slow its pace but not halt the broad planetary transformation underway. If we accept the reality that massive changes to the biosphere are inevitable, however, we can begin to develop strategies to channel that change actively towards outcomes we find desirable.

Often, attempts by individuals to solve global problems lead to direct approaches that ignore realities such as people's prejudices or their resistance to change. Metaman cannot ignore these realities, because it contains and reflects them. Naturally, its solutions are indirect and subtle. For example, it is the internal dynamics of Metaman, not human rationality, that have blunted the danger of global nuclear war – the ultimate threat.

So completely does military conflict pervade history that war seems almost an unavoidable product of human nature, but now the threat of global cataclysm is in sharp retreat. This development goes far beyond the sudden end of the Cold War; regional conflicts since the Second World War have been frequent, but the nearly five decades of relative peace since 1945 is the longest period since the Roman Empire without a direct war between major powers.[47] It is not mere chance that we are now in the midst of this long peace, powerful forces are at work.

The growth of international trade, the expanding reach of global communications, the blending of disparate cultures, and the increasing interdependence of nations are working against military conflict. And because these aspects of Metaman's ongoing development are re-inforcing one another, the current period of relative peace may long continue. The national economies of Western Europe are becoming so interwoven that the notion of a war there may soon seem as absurd as that of war between states of the US. In fact, strong interdependencies are rapidly spreading, so if nothing triggers a global war within the next few decades, one may *never* occur again.

As humanity leaves behind the threat of nuclear cataclysm, it is time for us to extend our gaze towards a more certain future. Today, humanity is better equipped than ever to deal with the challenges it is facing. Already, accelerating technological progress has produced the essential technologies to address the most important underlying global issues of the present – population growth and the rapid consumption of fossil fuels.[48] But technology alone cannot guarantee humanity's well-being; social mechanisms to direct and broadly apply technologies are also needed. This is what worries people. No wonder; at times government policies and individual choices seem so shortsighted as to make one wonder whether humans, as a species, are capable of setting aside their own immediate self-interests long enough to surmount global problems.

Understanding Metaman, however, reveals that hope for the future need not lie in some miraculous transformation of human nature. As a developing super-organism, human society has begun to regulate itself on the vast scale necessary to ensure its survival and vitality. Individual humans, though still actively pursuing their own immediate self-interests, are doing so within an ever tighter envelope of social controls. Restrictions on toxic-waste disposal, emissions standards for cars, a ban on CFCs – these and other efforts are not the result of individuals responding to immediate danger, but a collective response to chronic, distant threats. This response is the key to our future. There is no denying that we are living in tumultuous times, but this era of Metaman's birth is not an ending: humanity's future stretches far ahead and is filled with promise.

2

THE BIRTH OF METAMAN
Extending Life's Patterns

THE SCALE OF EVOLUTION is vast; it is hard enough to comprehend processes spanning thousands, much less millions and billions of years. To appreciate life's 3.5 billion-year history on earth, it is helpful to look at each 100 million years as if they were a single 'story year'. Doing this, life is now in its mid-thirties. It is robust and seemingly secure at present, but unless it one day moves beyond this planet of its birth, life must eventually perish when the sun finally exhausts its fuel.[49] By then, however, life will have reached the ripe old age of eighty-five, and a lot can happen in *fifty* years.

Life's origins were humble. It was born on the third planet of an unexceptional star near the fringes of the 200-billion-star cluster that is our Milky Way galaxy – one of some 100 billion galaxies in the universe. Our solar system condensed from a cloud of swirling gaseous debris left by explosions of previous stars, so our sun is at least a second-generation star.[50] In fact, were the earth not formed from stellar debris we would not be here because the carbon, oxygen, iron, phosphorous and other elements that are crucial to life as we know it are the products of atomic fusion within those long-dead stars. It is more than poetry to say we are children of the stars: the elements that make up our bodies were formed inside those blazing infernos.

After the formation of the solar system, the earth remained lifeless for nearly a billion years, ten years in our story. The planet's molten mantle took five or six of those years to form a thin solid layer on its surface, and for several more years, while volcanoes spewed lava and belched fumes into dense, swirling clouds of dust and gasses, giant

The Universe is inconceivably large. This photograph, made through the 4-meter telescope at the Kitt Peak observatory in Arizona, shows not stars but a cluster of almost one hundred galaxies, each containing billions of stars. So distant is this galactic cluster (Abell 2151) that the light from it, travelling 186,000 miles each second, takes 360 million years to reach the earth. Courtesy of N. Sharp, National Optical Astronomy Observatories.

comets and meteors intermittently crashed through this fragile new crust and vaporized any nascent seas.[51] But slowly, as the planet cooled, clouds of steam condensed into hot oceans beneath a heavy atmosphere. Lightning flashed, solar radiation beat down from space,[52] the earth eroded under torrential rains, and the seas became a cauldron of diverse organic molecules.[53] Then, about thirty-five years ago, this vital broth of reacting biochemicals bore life[54] – the first primitive bacteria.

During life's first few 'years', the earth's oceans and lagoons teemed with a bacterial scum thriving under a humid, oxygenless atmosphere. But just ahead was a major adolescent crisis: pollution of the planet's atmosphere. When blue-green bacteria evolved photosynthesis, they began releasing a waste product, oxygen, so reactive it could destroy unprotected cells. This gas, just as it quickly discolors the exposed surface of a cut apple, decimated many early bacterial communities. Free oxygen, however, could not accumulate significantly in the

Mound-shaped structures called stromatolites are formed by the progressive build-up of minerals deposited in matlike layers by growing bacterial communities. The oldest known fossils, they have been identified in geological formations 3.5 billion years old. Both modern and fossil stromatolites about a foot and a half high are shown here. Top: a living stromatolite reef at Shark Bay, Australia; bottom: a fossilized stromatolite reef in 2.3 billion-year-old formations near Cape Province, South Africa. Photos courtesy of J. William Schopf, UCLA.

atmosphere until all iron and other reactive minerals on the planet had been oxidized.[55] Essentially, only after the planet had 'rusted', a process that was completed by life's mid-teens, could oxygen's atmospheric concentration rise to what it is today.[56]

Oxygen brought more than destruction; it also created extraordinary new possibilities for life: the 'aerobic' metabolism that evolved to use this high-energy molecule was a powerful new way for cells to fuel their activities.[57] This metabolic process gave living things access to the same store of energy released as heat when wood burns.

By this point in its teens, life's long phase of biochemical evolution was largely over; almost all present-day metabolic chemistry had evolved. Life's second transition – the evolution of the complex single-celled organisms called eukaryotes – was therefore an organizational advance rather than a chemical one.[58] These new cells were more complex in form and more versatile in behavior than bacteria. The *Amoeba*, for instance, can both swim freely and glide along surfaces, and lives by enveloping and devouring bacteria.

As life approached twenty-eight, eukaryotic cells began to form multicellular organisms – the third of life's major organizational transitions.[59] The potential of these new living forms, called metazoans, proved immense, and soon a multitude of soft-bodied animals, some unlike anything living today, had evolved. This was just the beginning, though; by life's thirtieth birthday, animals with shells and skeletons had arrived and flourished. With scaffolding and armor, cells could form complex and powerful new forms.[60]

At this juncture, some five years ago in our story, life was still confined to the water. But soon, multicellular organisms pushed ashore. Plants moved onto the land some four and a half years ago and created a rich environment that animals would enter only a few months later. These first land animals were amphibian; they spent much of their lives on dry land but needed to return to the water to reproduce. The reptiles, with eggs that would not dry out in the air, had no such need. Appearing three years ago, they were so successful that they dominated the land within a year. Then, just eight months ago, the reptiles' reign ended abruptly. A large asteroid struck the earth at this time[61] and raised such a cloud of dust[62] that it eliminated about two thirds of all species, including the mighty dinosaurs. Called the Cretaceous extinction, this catastrophe presented a rich opportunity for any surviving organisms. Mammals, small warm-blooded animals that had evolved from reptiles only ten months earlier, stepped in to fill the void. Our distant primate ancestors entered the scene less than six months ago, the earliest hominid (*Homo habilis*) only two weeks ago.

Dinosaurs, dominating the planet's landmasses for some 150 million years preceding the Cretaceous extinction, ranged from mild herbivores to agile, aggressive carnivores like the warm-blooded, 9-feet-long Deinonychus. Shown here as an artist's rendition (top) and as a mounted skeleton (bottom), there can be little doubt as to how deadly its sickle-like talons must have been in an attack.[63] Courtesy of John Ostrom, Peabody Museum of Natural History, Yale University.

Late yesterday afternoon witnessed the arrival of the earliest *Homo sapiens.*

This morning was hectic. Less than an hour ago dawn broke, and with it came agriculture. Writing appeared about a half-hour later. The last twenty-five minutes have recorded the rise and fall of empires, the rapid proliferation of humans, and the technological advances that are now so changing life on the planet. The glory of Rome began eleven minutes ago and ended three minutes later. James Watt built the steam engine a minute and a half ago. And in the past thirty seconds, with human collaboration beginning to assume global dimensions, Metaman was born.[64] The development was momentous. When Neil Armstrong walked on the moon only eight seconds ago, life – through Metaman – had taken its first step towards the stars and begun a new phase in its evolution.

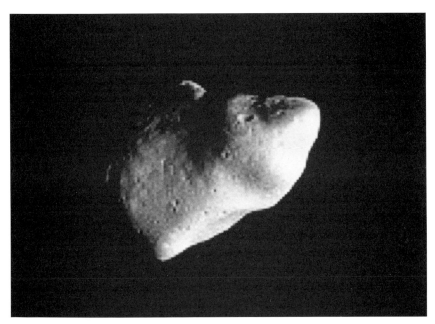

Gaspra, which hurtled past the Galileo spacecraft at 5 miles per second in the vicinity of Jupiter in 1991, is the first asteroid ever photographed at close range. This photo was taken from a distance of 3000 miles.[65] Gaspra rotates once every seven hours and is estimated to be about 12 miles long and 8 miles wide – about the same size as the meteor that crashed into the earth and caused the massive Cretaceous extinction some 65 million years ago.[66] Courtesy of NASA.

Although it may be hard to imagine what even the next 'minute' will bring, the morning has barely begun. A whole day lies ahead, and then another, and another, and another. Even while reshaping its birthplace, life, robust and still shy of forty, has begun to look towards the stars. It may be too early to see how the newly formed Metaman will spread beyond our solar system, or where its seeds will fall and into what they will sprout, but it is not too early to surmise that one day Metaman will move out into the galaxy.

OF LIVING THINGS AND HUMAN INTUITION

With any tightly linked group of organisms, identifying the functioning unit is often paradoxical. One way of seeing why Metaman – our strange amalgam of concrete, humans, computer chips, and various plants and animals – is a super-organism rather than merely an elaborate 'social grouping' of humans, is to look at another, far simpler grouping of organisms – a termite colony. Is the individual insect or the colony itself the important biological entity? At first glance, the individual termites seem to be as much 'individuals' as any other insects are, but close observation of a termite colony reveals a social organization so extraordinary that it is reminiscent of an organism. A colony of the termite *Macrotermes*, for instance, may endure for eighty years or more, despite the fact that few of its termites will survive even two years.[67] The several million termites constituting such a colony are differentiated into physically distinct castes whose relative numbers are regulated by chemical secretions that cause larvae to develop into workers, soldiers, nymphs or queens according to the colony's changing needs. A *Macrotermes* colony communally cares for its larvae, maintains the temperature and humidity of its nest, and shares food grown in humid subterranean fungus gardens tended by workers. Moreover, other than the single queen (and king), none of the termites reproduce. In essence, the termite colony is the real 'individual' here, and the scurrying termites but 'cells' within an insect 'super-organism'.[68]

How this termite super-organism manages to leave 'offspring' is particularly interesting. The colony intermittently hatches a swarm of winged queens, which disperse like seeds. Each queen that survives her nuptial flight alights, sheds her wings, lays eggs, and begins to build the foundations of a new colony. Should this new colony take root, the queen's many offspring will wall her into a special under-ground cell where she will swell to about the size of a person's thumb and lie immobile for up to a decade producing as many as 30,000 eggs a day.[69] Thus, each termite colony itself is the biological 'individual' that grows and reproduces.

With most animals there is little ambiguity as to what is the relevant biological entity. The creatures are not part of a complex social group, and the intricate interdependencies of the cells that make up their bodies are invisible to us. But were we able to see into the body of an animal such as a mouse at very high magnification, we would almost certainly find it as confusing as a termite colony. Absorbed in watching individual cells play out their own life dramas, we might never notice the higher mouse pattern they formed.

We face just this problem with our perception of Metaman. We are absorbed with occurrences at our own scale, not with those at the global level of the super-organism. With a bit of effort, though, we can transcend our relatively limited vision and life-span to view the large integrated patterns that make Metaman a being in itself.

This large Termitary in Australia is some 18 feet tall and probably houses more than a million termites.[70] Such colonies were first recognized as 'organisms' by the naturalist William Wheeler, who coined the term 'super-organism' to describe them. Photo by G. Hill, National Museum, Melbourne.

Living organisms from bacteria to elephants all share certain general qualities: each organism is made up of countless specialized parts united into a cohesive whole.[71] Each uses energy and materials to fuel its activities, maintain itself, and grow. Each senses and responds purposefully to what is going on around it. Each has a reproductive strategy that enables the species to persist and evolve.

Generally, of course, we need no such list to recognize life. The subtlest of signs is usually enough to tell us that something is highly organized internally and can behave purposefully to perpetuate itself. If one dark night you were walking through dense woods and heard a soft, deep snarl, you would know immediately you were in the presence of something alive, and might also guess it had a pretty active metabolism. We are experts at detecting all relevant life around us because the lives of our ancestors so depended on that talent.

We are less astute when life assumes a form beyond our experience. Here we are constrained by the limits of our knowledge and understanding, as well as our senses. Until 1674, when Antoni van Leeuwenhoek's microscope revealed the 'animalcules' in water,[72] people were completely unaware of the teeming 'invisible' life around them. Now, we are convinced that germs are everywhere, and combat them daily from kitchen sink to underarm. Or think again of the termite colony; only by virtue of the painstaking observations of generations of naturalists can we see it as a 'super-organism'.[73]

Recently, with a new perspective made possible by such products of technology as photographs from space and rapid global communication, humanity has begun to glimpse Metaman. That our intuition does not tell us that Metaman is a living entity is hardly surprising; after all, intuition alone would tell us the world is flat. Metaman is too diffuse, too dynamic, too discontinuous, and too large to recognize easily. Its parts, however, need not touch or even lie close together to be closely joined: individual telephones appear to be separate objects but are part of one global net. A bank's local branches *look* independent, but are firmly attached to each other and to the rest of the economy. Careful examination reveals that Metaman possesses each of the essential qualities found in all living things.

THE FUNDAMENTALS OF LIFE

A detailed look at the anatomy of any organism reveals a basic pattern: a host of specialized parts deftly woven into one functional whole.[74] A human being has diverse cell types, tissues, and organs, each with its own specific job; a termite colony has different castes integrated together. A piece of coral, however, does not have specialized parts; cut it in half and the countless nearly identical polyps that make it up will not be affected. Thus a coral is not a super-organism, and neither are the many social groupings of higher animals – flocks of birds, herds of antelope, and schools of fish. Only humans, among higher animals, have become significantly specialized within a social context.[75]

Human specialization is unique in that it is almost entirely behavioral. Being learned, it is both more flexible and more powerful than that occurring elsewhere in the animal world. A termite colony has a soldier caste, but human society can rapidly train and equip an army and then demobilize it when danger passes. The specialization and division of tasks has now extended into almost every human activity – a sports team, for example, depends not only on players and coaches, but on accountants, contract lawyers, publicists, travel agents, an-

The first views of our planet from space offered us all a new perspective on humankind's shared future. This earthrise was witnessed by the astronauts of Apollo 8 in 1968. Courtesy of NASA.

nouncers, physicians, trainers, talent scouts, and others.

Specialization within Metaman begins with individual humans but is even more apparent with equipment and organizations. Computer chips, for example, are inexpensive and reliable because organizations devoted exclusively to these devices make them by the hundreds of millions in specially designed factories. Extreme specialization of this sort would not be possible unless diverse activities could be effectively tied together by sophisticated distribution, transportation, communication and financial systems.[76]

Specialization and integration lead to dependencies at every organizational level. A city cut off from the outside would soon grind to a halt; a manufacturer deprived of its network of suppliers would have to halt production; an individual cut off from society would be hard pressed to find food. Biologically, humans have changed little since the beginning of civilization, so *theoretically* we could get along quite well on our own.[77] But socially, people have changed so much that most of us – especially those living in urban areas – could not survive in the wilds without modern devices. What do most people know about catching animals, recognizing edible plants, or even finding their way about while still protecting themselves from the elements? Today, if a plane went off course, lost power, and the crew bailed out in remote tropical jungle, it would be considered remarkable if they somehow managed to stay alive for a year and hike back to civilization.

Even if everyone knew how to survive in the wilderness, though, famine would be massive without the technology and division of labor within Metaman. The world just does not have enough game-filled forest or fertile farmland to support five and a half billion hunter-gatherers . . . or subsistence farmers.

Every living thing converts energy into internal activity, and raw material into its own internal form. This is basic to all life because any creature must not only fuel its activities, but also repair and maintain itself. Animals eat the tissue of living things and use the sugars, amino acids, and other molecules therein; Metaman feeds directly on both living and non-living materials. Its appetite is staggering. Each year it consumes energy equivalent to some forty trillion pounds of coal – eight thousand pounds for every human being on the planet.[78] Metaman also ingests annually some 1.6 trillion pounds of iron, 1.2 trillion pounds of wheat, 200 billion pounds of gypsum, 205 billion pounds of fish, and equally large quantities of many other materials.[79] After extracting raw materials from the environment, Metaman processes them to make the plastics, concretes, metals, ceramics, and other compounds used in its numerous constructions. Indeed, the entire process of consuming raw materials, converting them into products that are transported to where they can be used, and eventually discarding wastes, is the equivalent of digestion, circulation, and excretion within animals.

Although Metaman will continue to improve the efficiency with which it uses energy,[80] it will always need massive energy supplies to drive its expanding metabolism. But the earth's fossil-fuel reserves are finite and are being consumed. Even if the threat of global warming does not soon push Metaman to turn away from these fuels, at current consumption rates, oil and natural gas will be gone a century from now and coal will be depleted a few centuries later.[81] Fortunately, advancing technology has provided feasible alternatives to fossil fuels, including renewable energy sources such as solar power, wind and biomass fuels. Thus, Metaman's challenge for the coming century is not to discover new energy sources, but to effect a smooth, large-scale metabolic shift towards the alternative energy technologies already identified.

To survive, living things must sense and respond purposefully to relevant changes in their surroundings. Responses, however, need only be flexible and sophisticated enough to meet the challenges being faced. Some organisms must respond rapidly, others may do so quite gradually. Faced with rapacious predators, a rabbit must identify subtle sounds and scents and react quickly, whereas to avoid drying out at low tide, a mussel on a rocky shore need only be able to tell when it is out of water and slowly close its shell.

Metaman, too, is aware of the crucial aspects of its environment and is responding to them in its own self-interest. This 'awareness' does not require what we think of as consciousness, but merely a capacity to interpret sensory input. Countless non-biological innovations from radio telescopes to X-ray machines have enormously extended human senses, and this is only a hint of the vast sensory capabilities of Metaman. It observes the growth of a country's population, watches the concentration of carbon dioxide in the atmosphere rise, and traces the shape of an oil deposit miles beneath the ground. Continually monitoring both itself and its surroundings, Metaman uses what are essentially complex 'sense receptors' – large clusters of machines and people working together to collect, analyze and transmit information. One such cluster, the US Weather Bureau, employs 5,000 people at 300 weather stations and uses various communication equipment, computers, and weather satellites to keep track of weather patterns.

The weather bureau is only a preview, though; Metaman's senses are rapidly becoming more penetrating, more sensitive, and more far-reaching. Until the mid-1970s, the extent of global deforestation could be gauged only by contacting forestry officials in as many relevant regions as possible and assembling their assessments into what was, at best, a blurry and incomplete picture. Today, deforestation is computed from direct measurements of the changing vegetation patterns revealed in satellite photographs.[82] Such 'vision' is neither yours nor mine: it is collective; it is Metaman's. Humans can comprehend its complex images only after they have been processed and interpreted. We routinely use economic indicators, weather reports, atlases and census tabulations with little thought about the extensive underlying processes of Metaman required to prepare them, but even mapping the world has been a staggering collective accomplishment.

As each of us responds individually to fragments of this huge stream

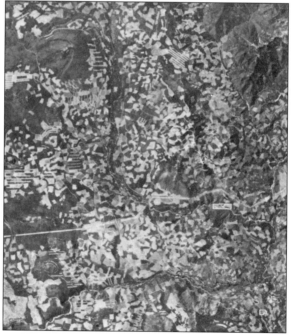

Opposite: *Sophisticated monitoring of our planet is now becoming routine. These satellite images of the Amazon basin north of Manaus (top) and of the Mount Hood National Forest in the Pacific Northwest of the United States (bottom) are typical of these regions and show deforestation clearly. Exposed soil in recently deforested areas appears white, regrowing forest shows up as light grey, and undisturbed ancient forest is dark grey. People in temperate lands often point to the destruction of tropical forests and yet ignore the destruction in their own backyards. Measurements show that less than 15 per cent of the pre-colonial Amazon rainforest has at present been destroyed; in comparison, 90 per cent of the old growth in the Pacific Northwest of America is gone yet clearcutting – even on public lands – continues.[83] Courtesy of NASA.*

of information, our responses couple and merge to create the large-scale adjustments that constitute *Metaman's* integrated response to information. Viewing social changes merely as trends in human lifestyles misses their larger significance: they are both Metaman's internal developmental adjustments and its adaptive responses to the immense changes taking place in the world – changes that are often the product of this super-organism's own activity.

A good example of such a response is the increasing awareness of, and reaction to, environmental issues such as global warming and ozone depletion. Detection of these effects is based on a huge global effort,[84] and Metaman's incipient response is also global. A surge of concern rises through societies throughout the world. Newspapers and magazines print stories about impending dangers, environmentalists push for government action, specialists appear on television, diverse scientific and political groups come together to confront the issue, politicians hold international conferences,[85] businesses tout the efforts they undertake. No single group of individuals is coordinating this response; it is a broad reaction bubbling up from many independent sources. Moreover, tangible changes in behavior are already occurring. The anticipated halt in the manufacture and use of ozone-destroying chlorofluorocarbons (CFCs) will reduce ozone depletion substantially and moderate – by some 15 per cent – the growth of our atmosphere's greenhouse capacity.[86]

Such changes, although they unfold much more slowly than the hectic pace of our own lives and show many twists and turns, are a large-scale response to sensory input about a potential threat. When seen from a perspective of many decades, Metaman's responses to such challenges are as directed and purposeful as the behavior of familiar organisms. To expect Metaman to make a rapid transition away from fossil fuels would be to expect this immense planetary super-organism to move at *our* pace rather than its own.

AN EVOLVING METAMAN

As we have seen, Metaman, though unusual in its form, composition and behavior, possesses the essential qualities of all living things: it shows extensive internal specialization, persists as an integrated whole, has an active metabolism, grows, evolves, senses and responds. Furthermore, Metaman's current gropings towards space suggest it will one day even reproduce, extending its form out into our solar system and beyond.[87]

For Metaman, however, reproduction is not a requirement for evolution; at this very moment, Metaman is evolving rapidly by reshaping itself through internal replacement and growth. Its full evolutionary potential can best be grasped by reflecting on the nature of its constituent parts. There are two general types: those that are *biotic* – the humans, crops and domesticated animals of Metaman – and those that are *abiotic* – the various technological constructions fashioned from metals, plastics, concrete, and other inorganic materials.

A union between far simpler biotic and abiotic materials occurred long ago,[88] when simple soft-bodied animals began to build bones and shells from the minerals being secreted by their cells.[89] This ancient expansion of the building materials available to life made possible a skeletal support system and allowed the evolutionary move from primitive worms to giant dinosaurs, soaring eagles, and human consciousness itself. And yet this previous union was paltry compared to the one now underway between the exceedingly complex biotic and abiotic materials of today. The eventual results of this present union are likely to lead to forms that transcend both human beings and today's computers by even more than we transcend the primitive worms and skeletons of the past.

3

A FUSION OF TECHNOLOGY AND BIOLOGY
The Non-human Constituents of Metaman

PEOPLE PLAY THE CENTRAL role in Metaman, but not all the other parts of this super-organism are merely passive and structural like the hair, teeth and bone of an animal's body, or the tunnels and hardened earth mounds of a termite colony. Various non-human components play active, dynamic roles in this planetary creature.

Most people get along today with only a slight understanding of the machines they use. Presented with a box of parts, few of us could assemble a clock, a telephone, or even a tumbler lock. With increasingly complicated electronic parts replacing mechanical ones, even when we do understand a device we can rarely fix it when it breaks. We routinely encounter so many complex devices that we cannot try to understand how each of them works. Most people have neither the time nor knowledge to learn the theory behind a microwave or a VCR, and, in truth, don't even care. Learn how a VCR works? It's hard enough to figure out how to operate all the controls. Machines are becoming just another familiar part of our surroundings, their inner workings as inscrutable as those of a budding rose, a sparrow's egg, or a bolt of lightning.

A 'machine' in its most general sense is any man-made device built for some purpose – whether a spoon, a book, a road or a computer. So routine is our association with them that it is natural to see machines simply in terms of the immediate services they provide, but machines are a new class of entity and have demonstrated an extraordinary ability to proliferate. That machines owe their existence to humanity does not mean these devices have no significance of their own.

Consider one of our favorites, the car. From a human perspective, its history is simple. People invented cars in order to move more easily from place to place, refined and improved them better to serve our needs and manufactured them in enormous numbers because of their usefulness.

But cars are more than a mere extension of humans; as a class, the devices seem almost to have a purpose unto themselves. In fact, if one didn't know that machines were mindless, one might imagine they were somehow executing a larger design of their own. If highly evolved vehicles of the year 3000 were able to look back and recount automobile history entirely from *their* perspective, the story might go something like this:

> The earliest automobiles – frail and unremarkable descendants of animal-drawn vehicles – appeared in Europe in the late nineteenth century. Theirs is a history without parallel. No-one could have predicted they would achieve global primacy, but within a single century cars had spread throughout the planet and multiplied from a few fragile individuals to a robust population of more than half a billion.
>
> Our ancestors enlisted humans in the enormous task of provisioning them with the primitive, carbon-based fuels then so abundant. The dependent human population explored for oil in remote deserts and cold northern seas, extracted it from wells bored miles into the earth, transported it across oceans, brewed it in huge refineries, and shipped it to countless scattered storage sites. Wherever cars roamed they could find sustenance.
>
> Early vehicles also induced humans to assist in the task of bridging rivers, tunneling through mountains, and lacing the countryside with paved pathways. And by the late twentieth century, 'off-road' vehicles had begun to appear and move beyond the paths once so essential to mobility. Hardy mutants such as 'jeeps' and 'dune buggies' were quite at home in parched and rugged wastelands too harsh for ordinary cars.
>
> How cars of this era enlisted and maintained the unwavering support of the human population is still something of a mystery. One popular theory is that the vehicles succeeded in inserting themselves into human-courtship rituals and male-dominance displays.

Humans devote enormous resources to cars, and, as a result, cars are thriving. So too are machines generally. They have become much more than human tools and appendages; in what has been only an instant in the history of life, machines have appeared, multiplied explosively, and spread beyond even the farthest reaches of the planet. These devices, almost like living things, have progressed from the most rudimentary of forms to extremely elaborate ones, and some of them (large computer networks, for example) may one day rival the complexity of biological creatures. No other type of entity – animate or inanimate – has succeeded in propagating itself and evolving so rapidly. For our story, I playfully breathed consciousness and intelligence into machines; yet it is quite probable that one day this will be a reality.

TOWARDS MACHINE INTELLIGENCE

Well before the modern computer, people wondered whether machines would ever be able to learn, think and feel. Would they ever be 'alive', and if so, would they one day be our rivals instead of our servants? In 1872 the English writer Samuel Butler wrote prophetically in *Erewhon*[90]:

> There is no security against the ultimate development of mechanical consciousness, in the fact of machines possessing little consciousness now. A mollusc has not much consciousness. Reflect upon the extraordinary advance which machines have made during the last few hundred years, and note how slowly the animal and vegetable kingdoms are advancing. The more highly organized machines are creatures not so much of yesterday, as of the last five minutes, so to speak, in comparison with past time . . . Where does consciousness begin and where end? Who can draw the line?

His questions are particularly relevant today. Recent developments in computers and technology have made it possible for machines to outperform humans in many specialized activities. Today many people will attempt only the most basic computations without a calculator. In fact, so few people can beat a good chess-playing computer program that it was newsworthy when, in 1989, Gary Kasparov, the world champion, soundly trounced Deep Thought, the best-playing computer, and reaffirmed – at least temporarily – human supremacy in the game.[91]

Will human intelligence soon be surpassed by machines? In the 1960s, many in the budding field of artificial intelligence thought so.

But at present, researchers are still struggling to develop computers that can perform such mundane tasks as recognizing simple objects,[92] understanding human language, or exhibiting 'common sense'. These general talents, which most of us take for granted, have proven extremely difficult for computers, while the highly specialized abilities we find difficult, such as playing chess, have proven relatively easy. The reason for this is that a task such as understanding speech is vastly more complex than anything computers now do and is easy for us only because the human brain has been so honed to the problem. If human survival had depended for hundreds of thousands of years not on communication but on playing chess, most of us would make contemporary chess-playing computers seem like rank novices.

A growing understanding of the amazing complexity of the human mind is showing that a huge gap still remains between the capabilities of the human brain and the most powerful computers.[93] Rigid computation, no matter how rapid, seems unlikely to be enough to produce qualities such as creativity, conceptual understanding, and perhaps even the ability to pick familiar faces from a crowd.[94] This does not mean that such capacities are beyond the reach of technology. Achieving them will simply demand the same types of 'massively parallel',[95] interactions that occur in the tissues of the brain. The brain's power emerges not from computational virtuosity, but from the rich interactions of billions of neurons whose synapses dance unpredictably to form and dissipate the complex patterns constituting human thought and perception. When electronic circuitry achieves the complexity to accommodate equally rich patterns of activity,[96] phenomena such as true machine intelligence, and even consciousness, will begin to emerge.

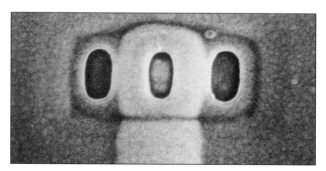

This experimental transistor has dimensions more than four times smaller than the devices being used today and has an area less than a 50,000th the cross-section of a human hair. Courtesy of Clive Reeves, IBM.

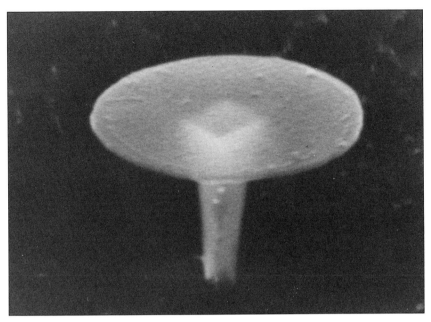

This microlaser is 100 times smaller than those currently in use and could fit inside a single red blood cell. The thumbtack-like disk seated on the pedestal of the laser is only some 400 atoms thick and about 2 microns across. Such tiny lasers may one day be used in optical computers based on light rather than electrons. Courtesy of AT&T Archives.

There is no doubt that such complex circuitry will one day be built. Today, less than fifty years after ENIAC, the first programmable digital computer, performed an astonishing 5,000 operations per second,[97] 'massively parallel computers' link together thousands of powerful processing units that operate simultaneously to perform tens of billions calculations per second.[98] The transistors on a computer chip are already less than a fiftieth the width of a human hair, and within a few decades might be a hundredfold smaller. At that size, a single human nerve cell lying on top of a circuit would cover a million transistors.[99] Were thousands of thin, richly interconnected layers of such circuitry laid one atop the other like pages in a book, the result would make today's fastest supercomputers seem puny and might rival the abilities of the human brain.[100]

The full potential of electronic processing is not yet clear, but there is no reason to believe its capabilities will not eventually far surpass those of the human brain. Keep in mind that computer circuitry is a processor of information, pure and simple, and its miniaturization –

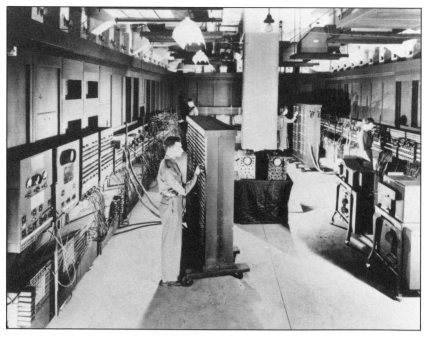

The ENIAC 'Superbrain', built in 1946, was the world's first programmable, digital, electronic computer. ENIAC (Electronic Numerical Integrator and Computer) filled a room with its 18,000 vacuum-tube switches but was far less powerful than a hand-held calculator of today. And a super computer might now contain 10 billion switches, the equivalent of a half-million ENIACs. Courtesy of the Boston Computer Museum.

unlike that of aggregates of living cells – theoretically is limited only by the random atomic movements that might make its switches noisy and unpredictable at extremely small dimensions.

Although *general* artificial intelligence does not lie only a decade or two away, most researchers active in 'AI' (though arguing about when and how) regard it as virtually inevitable. Today's ongoing debate about whether it is possible to build a computer with 'intelligence' is less about computers than about the ultimate nature of consciousness and mind.[101] Is consciousness at root a matter of complex signal processing or is something else involved?[102] Even those who maintain that machines will never achieve true intelligence, generally accept that computers will eventually be able to reproduce any *particular* human cognitive process. They believe that although a computer may be able to diagnose disease better than any physician,[103] perfectly interpret the spoken word, and even make convincing small talk, this does not mean that it will actually 'understand' what it is doing.[104] But this is a rather arbitrary distinction. To accomplish such tasks convincingly enough to equal the richness of human behavior will require data manipulation just as complex (and even unpredictable) as that going on in the brain; why *not* call it 'thinking'?[105] Marvin Minsky, the co-founder of MIT's Artificial Intelligence lab and a pioneer in the fields of both artificial intelligence and robotics, made the following comment:

> When intelligent machines are constructed, we should not be surprised to find them as confused and as stubborn as men in their convictions about mind-matter, consciousness, free will and the like . . . A man's or a machine's strength of conviction about such things tells us nothing about the man or about the machine except what it tells us about his model of himself.[106]

Machines have become too sophisticated and too essential to be viewed merely as adjuncts to human beings. So deeply are they now embedded in the technological society that creates, maintains, and uses them, that machines are more accurately viewed as products of Metaman itself rather than man. A single artisan might forge a knife, but to produce a new car model requires years of collaborative effort among countless people and machines. A vehicle exists because of research and development teams, computer-aided design tools, and materials and parts from widely dispersed manufacturing plants. The Toyota industrial group in Japan contains more than a hundred associated companies supplying components.[107] A typical Boeing 747 contains some 3 million purchased parts supplied by 2,500 different suppliers in fifteen countries.[108] Even the simple book you are holding in your hand involved diverse typesetting and photographic equipment, inks, printing and binding processes, as well as lumber companies, paper manufacturers, shipping and freight companies, bookshops and other enterprises. Thus, when I speak not of 'humans' or 'society', but of 'Metaman' accomplishing something, I do so to recognize implicitly the role played by these immense and complex collaborations now so ubiquitous in the developed world.

Machines are growing more specialized not because they could not be designed to perform many diverse tasks, but because each task is better handled by a machine specifically designed for that particular job. Given an automated vacuum cleaner that cleans floors and a telephone-answering machine that takes messages, who would pay much to combine them into a general-purpose device that could do both?

Thus, despite the growing power of computers, we are not moving towards the human-like robots of science fiction. What, other than novelty, would be the value of integrating generalized human capacities into a robot that could mimic human behavior? An intelligent computer companion would be cheaper and more useful if it were pocket-size rather than clunking alongside us in a humanoid frame.

Unlike biological organisms, individual machines generally do not need to move, repair, or power themselves; the surrounding structure of Metaman takes care of these functions. Thus, machines have no reason to move towards self-sufficiency. The progressively deepening union between humans and machines is symbiotic, and the question of who might one day be master and who slave is inapplicable.

IN BIOLOGY'S FOOTSTEPS

A critical dynamic driving Metaman's development is technological advance, a process with remarkable similarities to biological evolution. Machines can be said to 'evolve' because, like living things, they are shaped by an evolutionary process: they spawn new variants and copies that compete with each other for survival. The 'procreation' of any particular machine depends on a network of factories and humans rather than on biological reproduction, yet the number of offspring in the next 'generation' definitely hinges on a machine's success. Many performance factors go into determining that success, but ultimately, as with biological creatures, their success is gauged by their ability to survive and propagate. Machines that succeed multiply and spread. Machines that fail disappear.

Where competition is fierce, change is rapid. The six years of the Second World War produced radar, jets, amphibious vehicles, guided missiles and the atomic bomb. Not long ago, even a large camcorder seemed amazing; now one fits in the palm of your hand. Machines can proliferate so rapidly that successful devices, particularly those performing new tasks, soon become widespread. Fax machines, automated teller machines and credit cards were once found only in a few scattered enclaves, now they literally populate the world. Biological species make equally large expansions, but on a vastly longer time scale.[109] Where animal species tend to survive for millions of years, machine types now are often supplanted in less than a decade by social change or the arrival of new competitors. Where are the quill pens,

Shown here at the Raketenflugplatz near Berlin in 1930 is eighteen-year-old Wernher von Braun carrying one of the earliest rockets. So rapidly did this technology advance, that as an adult von Braun was playing a major role in NASA's moon program. Edward Pendray Collection, Princeton University Library.

steam engines, flintlock rifles and telegraph keys? A few linger on in museums, fossils from an earlier era, the rest are gone.

New machines, however, sometimes have nearly as much difficulty displacing already existing ones as animal interlopers do displacing firmly established species from their niches. Dial telephones are inferior to digital ones, but do the job and are still around. As with animals, though, where there is dramatic improvement, a new arrival will soon triumph. The slide rule once seemed secure and for decades dominated its realm, slapping at the hips of engineering students. Then, quite rapidly, it disappeared, vanquished by the far more robust hand-held calculator.

Technological advance is a powerful process so resembling biological evolution that it produces many of the same results: mimicry of form, lingering vestiges of ancestral features, structures exaggerated for purposes of display, and evolutionary convergence upon equivalent designs.[110]

Mimicry, for example, is found among even simple machines

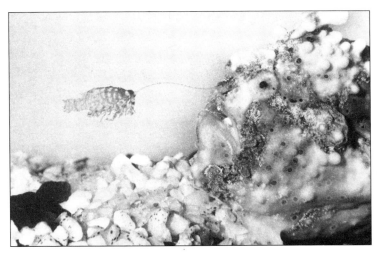

Closely resembling its surroundings of algae-encrusted rock, the warty frogfish lies motionless except for the fishlike lure (an extension of the dorsal fin) it dangles to attract potential prey. Mimicry and camouflage are also commonplace in the machine realm.[111] Courtesy of David Grobecker.

because – as with animals – the mimic gains by being mistaken for what it imitates. Molded glass resembling crystal, cubic-zirconia imitation diamonds, counterfeit currency, artificial sweeteners – each succeeds because it can fool the casual observer.

Similarly, vestiges of earlier forms – usually retained as ornaments – can be found in machines as well as animals. The existence of festive plastic candle-bases for flame-shaped electric light bulbs or of spoke patterns on car hubcaps would be difficult to understand without knowing their ancestry. Likewise, the human appendix and body hair are vestigial remnants of features no longer important and gradually disappearing.

Even the development of exaggerated features like the peacock's flashy feathers or the ancient Irish elk's giant antlers – both associated with mating – is mirrored in the machine realm. In the 1950s cars developed extremely large tail fins, which attracted attention and propagated rapidly. Though later replaced by other elements of visual display such as streamlining, for a brief moment the tail fin reigned supreme.

Different animal species sometimes independently evolve equivalent solutions to challenges they have in common. The reason is simple: often there are only a few good ways of doing something. Fifty million years ago, for example, when the mammalian ancestors of

The tail fins of this 1957 Cadillac Eldorado Biarritz show the same exaggeration that has evolved in peacock feathers, elk horns, and other animal features that figure prominently in mating displays. Courtesy of Archive Photos.

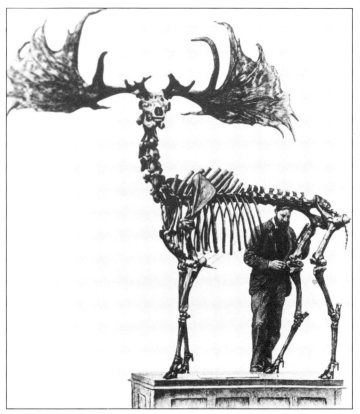

The Irish Elk, which became extinct 11,000 years ago, grew antlers measuring as much as 12 feet across. These antlers, shed and regrown annually, were probably important for male-dominance displays.[112] Photo by J. Millais, 1897.

whales returned to the sea, their feet gradually evolved into fins similar to those of fish; they 'rediscovered' this superior way of moving through water. Biologists call such evolution 'convergent', because it reaches the same end point from different starting points. The phenomenon is widespread among machines, too. Sails, which are the best way of using the wind to move across water, have evolved independently again and again in different cultures.

Predictably, machine evolution sometimes converges upon technical solutions evolved long ago by animals.[113] The radar systems used by ships and planes, for example, strongly resemble the sonar of porpoises and bats. When the military first started using radar to locate planes, engineers found that unless their receiving circuitry was momentarily turned off whenever loud outgoing radar pulses were emitted, the pulses would damage the sensitive receivers designed to detect faint returning echoes. It has since been found that some bats perform exactly the same trick by contracting muscles to desensitize their ears when they are emitting loud ultrasonic clicks.[114]

Natural selection directs change towards 'solutions' that are defined by the underlying nature of the challenges being faced.[115] That machine technology can in decades evolve the same solutions that biology required many millions of years to achieve is striking evidence of the awesome acceleration of evolution brought by the synergies within Metaman.[116]

Human and machine are now so inextricably bound together that the dynamics of technology have become even more important than those of biology in determining the future of humankind. The enormous technological strides that in recent decades have brought Metaman into being will soon be overshadowed by even greater advances, and by their resultant influences on society.

With the ongoing intrusion of machines into all aspects of human life, it is not surprising that some people fear technology might someday displace humans entirely, or leave them with nothing to do. This will not happen. Humans and machines are not competing; they are collaborating. A look at our planet affirms the enduring mutuality of this partnership within Metaman. The earth's surface is a wet, hostile place for machines, while for us it is the ideal home. Thus, on earth humans will *always* be essential to Metaman. In space, however, the story is different. Without gravity, water or air, the situation is reversed – humans (at least, as we now know them) are in hostile territory and electronic devices are in their element. In this region, abiotic forms are likely to predominate in the structures of Metaman. Even with the relatively simple computers of today, manned flights are generally not worth the expense and risk they entail; when technology becomes more intelligent and remote communication richer and easier, such flights may be more a recreation than a necessity for the development of space. Humans will journey through this realm and even establish colonies there, but Metaman's extensions into most of the region will be primarily technological. Ultimately, space and the barren asteroids, moons and planets will be the 'natural' realm of the machine.

THE LIVING PARTS

The tight, symbiotic union of machines and humans is central to Metaman, but this super-organism also has non-human biological parts – crops, livestock, pets, laboratory animals, and even 'pests'. Like humans and machines, these components are thriving because of their successful integration into the larger social entity. The domesticated dog, for example, is now by far the most successful canine. Until some 50,000 years ago when they began to associate with humans, wild dogs had to hunt for themselves; now, however, after millennia of working alongside people, many breeds do no work at all and have their meals served.[117]

Other domesticated animals are equally joined to the human endeavor. Although some of their fates seem much less appealing than those of pets, animals such as cattle, sheep, horses and pigs have achieved a large measure of security while so many other large mammals teeter at the brink of extinction.[118]

The story of agriculture is even more dramatic. The dominant plants on the planet are now corn, wheat, rice, potatoes and barley.[119] Forests are felled to make way for crops; minerals are mined and trucked to fertilize them; huge irrigation systems bring them water; their competitors are poisoned and their insect enemies slain. These plant species have become so dependent upon the workings of Metaman that many could not even survive on their own. Whether one flies over Canada, Ireland, Taiwan or India, the scene below is largely the same – a landscape of farmland. What were once forests or grasslands are now endless fields. In only a few centuries, the continents of the world have been transformed into nurseries for a relative handful of crops. Whether it is vegetables, fruits, grains or simply hay or cotton, these organisms, like humans, machines and domesticated animals, are now an integral part of Metaman.[120]

Not all living things associated with Metaman, though, have entered into a cooperative union. Many have achieved great success by developing other associations with Metaman: parasitizing it, feeding off its leavings, or exploiting its weaknesses. Rats feed on uncollected garbage, insects devour large grain stores;[121] weevils feast on huge fields of cotton. The success of these organisms, however, will probably prove transitory. As Metaman evolves, it will continue to reduce the impacts of such antagonists. The massive spraying of DDT and other early pesticides was but a clumsy early groping in this direction; now there are more selective chemicals being used, and far better methods are within sight.

The viral 'biopesticides' being designed to kill various insect pests illustrate the radical changes Metaman is bringing. One problem in reducing crop damage by using viruses has been the slowness with which they act; the infected insect pests continue to consume a crop for a week or more before dying. To remedy this, biologists have now taken the gene carrying the code for the paralyzing venom of scorpions and spliced it into the virus.[122] In consequence, when the genetically engineered virus – now part scorpion – fatally infects insects, it causes rapid paralysis. No longer can the insects feed prior to their deaths. This extraordinary manipulation of a living system offers a glimpse of what will one day be possible throughout the biological world. Broad success against Metaman's various parasites may take longer than the few decades suggested by some of today's optimists, but accelerating progress in molecular biology nearly insures this eventual result.[123]

Today's early efforts in bioengineering signify a fundamental change in the dynamics of the biosphere. Human society has long been reshaping the many organisms associated with it, selective breeding having produced domesticated animals and plants far different from the wild species from which they came. Now, by virtue of Metaman's emergence, the power to engineer and design consciously, which has so shaped machine evolution, is entering the biological realm and breaking down the division between biology and technology. Goats have been genetically altered so that their milk contains human proteins that can be purified and used medically; strains of microorganisms are being patented for use in industrial processes; plants are being given resistances to disease. Thus, at the same time that technological and biological materials are forming integrated systems within Metaman, these materials themselves are beginning to converge. Mechanical devices are becoming complex – perhaps even intelligent – and living things (including humans) are becoming subject to design.

4

INNER WORKINGS EXPLORED
Physiology of the Super-organism

WE RARELY PAUSE TO think of all that goes into bringing us running water at the turn of a tap or a friend's voice on the telephone, but a daunting maze of connections lies behind even the most commonplace activities in today's world. Consider, for example, what happened when I stopped for lunch at a small restaurant last year.

I was able to trade part of my labor on this book to get a meal from the restaurant owner. I didn't, however, give him any money from my publishing advance, I used a credit card. Essentially, he trusted some strangers at the credit-card company to pay him the money I was promising, and those strangers were counting on me to pay them at least some portion of their money when, at the end of the month, they would remind me about my promise. Of course, I wasn't actually going to *pay* those strangers; I didn't even know where they were. I was going to write a note to some bankers, whom none of us knew, and ask *them* to take money of mine and give it to the people at my credit-card company. The people at the bank were guarding my money for me – or rather they were using it themselves but had promised to give me someone else's money if I needed mine. I trusted them because some people in Washington said they'd replace my money if the people at the bank lost it. In truth, there wasn't any actual 'money' involved at all, but. . .

Back to the meal. Because I drank a German Rhine wine and ate some grapes from Chile along with my 'California cuisine' of Cajun chicken and a salad, getting my food to the restaurant involved complex arrangements among many people overseas as well as in the

US – truckers, farmers, manufacturers of farm products, and even the crews of cargo ships. And there were yet others involved: those who owned the building; those who had made the cutlery, plates, furniture and kitchen equipment; those who had laundered the tablecloth; the cook, waiter and cashier. And I drove my car to the restaurant, so. . .

Today eating is a far cry from walking to a neighbor's farm for a home-grown meal. Nearly everything done in the developed world depends on numerous strangers and organizations collaborating across time and space. This ceaseless activity, shifting continually yet held together by a rich social framework, constitutes the vital processes of Metaman.

ESSENTIAL SYSTEMS OF THE META-BODY

To sustain itself, Metaman consumes complex materials and converts them into simpler forms it can readily use – the same basic task performed by an animal's digestive system.[124] Beginning with a broad diversity of substances ranging from chromium ore to lobsters, Metaman ingests and transforms each of them in operations scattered throughout the world.

The production of steel is one example of this 'digestion'. A complex industrial process stretches from the explosive blasts that fragment iron ore at open-pit mines to the distant foundries that form the steel sheets, bars and rods that will later be transformed into parts for a multitude of devices and structures.[125] Metaman feeds itself through countless specialized coalitions of people and machines extracting materials at scattered lodes. Even the bread we ourselves eat depends on such digestive structures: vast tracts of farmland prepared, tended and harvested using tractor-drawn equipment; fertilizer companies, irrigation systems, and crop-breeding programs; milling factories and storage silos. And these elaborate networks extend beyond traditional crops and livestock: half the trout consumed in the US today is raised on trout farms.[126]

To use the many important products of its digestion, Metaman has a sophisticated 'circulatory system' that shuttles them to where they are needed. It is hardly surprising that the image of vehicles moving along highways branching into smaller roadways is suggestive of cells circulating through blood vessels.[127] A half-billion motorized vehicles move through an extensive road network linked to railways, shipping lanes and airline corridors,[128] and other flows augment Metaman's vehicular circulation. Pipelines are continually moving natural gas and oil through the world,[129] and in dry climates so much water for crops, industry and humans is diverted into aqueducts that entire rivers are emptied.[130]

Metaman's structure is so complex and discontinuous that undirected flows of materials would not be enough to satisfy its needs. If Metaman's circulation worked like our own, gigantic trucks of appliances, food and materials would be ceaselessly moving from door to door offering their fares to any takers. Metaman's circulation is more sophisticated: it generally addresses things to precise destinations.[131] It is this enormous innovation that allows intimate cooperation among widely separated entities.[132] Cars can be assembled from parts built in factories on different continents; retail stores can maintain inventories from all over the world.

Digestion and circulation supply Metaman with the energy and materials it needs for its 'metabolism' (to grow, repair itself, and carry on its many activities) so advances in these systems have been crucial to the evolution of a global super-organism. In fact, each time humankind has harnessed more energy, human life has been transformed.

Fire, tamed more than one million years ago by our ancestor *Homo erectus*,[133] gave primitive humans the first external energy that could be readily summoned and manipulated; it quite literally brought humanity out of the dark. Then, some fifteen thousand years ago, humans gained control of a second source of energy: draft animals. Using these animals, humans could move faster, go farther, carry more. The power of these animals built and maintained the first civilizations.

When James Watt patented the first practical steam engine in 1769, humanity commanded greatly increased energy for the third time.[134] Finally, the abundant energy trapped in wood and fossil fuels could do more than generate heat, it could produce controlled motion. The steam engine and its offspring transformed the globe's store of fossil fuels into a vast reservoir of manageable energy, and access to that energy became almost effortless with the generation of electricity and its delivery over power lines. After the first central generating station was built in London in 1882,[135] fuel no longer had to be hauled to wherever power would be used, only to a central plant.

Electricity, however, is more than an improved way of delivering the energy of fossil fuels; it fundamentally alters the way energy can

be used. By allowing the finer control and management of power –
even down to the microscopic levels of integrated circuits – electricity
has made possible both telecommunications and the computer. In
addition, electricity can be produced from almost any energy source –
falling water, thermal vents, nuclear reactions, wind, and even
sunlight; electricity makes it possible for Metaman's metabolism to
evolve beyond its current critical dependence on the earth's dwindling
store of fossil fuels.

Today, harnessed power permeates virtually all our activities, and
immense quantities of fuels and electricity flow the breadth and width
of Metaman.[136] At last, some 40,000 generations after fire was first
tamed, humankind can bend energy to its will and use it almost
anywhere.

Metabolic activity generates waste products. An animal has a distinct,
unchanging boundary separating inside from outside, so its excretion is
reasonably straightforward.[137] Metaman, however, has no sharp
boundary, so its 'elimination' is less easily assured. This issue is
extremely important because wastes previously thought to be
excreted are now proving to be less 'external' than once imagined.
Discarded chemicals leak into ground water and reappear in wells.
Automobile exhausts create noxious smog that hangs over cities.
Suburbs grow to surround once remote dump sites. Sewage and
industrial wastes pollute rivers. Even space debris has now become a
hazard to satellites.[138]

Global in extent, discontinuous by nature, Metaman is growing ever
more pervasive and now has no easily accessible 'outside' that will long
remain isolated. This is a very recent truth, because as long as human
civilization has remained scattered, there have always been places to
discard wastes and forget them. But toxic and non-toxic wastes alike
now must be encapsulated *within* Metaman if they are to be kept
separate from its 'internal' workings.

As Metaman develops, so does its excretory system: wastes are
being sequestered at a diminishing number of ever larger, more
sophisticated, and more remote facilities.[139] This natural consequence
of Metaman's need to expel metabolic byproducts from its spreading
active regions will afford humans more protection from dangerous
wastes than the more scattered disposal of the present. More distant
disposal sites, however, will necessarily cause larger quantities of
toxic and dangerous wastes as well as simple 'garbage' to pass through
Metaman's circulatory system – hauled by rail, truck or barge to those
sites. There are advantages and disadvantages for individuals in these

changes, but the overall process is essential for Metaman, and inevitable.

As concern about waste disposal has grown in past decades, Metaman's careless discharges into the planetary environment have sharply diminished. Nuclear wastes, once dumped injudiciously, are now the subject of heated debate as permanent repositories for their disposal are sought. Metaman's excretory system still has a long way to go in dealing effectively with the enormous quantities of waste passing through it, but the present system is unquestionably superior to previous times. The day-to-day reality of waste disposal in earlier eras is hard to comprehend fully in the antiseptic atmosphere of the present. In 1853, London had some 3 million inhabitants and no sewer system whatsoever;[140] garbage and raw sewage were routinely dumped in the streets. Now, unless a toilet clogs, sewage is nearly invisible to urban dwellers because it is so reliably shunted through a specialized excretory network to treatment plants.

In addition to improving its mechanisms for disposing of wastes, Metaman is beginning to diminish the overall volume of these materials. Metaman is reducing pollution, treating sewage more fully, and, in particular, increasing recycling[141] – which will eventually become routine. After all, internal 'recycling', because it so enhances metabolic efficiency, is commonplace in biological systems. The human body, which is continually breaking down damaged cells, doesn't excrete the resultant cellular debris but digests and reuses it, and Metaman, as a global super-organism, will eventually do the same.

Metaman digests and distributes materials, eliminates wastes, and metabolizes energy in ways that are suggestive of the workings of the human body. Each of these processes is essential to any large, living entity, and so too is homeostasis – the ability to maintain a stable internal environment. Any person who cannot keep his temperature within a few degrees of 'normal', maintain the salt balance of his blood, and avoid dehydration, will soon perish. Skin keeps us from drying out; clothes help us retain our heat. When hot, we sweat to cool ourselves; when cold, we shiver and pace to increase our metabolism, and rub our hands together for warmth.

Metaman, too, controls *its* 'internal' environment. Giant dams keep river basins from flooding; irrigation systems save crops during dry spells. Moreover, Metaman maintains countless 'mini-habitats' tailored to the differing needs of its diverse, individual parts. Mechanical and electronic components require particularly special care. Get a camera wet or set it in the sand at the beach and the device may never work again. The more sophisticated a device, the more sensitive it is likely to be. Computer chips require dust-free manufacturing facilities; highly sensitive photocells must be carefully protected from vibration. And to maintain the tissue cultures that are essential to medical research, frozen cells must be stored at liquid-nitrogen temperatures.

Metaman has created comfortable microenvironments for people too. Our homes – heated and cooled to our liking, sealed to keep out wind and rain, and artificially lit to give us day or night at any hour – enable people to live comfortably in climates far too harsh for unprotected humans. A person can lounge in a light robe at midnight reading a book and munching fresh fruit, while a blizzard with sub-zero temperatures is howling outside. This is extraordinary. And only in modern times have such microenvironments become possible, much less commonplace. One of the images in the film, *The Lion in Winter*,[142] is a powerful reminder of this. The scene begins with a close-up of a large basin of ice-covered water, then two hands descend, breaking the ice and flicking the pieces away. The next shot shows Henry II, King of England, dashing freezing water on his bearded face and casually chatting with his mistress. It is dawn in the castle bedchamber and he is washing. The year is 1183.

COMMERCE AND THE REGULATION OF METABOLISM

Metaman, like every other living thing, coordinates its internal activities so that they mesh and serve one another. Today's vast collaborations among millions of individuals are intricately regulated – by government, commerce, religion, custom and education. The most obvious of these agents is government, which generally maintains a social framework for human activity. But commerce, which orchestrates so many of our contemporary collaborations, is an even more important force regulating Metaman's metabolism.

Consider how effectively the marketplace manages the production and consumption of, say, fresh fruit. Prices balance production and consumption by integrating diverse factors such as the cost of labor and transportation, overall consumer demand, the size and timing of the harvest, and even the appearance and taste of the fruit. Change any factor significantly and the price will change too. The marketplace is a massively parallel processing system that is continually integrating and interpreting information. At every instant, vast numbers of transactions are occurring simultaneously throughout the economy.

This is what makes the system so powerful. Indeed, so potent is the
market system in integrating diverse information that attempts to
replace it with more centralized structures, such as government
bureaucracies, have had only limited success.[143]

Modern commerce, because it is constantly adjusting and coordinating Metaman's diverse internal activities, is central to Metaman's
physiology. Commercial activity is akin to the many nervous impulses,
hormones and chemical transmitters that regulate cellular behavior,
harmonize the activities of various organs, and generally keep an
animal's body functioning as an integrated whole. The rise of commerce has thus been a key ingredient in the birth of Metaman.

The origins of the economic devices now tying Metaman together
expose their enormous complexity. Paper money, for instance, seems
a simple thing, but only because of our familiarity with it. In the
thirteenth century, Marco Polo was so astonished by this Chinese
invention that he wrote:

> Of this money the Khan has such a quantity made that with it he
> could buy all the treasure of the world. . . . And no-one dares
> refuse it on pain of losing his life. And I assure you that all the
> peoples and populations who are subject to his rule are perfectly
> willing to accept these papers in payment . . . they can buy
> anything and pay for anything. And I can tell you that the papers
> that reckon as ten bezants do not weigh as one. . .[144]

Today, as never before, total strangers confidently and effortlessly
exchange goods and services using abstract monetary devices ranging
from installment loans to debit cards. The intricate patterns of
exchange so critical to Metaman can occur only because there is now a
sophisticated financial system to balance and track these transactions.
The most ancient way of exchanging things is pure barter,[145] but it is a
primitive tool. Money – transferable items of generally accepted
value[146] – is far superior and has been present in all complex
societies.[147]

Paper money – a mere symbol without intrinsic value – was a giant
conceptual step from coinage; it depended upon a general confidence
that this symbol could be exchanged for something of 'real' value.
Paper currency transformed money into a pure bookkeeping device.
People who accumulated these 'counters' had ostensibly supplied
more than they had consumed and thus had earned the promise of
future consumption. The key to paper money's success was that this
'promise' was not an individual's but all of society's and thus separate

from any particular transaction. Today this bookkeeping device is being superseded: financial transactions are increasingly being tracked electronically. This is unavaoidable because only by transcending the transfer of physical objects can global financial transactions keep up with the pace of activity generated by electronic communication.

The unseen activity we stimulate when we make a 'paperless' transaction is amazing. Consider one I once made at the San Francisco Airport: I went to an automatic teller machine (ATM) there, inserted a Diner's Club card, pressed a few buttons, and got five crisp 20-dollar bills. Simple enough, but here is what happened during the few seconds the ATM took to dispense the cash. First, the ATM identified the card by checking the leading digits of the account number encoded on the magnetic strip on the back of my card. Next, the ATM combined my withdrawal request with the security code I had typed, and sent them over the phone line to a switching company in Milwaukee. This company's computer read the transaction, looked up the account type to determine where to send my request, and forwarded the transaction by phone to Citicorp in New York. Here the account was identified as belonging to Diner's Club and the transaction was routed via Milwaukee to Denver. In Denver, where the Diner's Club data-processing center was located, the transaction was read again and my account was examined to determine whether I had used the correct security code and had enough credit there. Everything was fine, so my account was debited and a phone message was sent back to San Francisco via New York instructing the ATM to dispense cash. In about ten seconds, eight messages had travelled 10,000 miles and been examined by four different institutions. And half the transaction still remained to be completed. As I was turning towards my flight, the ATM was sending a message back to Denver to tell Diner's Club to begin the settlement process that would transfer 100 dollars from my account to the bank owning the ATM.

For all this, I was charged less than a dollar. My transaction was a 'simple' one; the global markets of today are filled with a bewildering array of complex financial instruments to move funds, hedge risks and raise capital.

Modern financial instruments are one element in the commercial system so integral to Metaman's metabolism, but there are many others – some so familiar they are easily ignored. It is easy to forget that even in the 1800s, most items were manufactured one at a time by individual craftsmen, had no brand names, and were not advertised.

Until the coming of steam, transportation moved at the pace of draft animals and the wind. Steam brought speed and volume to commerce, and this brought crisis: old commercial methods no longer worked; they were too slow and cumbersome. The ensuing worldwide transition to modern commerce is revealing of the workings of Metaman and is simplest to trace in the US, where the innovations of the Industrial Revolution were applied on a grand scale and did not displace an already entrenched system.

Advances in transportation came first. As the railroad companies began moving large volumes rapidly over long distances, their operations became too large and extended to manage and yet too interconnected to partition. Chaos ensued. The editor of the *American Railroad Journal* wrote in 1854 that so much confusion prevailed that 'in the greatest press of business, cars in perfectly good order have stood for months upon switches without being put to service and without it being known where they were.'[148]

The solution was bureaucracy – a military-like hierarchy with information flowing up through the ranks. Station managers sent hourly telegraph reports of the statuses of the trains in their vicinity to a large clerical staff that integrated the information and sent it on to supervisors. The organization itself now automatically gathered and interpreted information, making it comprehensible to decision makers. This is the essence of the bureaucratic form, which dominated business organizations until the superior processing power of the computer began to render it obsolete. The early crisis of the railroads reveals why Metaman's formation depended so critically on the emergence of modern tools for communicating and handling information. The rate at which materials flowed through society could be increased only by effectively managing much more information.

The crisis of the railroads next spread to manufacturing; though the challenges there were somewhat different, they too hinged on information processing. Assembling a car or a sewing-machine requires meshing numerous complex sequences of operations, so a large acceleration of production was a nightmare to coordinate. The answer was to reduce complex manufacturing processes to patterns of continuous flow between small well-defined operations. The epitome of this was the moving car assembly line, introduced in 1913 to produce the Model-T Ford.[149]

As innovations in transportation and production began to bring more and cheaper materials to market, the retail distribution system became a new bottleneck. Before society could become significantly more integrated, new ways of managing the flow of goods to market had to be found.

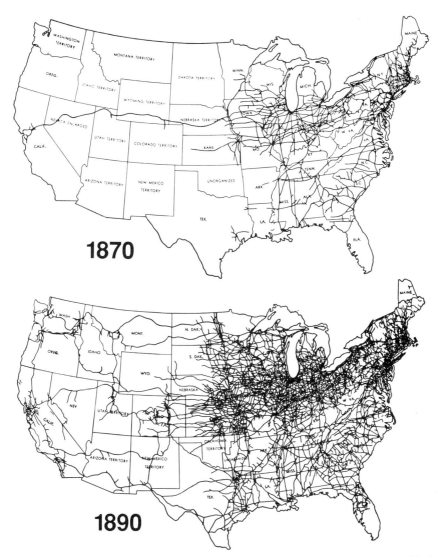

1870

1890

The arrival of steam rapidly accelerated the pace and scope of commerce and led to a crisis in the commercial system. The railroads were one of the first systems to feel the massive changes underway. Between 1870 (top) and 1890 (bottom), the rail network in the US expanded from 53,000 to 164,000 miles of track. Courtesy of the Association Of American Railroads.

In the early 1800s, goods arriving in New York were sold directly to shopkeepers at auction: as commerce accelerated, however, merchants were unable to keep up with the auctions and started hiring buyers. Within a few decades, however, these agents were replaced by wholesalers, and then mass retailers appeared on the scene.[150] Comparable changes were occurring in every aspect of the movement of goods to market, and by 1900 most of the innovations in distribution that are familiar today – cash registers, fixed prices, shopping baskets, vending machines, standardized container sizes, brand names, even product advertising[151] – had appeared. When, in the early 1900s, these innovations were joined by those of market research and sales analysis, all the essential features of a modern commercial system were in place.[152]

In Metaman, almost all people are now consummate consumers who depend upon others to produce most of what they eat, wear, use and own. The transition to mass consumption signalled the end of individual self-sufficiency and was at the heart of Metaman's emergence. In a single century, commercial systems in the world's most developed countries had sprouted into a complex structure capable of orchestrating the diverse activities and material transfers of Metaman's metabolism.

Now, this powerful commercial structure, by transforming the formerly centrally planned economies of China, the Soviet Union and Eastern Europe, has nearly completed its global spread. This present transition is very reminiscent of the one that followed the acceleration of commerce in Europe and the US in the nineteenth century. The current shift, like the previous one, is the result of technological advance. This time, high-technology has pushed commerce beyond the capabilities of bureaucracy and central planning by making products and production methods substantially more complex.[153]

AN INEXORABLE MARCH

In tracing the development of commercial systems through history, it is evident that technological progress shapes not only society, but the context for future progress. History is a cascade of interlinked developments, not a sequence of isolated events. The development of steam power, for example, led to more rapid transportation, and thereby set the stage first for progress in manufacturing and then for the transformation of the commerce system itself.

At first glance, human progress may seem uncertain – cultures flourish, then decline; regions prosper and expand, then move from center stage. Viewed from a larger perspective, however, progress is steadier. Particular kingdoms may pass away, but they leave their innovations behind to seed further development elsewhere. Writing, iron, gunpowder and the car soon spread from their birthplaces out into the world, severing their fates permanently from their creators. Moreover, such technological diffusion has grown extremely rapid. Writing took two thousand years to spread from the Middle East to China,[154] and gunpowder a few centuries to travel from China to Europe.[155] Now, computer technologies often take only months to spread globally.

Humanity's ongoing technological advance appears inexorable. But what then of the important events and personalities that constitute the human story? How much do they really influence the larger direction of history and shape the long-term character of society?[156] Imagine that history were a tape that could be rewound, altered, and then replayed as a new story. How would today's world be changed by returning to 334 BC and killing Alexander the Great as he was crossing the Dardanelles to begin his conquest of the Persian Empire? A more pivotal moment in history would be hard to find. Without the collapse of the Persian Empire, Rome might never have grown to dominate as it did; Christianity might not even exist.

Were history thus replayed, language, culture, people and power would not be distributed as today. But none the less, the essential character of human society – give or take a thousand years of development – would probably have moved towards its present form, and human civilization towards the formation of a global super-organism. The reason is that the character of human society is so strongly influenced by the technologies it produces.[157] Once developed, the steam engine was bound eventually to expand trade; telecommunications, to knit the world together; printing, to spread human knowledge; antibiotics, to increase life expectancy. Without Alexander, these major developments might have been delayed (or accelerated), but it is likely they would eventually have occurred.[158]

The timing of technological progress may be influenced by many social factors, but the specifics of new technologies are determined by the *nature* of the physical world rather than humanity's strivings. No matter how much effort was devoted to alchemy, lead was never going to be transmuted into gold. A century ago, no-one had good reason to predict the modern computer and what it has now wrought, but in light of what is now known about electronics and physics, it is reasonable to infer that, as science progressed, computers were certain to be developed and exploited. Likewise, the future of biotechnology is controlled less by biologists than by the potentials of technology and of biological organisms. Scientific endeavor probes broadly, but it merely *uncovers* truths that already exist and are thus, in a sense, predestined to figure in humanity's future.

The *detail* of history is inherently chaotic, but not its long-term course, which is driven by absolute truths about humankind and the world: a huge reservoir of oil lies beneath the Middle East. Mixing potassium nitrate, carbon and sulphur creates gunpowder. Bacteria cause disease. Crops grow well in river deltas. Burning coal releases carbon dioxide. These truths channel the flow of human history; we cannot escape them. Humanity's tightening global union and the emergence of Metaman is not a fluke that might easily be derailed; it is the expression of powerful evolutionary forces and a consequence of the very nature of human beings and the natural world.

5

THE MIND OF METAMAN
An Evolving Global Brain

METAMAN IS CEASELESSLY MONITORING itself and its environment, interpreting the information, and responding appropriately to it. This does not *necessarily* mean that Metaman is conscious, but this superorganism does have the functional equivalent of a nervous system. An insect with its tiny brain will take evasive action when it encounters danger, and a person who is standing erect is continually – and unconsciously – monitoring his or her body orientation and making the precise adjustments needed to stay balanced. Metaman is no less purposeful. When it finds itself running out of oil, it searches for more. When it feels itself edging dangerously close to nuclear catastrophe, it senses the threat and struggles to pull back.

The more complex the organism, and the more diverse its behaviors, the more sophisticated the integration of its diverse parts must be. It is no surprise that a mouse's nervous system is more complicated than an earthworm's. Nor should it be surprising that Metaman's 'nervous system' is immensely more elaborate than any animal's. Metaman processes huge amounts of information by combining human thought and computer calculation within the various organized networks of human activity. Such networks as science, government and business together constitute the broad cognitive systems that function as the 'brain' of Metaman. Any nervous system engages in three basic activities – sensing, interpreting and responding – and all three are present in Metaman, which houses countless sense receptors to monitor itself and its environment,[159] combines and interprets that information, and acts upon those interpretations.

SENSING AND INTERPRETING

Telescopes on the ground and in satellites gather information from space. Barometers, radar, drilling rigs and seismographs probe the earth's atmosphere and crust. Hundreds of laboratory techniques penetrate other realms: nuclear magnetic resonance imagers give accurate pictures of the inside of an organism's living tissue, DNA sequencers provide the details of a cell's genetic makeup, mass spectrometers decipher molecular structures, and giant cyclotrons explore the subatomic realm. Sense receptors of every shape and kind generate a stream of data about Metaman's environment and the physical world.

Metaman also monitors its own *internal* state: health organizations track disease incidence; intelligence agencies gauge military capabilities; government analysts measure unemployment. As Metaman gathers and retains ever more detail about economic, social and intellectual activity, the collection of these data is becoming increasingly automated. Computers tally financial transactions, monitors record which television programs people watch,[160] and sensors measure traffic on highways. No *individual* keeps track of the time we spend on the telephone, but we are billed for each of our calls, and anyone who wished could discover that there were 785 million minutes of outgoing international telephone calls from Italy in 1988.[161]

Reliable information is crucial to making projections and anticipating events, so as patterns of activity within Metaman grow more complex they rely more on the data being provided by the various clusters of humans and machines functioning as sense receptors. Inflation, trade, inventory and money-supply measurements produce the economic indicators that steer government policy; epidemiological information guides medical research.

Collecting data about human activity is of obvious importance to Metaman and has been expanding rapidly, so much so that many people are afraid of losing their 'privacy'.[162] But while blocking the collection or integration of certain specific data – whether financial, medical or social – may at times be a good way of protecting the individual, any widespread obstruction of the collection and movement of information would be counterproductive for humans as a whole. Without census data how can governments target resources? Without credit information, how can businesses make loan decisions? As Metaman grows and develops, it *needs* more information, not to regulate the individual, but to orchestrate its own metabolic activities.

Such nightmarish visions as Aldous Huxley's *Brave New World,* where individuals are tightly controlled by some all-powerful central authority, embody a basic fallacy: complex organisms do not work this way. An organism's many parts do not slavishly follow the commands of some central director. A heart needs no coercion to pump blood, a drone bee no duress to gather pollen. People's individual roles in Metaman are not rigidly determined by some higher authority and never will be. We each must find our own place, and as Metaman evolves, our choices about what we do and how we live are expanding not contracting. Because the free flow of information is so integral to Metaman's continuing development – and thus to humanity's well-being – in general, humanity would do well to enhance rather than inhibit these flows.

A stream of sights, sounds, smells and other sensory data continually flows into each of us. Little of it ever rises to conscious awareness, but every person's body is always screening, analyzing and integrating the data. A moment ago you may have been unaware of any sensations coming from your fingers turning the pages of this book, but now as you focus your attention you feel texture and thickness. It is easy to cross a room unaware of the floor's touch against your bare feet, but step into a tiny puddle and it will seize your attention. A person can even drive a car lost in thought, unconscious of what he or she is doing. Sensory data is processed where it is needed: sometimes locally (when someone jerks his hand away from a hot pan), sometimes at higher levels of integration (when a person tosses a ball to a friend, unmindful of the complex measurements and computations involved).

Likewise, sensory data is continually streaming into Metaman and being examined locally or passed to more powerful processing centers. The stock and commodities markets are good examples of how rapidly and efficiently disparate information can be integrated. Buy and sell orders from throughout the world drive price movements, and anything relevant occurring anywhere is soon reflected in a stock's price. With an air traffic control system, however, *local* weather conditions and airplane traffic govern the assignment of flight paths.

Information must be gathered together before it can be usefully integrated, so telecommunications has become a key part of Metaman's nervous system. The 'phone' system is an immense global network shunting information over diverse paths.[163] Banks wire money, computers transmit data, stores verify credit, and individuals converse. Today many people who live by themselves spend more time on the telephone than in face-to-face contact with others. On average, some 5 million pairs of locations in the US are coupled in intimate dialogue at any moment, and half of the volume of telephone traffic is data transmission rather than voice.[164] Moreover, with the spread of cellular phones, the telephone system itself is becoming mobile and able to attend people during their everyday activities. One day people will not only move freely and still have anyone, anywhere, within reach; they will be so used to the technology as to take it for granted, much like indoor plumbing and household electric power today.[165]

Telephone lines carry directed individual communications much as neurons conduct messages within the human body, but this 'neural' network of Metaman has capacities far beyond those of animal systems. Not only do telephone calls carry much more information

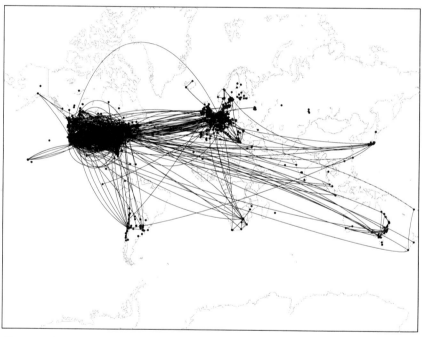

Communication within and among computer networks still makes up only a tiny part of the information flowing within Metaman, but such communication is expanding rapidly. Shown here are the most active communication paths within Usenet, the largest global network for broadcasting information among computer users, networks and organizations. In 1992, Usenet connected some 54,000 organizations, 11 million users, and 600,000 computers globally. The amount of information broadcast through Usenet has been increasing some 70 per cent a year since measurements were first taken in 1988.[166] Courtesy of Brian Reid and Digital Equipment Corporation.

than the firings of individual nerve cells, but these communications can be directed to *any* specific party. Such communication, however, makes up only a part of the information flowing within Metaman.[167]

The broadcast and print media spread their messages widely. In speaking to the crowd, they resemble the hormonal communications within animals. When sex hormones course through humans at the end of childhood, many tissues respond and adolescence begins, and when a person is greatly startled, a jolt of adrenaline alerts the heart, brain and other organs to possible danger. Similarly, in Metaman, images such as the 1986 Chernobyl disaster or Iraq's 1990 invasion of Kuwait immediately resonate through the media and seize the world's attention.

Overnight, such information provokes widespread responses ranging from swings in financial markets to changes in individual travel plans. Governments confer, people argue – the whole world watches. In a sense, Metaman focuses its 'attention' on what is happening and brings powerful forces to bear on it. Once the crisis passes, however, this collective attention rapidly dissipates. We all move on to other concerns – a sporting event, a financial scandal, or perhaps some new disaster or crisis. Significant effects may linger for decades, but the world at large soon forgets.

On a much shorter time scale, a person's attention will similarly skip from one thing to another. During a walk along a street, you might fix momentarily on a bright sign, then drift into musing about a memory or idea only to be startled by the screech of a car's brakes, look up, and find yourself focusing on the face of an interesting stranger who has caught your eye. Any complex nervous system, by virtue of the intricate interplay of patterns continually occurring within it, almost certainly exhibits this same dynamic, unpredictable quality.

FROM HUMAN BRAIN TO GLOBAL MIND

Continually sensing, transferring, and manipulating information, Metaman does more than just shuffle and store data, Metaman interprets and processes it. In essence, Metaman actually 'thinks' by using a 'brain', that literally is all around us. And that brain contains within it the functional equivalent of a global 'memory' housing all of humanity's accumulated knowledge. Examining the evolution of this global memory reveals its nature and its future.

The ability to preserve what is created and to bequeath it to successive generations is the foundation of civilization. Without this, there would be continual repetition. Physical constructions deteriorate and must be replaced again and again,[168] but knowledge – whether a technological insight, an idea behind a social system, or an understanding of the natural world – gives rise to more knowledge. Humanity's collective knowledge at any moment may differ only minutely from what it was previously, but the overall accumulation has been inexorable and is the key to human social evolution and to the formation of Metaman.

Humanity's ability to gather, store and use information has taken several leaps of enormous consequence. The first leap, the development of language, provided the very foundation of human society.[169] The second, the development of writing, allowed information to be stored in a durable form outside the individual.[170] No longer was the knowledge a community could preserve limited by human memory. The arrival of movable type brought a third immense leap in information handling.[171] With this advance, written information could begin to diffuse broadly.[172] Fifty years after Gutenberg published his Bible in Mainz in 1455,[173] the number of books in Europe had expanded a thousand-fold, from tens of thousands to tens of millions.[174] Today, it is a challenge just to dispose of the mountains of newspaper spewed out by one giant rotary press printing six million pages an hour.

And now a fourth great leap is underway: electronics is converting information from the static patterns of previous media into dynamic ones. Over the past century, humans have gained the ability to capture sounds, images, and motion directly. Now, we can extend our senses by realistically conjuring up distant events, experiences and locations. Film footage can re-create scenes we would never otherwise encounter – a festival in a distant land, an animal deep in its burrow, even a battle long past. In essence, people now can breach previous barriers of space and time to share the visions and experiences of others, and this information – encoded in vibrant patterns of electricity, magnetism, and light – can be transmitted and duplicated without moving physical materials.

These technological advances have led to the global integration of human activity that has been crucial to Metaman's birth. Today, communication satellites allow complex information to move nearly instantaneously anywhere on earth, and the complexity of what is stored and transmitted has no clear limits. Indeed, the entire library of the Sorbonne of fourteenth-century Paris – housing some 2,000 books – could now fit on a few computer disks the size of music CDs, and a few keystrokes could summon any passage from the library.

Electronics, which has so revolutionized the transmission and

Found in 1799, the Rosetta Stone, which is inscribed with Egyptian hiero-glyphics, demotic characters and Greek, led to the deciphering of hieroglyphics. Writing was the embryo of a global memory transcending human biology. With the advent of writing, no longer was human knowledge limited by human memory, and no longer was human communication limited by the need for face-to-face contact. Courtesy of the British Museum.

storage of data, is also transforming its use. But preserving and disseminating vast amounts of information cannot alone create a functional global brain for Metaman; it is also essential to be able to sort through this morass of information to find what is needed. Computerized airline reservation systems, for example, must be able to display instantly at countless locations the full, up-to-the-minute information about any particular ticket or flight.

Optical and magnetic storage devices, computers and large communication networks are already beginning to make the vast, dispersed store of information in Metaman readily accessible. One day it will be possible to have at one's fingertips any information contained in any library or data base anywhere in the world, perhaps simply by verbally asking a question.[175] Globally integrated information will be of extraordinary value. Consider, for example, what might be learned about the subtle long-term effects of prescription drugs by correlating the hundreds of millions of medical and pharmaceutical records that exist globally.[176] The link between cancer and smoking now may be clear to almost everyone,[177] but even in the 1950s tobacco was not yet established as a serious danger. The threat is too delayed and subtle to be readily apparent to an individual observer and could be clearly perceived only through broad correlations of information.[178]

The journey from language to writing, to printing, to electronics has, in one essential way, brought information storage full circle. In the human brain, information consists of dynamic patterns of electrical and chemical activity that interact in rich, complex ways – we *think*. But human memory is limited in capacity and its contents are easily lost. Storing information on physical materials such as paper and film overcame these problems by creating unlimited amounts of secure storage, but it carried a price: unlike the information in the human brain, information contained in external storage was static and could not easily be manipulated or retrieved.

Now, externally stored information is being returned to dynamic patterns of activity that can combine and interact in increasingly complex ways within Metaman's network of global connections. The term 'global memory' is more than metaphor.[179] Such processes as climate simulations, election tallies, telephone switching systems, and global banking systems, are early glimmers of 'meta-thinking'.[180] When Metaman's global store of information exists largely as electronic patterns that are as readily manipulated as the volatile patterns in the human brain, Metaman will truly have a 'mind' of its own. Indeed, as its 'meta-thinking' becomes ever richer and is coupled with an ever fuller 'self-awareness'[181] provided by its evolving sensory system, Metaman may eventually evolve a sort of planetary 'consciousness'.

The electronic manipulation of information is only one part of Metaman's mental activity; Metaman also processes information through us! Each of our minds is an internal resource for the super-organism to use. From interpreting satellite photos to looking for product defects on an assembly line, humans process information and do it extremely well. Generally, however, the human mind – as powerful as it is – is only a tiny cog in some far more elaborate information-processing structure in the mind of Metaman. Machines do the real analysis at the US Internal Revenue Service; the 120,000 employees[182] essentially support these devices and link them to taxpayers and policy makers.

Even people who seem to be making decisions entirely on their own are in reality part of a much larger effort. When deciding what to plant and when to plant it, a farmer looks at long-range weather forecasts, general economic indicators, commodity price projections, government policies and many other factors. Farmers sit atop a huge pyramid of organizations collecting and interpreting information. What is important to Metaman is not the decision of a particular farmer, but the aggregate decision of *all* farmers, consumers, bankers, politicians and others who together constitute the global system for making agricultural decisions.

In science, the role of individuals – designing experiments, interpreting results, and achieving insights – is particularly critical. But scientists, too, are supported by a dense technological network of telecommunications, research journals, conferences and administrative processes that integrate their disparate activities. Individual scientists come and go, but the ensemble endures. Scientific ideas are the collective product of modern science. Flashes of insight are individual but grow out of the interplay of personal communications among scientists, vast stores of information archived in journals and books, and analyses and data provided by complex machines. The immensity of some of these collaborations is shown by the listing of 147 co-authors from 37 institutions in 11 countries on the 1992 paper describing the first complete sequencing of a chromosome – the 315,000 base chromosome III of yeast.[183]

With the arrival of Metaman, the sharp boundary between manipulating information inside the human mind and outside it is disappearing. When a person sits before a video console and interacts with a computer program, his or her labor is intimately joined with the computer's. Similar, but larger collaborations occur within most organizations, essentially transforming them into intelligent, integrated complexes of humans and machines. Some of these complexes have more technological content,[184] some less, but this joining of human and machine is real and is an essential feature of the emerging mind of Metaman.

RESPONDING

Metaman, which could not function as an integrated whole without continually gathering and interpreting data, uses the information in a variety of ways. At the most basic level, this information is what allows Metaman to regulate its underlying metabolism as discussed earlier. When consistent shortages of particular materials develop, enterprises detect these 'opportunities' and direct their efforts towards them. When a region is suffering a labor shortage, that information spreads and people gravitate there.

At a slightly higher level, the information guides Metaman's physiological adjustments – reactions to trauma, for instance. When there is an earthquake or other natural disaster in the developed world, a broad effort quickly assembles to provide assistance. Some of the response comes from organizations specially designed for the purpose, other help is 'spontaneous'. That humanitarian aid is the product of individual concern does not preclude it also being part of *Metaman's* response to trauma. A disaster-relief operation is an organized, coordinated behavior that is no less 'purposeful' than a human being's physiological response to a cut finger. After all, the body heals its wounds through the actions of individual cells – each with a perfectly good reason to do what it does. Taken together, these individual cellular actions constitute the body's response to the injury. If a healing wound could be probed to find out why particular cells in the scar were dividing, their reasons might range from the specifics of local chemical conditions to the signals sent by their immediate neighbors. The importance of sealing wounds to prevent infection would not be one of these reasons, however, because that process is meaningful at the human level not the cellular one.

Seeing disaster relief as a physiological response by Metaman rather than merely a human response to tragedy explains why the developed world responds so mildly to most disasters in less-developed lands. A million people drowned by floods in Bangladesh or perishing from drought in Africa elicits a modest reaction compared to the massive mobilization of resources that would ensue if an equivalent disaster were to strike Australia or Italy.[185] The meager global response to disasters in less-developed regions comes not from a lack of individual sympathy for the victims, but from the as yet loose integration of these regions with the functional core of Metaman. There is little way for such an event to provoke a response from the super-organism: the broad communications connections that could build media attention are lacking. The economic and political ties that would send a ripple of secondary effects out into the world are meager. And the basic infrastructure that would be the conduit for any relief is ill formed.

Beyond such essentially physiological reactions, Metaman also responds to information at a yet higher level by exhibiting large-scale behaviors that are analogous to the conscious actions of human beings. The recent global response to environmental challenges is an example of this. Concern for the natural environment is hardly unique to the present era, but the outpouring of such concern in the developed world is unprecedented. Clearly, individual human experience is not the sole driving force. A century ago, when urban living conditions were abominable by today's standards, what outcry there was caused little change. Why is there a growing response to environmental problems now instead of a decade or a century ago? The answer lies in Metaman's growing ability to understand and respond to such issues. Only recently has Metaman had a nervous system sophisticated enough to begin to integrate individual human concerns about such issues as pollution into a larger awareness of these threats and translate it into coherent action.

A well-honed survival instinct is almost universal among living things. The reason is self-evident: animals that are better at surviving, survive. Thus, animals have become particularly adept at avoiding the dangers they (and their ancestors) regularly encounter, but often fare poorly against unfamiliar threats. A rabbit, though expert at evading a hungry fox, will stand transfixed by the headlights of an oncoming car. A moth whose perfect camouflage hides it from hungry birds will seek out a bug light. A snake will flee from a dog but sun itself on a nice, warm highway.

The more sophisticated a creature's nervous system, the more it can learn to recognize unfamiliar danger. Humans routinely avoid hazards they have never personally experienced. Generally, it is not experience but knowledge that deters people from swimming during a lightning storm. In trying to assess humanity's chances for survival, it is common to question whether humans, as individuals, are up to the challenges involved. Can we transcend our aggressive nature and learn to live together? Can we subordinate our own individual self-interest to the larger good? The feeling is often expressed that somehow the problems facing the world have grown too large for humans to solve. Such doubts are justified: today's problems *are* too big for individuals. After all, in many ways we are but hunter-gatherers in modern garb. Fortunately, though, humanity's fate rests not on the ability of *individuals* to perceive and circumvent global dangers, but on the capacity of Metaman, a complex super-organism, to do so.

If human beings can understand and respond to danger without experiencing it, Metaman too is certainly capable of doing so. As individuals, human beings may have great difficulty responding adequately to dangers as far removed from everyday experience as 'nuclear war' or 'global warming', but Metaman's capacity is larger. Already, many decades before individuals could possibly detect any global climatic change,[186] Metaman has discovered warming of about one degree Fahrenheit during the past century[187] and begun to respond to the potential problem. Some people may fear that Metaman is moving too slowly, or too equivocally, but it is important to remember that we are operating on a very different time scale than Metaman. Often when people become aware of fragments of information within Metaman's huge nervous system, they expect Metaman to respond instantly, but its size embodies a certain inertia. In Budapest in 1990 shortly after the Berlin Wall fell, I was talking enthusiastically with some acquaintances about how well Hungary would be doing in a mere decade or so. A twenty-five-year-old woman who was hoping to emigrate to the US looked at me and said sadly that ten years might be a short time for Hungary, but it was a long time for her. How true.

It takes significant effort to see the human enterprise from the larger perspective of Metaman, but doing so helps make sense of the underlying forces shaping our world. If we choose to ignore this perspective, we risk serious consequences. These forces are not distant; the currents they create are shifting the ground on which we stand and moving our lives.

METAMAN TODAY

It is Mankind as a whole, collective humanity, which is called upon to perform the definitive act whereby the total force of terrestrial evolution will be released and flourish; an act in which the full consciousness of each individual man will be sustained by that of every other man, not only the living but the dead.

Pierre Teilhard de Chardin, 1920.[188]

6

THE FOUNDATION FOR OUR FUTURE
Accelerating Towards Global Union

PROFOUND CHANGES ARE UNDERWAY: advancing technology, expanding trade, and ever more pervasive telecommunications are giving society a form and character without historical precedent. The same evolutionary forces that bore Metaman are now effecting a broad global integration of all humankind and providing Metaman with the cohesion to address the challenges it faces. Global union, like all profound change, inevitably leads to some loss; the new possibilities it is offering us, however, are immense. 'Globalism' is a popular topic: global economics, global culture and even global government are routinely discussed. Naturally, this planetary integration is a complex process. Our challenge is to understand how it is being manifested, where it is leading, and what it means for humanity.

TRIBAL STATES AND GLOBAL GOVERNMENT

Powerful regional movements for self-rule have torn apart many nations in the past few years. In 1991 when the Soviet Union splintered, it managed largely to avoid bloodshed, but when Yugoslavia came apart at the seams, Croats, Bosnians and Serbs were soon engaged in a bloody struggle. Meanwhile, Kurds battle Turks; Tamil and Kashmiri separatists clash with Indian troops; Quebec threatens to leave Canada; and even Scotland pushes to split from Britain.[189]

Although some long-standing animosities have erupted violently where ethnic tensions have previously only simmered, the world as a whole is not fragmenting into antagonistic enclaves. The stories of ethnic strife that intermittently fill the news paint a distorted picture; the actual global reality is one in which silent, undramatic changes are irresistibly pushing peoples towards broad international cooperation. In 1991, the headlines proclaimed that Slovenia had asserted its independence, but the country's concurrent requests for admission to the European Economic Community went nearly unnoticed.

Two powerful trends are evident today – one towards local autonomy, the other towards international regulation. Though appearing to be in opposition, they are not; they are different manifestations of the same phenomenon – Metaman's growth. Therefore, both local *and* global forces will increasingly influence human activity.

Every living system regulates 'global' functions globally and 'local' ones locally, and this pattern is becoming evident in Metaman. Activities involving diverse peoples and regions (matters of trade, communications, finance and security) are being managed more globally, while many other activities are coming under greater local and individual influences. Throughout the developed world regulatory structures are fragmenting and realigning as additional layers of organization spontaneously form. GATT (The General Agreement on Trade and Tariffs) moves to expand its regulation of international trade, a city sets up a commission to manage its growth, or citizens form a coalition to oppose a nuclear power plant. Some activities such as health care, which were once entirely the responsibility of the individual, are now becoming the province of government; others, such as religion, are becoming individualized.

The nation-state is being eclipsed. National governments are no longer the pinnacles of power in the world. Not only are local demands eroding their strength and challenging their authority, but in economic, political, scientific and social realms, international organizations are transcending nations and making national governments just one organizational level among many. In theory, of course, nations still hold the reins within their own borders, but in practice their influence is severely constrained by an international environment largely beyond the control of any individual nation.[190] Despite all its efforts, the US is unable to halt the flow of illegal drugs across its borders. A recession in America is felt by Japanese and European industry alike. As economic interdependence grows, national political power becomes more elusive.

Enterprises that reach across national boundaries are difficult for governments to regulate. Censor the news and it leaks in from elsewhere; bind an industry too tightly and it migrates to friendlier turf; block a field of research and scientists go elsewhere. In 1990, for example, Germany enacted a comprehensive and restrictive law to regulate research in genetic engineering and is now finding that the result has been merely to reduce German competitiveness in this important field.[191]

The broad linkages forming within Metaman are particularly evident in business. Sony is thought of as a Japanese company, but it has operations all over the world, and some 45 per cent of its employees are non-Japanese. In fact, Sony was the biggest *exporter* of televisions from the US in 1989.[192] Similarly, the Coca-Cola company now derives more than 80 per cent of its income from operations outside the US and many of its top executives are non-American.[193] When it comes to commerce, it is becoming difficult to determine what is in a particular nation's interest. Honda is now the number three US car producer and is exporting cars produced in the US to Europe and Japan.[194] Is Honda's continued success 'good' or 'bad' for Americans? Some US citizens hope to help their country by purchasing 'American' products, but in the interdependent world of today it is no easy task to determine where a product has been produced.[195] Certainly a name is not enough. I picked up some batteries being sold under the General Electric label and they were stamped 'Made in Korea' and had 'Produced in Taiwan' on the packaging. The Firestone Tire Company is a Japanese company (owned by Bridgestone); Jaguar is a General Motors subsidiary; Zenith Computers is owned by Group Bull of France. Today, almost any large manufacturer that hopes to compete effectively must have operations, suppliers and customers scattered throughout the developed world.[196]

National governments may struggle to maintain their authority over local regions that are pushing for autonomy, but these same governments also voluntarily relinquish authority to international bodies. The member states of the European Economic Community (EEC), for example, are giving up much of their control of tariffs and agricultural policy, and they may one day do so even with their power to manage their currencies.[197] The dynamics of Metaman's evolution are driving such developments. Nations, however reluctantly, are being swept along by the consequences of proliferating long-range economic ties.

Commerce is a powerful force driving the world towards global integration, because as countries join together economically they cannot avoid joining in other ways as well. When 'global government' eventually develops, it will not be imposed from above; it will arise from below as a natural outgrowth of economic and cultural interdependence. The United Nations, invaluable as it may be as an instrument for resolving regional disputes, is limited by a focus that is political rather than economic. The move beyond the nation-state is not driven directly by politics but by the underlying economic and technological changes that are reshaping the political landscape.

As a creature of commerce, the EEC exemplifies the physiological workings of Metaman. This union is prototypic of the organizational structures likely to exert great influence over human affairs in the future. Indeed, the EEC may ultimately become the first global power that is truly multinational. By 1994 this free-trade zone is expected to include eighteen countries and more than 380 million people,[198] and several decades hence it may well stretch from Iceland to Russia and include some 900 million.

These European nations are leading the way in confronting the many daunting political challenges posed by broad multilateral economic integration. Because such integration is an essential feature of Metaman's ongoing development, the institutional structures Europe develops in the process may serve as a nucleus in extending the pattern worldwide. From our vantage point in history, it might seem that sovereign states would never agree to relinquish their control of currency and other important economic matters, but the move is less radical than it may seem. For years, national governments have been losing their ability to manipulate their economies independently. With the globalization of capital markets, for example, the ability of a nation to modify its interest rates freely has greatly diminished. If one nation sets its prime rate too high or low by global standards, disruptively large cross-border flows of capital result. Thus, even now, international markets greatly constrain national economic policies. There will undoubtedly be many setbacks and delays in the move towards European economic union. The process cannot be as straightforward as once imagined at the 1991 Maastricht meeting,[199] but the move towards union is being driven by powerful economic forces and its fulfillment is only a matter of time.

The EEC, Japan and the US are the three principal economic powers today. A traditional view suggests that they, like the colonial powers of previous centuries, will struggle to carve out spheres of geographic influence. But Metaman's development is not moving in this direction. Global competition will increasingly be between corporations and corporate alliances rather than nations.[200] Announcements of strategic collaborations in the corporate realm are nearly a daily occurrence. AT&T, Sony, Apple, Motorola, Phillips and Matsushita form an alliance to speed the development of mass-market products for computer networks; Daimler-Benz and Mitsubishi work out a cooperative marketing arrangement; IBM and Siemens decide to build a 700 million-dollar French factory to produce advanced chips.[201] In the 1980s European, Japanese and American corporations formed some 1800 alliances: 53 per cent between European and US companies, 14 per cent between European and Japanese ones, and 33 per cent between Japanese and US companies.[202] Japan and the US may engage in polemics about trade imbalances,[203] but while they are quarrelling, their economic integration continues.[204]

With the formation of Metaman, global economic necessities are overpowering insular national policies. Obstacles do arise in difficult negotiations such as those to expand GATT to cover services, foreign investment, farm products, and intellectual property rights, but the larger trend is evident in the relative success of the EEC, the diminished trade barriers in both North and South America, and the end to the economic isolation of Eastern Europe, China and India. Ultimately, global economic interdependence is inevitable because it is a consequence of the technological progress in transportation and communication inherent in Metaman. It is self-defeating for a nation to try to hold itself apart from the world economy: no single country can match the pace of technological advance in the world at large; so a country that isolates itself must gradually fall behind. Moreover, many of today's most challenging endeavors require more resources than any single nation can supply.[205]

TOWARDS GLOBAL CULTURE

A few centuries ago, the world brimmed with rich, distinctive cultural traditions. Not only were Zulus, Eskimos, Maoris and other native cultures still largely isolated from outside influences, but the differences between developed lands were pronounced.

Today, such diversity is mostly a thing of the past. A few traditional native cultures still persist, but their days are numbered. They cannot long withstand the seductive influences of tourists and modern communications, nor effectively isolate themselves in remote preserves. Inevitably, they too will be transformed, because mass production, instantaneous communication, specialization and rapid change are largely incompatible with the social order of the pre-industrial age. A traveler who climbs into the mountains between Thailand and Burma may still find villages of the Akka tribe, but he or she will be greeted by women hawking souvenir bracelets and necklaces.

The fashions of youth protest today are global. It would be hard to guess that these are Czech kids; the photo was taken in Prague only six months after Vaclav Havel's rise to power in December 1989. Courtesy of Larry Boyd, Impact Visuals.

The effects of Metaman's birth on the cultures of the developed world have been equally potent. Throughout these lands people increasingly use the same products, hear the same music, see the same images of world events, study the same subjects, and watch the same films and television shows.[206] Students in Prague celebrated Communism's 1990 fall by playing Beatles music. Children eat Big Macs in Tokyo. I pick up sushi at my grocery store in Los Angeles.

As cultural environments around the world become more similar to one another, so too do people's lifestyles. But we need not fear that society is headed towards an eventual homogenization that will reduce life to a boring sameness everywhere. Individuals are enjoying more – not less – choice and variety in what they experience. This is because modern communication, trade and travel are bringing a rich cosmopolitan culture into being by making the world's broad diversity accessible to everyone.

People of ethnic minorities may feel they are losing their cultural identities, but ethnic majorities are sharing this experience. As the world's peoples become tied together, every culture inevitably is finding itself a minority culture. Though each may retain many special qualities, it will none the less become a variant of a larger pattern common to all. For example, Japan, though ethnically homogeneous, is changing significantly as its international ties multiply. Japanese attitudes about employment, material consumption, and the role of women are moving towards those typical of other developed countries.

The growing exposure of individuals everywhere to diverse cultural patterns is diminishing the strength of traditional lifestyles and cultural identities. When this leads to disturbing social transitions or to conflict between generations, it is tempting for communities to try to block the 'outside' influences. But the spread of global culture is not a matter of political choice, it is – like the transition to a global economy – intrinsic to Metaman. The continuing evolution of this planetary being – the mingling of peoples, the diffusion of imagery and ideas, the spread of modern products and technologies – is bringing this transformation.

The broad replacement of local cultural patterns by a rich, global one is evident throughout the body of Metaman – in clothing, music, television, film, science and even architecture. For example, architec-

The emergence of international culture has been accompanied by the rapid spread of global icons. This statue of Colonel Sanders stands outside the Kentucky Fried Chicken fast-food restaurant in Peking; in the background is the Zhenyang Gate of Tiananmen Square. Photo by Mark Avery, Bettmann Archives.

tural norms in the developed world today are a far cry from the geographically distinct styles of the past. Swiss chalets, adobe ranches, and thatch cottages all reflected their particular cultures and the building materials available locally. Now an architect looking at a photo of a recently constructed high-rise apartment building would have great difficulty identifying the country in which it stands.[207]

As to clothing, the colorful and varied folk costumes of times past may mainly be relegated to special festivals and dance performances,[208] but the diversity of color, form and fabric seen at some gatherings in New York is probably greater than all the variation offered by any *single* culture of the past. Interestingly, people's attire is becoming specialized more by activity than locale or social status. A photo may give only subtle clues as to a person's nationality but reveal clearly if he or she has just been skiing, playing tennis or working in an office.

One reason for the richness of the global culture now emerging within our planetary super-organism is that modern culture incorporates and extends, rather than simply supplants, elements from traditional cultures. The process is clearly revealed in today's music and food. Paul Simon's record, *Graceland*, for instance, blends rock 'n' roll chords and African tribal chants with strains from folk songs, blues and jazz. Such cross-fertilization is widespread and is expanding musical diversity by creating new forms and styles out of diverse local idioms. The unprecedented variety in today's cuisine emphasizes the depth and history of this process. Not only is the mutual contact between formerly isolated ethnic cuisines enriching contemporary dishes, but the so-called 'traditional' cuisines are themselves actually recent arrivals. They are the product of the beginnings of global commerce and the voyages of the European seafarers of the sixteenth century. Prior to that time, Italian and Spanish dishes had no tomatoes or red pepper, the Indians no curry, the British no potatoes, and there was no beef, pork or lamb in the New World.[209]

Of all the forces pushing humanity towards a common culture, the most powerful may well be radio, film, and television. During the Persian Gulf War, humankind sat together to watch events as they were occurring. Cable News Network's coverage was a dramatic demonstration of how far worldwide communication has advanced, but the routine day-to-day broadcast images permeating Metaman have a much greater cumulative social effect. The global character of such programming is seen in the fact that foreign syndication receipts for many American television sitcoms exceed their domestic receipts.[210] France, for example, is particularly zealous in protecting its culture, yet 47 per cent of the fiction programs broadcast on French television in 1990 were American.[211] Moreover, even when television shows are created in different countries, their themes are generally similar. The production and 'packaging' may be different for each country's soap operas, panel shows, situation comedies and game shows, but the content is not. A luxury car beside a beautiful home, a view of earth from space, Mickey Mouse, a starving child in Africa – similar images and symbols fill people's lives and help define the global culture now forming.

Whether through worldwide telephone links, television broadcasts by satellite, global financial markets, or international scientific conferences, a massive flow of information is strengthening Metaman by drawing humanity into an ever-tighter network of activity. Modern communication technology is mixing more than cultures; it is breaking down divisions between religions, professions, social classes and even scientific fields. Today archaeologists use the techniques of molecular biology to trace the origins of different ethnic groups; biochemists use X-ray crystallographic techniques from physics to study proteins; artists use computers to produce special visual effects; and individuals draw selectively from Buddhism, Christianity and Muslim faiths as well as natural science to form their personal philosophies.

The development of our global super-organism is augmenting rather than reducing the range of possibility in people's lives. Although the distinctions *between* different cultures are shrinking, the diversity *within* each culture is greatly expanding. London and Madrid are more alike today than they were a century ago, but each city is itself more diverse now. People have more choice than ever before in food, books, clothing, music, sports, travel and even careers.

Improved communication has been central to the coalescence of the human enterprise, and the synergies of Metaman are in turn greatly enhancing communication. Generally accepted standards, whether concerning the diameters of bolts or the protocols of computer networks, are communication tools that ease the task of cooperation. Thus, such conventions are multiplying in all fields.[212] The standards that are adopted are not necessarily superior, they may just happen to be most prevalent when alternative systems begin to compete. Language, of course, is one of the most important communication conventions. The dominance of the English language, now the *de facto* international standard for business and science,[213] illustrates the phenomenon. International meetings are usually held in English, and the most important research in many countries is now submitted to

English-language journals.[214] English owes its favored position not to its intrinsic qualities, but to its wide dispersal by a colonizing England followed by America's preeminence at the time of the advent of global communications and trade. Had global integration occurred at some previous historical period, however, the world might now be conducting its business in French, Spanish or Chinese.

As English and several other major languages have become firmly entrenched, minor languages throughout the world have been disappearing. Linguists estimate that most of the world's 6,000 existing languages will be gone within a century or two,[215] because when a small isolated population is assimilated into a larger economy and culture, local languages generally disappear within a few generations. Even among large populations whose languages are under no immediate threat, however, the incentives to learn a major world language will grow because the world's burgeoning information store is available in only a few languages.[216] Over 60 million people speak Tamil, but how many biology papers, physics texts, or even films will ever find their way into this language, and how up-to-date will they be?[217]

Language is a key aspect of traditional cultural identity, and its loss – which necessarily obliterates people's poetry, songs, and even their

---

III. 結 果

1. 原発巣の腫瘍血管

直径 10 μm の腫瘍血管では，内皮細胞は比較的厚く，surface は比較的 smooth で，多数の pinocytotic vesicle を認めた．basal lamina は明瞭で，この type の腫瘍血管を多数認めた (**Fig. 1 a**)．直径 6 μm の腫瘍血管では前者と異なり，内皮細胞に surface infolding が見られ，vacuole も多数認めた．basal lamina は不明瞭で，perivascular space は拡大していた (**Fig. 1 b**)．Desmoplastic variant の腫瘍血管では，内皮細胞は菲薄化し，short な intercellular junction が見られたが，opening は認めなかった．また，多数の tubular body を認めた．basal lamina は不明瞭で一部多層化しており，周囲に多数の collagen fiber を認めた (**Fig. 1 c**)．レプリカ像では pinocytotic vesicle は 1 平方 μm 当たり平均 23 個に増加

していた (**Fig. 1 d**)．また，5 - 7 条の tight junction が見られた (**Fig. 1 e**)．

2. 播種巣の腫瘍血管

脊髄腔播種巣の直径 8 μm の腫瘍血管では，内皮細胞は不規則で，surface infolding も目立ち，endothelial proliferation を認めた．intercellular junction は short なものが多かったが，明らかな opening は見られなかった．basal lamina は不明瞭で一部多層化しており，perivascular space は拡大していた (**Fig. 2 a**)．同症例の右シルヴィウス裂播種巣の腫瘍血管では fenestration を 3 箇所に認めた (**Fig. 2 b**)．大脳縦裂播種巣の直径 13 μm の腫瘍血管では，内皮の菲薄化した部分に fenestration を認めた (**Fig. 2 c**)．

3. 遠隔臓器転移巣の腫瘍血管

リンパ節転移巣の腫瘍血管では，内皮細胞の肥厚，菲薄化と surface infolding が著明で，fenestration も認め

This excerpt from the Japanese medical journal, Noshinkei Geka *(Neurological Surgery), is sprinkled with English phrases embedded in the Japanese text. Though understood worldwide by specialists, these phrases are obscure to most English-speaking natives. In field after field, this trend towards extreme specialization of content and vocabulary is accompanying an increasingly international usage of English.*

vocabulary – is sure to be accompanied by profound cultural change. Undeniably such change includes loss; this is part of the trauma of Metaman's birth. But the collapse of cultures and societies is not new to the present era, only our general awareness of it and the frequency with which it is occurring is unprecedented.

While recognizing this loss, it is important to be conscious of the enormous opportunities Metaman is creating. The emerging global culture is being broadly embraced – especially by the young – because it offers a vision of equality, individual fulfillment and a better future. So alluring is the theme of 'globalism', it is already beginning to be used in marketing campaigns – 'The United Colors of Benetton', for instance.

In many ways, 'idealized' American culture – a multi-ethnic, egalitarian, technological and materially affluent celebration of growth, change, and individual freedom – is the prototype of the evolving cosmopolitan culture of Metaman. The US is prototypic, however, not because it is shaping the world, but because the forces shaping Metaman have been transforming America faster than other places. Why? First, America is more socially malleable because it has had fewer entrenched traditions to displace and has known a long history of cultural change brought by the influences of successive waves of immigrants. Second, America, by escaping the general destruction of the Second World War, began to experience the social effects of general affluence, modern communications and advanced manufacturing technologies before most other nations.

America, unsurpassed in embracing diversity, has taken different peoples and cultures and forged an identity that largely transcends ethnicity. A major appeal of American culture is that it is virtually all-inclusive. Not only are pizza, hot dogs and jazz all seen by Americans as typically American, but a Chinese, Nigerian or Iranian immigrant, though he or she would never fully be accepted as 'British' or 'German', can become as much an 'American' as anyone else.

The reality of America may fall far short of the ideals of personal fulfillment, individual freedom, social equality and opportunity that lie at the core of *idealized* American values, but these ideals are none the less embodied mythically in film and on television and have broad appeal worldwide. It is this mythos rather than American culture *per se* that is so appealing as a vision of the future. To some people, this vision means simply enough food to eat, to others, material affluence, to still others, freedom of expression or release from rigid social constraints. But more than anything else, the evolving global culture embodies the concept of a better life for the individual.

Not surprisingly, rock music, Coca-Cola, McDonald's, television situation-comedies and other signs of 'popular culture' are sometimes enthusiastically welcomed and sometimes bitterly attacked when they spread into new regions. Some people see the promise they symbolize, others the losses they will cause. In more-developed lands such products are often seen as symbols of cultural decay, in less-developed countries, as the harbingers of jarring changes that will eventually displace existing modes of life.

The struggle between traditional values and the forces of Metaman is particularly evident in the collision between Muslim fundamentalism and modernism in the Arab world. Iran's tumultuous return to parochialism and rigid orthodoxy with the overthrow of the Shah in 1979 did provide temporary refuge from the cultural influences being brought by Metaman's growth, but in Iran, as elsewhere, the patterns of our planetary super-organism are certain to dominate eventually. In fact, pressures for increased moderation in Iran are already building.[218] As communication, travel and trade continue to expand, cultures will be ever less able to isolate themselves from the pervasive influences of the world at large.

Humankind's increasingly shared culture and experience is expanding individual perspective beyond narrow regional and ethnic bounds and forming a human community capable of confronting the larger challenges facing the world. Of all the challenges for humankind, however, the greatest may well be the social and psychological adjustments Metaman is demanding of us.

THE DYNAMIC OF METAMAN

Many ongoing developments such as the emancipation of women, the spread of human rights, the breakdown of class boundaries, and the democratization of society appear to be matters of social 'choice'. This may be true in the short term, but over the long term, these developments are inevitable consequences of the basic forces moving Metaman forward.

Slavery disappeared by just this process. This practice, which has been a nearly universal institution since the beginning of history, existed in Greece, India, Africa, China, the Middle East, and even Renaissance Italy.[219] In 1395, for example, a merchant near Florence wrote to his partner in Genoa, 'Pray buy me a little slave girl, between eight and ten years old, and she must be of good stock.'[220] Until a few

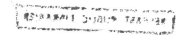

centuries ago most people, including even the framers of the US Constitution, accepted slavery as natural.[221] Then, quite suddenly, the practice was gone.

The reason for slavery's virtual disappearance is not that humans have grown more ethical, but that the nature of human endeavor has changed. Athens during its 'golden age' was supported by a large slave population because it had to be. No feasible alternative then existed for an affluent democracy with equality among its 'citizens'. If one group – in this case some 30,000 citizens – was to have time for philosophy, art, science and war, another group had to do the work. Consequently, societies needed slavery or some hierarchical social structure like that of feudal Europe. The Roman Empire, for example, took a middle path: rural Italy had both a vast peasantry *and* large numbers of slaves.[222]

The coming of the Industrial Revolution permanently changed the social equation: harnessing fossil fuels raised human productivity enough to make possible a civilization not supported by a large human underclass. Furthermore, as jobs became more complex, direct coercion of workers became less useful. Forcing large numbers of slaves to harvest crops or to work quarries is different from making them do complex tasks requiring individual initiative and years of education. As economic systems evolved, they soon proved better than slavery at organizing and controlling labor.[223] The workers in Britain's early textile mills were paid such pitiable wages that slaves would have been far more expensive. Slaves had to be fed, housed and cared for, or replaced at significant expense, but employers had no responsibilities to hired laborers. Indeed, immediately prior to the American Civil War, Irish laborers were frequently used for jobs considered too dangerous for slaves,[224] who were a capital asset that owners were loathe to risk.

In the world of today, it seems so self-evident that slavery is wrong that it is hard to imagine viewing the practice any other way. But attributing slavery's banishment to *our* moral superiority would imply that Thomas Jefferson, Hammurabi, Socrates and Cicero were less 'ethical' than the ordinary person of today. This is unlikely, particularly since we tolerate so much unnecessary human misery in the midst of plenty. In truth, outlawing slavery could not become a feasible political objective until advancing technology and new sources of power (the same essential forces responsible for Metaman's emergence) brought the increased productivity and expanded commerce that made slavery economically unnecessary and socially undesirable. Until recent times, *universal* human equality was not a possibility for human society. The

Bronze slave-collar (top) found around the neck of a skeleton in southern Rome. 'If captured return me to Apronanus, minister in the imperial palace, at the Golden Napkin on the Aventine, for I am a fugitive slave.' Bronze plaque, 3rd-4th century (bottom); 'I am Asellus, slave of Prejectus attached to the ministry of markets and I have escaped the walls of Rome. Capture me, for I am a fugitive slave, and return me to Barbers' Street near the Temple of Flora.' Courtesy Dutuit Collection, Petit Palais, Paris.

concept may have been appealing, but why would it have been taken any more seriously than other idealistic and impractical notions?[225] For example, almost everyone in earlier ages would undoubtedly have welcomed the disappearance of starvation and disease but would not have imagined such goals to be possible. Only today – by virtue of Metaman – have these become realistic possibilities, and only recently have these goals, like slavery before them, begun to be viewed as moral imperatives.

The collapse of European Communism is a recent demonstration of how humanity is swept along by the larger currents of Metaman – this time, global trade and electronic communication. Ultimately, Communism failed because central planning was not up to the immense task of orchestrating a modern consumer-based economy. The Soviet leadership saw that, without a change in direction, their nation was destined to become irrelevant economically – and eventually politically. Knowing they could never match the accelerating pace of technological advance in the robust global economy, the Soviets embarked on their program of economic restructuring, 'perestroika', to try to stave off an otherwise inescapable decline.

Economic necessity explains why reform was attempted, but it does not explain why Communist regimes throughout Eastern Europe toppled like dominoes once direct Soviet power was withdrawn. Clearly, this disintegration was not part of Gorbachov's original plan. Why did it happen? Neither starvation nor unemployment stalked the Eastern Bloc countries. Other peoples – in India, China or even in Eastern Europe before the First World War – have suffered much more and remained compliant. Unlike those countries, however, the Eastern Bloc was tied into the global network[226] and could not hide its failures. East Germans could watch West German television and see how well their kinsmen were faring. Hungarians and Czechoslovakians could compare their post-war progress to Austria's.

The sudden disintegration of European Communism surprised almost everyone, everywhere. Governments, unable to control such events as the massive exodus of East Germans to the West, could only scramble to try to respond to what was happening.[227] Their efforts were futile. Each clash augmented the next, and each reform movement drew strength from the others. Far-reaching changes, following a course of their own making, swept through Eastern Europe and then into the Soviet Union itself.

Today, as a result of the electronic linkages of Metaman's evolving nervous system, events often rapidly cascade towards critical climaxes. The lag between action and reaction is shorter than ever before because instantaneous communications force all involved parties to react to events as they occur. The attempted Soviet *coup* of August 1991 stands as a perfect example: it telescoped the demise of the Soviet Union into a few intense days. Political maneuvering did not drag on for months while rival factions jockeyed for position and tried to gauge how key groups would react; the allegiances of all important players became obvious almost immediately.

CHANGE IS THE ONLY CONSTANT

Metaman's birth is bringing tumultuous social change that many people would rather avoid. Thus, governments sometimes try to maintain the *status quo* by protecting their markets, delaying new technologies, blocking foreign investment, censoring films and music, mandating national languages, or even forbidding overseas travel. Such policies are in opposition to the forces working within Metaman. Societies cannot long isolate themselves from the outside world. Time after time regimes have tried and failed. In the 1940s Argentina nationalized many industries and erected stiff import barriers to protect itself; now, with a decrepit economy, it has been forced to backtrack and privatize scores of inefficient state-owned industries. South Africa created a powerful police state to preserve white supremacy, but after decades of economic and political isolation, the country is ending apartheid and beginning to rejoin the world community. In 1992, South Africa's whites voted overwhelmingly to continue the process, and the country fielded an Olympic team for the first time in thirty years.[228]

For a society to remain healthy in today's world, flexibility is essential. Metaman is not static, it is continually renewing itself, adjusting its form, and adapting. Its vital, organic nature has obvious implications for present-day economic policy. The continued transformation of our global economy is inevitable, so there will always be industries that are thriving and growing, and ones that are withering and dying. Government cannot stop this process. The public policies that best ease society's ongoing transformation are not those that resist change, but those that embrace it by facilitating the redeployment of human or other resources that are displaced. A competitive economy no longer demands bountiful natural resources – the Japanese have few, and Singapore, Taiwan and Hong Kong almost none. Economic success within Metaman grows from a well-educated[229] and productive population, modern communication and transportation networks, and a stable political environment that fosters competition. These are the new 'natural' resources in the Age of Metaman.

7

RITES OF PASSAGE

Perspectives on Global Concerns

IN 1988 NORTH AMERICA suffered a hot, wilting summer and extensive crop failures.[230] Was it a harbinger of global warming and agricultural shortages? In 1992, the concentration of ozone-destroying chemicals above Northern Europe and Russia rose sharply.[231] Would atmospheric ozone depletion be far more severe than previously projected? Today, the barrage of dire predictions about humanity's future is so unceasing that even the inhabitants of a remote tropical paradise worry about what lies ahead. In 1987 the Maldives, fearing that rising sea-levels would submerge their beautiful archipelago in the Indian Ocean, petitioned the UN to declare the country endangered.[232] These collective fears, however, do not mean that humanity is moving towards some planetary disaster. Our influences are not an intrusion on the earth's ongoing pattern of biological change; they are an extension of that pattern.

Implicit in most current visions of humanity's future is the idea that we are a species out of control and rapidly devouring the limited store of global resources available. This perspective offers no reasonable hope that humanity's fate will differ from that of any other species suddenly unchecked by natural constraints. Eliminate the snakes and other predators from an island inhabited by rabbits and it will soon be overrun; but once the island has been stripped bare, the rabbit population will crash. Under equivalent conditions, bacteria, insects, deer and other animals will invariably follow similar paths. On what basis can one contend that this will not be humanity's fate? Some optimists maintain that the world's resources are unlimited; others hope for some miraculous change in human behavior; still others predict that amazing technological breakthroughs will save humankind. Yet none of these notions holds up to scrutiny – from a traditional biological viewpoint humanity's future looks grim.

An alternative perspective, one that acknowledges the existence of Metaman, however, suggests bright prospects because it recognizes that the emerging global network of human activity is becoming self-regulating. Many people blame today's environmental problems on the rise of our high-technology society, but humanity has long exerted strong influences on its environment. Some ten thousand years ago, humans brought about the extinction of the woolly mammoth, large-horned bison, ground sloth and other large mammals of North America.[233] The deforestation of much of Europe, China, India and North America was by human hands. Admittedly, Metaman can bring about such changes in decades rather than centuries or millennia,[234] but what is really new is not the existence of environmental problems, but the existence of *solutions*.

Imagine how dismal our future would look if technological progress had stalled before the Second World War. Our underlying challenges would be largely unchanged: humankind would still be consuming the planet's precious fossil fuels and other resources; the level of CFCs and other greenhouse gases would still be rising; human population would still be multiplying; nations would still be at war. Without the 'senses' of Metaman, however, humanity would be largely unaware of its problems: there would be no adequate projections of vital resources or agricultural production, no satellite surveys of disappearing forests, no detailed measurements of atmospheric change. Furthermore, even if humanity could somehow figure out what was happening, it could do little without modern technologies and global communications. There would be no replacement for fossil fuels when they were finally exhausted and no way to halt population growth without a rise in death rates.

This, however, is *not* the situation today. Humanity's problems are generally known and solutions are understood. Renewable energy sources could largely replace fossil fuels; birth control could check population growth; new technologies could control pollution and environmental destruction. The challenge to humanity is not to *find* solutions but to *implement* them, and Metaman's role will be central in this. Isolated individual behavior is often unresponsive to distant indirect threats, but Metaman possesses the mechanisms broadly to coordinate human activity and therefore can address these matters. In fact, it is making remarkable progress already.

THE FADING THREAT OF NUCLEAR WAR

For nearly four decades, the specter of global nuclear cataclysm has hung over humanity.[235] Of all the menaces that have faced humankind through history, this alone has been capable of suddenly obliterating its long progress. Now, this threat may be disappearing for ever, not as the harvest of arms-control treaties carefully negotiated among world leaders, but as a secondary consequence of far deeper currents. Recall that humanity is in the midst of a nearly fifty-year period of relative peace – the longest without a direct war between major powers since the Roman Empire,[236] and today this peace is more secure than ever. This is not just some historical anomaly – a lucky break that must eventually end – it is a manifestation of the enduring changes in human society accompanying Metaman's birth.

One deterrent to global war is, of course, technological advance: nuclear weapons make absurd the idea of victory in all-out war. But major powers have also stopped battling one another because the economic incentives for conquest and territorial expansion have largely disappeared. Since the Second World War, Metaman's proliferous growth has tied nations together as never before, and their actions have begun to reflect this interdependence.

Historically, commercial competition has not brought peace, but war, with kingdoms battling to gain markets, raw materials and tributes. Carthage and Rome fought bitterly over Mediterranean trade. England and Spain clashed over their colonial empires. The speed with which the world has changed can be seen by considering that in 1939 Hitler, to build a German empire, seized Poland and Czechoslovakia and precipitated the Second World War. But now, some fifty years later, if Poland were to *petition* Germany and plead for union of their two nations, the request would almost certainly be denied. Germany would gain little by taking on the financial burdens of Poland, a country in which it already enjoys ample influence without the responsibility of governing. Indeed, many West Germans were unenthusiastic about even *German* reunification. In the developed world of today, unless a foreign country has few people and possesses considerable resources, it is no prize.

In essence, economic and military power are decoupling: no longer does military might guarantee economic strength, nor economic strength rest on military power. Actually, the two are increasingly in opposition because war diverts resources away from areas now crucial to economic development – education, research and capital investment – and leaves little economic benefit in its wake. Even before the 1991

Gulf War began, the US was pressuring other nations to help finance the undertaking. Far from viewing this war as a desirable economic stimulant, the US saw it as an economic burden to be shared.[237] Nor does a lack of open conflict relieve the costs of military preparedness. The arms race has been such a drain on the Second World War's victors that it hastened the collapse of the Soviet Union. That two of the most robust economies in the world today – Germany and Japan – are powers that were forced to limit military spending for nearly fifty years is more than coincidence;[238] it is testimony to the shifting nature of international competition within Metaman. Ironically, forcing these countries to concentrate on commerce, which is so central to the metabolism of Metaman, enabled each to gain the regional primacy it could not achieve by military means.

As economic interdependence increases, armed conflict between major powers becomes ever more self-destructive. The French and Germans have been at war repeatedly during the last two centuries,[239] but in the last two decades they have become so economically joined that armed conflict between the two nations is nearly unthinkable. Were they ever to stop trading with one another abruptly, the economic disruption would be so severe it would generate strong internal pressures to restore commerce. The same is true for the US and Japan, and for many other countries as well. With ties proliferating between the former antagonists in the Cold War, the prospects for permanent peace between major powers are excellent.

Global communication and culture are two more of Metaman's 'mechanisms' for deterring military conflict. In the nineteenth century, the great powers could routinely use war to effect their policies; today their range of action is sharply limited by world opinion, the very existence of which is a direct result of Metaman's evolution. The term 'world opinion' is actually a way of referring to a host of newly formed interdependencies that restrict unilateral action within Metaman. In 1845 the US could invade Mexico with impunity and seize what is now the American Southwest,[240] whereas in 1989 the US felt it needed to go to great lengths to justify a limited action against President Noriega in Panama.

Television is one of the most powerful influencers of world opinion. It has figured prominently in transforming our experience of distant war from an abstract exercise in patriotism to a visceral barrage of images of carnage and grief.[241] This vicarious involvement makes it harder for domestic audiences to be manipulated into tolerating heavy casualties or feeling blind hostility for an 'enemy' population.[242] Thus, television makes it difficult for a major power to sustain support for an extended war, even one it could easily win.

Without widespread modern communications, the strategic maneuvering to influence public opinion during the 1991 Gulf War would have been unthinkable.[243] Iraq's Scud missile attacks on Israel had no *direct* military importance; they were an attempt to provoke an Israeli retaliation that might incite Arab demonstrations, fracture the UN coalition, and force the US into a political settlement. Another demonstration of the ability of modern communications to inhibit military action by superior forces took place in Lithuania: with no weapons whatsoever, it defied Moscow and eventually gained its independence.

Humanity's current relative peace is not fragile: it is the product of progress in technology, communications and commerce. Not only is all-out war between major powers a thing of the past, regional wars too will gradually fade as less-developed lands join more fully with the global network.[244] Ending war is a goal that once was seemingly insurmountable, yet it is well on the way to being accomplished by the internal dynamics of Metaman's development. This exemplifies the subtle, yet powerful mechanisms that are now in the process of resolving humanity's fundamental challenges.[245]

POPULATION GROWTH – THE CHALLENGE OF OUR ERA

With the threat of nuclear war receding, the central challenge facing humanity has become its growing population.[246] Our numbers are swelling by some 95 million people each year[247] – another France every seven months, another Mexico every year, another India *and* Pakistan every decade. Many people would like to ignore this difficult issue and behave as though it is far from their lives, but this problem belongs to us all; it belongs to Metaman. The most direct consequences of overpopulation are largely localized, but the indirect effects of burgeoning population growth are creating deep social tensions and blocking enduring progress on global environmental challenges. The biosphere itself feels the strain: overgrazing causes desertification;[248] overpumping empties aquifers;[249] cultivating fragile mountain slopes erodes topsoil;[250] and burning more fossil fuels adds to global warming. Most of the dangers of overpopulation are not new revelations though; Paul Ehrlich catalogued them in *The Population Bomb*[251] twenty-five years ago, when there were 'only' 3.5 billion people on the earth. Today, there are 2 billion more!

Achieving 'zero population growth' is a wise immediate goal for humanity. Human numbers, however, will not remain static when this goal is finally reached. Population will move towards whatever level proves to be most optimal for Metaman. Perhaps, the most desirable global population will be one billion – enough people to allow industry to realize scales of economy, yet not so many as to cause overcrowding. Or perhaps powerful new technologies will allow 10 or 15 billion people comfortably to inhabit the earth. Regardless, as Metaman matures and human reproductive decisions become largely divorced from sexual activity, individual choices about childbearing will be strongly influenced by broad social policies.

The key to understanding the present population problem is to realize that it is not an issue of population *density* but of limited resources. Hong Kong holds 250,000 people per square mile, twenty times even New York City's density.[252] People get along well in cities and heavily populated countries, but such places are not self-sufficient – they must draw upon the reserves of the rest of the world to survive.[253] The Dutch, for instance, live comfortably with a thousand people per square mile, but that is possible only because Holland

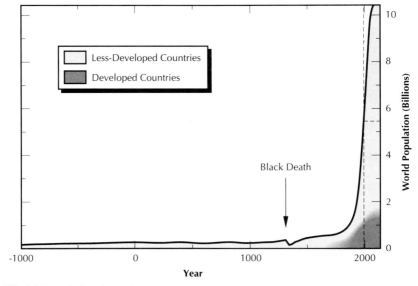

World Population has risen exponentially with the spread of modern medicine and health practices throughout the world, and at current rates the human population of 5.5 billion will exceed 10 billion by about 2040. More than 90 per cent of population growth is now in the less-developed world.

imports millions of tons of cereals and minerals annually, takes a half-million tons of fish from the sea, and extracts large deposits of off-shore gas. The globe as a whole, however, has no immediate prospect of using significant *external* resources, so if there are too many people, then many will have to live in abject poverty or die.

At its present level of technological development, Metaman cannot adequately support even the present human population. The super-organism's activities already tax the globe's ecological systems, and hunger and poverty are widespread. Global production of goods and services would have to increase four-fold just to raise the average income of the world's *existing* population to the level of present-day Western Europe. This is the crux of the population problem: the 'quality' of life for humankind as a whole.

If human population were to continue to grow at its present pace, the world would house some 40 billion people by the end of the next century, and some 200 billion a century later. This is impossible. There are only two alternatives: a drop in birth rates or a rise in death rates.[254] Some world leaders say that there is no crisis yet, that there is enough food to feed the world and that the only problem is distributing it. This was largely true in 1960, when world population was only 3 billion, but today it is true only when harvests are good, and soon it will be patently false. The burst in agricultural production brought by irrigation, new crop varieties, fertilizers, and increased agricultural acreage has slowed,[255] and biotechnology's 'green revolu-tion' still lies in the future.[256] Not only is erosion, salination and encroaching urban growth now removing land from agricultural pro-duction, but crop yields have stabilized and fertilizer is so common that its use cannot be expanded much further. The total amount of food produced, if there are no droughts in major agricultural regions, is still adequate to feed the world's population, but for how long? Humanity's major buffer against misfortune is that about a third of the world's grain production is now fed to livestock. But eating less meat,[257] an oft proposed 'solution' to world hunger, would be no more than a stopgap measure: the temporary surplus it supplied would be offset by population growth within little more than a decade.

Controlling human numbers is clearly a necessary step in the evolution of Metaman. On the surface, the super-organism's response to the challenge may seem nearly non-existent: human numbers continue to rise at an unprecedented rate. A deeper look, however, shows that clear progress is being made.[258] Population growth is already compara-tively low throughout Metaman's core in the developed world, and not because of broad *human* awareness of the 'population problem', but as a consequence of the social changes that have attended Metaman's formation.

The primary difficulty today is at Metaman's periphery, the less-developed world where more than 90 per cent of the increase in population is occurring.[259] But here too, there has been progress: birth rates in these regions have fallen by about a third since 1950. This reduction, however, has been obscured by the even more precipitous drop in death rates that began a generation earlier.[260] In 1915, for example, life expectancy at birth in India was only twenty years and India's population was stable at 250 million; by 1990 life expectancy had risen to fifty-seven years, and the population had more than tripled, to 850 million.[261] It is ironic that the overpopulation now causing so much misery in less-developed regions of Africa, Asia and South America is the result of the gains in life expectancy produced by modern medical and sanitation practices specifically intended to *relieve* hardship in these lands.

The present ravages of overpopulation in these countries are analogous to the devastation caused by modern military technology, which has made the conflicts in these regions so destructive. At times, painful social trauma and individual tragedy attends Metaman's spread, but it is worth remembering that this is but a stage in humanity's journey. The elimination of both war and population growth, which is now largely completed in Metaman's central regions, is sure to spread towards its periphery.

The control of population in the world's less-developed regions cannot occur, however, through the 'demographic transition' that occurred in Europe a century ago when rising standards of living led to a gradual drop in family size. Population growth in the less-developed world has been reducing standards of living there, so to halt that growth will require another mechanism – the widespread application of birth-control technologies. Very powerful tools are on the way:[262] significant progress, for instance, has been made towards developing a vaccine to 'immunize' women against conception.[263] A single pill or injection might prevent pregnancy for several years.[264] Enormous ethical dilemmas obviously lie just ahead, because the temptation for governments to employ these powerful tools aggressively to manage fertility problems will be nearly overwhelming, particularly in regions choked by overpopulation.

There can be no doubt that one way or another population growth will cease. The question is not *whether* Metaman will control human population growth, but *when* and *how*. How much famine and pestilence[265] will it take to prod humanity into embracing concerted family-planning efforts? What methods will be employed?

Before looking at the immediate prospects for aggressive action by Metaman, consider the nature of the challenge. It is commonly believed that the main obstacle to reducing birth rates is people's unwillingness to have smaller families. The data from family-planning efforts suggest otherwise. The primary reason that progress has been so slow in recent decades is not the difficulty of the task, but the meager resources devoted to it. Total international assistance for family-planning programs in the four decades from 1950 to 1989 *totalled* less than 10 billion dollars.[266] In 1988, for example, the assistance from all developed nations combined was only 660 million dollars – less than Americans spent on Hallowe'en costumes that year.[267]

Additional funds alone could have an enormous impact. The United Nations Population Fund estimates that global population could be stabilized at 9 to 10 billion people if, by the year 2000, the total annual contribution of the developed world were gradually raised to 5.5 billion dollars,[268] about a half of a per cent of the world's military expenditures in 1990.[269] Rapid progress in family planning is possible because large numbers of women in the less-developed world want to limit the size of their families but have no ready access to contraceptives. Half the women in South America with three or more children want no more babies,[270] and three quarters of the married women in Africa who want no more children are not using contraception.[271] A major reason for this situation is that the cost of contraceptives is often 10 per cent or more of average annual income in these regions.[272] The most compelling evidence of the need for better access to contraceptives, though, is not survey data but the 40 to 60 million abortions performed in the world each year[273] – many illegal, dangerous, and on women who already have many children.[274]

With effective family planning so 'easy' a task and one that is so critical to the transition of developing countries into Metaman's pattern, why is so little being done now? The answer lies in the nature of the population problem. The most immediate effects of overpopulation are largely manifested at the super-organism's periphery; the effects felt in its core regions are subtle and indirect. Thus, responding to this problem requires a more sophisticated global awareness than was necessary for a threat such as nuclear war. Metaman's response to population growth, much like that to other global environmental issues, understandably lags behind its response to more direct dangers. Concern about population was building in the early 1970s, but the acrimonious debate over abortion in the US[275] effectively interrupted international efforts in the area.[276] Now, however, population growth is once again receiving attention from environmental groups and the media,[277] and progress may prove surprisingly rapid.

War and population growth are both issues that relate to how Metaman regulates its own internal form: how it reshapes its body, renews its flesh, and grows. War has been the most obvious force in the struggle among cultures and peoples, but disease and famine and the abrupt population collapses that attend them can exert even stronger effects. The Aztec civilization was destroyed less by the military power of the Spanish conquistador Hernando Cortez and his few hundred men than by the ravages of smallpox and other diseases they brought.[278] The epidemics immediately following Cortez's arrival in 1519 killed about a third of the more than 25 million Amerindian population of Mexico and introduced diseases that within fifty years had eliminated nearly 90 per cent of that population.[279]

Throughout history war has been considered natural and unavoidable, only recently coming to be seen as a preventable evil.[280] Now an equally revolutionary change in humanity's view of disease and hunger is underway. Until the last few centuries, human life expectancy at birth was appallingly low; a baby boy born in France in 1740 had an average life-span of only twenty-four years.[281] No longer does it seem inevitable that many children become ill and die, that people starve to death, or that epidemics periodically sweep away millions. Just as economic, technological and social forces are now eliminating war as a significant competitive mechanism within Metaman, so too are these forces eliminating disease and hunger as the major constraints on human numbers. Metaman is now in the process of making a fundamental shift in the way it regulates its form and development. It is replacing clumsy, destructive mechanisms such as war and famine with more sophisticated ones such as economic competition and birth control. To accelerate that shift is the challenge of our era.

GLOBAL WARMING – LARGER PERSPECTIVES

Economics and birth control are refining Metaman's internal regulation, but it must also manage its external interactions. The threat of global warming exemplifies the new level of interplay between humanity and its environment. Responding to this potential danger is a task for Metaman as a whole, because significantly reducing the release of carbon dioxide and other greenhouse gases calls for more than the isolated actions of individuals or even the mandates of government; it requires fundamental changes in society.

'Global warming' is on today's public agenda not as a result of the pronouncements of farsighted government commissions. The issue grew out of mounting general concern prompted by scattered scientists and environmentalists in the early 1970s, and taken up by the media and the public. The activity percolating through society now includes scientific meetings, research projects, political lobbying, government commissions, international meetings . . . and even a little government action. This response is not orchestrated by any individual group; Metaman itself is beginning to stir.

The debate over 'global warming' has been acrimonious: some experts proclaim that humankind is on the brink of disaster, others that the dangers are grossly exaggerated.[282] There can be little doubt that *some* warming of the earth will occur from increased greenhouse gases.[283] The real questions are 'How much?', 'How soon?', and most importantly, 'What will the consequences be?' Record temperatures of the past few years suggest that the climate is already showing the effects of human activity,[284] but this is far from certain.[285] The consensus among atmospheric scientists in 1992 was that greenhouse warming during the coming century would be between 3 and 9 degrees Fahrenheit.[286] At present, Metaman can make no better judgment than this, but as its sensory systems improve and its analytic capacities expand, so too will its predictive powers.

A larger perspective helps clarify the possible impacts of climate change of this magnitude. Importantly, this potential warming is *not* beyond what the earth has known before. A hundred million years ago, when the dinosaurs reigned, carbon dioxide was as much as seven times what it is today, and global temperatures some 10 to 15 degrees above current levels.[287] Only 18,000 years ago, when the world was in the depths of an ice age,[288] global temperatures were some 9 degrees colder than today and glaciers more than a mile thick reached to where St Louis and Berlin now stand.[289] The ebb and flow of the ice-ages is governed largely by cyclical changes in the earth's rotation and orbit,[290] and the current 'interglacial' (the interval between ice-ages) is nearing its end. Thus, it is possible that within a few thousand years frigid conditions will return to our planet.[291] Of course, it is also conceivable that a Metaman-induced global warming will delay, or even block, the end of the current interglacial.

We might wish that the world's climate would always remain more or less as it is now, but this won't happen. Even if we were somehow immediately to stop altering the earth's atmosphere, humanity would still have to contend intermittently with large, sometimes rapid, 'natural' climate changes.[292] Therefore, should significant global warming occur, adapting to the change would only be the first of many similar challenges Metaman will face in the millennia ahead.

Just because 'global warming' does not carry the menace of impending planetary disaster,[293] though, does not mean that the threat is to be taken lightly. The potential effects are serious ones that would be greatly mitigated if Metaman were to reduce its production of greenhouse gases significantly. This would require widespread conservation of energy,[294] increased fuel efficiency in transportation, and a significantly reduced use of fossil fuels to generate electricity. Such changes are impossible without an enormous mobilization of resources over many decades.

Metaman's technological capacity to move beyond fossil fuels is indisputable. Alongside alternatives such as nuclear power, there are renewable energy sources such as biomass fuels,[295] wind and solar power poised to make significant contributions to our energy needs.

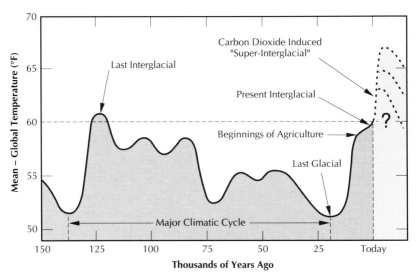

Planetary glaciation and deglaciation follow a cyclic pattern with a period of slightly more than 100,000 years.[296] The globe is now at the end of one such period and, in the absence of global warming, would move towards another ice age within the next few millennia. Whether renewed glaciation will be delayed, or even prevented, by greenhouse warming is as yet unclear. Note that the mean global temperature shown here ignores short-term fluctuations. Redrawn with permission of Enslow Publications.

Solar energy is close enough to being cost-competitive that mass production coupled with continuing technical advance could make it an important source of power in a few decades.[297] Moreover, in windy regions such as the Great Plains of the US, electricity from wind turbines is already cheaper than power from new coal-burning plants.[298] Studies suggest that with a concerted effort, half of all electrical power in the US could be derived from renewable sources within forty years.[299]

Transforming industrialized societies, though crucial in reducing the release of greenhouse gases, is only part of the challenge. The threat of global warming uniquely exposes the interdependence of all the world's peoples, because atmospheric pollution demands global solutions. No one country, no matter how completely it changes its own behavior, can escape the effects of excesses elsewhere. At present, the developed world is the major producer of greenhouse gases, but the less-developed world is catching up. In 1987 they produced 20 per

This windfarm is located in Altamont Pass, California, where there are some 7,500 wind turbines. In 1991, California had a capacity of more than 1,700 Megawatts, three quarters of the world's total generating capacity from wind and enough to meet the residential electrical needs of a city of a million people.[300] Today's most efficient wind turbines can generate electricity at 5 cents per kilowatt hour, the same cost as coal-generated power.[301] Photo by George Steinmetz, courtesy of Kenetech/US Windpower, Inc.

cent of the world's carbon-dioxide emissions; by 2010 they may account for 40 per cent.[302] China possesses more than a third of the world's coal reserves[303] and is pushing to industrialize; it is not going to slow its progress because of concern about global warming. Without viable alternatives, China will continue to build coal-burning power plants.[304] Hunger, poverty and economic growth will always be of more immediate interest to the developing world than carbon-dioxide emissions. Thus, if global emissions are to be reduced, the industrialized core of Metaman will have to provide less-developed regions with technologies that enable them to reduce emissions without retarding their development. And this appears feasible. Experts estimate that if the developing world could halt population growth and apply the most energy-efficient technologies currently available, it could achieve the standard of living enjoyed by Europe in the 1970s using only *10 per cent* more energy than at present.[305]

The complex interplay of government, science, business and the media about global warming shows the process of change within Metaman. A gradual realignment slowly emerges from the seemingly contradictory actions of its many parts. The super-organism may appear to be moving slowly, but the task of modifying its own metabolism is enormous. To imagine that it could substantially reduce its carbon-dioxide emissions easily is a little like maintaining that a chronic depressive should 'just cheer up'. Metaman's measured pace, however, does not mean it is not responding: some steps have already been taken: The 1987 Montreal protocol gradually phasing out Chlorofluorocarbons (CFCs) was strengthened in 1990 and again in 1992 to eliminate CFCs by the year 1996.[306] These policies will both reduce greenhouse warming *and* limit ozone depletion.[307] Further, in 1992 more than one hundred heads of state gathered in Brazil and pledged to attempt to slow the release of greenhouse gases.[308]

As improved climate projections become available in the next decade, policies in this realm are likely to become much more consistent than they are now. Either the threat will be found to have been overstated, and Metaman's current agitation will subside, or evidence of warming will be bolstered and the present response will have been the prelude to more aggressive action. To date, the policy directions under serious consideration – improving car fuel efficiency, increasing research on renewable energy, and reforestation – would be desirable even in the absence of global warming.[309]

The task of reducing mankind's dependence on fossil fuels is so tremendous, however, that regardless of how aggressively humanity moves in this direction the transition will take at least a half century.[310] Thus, if present projections are on target, Metaman will *have* to respond to broad climate change whose impacts would be large but not catastrophic. The most significant effect of 9 degrees of warming during the next century (the upper range of projections) would be to alter animal and plant communities greatly. Each degree of warming shifts the distribution ranges of species by some 60 miles, and a forest, which is particularly slow-moving and can migrate only about 100 miles a century by natural seeding mechanisms, could not keep pace. Metaman would undoubtedly do a lot of replanting, but such warming would none the less alter many local ecologies sufficiently to drive some plants and animals to extinction, especially those that are already narrowly distributed. But nature is resilient, and rapid changes such as these are not new. For instance, temperature shifts of this magnitude also occurred over only a fifty-year period at the end of the most recent ice age.[311]

Climate change taking fifty to a hundred years is rapid for natural ecosystems, but Metaman itself would have an easier time. Human society has demonstrated rapid, large-scale change time and again. Almost the entire 4-million-mile road system in the US was paved in the sixty-five years from 1920 to 1985.[312] Thirty years after nuclear power generation was developed in the late 1950s, France was generating some 70 per cent of its power from this source.[313] Berlin and Tokyo, two decades after being devastated by the Second World War, were vital and thriving. Human society is not static; Metaman is continually replacing and reshaping itself. The world's entire automobile fleet is largely replaced every fifteen years.[314] Industrial equipment lasts ten to twenty years,[315] buildings and other constructions generally less than a century. In fact, two thirds of Germany's capital stock (its buildings, highways, power lines and other infrastructure) is less than twenty years old.[316]

Climate changes occurring over many decades would be taken in stride by Metaman, because the continual turnover of its constituent parts enables it to transform and adapt. The activity of the superorganism that is most vulnerable to large changes in temperature and rainfall is agriculture.[317] Various crops would have to be moved into new geographic regions, and unfortunately, any major agricultural disruption lasting a few seasons might cause famine.[318] Such a tragedy, however, would be more appropriately attributed to overpopulation than to 'global warming' *per se*. As long as human numbers keep agriculture pushed to its very limits, humanity will remain vulnerable to intermittent famine. The most feasible solution is to control human

Metaman is continually renewing itself. Tokyo is one of the world's most vital cities, yet less than fifty years ago this was the Ginza, Tokyo's main shopping district. The photo was taken at the end of the second World War in December 1945 by David Davis. Courtesy of Bettmann Archives.

reproduction, not the earth's climate or the metabolism of Metaman. After all, if you built your house barely above the reach of high tide and then saw it swept away by a storm, the tempest would not be the cause of your misfortune.

The Imax film, *Blue Planet*,[319] shows the earth, as seen from the space shuttle, in breathtaking images projected on to a four-story screen.[320] Watching giant storm clouds swirl in a vortex a thousand miles across evokes a feeling of the utter immensity and beauty of our planet. Even Metaman's activities remain dwarfed by the earth's larger flows and rhythms – the ocean currents, the streaming clouds, the seasons, the slow creep of the continents themselves. As we reshape the natural world around us, we must not lose sight of the limits of Metaman's current powers. Though extraordinary, they are not yet up to the task of regulating the earth's atmosphere and climate. A complicated interplay of land, sea, atmosphere and living organisms keeps the conditions on the earth's surface stable even in the face of so cataclysmic an event as the impact of a giant meteor.[321] And a meteor a kilometer or more in diameter strikes the earth every few hundred thousand years with an explosive force that is some 5,000 times larger than the nuclear arsenals of all nations combined.[322]

Drastically altering the planet's resilient natural systems without understanding their subtle complexities is foolhardy. As humanity discovers the ways it is most altering the global environment – for example, burning fossil fuels or adding CFCs to the atmosphere – it would do well to moderate these activities, at least until it learns how to compensate for them. High-technology climate-management schemes like spreading aerosols in the upper atmosphere to reflect the sunlight or dusting the southern seas with iron to feed plankton blooms that absorb carbon dioxide[323] may be seductive, but at this early stage in Metaman's development, they would surely have unforeseen consequences that would have to be alleviated by yet further interventions. Such schemes would therefore invariably lead to a jumble of technological 'fixes' unable to regulate climate effectively.

The path towards planetary regulation should be approached with the utmost caution. After all, if you had a little dial to control your pulse rate, you would eventually find its use an onerous burden because what was once automatically regulated would demand constant attention. The same applies to global climate. Until Metaman has evolved to the point where it can create a *self-regulating* planetary system as robust as the one which now exists, its best interests lie in protecting the 'natural' systems that have worked so well. Perhaps one day this planetary creature will manipulate the climate;[324] certainly, if faced with the onset of another ice age, Metaman would try to ward off glaciation any way it could. But by that time its knowledge and power may be equal to the task.

DAWN OF THE SOLAR AGE

The major remaining challenge for Metaman is to assure its continued nourishment. Because its activity depends almost entirely upon the consumption of fuel and mineral lodes built up by geological processes over hundreds of millions of years, today's hectic activity appears to be 'unsustainable', destined eventually to grind to a halt as these resources are exhausted. One solution might be the popular 'New-Age' vision of a transition to a 'sustainable'[325] society through the dawning of an age of reduced material consumption, simpler lifestyles, and harmony and balance with 'nature'. This may be an appealing image, but Metaman's transition from its current pattern of activity will not lead towards some idyllic recasting of a bucolic past, but towards a world that makes full use of advanced technology and is far different from anything that has gone before. At this point, our ability to live in harmony with nature depends on technological advance, not simpler human lifestyles. In 1975 half of the deforestation in the world was to produce fuel for cooking and warmth.[326] The inescapable reality is that the human population is already far too large to return to pre-industrial patterns of production and consumption.

The key to development and growth – to life itself – is energy. This is as true for Metaman as for any living organism, so if energy were to become scarce, Metaman would be imperiled. But this planetary being will almost certainly have *more*, not less, energy at its disposal in the future, so humanity is not approaching an age of scarcity.

This rosy outlook is warranted by two factors. First, the availability of fossil fuels and other existing energy sources is likely to be more than adequate for at least the next century;[327] second, dramatic progress in the development of new sources of energy makes it clear that the move beyond fossil fuels is imminent.[328] 'Renewable' energy sources[329] such as the wind and sunlight are essentially unlimited ones that will never cost more to harvest than they do now. Rather, the more they are used, the cheaper they become. Mass producing solar cells, for example, would both reduce the cost of cells and spur their improvement – the same effects that have been so apparent with

This ten-megawatt power plant in the California desert, Solar I, generated power by using sun-tracking mirrors to focus sunlight on to the central collector and produce steam that would drive a turbine. Solar II, a more efficient plant that will use molten salt instead of steam in its central tower, is scheduled for completion by 1996 on the same site. Solar II will employ technology capable of generating electricity for about 7 cents per kilowatt hour, which approaches the 5 to 6 cents/kwh cost of power from coal and natural gas.[330] Courtesy of Southern California Edison.

computers, televisions and countless other devices.

Because these new energy technologies have the potential to supply so much power, they place an effective ceiling on the cost of energy. If, for instance, energy ever began to be sold above the price at which it could be generated by solar power, solar-power generators would soon be built to meet this demand.[331] Moreover, as these new technologies improve, this ceiling is bound to descend, until it eventually forces down the price of other energy sources. It is even conceivable that with so much capital invested in equipment to pump, refine and transport oil – which is often brought to the surface for less than 5 dollars a barrel[332] – falling demand might one day lead to a glut and tumbling oil prices. In any event, once alternative sources of energy begin to reduce the demand for oil,[333] a long-term rise in

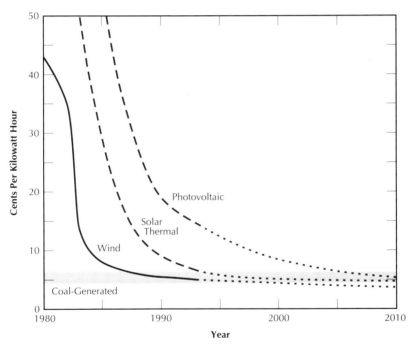

The cost of generating electricity from wind and sunlight has rapidly declined in the past decade. Wind-power costs (solid line) are those measured on existing installations. Costs of photovoltaic and solar-thermal generating plants (dotted lines) are derived using data from test plants and prototypes to estimate what would be possible for full utility-size generating facilities built from components manufactured in quantity. Such facilities, because they are as yet unable to compete with existing power-generating technologies, will probably not be built for at least a decade.[335]

energy prices will be virtually out of the question.[334]

In addition to energy, Metaman requires a continuing supply of the raw materials that form it. The potential exhaustion of key mineral resources does not, however, hang like a dark cloud over humanity's future, because mining is so energy-intensive that falling energy costs will make ever lower-grades of ore deposits usable.[336] In a sense, technology rations what can be used in any given era. Many reserves that are not 'economically' recoverable today will become so tomorrow,[337] and because lower-grade deposits are generally far more abundant than higher grade ones, the total 'recoverable' mineral resources will rise over time.

Another cause for optimism is that the material content of finished products is declining as smaller, more compact devices replace larger, heavier ones. This is happening not only in consumer electronics, where today's laptop computers are much more powerful than the early mainframe giants; but in telecommunications, where thin glass fibers now carry hundreds of thousands of times the information that large copper cables once did;[338] in transportation, where vehicle weight is declining and fuel efficiency rising;[339] and even in construction, where strong new concretes and girders are reducing structural bulk. Not only is overall weight decreasing, but plastics, silicon, fiberglass, ceramics and other materials derived from abundant planetary resources are replacing less-abundant resources such as metals.

The extraordinary 'metabolic' efficiencies that might eventually be possible for Metaman can be judged by considering how effectively evolution has honed the metabolism of biological creatures. A human being performs its many feats with an average rate of energy consumption less than that of a single 100-watt light bulb! So efficient are our bodies that the total caloric intake required to fuel the all-important human part of Metaman's metabolism accounts for less than 1 per cent of the energy used by the super-organism as a whole.[340]

Metaman still wastes a large portion of the energy and material it consumes, but its metabolism is growing ever more efficient. For example, a kilowatt-hour of energy can now be generated with only one-seventh as much fuel as in 1900,[341] and a new refrigerator consumes only half the electricity that one did twenty years ago.[342] Recycling materials is not only further improving energy efficiency, it is also reducing the consumption of raw materials. The potential impact of this metabolic adjustment is seen in the fact that recycling aluminum uses only one twentieth the energy it takes to smelt the same amount from bauxite.[343]

Reusing basic materials makes strong economic and environmental sense, but the growing popularity of such activity runs beyond simple economics or environmental awareness.[344] The recycling revolution reflects Metaman's natural tendency towards greater metabolic efficiency.

LIVING WITH SECURITY

A variety of hazardous materials, social tensions and environmental effects are largely new to our era. With the enormous media attention devoted to dramatic issues such as radiation from nuclear wastes, toxic chemical pollutants, pesticides, international terrorism, a weakening ozone layer, and even grisly mass slayings, it appears that we are rapidly transforming our world into a dangerous and uncertain place. This is far from true. The developed world has become so safe that a one-year-old now has a 98 per cent chance of living past the age of thirty,[345] that someone cut down by a heart attack at the age of fifty is thought to have died prematurely, that those over the age of sixty-five will comprise a fifth of the population in the US by the middle of the coming century.[346] As Metaman develops, the world is becoming ever safer and more predictable for humans.

Consider the many carcinogens that receive so much attention. Epidemiologists believe that the number of cancer deaths resulting from substances covered by environmental, food or workplace regulations in the US total only 7 per cent of all cancers.[347] We may be afraid of the chemicals we eat or the radiation we cannot see, but some 30 per cent of all cancer comes from smoking, something we ourselves control.[348] In addition, though many people die of cancer, it is largely a disease that threatens us after middle age. If cancer disappeared entirely, it would increase human life expectancy by only three years[349] – a minor fraction of the twenty-five-year increase the developed world has seen since 1900.[350] In truth, few people in previous eras lived long enough to get cancer.

Similarly, look at the dangers we may face from depleting the ozone layer. A United Nations' panel estimated that if humans made no compensating behavioral changes,[351] a 10 per cent ozone depletion – which would take some twenty-five-years at current rates[352] – would cause more than a million cataracts globally each year and 300,000 additional cases of skin cancer. These are significant figures, but they are low compared to many of humanity's other health problems. Remember that we live in a world where 14 million babies die each year of hunger-related causes.[353] Whatever the future hazards of ozone depletion prove to be,[354] however, the problem will be temporary: public policies already in motion are projected to return atmospheric ozone to its present level by the middle of the next century.[355]

We might also reflect on the problem of violence and crime in many cities. The US has the highest murder rate of any industrialized country[356] – some 20,000 murders occurred there in 1989 alone.[357] However, despair took a higher toll – there were some 28,000 suicides.[358] And many countries have even higher suicide rates than the US; Hungary's, for example, is nearly four times greater.[359] In short, we may feel threatened in many ways today, but generally it is not because the world has become a more dangerous place. The world was once poetically described as 'this vale of tears',[360] but in the developed world of today, many people think of *want* and *need* as nearly synonymous and expect somehow to escape the normal vicissitudes of life. That such attitudes exist reveals how far humanity has come.

Nuclear war, population growth, global warming, and the exhaustion of natural resources are generally perceived as the most serious long-term threats facing human society, yet it is clear that all are manageable. Humanity's long-term future is secure and does not hinge on any miraculous transformation of human nature. Metaman is enabling humankind to surmount its larger challenges despite the limitations of human beings as individuals. But what about the immediate decades ahead? What can *we* do to accelerate Metaman's resolution of its long-term problems and thereby improve our lives and those of our children?

The first thing is to permit ourselves to lay down a heavy burden – the notion that we humans are in the process of devastating our planet and the well-being of all future generations. We are in the midst of a difficult passage for humankind, but it is just that – a passage. And it is one that we can shorten if we try. By approaching the global and individual challenges before us with full comprehension of the larger currents shaping them, we *can* make a difference. Controlling population is clearly the one underlying issue that will most affect the quality of human life in the decades ahead, but there are many other critical matters that would benefit from our attention. There is much to be done, and whatever the part we choose to play, the effort is one that embraces us all, because it is the totality of all our individual actions that constitutes the behavior of Metaman.

8

MAN AND METAMAN

The Individual and the Super-organism

CIVILIZATION HAS PROVED REMARKABLY resilient. Even history's darkest episodes have only briefly stayed the continuing expansion of the scope and complexity of human activity. Between 1331 and 1360, the Black Death cut a broad swath from India and China to Europe, killing about a third of the 300 million people living there.[361] Sudden, horrible death was so common that it seemed as though the apocalypse had arrived . . . yet civilization did not crumble.[362] In fact, its essential character shows few enduring marks of the plague's passing, and from our vantage point six centuries later, this immense human tragedy is but a wispy shadow.

Civilization's resilience is also obvious in the lesser ravages of recent times – such episodes as the great depression of the 1930s, the worldwide influenza epidemic that killed some 20 million people in 1919, and the world wars.[363] None even came close to 'threatening' civilization, and within a few generations, each began to fade from humanity's collective memory.

With the emergence of Metaman, civilization has become even more robust. There is little question that the middle of the next millennium will not reveal a Metaman battered and tenuously clinging to life as commonly portrayed in our twentieth-century post-apocalyptic films, but rather a healthy and growing Metaman, with human society thriving and the basic problems we face in the year 2000 long since solved. Such optimism about Metaman's future, however, in no way diminishes the import of today's many significant problems for *us*. Although humanity can rest easy about its overall

The traumatic impact of the plague on the psychology of the fourteenth and fifteenth centuries can be seen in the macabre themes that characterize European art from this period. Yet even this immense tragedy, killing about a third of the human population, has left few enduring marks on human history. Shown here is the etching 'Dance of Death', 1493, Nuremburg Chronicle.

survival, we cannot afford to be complacent. Metaman might barely be troubled by the starvation of a few hundred million people, but the immediate human impacts, even for the survivors, would be immense. Thus, it would be foolish to let confidence in humanity's long-term future lull us into believing that all will be fine, regardless of our own actions. Our confidence about the future might better lead us to ask why problems that will one day be solved should not be solved sooner rather than later.

Present threats are not to Metaman, nor generally even to society, they are to the overall quality of human life today and in the decades immediately ahead. Most of the now familiar litany of problems confronting us – soil erosion, ozone depletion, species extinctions, rising sea levels, acid rain, global warming, population growth, industrial pollution, pesticide residues, nuclear waste disposal – are of concern today primarily because humans within the core of Metaman have grown to expect so much from life. Parents once would expect several of their children to die during childhood, and people knew that infectious diseases and accidents might prove fatal. Mozart died at the age of thirty-five and we think it tragic, but he was lucky; five of his six brothers and sisters died in infancy.[364] This is not to minimize today's problems, only to suggest that we are privileged to be able to view them as our primary concerns; many peoples at the fringes of Metaman would feel themselves blessed if they could do the same.

A PLACE FOR INDIVIDUAL ACTION

Local matters strongly influence our lives, but Metaman is concerned about such issues only in the aggregate. It does not consider our individual fortunes any more than we ourselves think of the many cells that die when we go for a hike and get a blister. Metaman is indifferent to whether your community is safe or your neighborhood school is a good one. Such matters are up to each of us, yet they are the very problems that many people now ignore. There is a joke in which a man says that in his family, he decides all the 'big' issues: what should be done in the Middle East, how international drug traffic can be stopped, what is ailing the healthcare system. His wife, he maintains, deals with only the 'minor' things: what the family eats, where they go on vacation, what they do on the weekend, what schools the kids go to. This sounds silly, but in the world of modern communication it is easy to become seduced by global issues that affect us only indirectly, and to neglect the local matters that touch us more immediately.

None the less, to be effective in our actions we must comprehend how the basic currents of Metaman – such things as expanding technology, global communication, and international trade – influence our lives. If we disregard such realities, we condemn ourselves to difficult future adjustments: a car manufacturer that neglects to raise the fuel efficiency of its vehicles will eventually find itself struggling against regulations. A person who shuns technology will have to live in a society that is increasingly alien.

Problems such as urban air pollution, crime and waste disposal are never entirely under local control, but they arise largely from localized activities and can be addressed by local action. A city that enforces strict emissions standards for automobiles can dramatically reduce its air pollution. One that develops recycling programs will have less rubbish to eliminate. One where neighbors get to know each other will have less crime.

Other problems, though, are caused by more distant activities that cast long shadows. Dumping wastes in a river poisons those downstream; industrial air pollution in Detroit causes acid rain in eastern Canada. These matters cannot be solved through local action alone; addressing them requires regional cooperation. Metaman's growth, cutting across regional boundaries as it does, makes such agreements ever more attainable.

Still other problems result from activities that are so widespread and have such diffuse effects that they are truly global in nature. Climate change, population growth, ozone destruction, and the depletion of global resources can be adequately addressed only on a global scale. Moreover, these matters threaten consequences that eventually may overwhelm local and regional efforts. What good is it to set aside a preserve to save a forest from urban encroachment if the area will soon grow too hot and dry for the forest to survive?[365]

By their very nature the impacts of global problems are indirect and delayed, so their solutions are largely beyond the reach of individual action. What can a single community, much less an individual, do to keep the atmosphere from changing? The answer, of course, is very little. Only the entirety of Metaman can solve these global problems or even perceive them during their early stages. Thus an isolated individual action like purchasing a more fuel-efficient car or saving electricity by using fluorescent lights may make us feel better, but it will not have a meaningful impact on global warming. If we wish to try to influence global issues more significantly, we must somehow amplify our energies – generally by harnessing media or government.

Because Metaman derives its health and vigor from the connections linking human activity, the super-organism's capacity to move towards resolution of global issues is strengthened when the trade and communication that bind us together are reinforced. The notion that the world as a whole would somehow be better off if regions were more self-sufficient and independent is at odds with the realities of Metaman's development. We must learn to embrace international interdependence, despite the uncertainties that accompany it. 'Bioregionalism' (the concept that to reduce wasteful shipping costs, regions should rely upon food grown locally) is an excellent example of a well-meaning but flawed approach to world problems. The idea may sound good, but the long-term effects of greater regional self-sufficiency would be counterproductive. Reinforcing an illusion of independence weakens the drive to solve the problems that – regardless whether we individually contribute to them – affect us all.

Global challenges can be met only through broad changes in the shape of society.[366] Thus, the effectiveness of our individual actions on population growth, global warming and other planetary issues is determined largely by how much we influence others and affect institutions and public policies.[367] For instance, we may go to great lengths to always recycle glass and newspapers or to use a bicycle instead of a car,[368] but we would probably have more overall impact if we were to expend half as much energy writing letters to try to raise taxes on petrol or get our municipality to begin curbside collection of recyclables. Likewise, if one person in twenty – over 250 million people worldwide – quietly had himself or herself sterilized in order to reduce population growth, the impact on human population would be small;[369] but if these same people instead loudly struggled to focus attention on family planning, humanity would soon be spending far more on such programs than the roughly 10 billion dollars needed annually to brake population growth.[370]

Change is frequently effected using the tools of government. The most common present approach is to promote or discourage specific activities *directly*, through legislative action. This works well where the path to achieving a goal is straightforward – preventing the dumping of toxic wastes, for example. But laws and government programs are notoriously slow to respond to changing conditions. California's water shortage was so severe prior to the rains of 1992 that water was rationed in both Los Angeles and San Francisco, yet precious water supplies continued to be used to grow wheat and barley in the desert. These crops, which could be grown more cheaply elsewhere, were profitable largely because of long-term water subsidies negotiated in the 1940s and 1950s when efforts were being made to expand agricultural production in the region.[371]

Where complex tradeoffs must be made, for example on many environmental issues, a more flexible approach is evolving – the use of market forces. If prices are adjusted to include the *indirect* social and environmental costs of products and practices, then the 'market' can balance 'costs' and 'benefits' to eliminate practices not worth the destruction they cause.[372] With this strategy, if society must pay tens of billions of dollars to dispose of nuclear wastes, the price of nuclear power is raised to reflect this liability; if coal burning is causing large expenditures to control pollution, the price of coal is set to reflect this; if cattle ranching is eroding land and polluting rivers, the price of beef

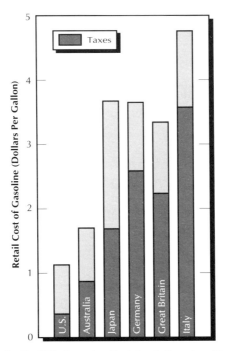

Gasoline prices in the US do not reflect the full costs of protecting oil supplies, maintaining a highway system, and cleaning the environment. Other nations, by imposing heavy gasoline taxes (shading), force consumers to pay more of these costs.[373] The low US gasoline prices are largely responsible for the relatively poor fuel efficiency of vehicles in the US.

is set high enough to pay these costs.[374] These links are important not because they raise revenues, but because they enable society to minimize such activities. This general approach has enormous potential because it represents an extension of the basic physiological mechanisms Metaman already employs to coordinate its activities.

Linking activities and their indirect costs, however, is simple in theory but very difficult in practise.[375] Not only must subtle indirect effects be uncovered, but prices must be selectively modified without blocking general market forces. The sophisticated commercial and government systems necessary to bring about these linkages are becoming more common as Metaman develops. Early moves in this direction are already evident: Germany charges 'environmental' surtaxes to ensure that products are recycled, and Los Angeles is using a market in 'pollution credits' to try to improve air quality more cheaply than would be possible with mandated emission levels.[376]

The long-term directions of Metaman are unfolding largely beyond individual control as Metaman discovers its own global necessities and acts accordingly. Certainly, Metaman's development is not playing out some human 'plan'. But in the short-term, individuals can strongly influence the shape of society, especially when their actions reinforce rather than oppose Metaman's natural tendencies. Look, for example, at the enormous influence of those scientists who detected ozone depletion in the atmosphere and spurred action earlier than would otherwise have occurred. Or consider how Gorbachov, when he was the president of the Soviet Union, paved the way for the economic changes that were to sweep through the Communist economies. Expanding global economics and communications guaranteed Communism's eventual fall, but without his individual actions, Communism might have struggled on for decades and ended with a world-wrenching spasm.

When we walk along the beach, our footprints leave no lasting trace because they are soon washed away by the lapping waves. Stronger, heavier steps will not alter this reality. Likewise, in realms where society is largely at equilibrium, our individual actions soon fade and leave no mark. It would be easy to conclude that society is too large for individuals to make much difference outside of their immediate personal environs, but this is not the case. In unstable realms – and this includes many aspects of society – small individual actions can ripple larger effects. A single footprint in the right place on a hillside path can start a new channel of water runoff and eventually create an entire stream bed; and in the same way, the strategic actions of a solitary individual can channel larger social currents.

The institutional structures of Metaman strongly influence our lives, so it is important that we hasten the refinement of the mechanisms that enable institutions to serve us. In government, for example, 'economic growth' is often used as a key measure of the health of a nation. At first glance this appears valid, because where economies are rapidly expanding, individual standards of living are generally rising. But within an integrated organism, unregulated growth creates imbalances that are harmful, not beneficial, and the same is the case with Metaman. Were overall growth to continue at present rates, the planetary super-organism would be using more energy by the year 2500 than reaches our *entire* planet from the sun.[377] Thus, 'growth' is sustainable only when its character continually adjusts to channel activities towards greater efficiencies in the use of energy and resources. And this increasing internal regulation of Metaman's growth will be able to enhance the quality of human life far more effectively when current economic tools are refined with this in mind.

Growth in Gross National Product (the total goods and services a nation produces), for example, is a blunt and inappropriate measure of the general well-being of a people.[378] GNP does not distinguish between activities that improve our lot and those that do not. GNP counts additional health care expenses no differently from greater educational or recreational outlays. Nor does GNP differentiate between products created from plentiful resources and those made from scarce ones. Making glass from sand is very different from clear cutting an old-growth forest, yet each raises GNP. Depleting natural resources does not add to a society's wealth any more than selling a home makes the owner richer than keeping it. Such transactions simply transform fixed assets into ready cash. Thus, when Indonesia cuts down tropical rainforest and leaves behind denuded, eroding landscapes, the one-time bonanza of valuable lumber temporarily raises GNP but produces no net gain.[379]

Most present-day economic models oversimplify both human society and the biosphere. In the era of Metaman, it is imperative to view the planetary surface as an integrated system, and economic theory is now evolving to encompass that reality. In recent years, for example, some economists have developed new measures of society to replace GNP.[380] Measures such as the Physical Quality of Life Indicator (PQLI) assign activities positive or negative contributions depending on whether they seem to add or reduce human well-being.[381] It is tools such as these that will enable Metaman's 'growth' to serve human 'needs' more completely as we collectively define and redefine them in the years ahead. And as Metaman's analytic capabilities develop, such measurement indices will undoubtedly become ever more sophisticated and influential.

AT THE PERIPHERY

With transportation and communication systems, power grids, manufacturing capacity and educated populations, the industrial world has large reserves to draw on during any crises of the next century;[382] Africa and some other regions have almost none. The question of what will become of these fragile, precarious nations at the margins of Metaman gnaws at even the most complacent of societies. For every Korea or Thailand that is rapidly progressing, there appear to be two Kenyas, Bangladeshes or Perus that are falling back.[383] There are no easy answers for these reservoirs of poverty. Strangled by overpopulation and political instability, they are not attractive sites for foreign investment;[384] saddled with backward economies and deteriorating natural environments, they bear the brunt of any shortages in world resources and have little cushion against natural catastrophe.[385] How can these regions ever make a transition to the pattern of the developed world?[386]

While the birth pains of Metaman may well devastate some cultures and populations in parts of Africa,[387] Asia and South America, the long-term prospects of the vast periphery of Metaman are hopeful. Metaman's rapid pace of technological advance is creating the tools to enable these lands to make the difficult transition they are struggling with today.

Until population growth in a developing country is halted, its economic programs to raise standards of living must labor under a debilitating handicap, but once population stops rising, solid long-term progress is virtually guaranteed. Economic growth (blunt as the measure may be) shows this clearly; at even a paltry 2 per cent a year, growth would raise real incomes sevenfold in a century.[388]

As Metaman continues to become more integrated, more organized and more aware, an increasingly cohesive approach to world problems is prevailing. Perhaps modern communication, by reinforcing the psychological and cultural ties between people at Metaman's core and its periphery, will stimulate the economic connections that can hasten development. Regardless, however, the process of change is already well underway.

Modern technology is the key to the transformation of Metaman's periphery into the rich patterns at its core. Historically, the acquisition and improvement of the basic infrastructure of society – telephones, trains, highways, schools and electrical power – has been a slow, expensive and difficult process taking many generations. Now, however, the cost of building the foundations for a modern society is falling sharply; soon the developed world may have the means to supply the power, communication, and even educational foundations for modernizing less-developed countries. Instead of painstakingly following the long developmental paths taken by today's advanced nations, societies could import the technology and expertise that would enable them to race ahead.

Generating electricity, for example, previously meant not only giant power plants or hydroelectric projects but also vast networks of high-voltage power lines that are generally beyond the means of rural areas and poor countries. Now, technologies for the inexpensive, small-scale generation of solar and wind power are beginning to provide cheap energy to isolated regions without existing power grids.[389] In fact, because the developed world has a sophisticated infrastructure already in place, this new technology is being used more widely in less-developed lands.[390]

A similar transformation is also underway in telecommunications, another essential internal element of Metaman. The price of equipment is rapidly falling and its reliability improving. The cost per unit of information transmitted by cable, for example, has fallen nearly a thousandfold since the introduction of fiber in 1977.[391] Not only do fiber optics allow trunk lines to handle huge numbers of intercity calls, but today's transoceanic fiber cables and satellite-based technologies are drastically lowering the cost of connecting less-developed regions to the rest of the world. In 1956, a transatlantic coaxial cable could handle only a dozen simultaneous voice calls; today a fiber-optic cable can handle 80,000.[392] Prior to such technological advances, the cost of tying developing regions into the global communications network of Metaman was prohibitive. Now, the penetration of cheap, reliable telephone communication into less-developed countries is on the immediate horizon.[393]

So too is widespread education. This critical component of making a successful transition into the 'modern' world of Metaman has been a stumbling block in many lands. Countries with few teachers and educational materials cannot educate their largely illiterate populations. At last, however, computer technology is beginning to offer the possibility of spreading up-to-date knowledge broadly in a usable form. Not only are software improvements making it much easier to interact with computers, but leaps in hardware technology have created small, powerful and reliable machines. A twenty-five-pound computer easily damaged by power surges could never be a useful educational tool in the less-developed world, but a hardy, six-pound, battery-powered laptop computer capable of accessing a several-thousand-volume library of books in a small box of optical computer discs (CD-ROMs) begins to have real potential.[394]

Tragedy and human suffering are not new to our era, but the potential to eliminate much of this suffering is a revolutionary development. Some 1 billion people now lead lives of relative affluence, and it is not yet clear how long it will take for all humankind to enjoy this prosperity. What is astounding is not that society has not yet managed to halt population growth or broadly distribute wealth, but that today – for the first time ever – there are mechanisms to bring this about. At this point, social progress *is* lagging behind technological progress, and

Solar Panel in Somalia. This solar panel provides power to a remote refugee camp in northwestern Somalia. When limited amounts of power are needed at sites far from existing power grids, photovoltaic cells are now often the most economic and reliable source. Photo by J. Dohnanyi, 1980, courtesy of the Food and Agriculture Organization of the UN.

because of the rapid pace of change, the gap has never been larger between what could be and what is.[395] There are famine, pain and wretchedness in many parts of the world, and it need not be so. But as never before there is also abundance that will spread as Metaman continues to grow.

In this time of widespread concern about social decay and imminent environmental catastrophe, optimism seems out of vogue. But there are some signs that high expectations for the future lie just beneath the surface. The broad and vehement opposition to anything but 'permanent'[396] disposal of nuclear-wastes is one such sign. Despite a plethora of present ills going unaddressed, billions of dollars are now being spent to ensure the containment of radioactive wastes for tens of thousands of years rather than 'mere' centuries. A young adult suffering from leukemia does not worry about the possibility of getting arthritis decades hence, but our society is showing deep concern about potential low-level radiation millennia from now. Clearly, there must be an underlying faith that the future will be a positive place where such a danger might make a difference.

The overwhelming evidence is that this faith is fully warranted. From a perspective of centuries rather than decades, the current turbulence inherent in the transformation of human society and the globalization of Metaman will soon be fading from view. Future humans will likely remember the twenty-first century not as a troubled, unfortunate period, but as the time when humankind burst forth from its ancient patterns and made the fundamental transitions that redefined life as it had hitherto been. Those of the future will see our epoch as a wild and glorious one that spawned the seminal developments of solar power, computer intelligence, space exploration and genetic engineering – the foundations of *their* civilization.

THE FUTURE

Come senators congressmen
Please heed the call
Don't stand in the doorway
Don't block up the hall.
For he that gets hurt
Will be he who has stalled.

For the times they are a-changin'.

Bob Dylan 1963[397]

9

BEYOND *HOMO SAPIENS*
Intimations of Humanity's Future

WHEN WE LOOK INTO the future, we tend to focus on the years immediately ahead, because these – unlike hazy distant centuries – seem relevant and nearly discernible. But on this time scale the march of history is chaotic – a recession, a new technology, or a change in government policy can shatter even the most careful projections. We need a larger perspective to see the patterns that transcend these fluctuations and to discern the forces that are shaping our present and future.

To glimpse Metaman's immense potential, recall the history of life recounted earlier; each story 'year' was 100 million actual years. By this clock, life is now a robust thirty-six-*year*-old with *decades* ahead of it. Humans began to form large clusters less than an hour ago with the coming of agriculture; Metaman emerged as a global super-organism only in the past minute, and is likely to live for weeks or even years rather than 'hours'. This may sound like a short time, but each of these 'hours' of Metaman's existence will span some twelve millennia and each 'week' some 2 million years. And yet to extend humankind's current trajectory even a few centuries into the future is enough to make the mind reel.

The most interesting questions do not concern *when* various developments will occur but *whether* they are possible: can genetic engineering significantly enhance the potential of the human mind or body? Can computers be made to 'think' as creatively as humans? Can the human cerebral cortex interpret complex information sent directly through an array of implanted microelectrodes? Can aging be significantly slowed or even halted? Such questions, because they are about the nature of the physical world and life itself, have definite answers, and the shape of humanity's future hinges on them. Although we do not yet have the answers, we do know enough for intelligent conjecture.

We will leave such concepts as warp speeds, anti-gravity, time travel and mental telepathy to science fiction; humanity's future needs no such fantasies to reach the limits of our imaginations. So rapid is current progress in molecular biology, computer science, communications, chemistry, materials science and other fields that profound change is inevitable even without any dramatic new 'breakthroughs'. Breakthroughs will come – unanticipated developments such as 'perhaps' high-temperature superconductors or sophisticated microscopic machines[398] – but these cannot be foreseen. Why even try? What already is well underway is sufficient to make the coming centuries strange indeed.

In the seminal areas of computers and biotechnology, innovation shows no sign of slowing and may well be accelerating.[399] For example, using X-rays instead of visible light to etch circuits on computer chips, promises to expand memories a thousand-fold in coming years,[400] and linking together thousands of micro-processors to work in parallel is producing equivalent gains in processing speed.[401] Tomorrow's desk-top computers will be as powerful as today's supercomputers, and devices will speak to us and understand what we say. In biology, the barriers to genetic manipulation have been overcome so rapidly that today's trickle of medical applications (new drugs and new insights into human biology and disease) will soon become a flood. Already, biotechnology has moved to the point where biologists can use simple commercial kits and cookbook-like procedures to extract a specific gene from its chromosome, sequence the gene to determine its precise structure, splice in new segments to change its character, and then reinsert it into a chromosome. Tomorrow we will not only understand and cure today's intractable diseases; we will 'design' new plants and animals.

Both society and the natural environment have previously undergone tumultuous changes, but the essence of being human has remained the same.[402] Metaman, however, is on the verge of significantly altering human form and capacity. So new is this prospect that as yet few of us have recognized it fully or faced its larger implications. But we need to do so, because understanding how Metaman's evolving technologies will affect human beings brings perspective to troubling medical and philosophical issues now facing

This tiny motor, built to high tolerances using X-ray lithography techniques, is slightly thicker than a human hair and has been operated at rotor speeds of 8,000 RPM. Such devices, which could be closely linked to computer chips, may eventually prove useful in various types of sensors.[403] Courtesy of H. Guckel, University of Wisconsin.

us. Today we peer into a future so strange it is nearly unbelievable: people with mechanical organs and electronic hearing and vision, babies conceived in test tubes and grown in incubators,[404] and human beings who are the product of conscious biological design. Medical developments are already challenging our fundamental ethical frameworks. A poor man tries to sell one of his kidneys to a wealthy individual who will die without it,[405] a hospital refuses to disconnect a brain-dead patient from life support and year after year the patient's body lingers on at great expense; a mother learns the gender of the child she has conceived and decides to abort the pregnancy.[406] These issues may be troubling, but they are here to stay. And they are harbingers of the major transition rapidly approaching humankind.

HUMAN-MACHINE HYBRIDS

As the nature of human beings begins to change, so too will concepts of what it means to be human. One day humans will be composite beings: part biological, part mechanical and part electronic. This idea may conjure images of unworldly androids, but the transition will not be as jarring as we might imagine. Replacing or modifying parts of the human body is already commonplace, and neither false teeth nor artificial knees make people feel less human. Pacemakers, hearing aids and prosthetic limbs are still relatively simple devices, but advances in biology, electronics and the material sciences soon will offer much more. Eventually, when such devices become superior to the body parts they replace, will humans spurn them? Not judging by our history.

Think about the clothing we take for granted. Large portions of the globe would be uninhabitable without it. Clothing is removable, but our association with it is now both a physiological necessity and a legal requirement.[407] Far from rejecting this ancient association with fur and cloth, we revel in it; we feel reduced and 'naked' when denied it. Clothing effectively has become a functional part of us. The same is true of eyeglasses. Many people could not get along without them, and as these devices have progressed, humanity's link to them has grown increasingly intimate. What a difference there is between a hand-held monocle from the 1800s and the extended-wear contact lenses of today.

Humans have many mechanical and electronic extensions of themselves: wristwatches, phones, pagers, even radios and televisions. Though external to the human body, these devices are becoming so miniaturized and important to life within Metaman that they, too, may one day go the route of eyeglasses. It is quite conceivable that eventually we all will wear tiny lapel-phones linking us to any other person at the call of his or her name. After all, when vocal commands are used to summon phone numbers, a phone will need no keypad.[408] Told to call someone, it will. Today's six-ounce cellular phones, speed dialers and voice-recognition software suggest that such future devices are not far away.

Considering that many people already feel anxious when they are separated from their pagers and cellular phones, it is likely that future generations, who since early childhood will have routinely chatted with friends whenever and wherever they wished, will feel unbearably isolated when they are 'phoneless'. Such a tight behavioral association with a technological device, though still a far cry from man hybridizing with machines, is definitely a step in that direction.

The deepening human association with non-living materials has proceeded naturally from clothing to eyeglasses to mechanical and electronic devices. Some, such as contact lenses and false teeth, have become essential to human activity but remain removable, others are already becoming permanent parts of the body. The first implant was the gold filling, which was used as early as the ninth century by the Arabs.[409] But teeth are at the body's boundary; completely *subcutaneous* implants did not arrive until the late nineteenth century when pins, screws and plates were used to hold fractured bones in place. Only since the 1930s, with the advent of modern materials and surgical techniques, have these simple fasteners given way to artificial hips and knees,[410] heart valves, pacemakers, and even lenses for the eye.[411] By 1988, more than 11 million people in the US had permanent medical implants.[412] The trend is unmistakable. Just as biology and technology are becoming ever more tightly united within Metaman, they are uniting within human beings themselves.

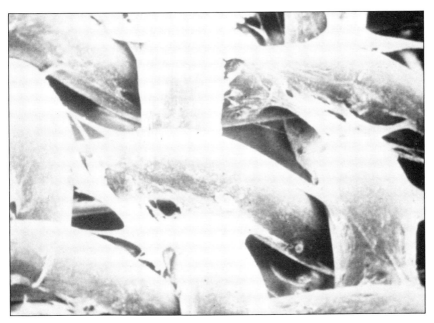

Living human skin tissue can be created by culturing human skin cells on a nylon-mesh support matrix. This scanning electron micrograph shows the first few cells adhering to the mesh. As such cells proliferate, they build their own extracellular matrix to create functional physiological tissue. Courtesy of Advanced Tissue Sciences, Inc., La Jolla, California.

Implants still by and large attempt to replace or repair defective human parts. Machines designed to overcome deafness, blindness, bone injury or paralysis need not match the workings of biology: a paraplegic who regains even a small amount of limb movement is much better off, and so is a deaf person who recovers a modicum of hearing. Failing vital organs, however, require replacements that come closer to equalling biological systems.

The technology of organ replacement is advancing rapidly. Artificial heart-lung bypasses are used for many hours during operations; portable mechanical-assists for the heart are now reliable enough to reside in the body and keep a patient alive for several months; dialysis machines can substitute for the kidney permanently. Further, patients can be intravenously fed glucose and nutrients indefinitely, thereby essentially replacing the entire human digestive system with the external manufacturing systems of Metaman. Where might all this lead in a century or two? One day an accident victim might lose heart, lungs, kidneys, stomach and intestines and survive by using a portable heart-lung-dialysis machine that adds nutrients, fluids and oxygen to the blood, and also cleanses, regulates and circulates it.[413] The unnerving image of a 'person' who neither eats, drinks, nor breathes, but instead consumes bags of nutrients and gets air through an intake hose, is a vision straight out of grade-B science fiction, but it drives home the point that the boundary between human and machine is collapsing throughout Metaman. The technology for a hospital-room version of such a machine is already nearly here. Technology and medicine are progressing so rapidly that the question of whether a *portable* device like this will one day be developed hinges less on its feasibility than on its economics.

More intriguing than replacing human organs is the possibility of extending human senses. The first steps towards linking powerful sensory devices directly to the brain have already been taken. Electrodes have been implanted in the cochlea of the ear to stimulate the auditory nerve and enable the deaf to understand speech.[414] These implanted electrodes are wired to a subcutaneous radio receiver that picks up transmissions from a pocket-size, portable sound analyzer.[415] With this 'electronic ear', some individuals who became deaf as adults[416] have learned to understand more than 90 per cent of spoken words, even without visual cues. They can recognize a person's voice, hear when a friend has a cold, and converse on the telephone.

The cochlear nerve is not the only place where a useful interface between the human nervous system and electronics is being formed;

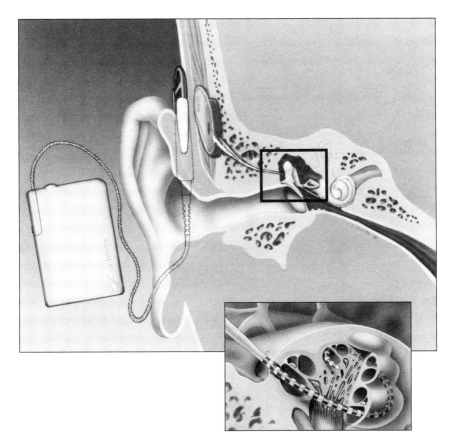

Auditory electrodes can now be implanted in the spiral of the cochlea (inset) to enable the deaf to hear. Activated by radio transmissions from a separate sound analyzer, each channel of such an electrode responds to different sound frequencies and stimulates a different part of the auditory nerve – much like what happens in a healthy ear. Courtesy of Cochlear Corporation, Colorado.

this nerve just happens to be the easiest to reach.[417] With less success, electrodes also have been placed directly in the visual cortex. Subjects report seeing discrete spots of light when these electrodes are stimulated,[418] so connecting an array of them to a camera-like artificial eye might one day give a blind person rudimentary vision.[419]

Efforts to make paralyzed limbs functional and to replace missing limbs with useful prostheses are also advancing.[420] When paralysis is caused by spinal damage that severs a limb's neural link to the brain, electronics can be used to bypass the spinal-cord injury and partially restore limb function. For example, shoulder movement has been used to control a radio signal that stimulates electrodes near the nerves of a paralyzed hand. Using this apparatus, a paralyzed patient can learn to grasp objects by moving a shoulder.[421]

Complete limb replacement is possible too. As industrial robots proliferate and their control systems improve, robotic arms may be used as human prostheses, probably controlled by transmitters in the limb stumps or the brain itself. Conceivably, such devices might eventually seem almost to respond directly to one's will. Couple such a prosthesis to electronic sensors sending the brain information about the artificial limb's position and orientation, and eventually the device might feel like part of the body – especially if it has been used from early childhood. The human brain is quite adaptable, and long familiarity and practice with a tool or piece of sporting equipment can occasionally promote such deep rapport that the device feels like a living extension of one's body.

Today, implants restore diminished capabilities, tomorrow they will enhance normal ones. Putting an anti-cavity coating on teeth is a rudimentary present-day improvement upon nature, but the future will bring more interesting advances: tiny ultrasound detectors to increase the range of human hearing and devices that enhance human smell or sharpen vision.

Meaningful extensions of human senses are more likely than improvements in such physical attributes as strength. The science-fiction images of powerful, human-like cyborgs crushing mere mortals with their bare hands are unrealistic, because even if such strength were possible, it would require a fundamental redesign of the body that would undoubtedly have many undesirable side effects. Considering that fork lifts, backhoes and other power tools are so readily available and that people rarely use what physical strength they have, who would need or want to lift giant boulders with massive artificial limbs that couldn't be detached when the work was completed?[422]

In contrast, tiny electronic implants to extend our senses or alter our moods would require no broad restructuring of the body. Because placing an array of electrodes in the brain almost certainly will be a simple and safe surgical procedure one day, the key question is whether such implants will prove useful. People may eventually use direct brain stimulation to calm themselves, go to sleep, stay awake, feel pleasure, concentrate their attention, or banish depression. Such brain electrodes are not on the immediate horizon; they would require a deeper understanding of the brain than now exists, and drugs are more effective tools that accomplish much the same things. But the potential of implanted brain electrodes goes far beyond mood alter-

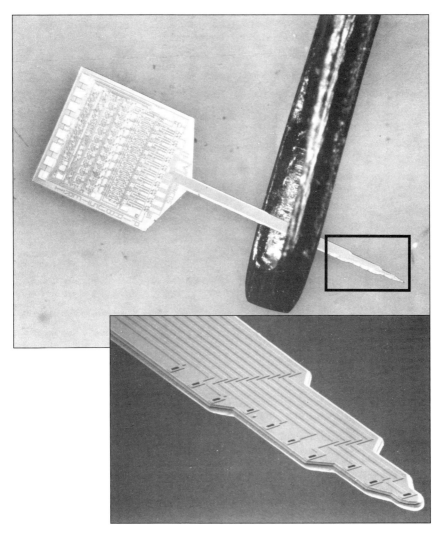

This tiny electrode pushed through the eye of a needle is a far cry from yesterday's recording devices. The circuitry at the electrode's base amplifies and processes the signals coming from the leads of the ten recording channels (inset).[423] *Such an electrode, which might be permanantly implanted to record the activity of several cells simultaneously and yet leave tissue undamaged, could one day figure prominently in the control of human prostheses. Courtesy of Najafi Khalil, University of Michigan.*

ation. By monitoring and stimulating brain cells and also communicating with external devices, it might eventually be possible to establish complex links between computer circuitry and the human cerebral cortex. This would give humans direct mental control over various machines and also expand mental capabilities with powerful enhancements of memory, communication and computation. Given Metaman's rapid pace of technological advance, it is no longer absurd to ask whether human and machine will eventually merge. Current understanding of the brain is too rudimentary to know whether a direct channel between electronic devices and the brain would be usable, but if it is, the division between human and machine may eventually all but disappear.

Even if electronic links to the mind continue to be restricted to the various sensory and motor nerve fibers of the brain, however, the possibilities are still incredible. Cochlear implants, for example, would provide a rich input channel to the brain. These implants might receive information from many sources – an ultrasound detector that hears high-pitched noises and gives a human better hearing than a dog, a fire alarm that shouts 'fire!' in someone's ear, an electronic organizer that reminds a person of his or her appointments. A cochlear implant might even receive telephone calls. To most of us, an implanted telephone initially seems absurd, but for a person who had a cochlear receiver and was accustomed to using a tiny lapel phone, it would seem quite logical. Of course, an implanted phone that could not be *turned off* would not be a high-technology marvel; it would resemble some cruel torture designed by demented engineers. We needn't worry; by the time a cochlear phone can be implanted, screening the calls should be easy. There already exists a hearing-aid that is embedded in a tooth and conducts vibration directly along the jaw, so a solid-state answering machine in a wisdom tooth would not be much of a challenge.

Establishing electronic connections with the nervous system eventually will confer on us some of the 'psychic' powers we have long dreamed of. Having transmitting electrodes controlled by our thoughts and able to operate electronic devices around us would give us an ability akin to telekinesis, and implanted phones would allow communication not far removed from telepathy. Today various businesses have dedicated communication links tying together distant sites. Perhaps future humans will create similar links to those they love. Such intimate ties will be feasible; whether they become a reality hinges upon whether people want them.

The union between electronics and humans does not require any fundamental new scientific breakthroughs, but it does demand that existing technologies be pushed forward substantially. Progress in medicine and electronics is now moving ahead on so many fronts, however, that this development may not be particularly distant even though the path there is still obscure. For example, although technical obstacles to direct electrode links between brain and computer could prove insurmountable at present,[424] other developments could just as easily supersede the technologies discussed. One thing is clear: the advancing technologies that have been so profoundly reshaping human society are starting to reshape human beings as well. Where future advances will lead is not yet clear, but there can be no doubt that the bodies and minds of human beings will be considerably altered in the coming centuries and millennia. Humanity cannot escape the reality that humans are becoming the objects as well as the agents of change within Metaman.

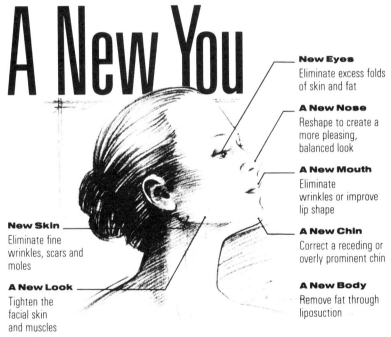

Early efforts to sculpt human form and potential have already begun, and the concept is becoming increasingly acceptable. Many cosmetic surgeries that are now commonplace would have been considered shocking a century ago had they then been feasible. Shown here is an advertisement that runs regularly in Los Angeles. Courtesy Lawrence Stein.

BIOLOGICAL DESIGN COMES OF AGE

Integrating mechanical and electronic devices into the body is one way of enhancing human capabilities; the other is through direct biological manipulation. Metaman's first gropings towards biological engineering and design rest upon enormous scientific advances in chemistry, molecular biology and genetics, as well as instrumentation and technology.

Central to this effort is the application of 'drugs', which in the general sense means any chemicals used to alter the internal functioning of living organisms. Our bodies are already brimming with such chemicals, orchestrating and coordinating our internal workings – vitamins to mediate our cellular metabolism, hormones to control our development, stimulants to make us alert in the face of danger, depressants to let us relax and fall asleep, narcotics to block pain and make us happy, antibiotics to kill bacterial invaders. These drugs are internal and 'natural', and their release is integral to the operation of the body. Both the pharmaceutical and illegal drugs now widely obtainable are close cousins to these natural substances; in fact, this kinship is what enables synthetic drugs to affect the body so strongly.

Because the range of available drugs has been increasing for many decades, the current products of biotechnology possess a familiarity that belies the dramatic new possibilities they herald. New ways of identifying and synthesizing drugs are moving humankind into entirely new territory.

The widespread use of pharmaceuticals is another aspect of humanity's tight association with machines. In this case, however, the connection is indirect, because the substances altering the body's workings are the product of Metaman's extended industrial processes, which thus serve as a sort of immense, collective, external prosthesis for humankind. And some of us are completely dependent on this structure for our survival.[425]

As with electronic prostheses, drugs are primarily used today to *restore* function – to alleviate chronic depression, fight off a disease, compensate for weaknesses in the immune system, or regulate an erratic heartbeat. But in the future drugs will also extend and manage normal human functions. Indeed, this is already happening – although in relatively crude ways. Anabolic steroids build muscle mass, barbiturates control sleep, immune-suppressants permit organ transplants, while other drugs promote the healing of wounds, ease motion-sickness, regulate fertility. In these early attempts, there are often negative side effects, but these are not intrinsic to the modifications themselves. As the body is better understood, drugs will be more specific and effective in their actions.

Apprehension about drugs and what they can do is natural. After all, with a physical prosthesis, effects can be more controlled and localized. Moreover, we are used to the idea of using machines to engineer the world around us. Drugs are a different story. They are unfamiliar 'engineering' tools that operate invisibly, using mysterious mechanisms we cannot fathom, and at times they alter our bodies in dramatic and unexpected ways. Even a simple vaccination can on occasion provoke a powerful allergic reaction.

One reason for side effects with drugs is that these potent substances generally reach their ultimate target by meandering through our bodies. But drug delivery will eventually become highly targeted. There are already techniques for poisons to be used so selectively they excise single cells – something the tiniest surgeon's blade could never do. For instance, certain antibodies, when prepared so they will attach to a unique site on the cells involved in arthritic inflammation, can carry toxins to those cells and kill them, thereby reducing the inflammation. Using the same strategy, toxins are beginning to be targeted at cancer cells.[426]

To understand the immense possibilities for human engineering using biological tools, it is essential to comprehend how these tools themselves will be designed and developed. Humans once found their medicines primarily by observing animal and human reactions to various plants. Although such 'trial and error' could identify sleeping potions, remedies for cramps, narcotics and ways of lowering fevers or fighting infection, the method could never have been much help in combatting uncommon diseases. Be that as it may, herbal cures passed down from generation to generation represent thousands of years of observations and have been the basis for many modern medicines. The heart medicine digitalis, for instance, is the active ingredient in the medicinal plant foxglove, and aspirin comes from the bark of the willow tree.[427]

A trial-and-error approach to finding therapeutic chemicals is a bit like banging a television set to 'fix' it.[428] The shock will sometimes jar a component back into place and solve the problem, and we may even discover precisely how to strike the set to fix some recurring failure. But such an intervention is crude and traumatizing. Now Metaman is opening up the set, learning how the parts work, and developing the tools to alter them individually. Using the powerful new techniques of molecular genetics to unravel the intimate workings of the human body and biological systems in general, the scientific enterprise is beginning to understand disease processes well enough to identify their key biochemical steps at the cellular level. Curing disease is becoming a targeted effort to find ways of blocking or altering specific biochemical steps or correcting other basic cellular deficiencies.

These procedures are still largely trial and error, but the focus is now much narrower. Rather than looking directly for a cure, companies can work to identify a key biochemical reaction in a disease process and then look for compounds that affect that particular reaction.[429] Moreover, with the advent of technology, initial drug screenings can examine many thousands of compounds using auto-mated assays executed by robotic devices. Whenever a promising chemical is found by these immense screenings, it becomes the starting point for further investigation. Chemists first determine its structure and attempt to understand how it works; then, if it still looks promising, they try to design similar chemicals that are more effective and have fewer side effects. A good example is the broad-spectrum antibiotic, Primaxin, which the Merck Corporation developed from a naturally occurring compound by chemically modifying it to increase its stability during storage and its resistance to degradation by the kidney.[430]

Supplementing these powerful brute-force searches for drug proto-types is a more selective approach. As modern biology elucidates life's inner workings, genetic-engineering techniques[431] are giving humanity access to the specific biochemicals being revealed. Biologists can now isolate the gene for almost any protein in an organism and make that protein in quantity. A major consequence for drug development is that proteins that could never possibly have been obtained in large enough amounts to use medically can now be manufactured by isolating their genes. All of nature is becoming the showroom for the drugs we will use.[432] The vampire bat has a pretty trick: in its saliva there is a chemical, Bat Plasminogen Activator, that keeps a victim's blood flowing while the bat drinks. Courtesy of the bat, this anticoagulant is now being synthesized for use as a drug to dissolve blood clots responsible for heart attacks.[433] This would be impossible without genetic engineering; imagine trying to collect enough bat saliva to produce a drug commercially.[434]

Efforts consciously to design and improve drugs are known as 'rational drug design'. Today, most such design efforts try to enhance com-pounds found by screening or genetic-engineering techniques, but biochemists are also learning to design from scratch the specific biological molecules that will alter key biochemical reactions.[435] This profound development marks the beginning of the transition beyond trial and error. Eventually, when a critical cellular mechanism is understood, scientists will not search for a biological molecule to control it, they will design one. The most notable early success in this approach was Tagamet,[436] a drug designed specifically to combat ulcers by reducing acid secretion in the stomach. This compound, released in 1974, was a relatively small compound, but by 1990, biochemists had synthesized a much more challenging molecule: for the first time they were able to design and synthesize an enzyme (a protein that catalyzes some specific biochemical reaction).[437] With progress in organic chemistry now making it feasible to synthesize any but the most complex of chemical molecules[438] and molecular biology rapidly unraveling the cell's workings, rational drug design appears poised to make a powerful contribution to pharmacology within a matter of decades.

A pill (RU486) to abort pregnancy or a growth factor (erythropoetin) to raise red blood cell production[439] is just the beginning: an Alice-in-Wonderland world is opening before us. In the decades ahead, we will develop the power to manipulate our internal chemistry safely to regulate our bodies as we wish. We will be able to gain or lose weight, manage our moods, improve our mental or physical performances, heal injuries, and perhaps even regenerate parts of our bodies. Moreover, such 'interventions' will become an accepted and routine part of everyday life, allowing us to adjust our work, play and sleep to serve best whatever lifestyles we choose. Conditions ranging from jet lag and sleep disorders to allergies and compulsive behaviors will, one day, be easily managed.

Dealing with the moral and emotional issues surrounding the use of ingested chemicals will be an immense challenge for society. The new reality of drugs is only now becoming fully apparent, and public policies and attitudes about them are still rife with inconsistencies. On the one hand, there are pharmaceuticals that are in wide and routine use; on the other hand, there are the illegal 'drugs', generally viewed with fear and loathing. But the distinction between these two realms is arbitrary: caffeine, nicotine and alcohol are drugs that are every bit as powerful as the illegal ones. And cigarettes and alcohol, which together cause some 60 per cent of preventable deaths in the US, are certainly as destructive.[440] Further, many people are addicted to 'prescription drugs', which are as easily abused as illegal substances.

The concept of a 'drug-free' society so oversimplifies the challenges of balancing drug 'use' and 'abuse' as to be extremely counterproductive. Drugs are not new to our modern society, such substances are used by primitive societies and even by animals in the wild. As the powers of Metaman extend our ability to manipulate human biochemistry, ever more drugs will definitely be used. Increasingly complex challenges lie ahead in dealing both with the medical issues associated with these drugs, and with the social issues related to our access to them. An even more fundamental challenge, however, will be in dealing with the extraordinary new possibilities these chemicals embody for humankind. Today's rapid advances in drug design are an opportunity we can embrace, not a danger we must escape.

Metaman's abilities to understand and manipulate living cells and to design and synthesize chemicals are now being yoked together with great effect. They are enabling us to understand the workings and failings of the human body at the biochemical level, to isolate unique biochemicals from any living system, and to use these and specially designed molecules to alter the human mind and body.[441] These abilities alone would be enough to transform human life in coming decades, but they are being augmented by a technique with even greater potential – the engineering of human genetics.[442]

REWRITING THE CODE

Intentional design, which is one of the driving forces of Metaman's technological advance, will in the future be applied not only to chemicals but to entire organisms. This presages immense long-term changes in the living parts of Metaman, including human beings. As humanity becomes accustomed to biological manipulation, a person's genetic endowment will no longer seem an immutable given. *The Rubáiyát of Omar Khayyám*,[443] states,

> 'The moving finger writes; and, having writ moves on; nor all your Piety nor Wit shall lure it back to cancel half a line, nor all your Tears wash out a Word of it.

But at least our genetic story will be subject to editing.

Genetic modifications to correct the underlying causes of chronic illness will eventually replace many drug treatment regimes.[444] This is already underway with Adenosine deaminase (ADA) deficiency, a disease that has generally led to early death because children who lacked this critical protein in their immune systems could not fight off infections. In a new treatment, white blood cells are withdrawn from an afflicted child, multiplied in a culture, and mixed with an engineered virus that has been given the ADA gene. When the newly grown cells are put back in the body, the child's immune system is repaired because some of the cells, having picked up the gene from the virus, can produce the much-needed ADA.[445]

Modification of humans *after* birth, however, is likely to be just a prelude. By applying biological techniques to embryos and then to the reproductive process itself, Metaman will take control of human evolution. Genetic changes that are inherited by future generations build, one upon another, and so their effects will eventually dwarf those of biological interventions not passed to one's offspring. Although manipulating human hormones and cells has the potential to regenerate new tissues, alter growth, or even slow aging, such interventions will not challenge the basic concept of what it is to be 'human'. However, altering the human genome might do just that one day, by 'inventing' new and more powerful beings who are very different from today's humans.[446]

The accomplishments of traditional animal and plant breeding hint at the magnitude of what might be possible when the techniques of molecular genetics are focused on the human genome. The enormous differences between a Great Dane and a poodle are the product of nothing more than carefully selecting and pairing offspring over hundreds of generations. Far more would be possible if each new generation were produced by conscious genetic design, especially if genes were drawn not only from other individuals but from other species as well. Who can say what new potentials a hundred generations of such design might yield?

To picture the extraordinary possibilities of the future, one need only look at what is happening today. Human genes have been inserted in a mouse embryo to create 'transgenic' mice that breed normally but are no longer strictly 'mice'. These hybrids are part human and provide animal models for studying such human diseases as Alzheimer's,[447] cancer,[448] and diabetes.[449] The human component of such hybrids may still be minuscule, but the conceptual step is immense. Gene transfers between species are becoming routine: over a thousand papers have been published in the last few years on medical developments in transgenic systems.[450] Similar gene transfers are occurring in the plant kingdom too. Genes for bacterial toxins have been added to cotton to provide resistance to bollworms, and to potatoes to kill Colorado potato beetles.[451] Eventually, humans also will incorporate genes from other species.[452]

Today, human beings may vary in intellect or stature, in race or ethnic background, but we are all essentially the same – we are *human beings*. In a world that is rapidly changing in so many ways, this knowledge is a comforting anchor. The idea of human-machine hybridization does not dislodge it because there is so little question of which parts would be 'ours'. But once humans begin to reshape themselves through biological manipulation, this anchor is dragged free, and the definition of what is 'human' begins to drift. So far, the drift is barely discernible: using growth hormones to become a few inches taller or steroids to increase muscle size is merely expressing existing potentials; having an organ or bone-marrow transplant merely replaces a failing body part; even curing a genetic disorder by introducing someone else's genes[453] into our chromosomes is just a molecular transplant. But much greater changes may lie ahead.

Altering even a small number of the key genes regulating human growth might change human beings into something quite different. For example, at the heart of 'humanness' lie the qualities of the human mind, not the strength, agility and size of the human frame. Our intellect, creativity, imagination, humor, even our hopes and fears are all rooted in the mind. To concretize the idea of reshaping human beings, consider the notion of increasing the size of the adult human brain by half. Whether such an enlargement would actually enhance human *mental* capacity is unclear, but thinking that it might do so is not unreasonable because the behavioral complexity of animal species generally increases as the ratio of brain to body weight does.[454]

The idea of expanding human mental capacities using the techniques of molecular genetics may sound absurd, but there are several clues to suggest that such an enhancement, whether by increasing brain size or by some other manipulation, might be possible: first, it is known that human mental capacity strongly depends on genetic endowment.[455] Second, there exist enough geniuses, people with photographic memories, and individuals with phenomenal gifts in language, art and music to demonstrate that even subtle changes can endow the brain with extraordinary powers. Finally, the primate brain has been evolving for more than fifty million years. The human brain is but a stage in a continuing progression that is poised to accelerate sharply as a result of the evolution of Metaman.

One might guess that human evolution is so complex a process that increasing the relative size of the brain would be almost impossible, but evidence suggests otherwise. The large brain that characterizes *Homo sapiens* probably resulted from relatively minor genetic changes to prolong the period of childhood (which is when the brain grows) in our primate ancestors.[456] Human adults are in a way baby chimps that have continued to grow without maturing, which is why we, as adults, retain the juvenile features of other primates.[457] Because the genetic changes that prolonged the juvenile period may have involved only a few genes,[458] it is quite conceivable that a further extension of brain growth would be relatively easy.

How far might the human brain be increased by genetic manipulation without serious negative consequences? There is no way of knowing, but before the emergence of Metaman, an increase in brain size would not necessarily have been beneficial to humans. Infants were born into a very dangerous natural environment; in fact, some of the earliest reliable mortality statistics, those from seventeenth-century Europe, show that more than 40 per cent of children died before their sixth birthday.[459] Although a larger brain might have served adults, an extended adolescence would only have increased the chance that a child would not live long enough to reproduce. Now, however, with infancy and childhood extremely safe,[460] there is no such obstacle to increased brain growth.

If *engineered* genetic change is eventually used to increase human mental aptitudes, future humans may make even the greatest geniuses of today seem like simpletons.[461] Rapid progress in genetic engineering generally, and in the human gene project specifically (which is attempting to decipher the entire human genome by the year 2005)[462]

The period of brain growth during primate development has become greatly prolonged in human beings. Thus, our juvenile facial features, which are so like those of a juvenile chimpanzee (left) remain unchanged during human development. Even when old we are young. An adult chimpanzee is shown on the right. Drawn by Margaret LaFarge.

suggests that extraordinary alterations of human biology will be feasible within the next century.[463]

Bioengineering is also likely to affect the human life-span. Science is only *beginning* to understand the process of aging, but clearly aging is under significant genetic control[464] and not merely the product of accumulated wear and tear. Some animals do not age detectably at all – as they grow older, they show no increased mortality or loss of function. Many mollusks live for more than a hundred years, and ocean quahogs (clams) have been found with growth rings indicating they are 220 years old.[465] Conceivably, the maximum human life-span is governed by a relatively limited number of genes.[466] Over 98 per cent of a chimpanzee's DNA is the same as a human's,[467] yet chimpanzees usually die before the age of sixty, even in zoos.[468] Thus, a few million years of evolution, changing little more than 1 per cent of primate DNA, has increased human life-span by more than a third.

The processes underlying aging are not unique to adults. Even in a child's body, the cells and their constituent parts are constantly wearing out and being replaced: genes mutate, proteins degrade, cells die. These processes do not present a problem because cellular systems actively compensate for them by replacing proteins or even whole cells and by finding and repairing genetic copying errors. Later in life, however, such repair systems seem to weaken and people's bodies begin to deteriorate. Must this happen?

Some signs suggest that aging may lie within the realm of medical manipulation. The gradual atrophy of skeletal muscles has long been viewed as an unavoidable consequence of growing old, but the onset of these changes in humans coincides with the pituitary gland's diminished secretion of growth hormone as we approach the age of forty.[469] Recently, when a group of men in their sixties and seventies were given regular growth hormone injections, their muscles grew, their skin thickened, and they lost fatty tissue[470] – all symptoms of increased 'youthfulness'. Experiments[471] such as this are tantalizing, but hardly convincing. If, however, continuing research begins to show that the limits of human mortality might be rolled back, there will be enormous energy focused on this. Who, after all, would want to be among the last to live a 'normal' life-span? If future humans are able to live actively for 150 years, death at the age of eighty will seem premature indeed. Extending human life by a few decades, however, does not adequately represent the full implications of understanding aging. If the process can be controlled, it may be no more difficult to extend life by centuries than by decades. Will aging one day be conquered? There are as yet no convincing indications one way or the other, but within the next few decades we will almost certainly know the answer.

No-one can know what humans will one day become, but whether it is a matter of fifty years or 500 years, humans will eventually undergo radical biological change. Competitive pressures within Metaman will ensure the spread of any useful ways of significantly enhancing human capabilities. Populations that adopt such techniques will generally outdistance those that do not, just as has been the case with other technologies. The computer has become a necessity for any modern society, and if a process were developed to triple human intelligence or to enable people to get along with no sleep, these too would soon become 'necessities'.

Such changes will not be painless. Like all major developments, they will cause great stresses within society. But asking whether such changes are 'wise' or 'desirable' misses the essential point that they are largely not a matter of human choice; they are the unavoidable product of the process of technological advance intrinsic to Metaman.

The emotionally charged example of eugenics illustrates some of the pressures that might bring about changes that are presently nearly unthinkable. Already, there are numerous sperm banks that purchase sperm from selected donors who are screened for a variety of general physical attributes, and there is even one bank that offers sperm from reputed 'geniuses'.[472] As more is learned about human genetics, and as techniques for genetic testing improve, such offerings are certain to become more sophisticated and even extend to embryos for implantation. Indeed, as it becomes technically feasible for any society to undertake a wide range of eugenic programs to enhance the inherent capabilities of its children, it is certain that some society will choose to do so.[473] But once begun, the practice would inevitably spread, because modern tools would make it so effective. For example, if a government cloned tens of thousands of geniuses, treated the children as a national treasure, and lavished education and care on them, how could other societies compete effectively in science and technology without doing something similar?

Procreation is so central to life that interfering with individual reproduction has been a taboo. In the past, any such interference was only possible through abusive control over large aspects of people's lives.[474] But as we increasingly intervene in our own reproduction with birth control, Caesarian operations, intensive care of premature babies, and therapies to cure sterility and infertility, this stricture will weaken. Add the growing sentiment to limit population growth, and it seems clear that various eugenic efforts will soon arrive – if not by government, then by individuals and private organizations.[475]

Neither changes in human biology nor links between humans and high-technology devices would be conceivable outside of Metaman. Whether humans remain largely biological or become progressively more machine-like depends primarily on the pace at which the biological and non-biological technologies of Metaman progress. Because the immense potential of computers is already obvious and that of molecular biology not yet fully apparent, it is still unclear whether in the future people will surgically repair a badly damaged hand, grow a new one as a salamander does, or install a prosthesis;[476] whether people will cure a diseased heart with drugs, implant a new one grown in a laboratory, or install a mechanical one.

Whatever the direction, it is likely that there will be not one but many 'human' forms in our future. As humans become more engineered, why would *we* not begin to manifest the same level of diversity seen in clothes, cars and other designed objects? Even without biological design, individual specialization is ever more the rule: few professional athletes play more than one sport, and few academics contribute to more than a small cluster of disciplines. It would be surprising if the ability to reshape and extend human capacities did not further promote such individual specialization.[477] By the standards of the future, a multi-ethnic society like the US will seem extremely homogeneous.

How different might 'human' forms eventually become? Even science fiction's macabre brain-in-a-bottle – a bodiless brain sustained by circulating nutrients, and able to sense and communicate through electronic links – is no longer an absurdity. Keeping such a brain alive would be a challenging but not implausible extension of today's tissue-culture technologies,[478] and sending such a brain information from artificial sensors would not be an insurmountable obstacle either. The tissue would be in such a controlled setting that implanting electrodes would be easier to do than today's cochear implants. Even monitoring the brain's activity in such a way that it could communicate appears possible; signals bound for the mouth and larynx might be detected in nerve stems and converted directly into speech.[479]

I am not suggesting that such a creature will ever exist, but its feasibility emphasizes just how enormous may be the changes ahead. Whether a bizarre creature such as a brain-in-a-bottle eventually appears will probably not hinge on technical constraints but on whether enough people would find such an existence desirable, or at least preferable to death.[480]

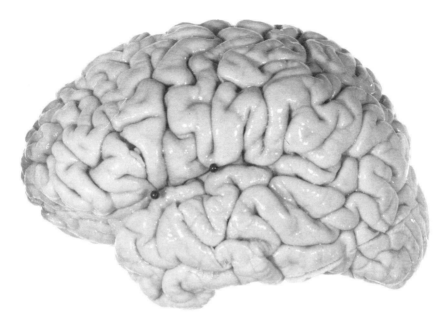

The left-side hemisphere of a human brain. How will this source of human character and identity be altered when it, like other human organs, becomes the object of direct manipulation? Will it one day be equipped with sophisticated electrode implants linking it to electronic circuitry? Will its growth or aging be modified through bioengineering? Will it one day be maintained alive outside of the skull? Courtesy Science magazine and Sandra Witelson, McMaster University.

Will the wedding of modern technology and genetics mean the eventual disappearance of humankind as we know ourselves? Perhaps, but it would be more of a beginning rather than an ending. When a species disappears we say it is 'extinct', yet we use the term for two very different types of disappearance. The first is a biological dead-end that leaves nothing behind – for example, the saber-tooth tiger or passenger pigeon; the second is really a 'pseudoextinction', the disappearance of a species that is supplanted by the new forms it produces. *Homo erectus* is extinct but not gone; it lives on in us, *Homo sapiens*, its direct descendants. Similarly, *Homo sapiens*, though likely to be transcended by its offspring, will not mark the end of a genealogical line but a point of great branching.

The coming transformation of humans may well surpass any previous biological transitions in both speed and extent. Future humans will not constitute a sequence of stable, clearly defined forms such as the ones seen in typical evolutionary trees. The human 'form' will instead come to represent a broad variety of potent hybrids between biology and technology – beings that can only survive within Metaman.

10

ENVIRONMENTAL TRANSFORMATIONS

The Changing Nature of Nature

ONCE HUMANS LED THEIR lives according to nature's cycles. People rose with the sun, went to bed after nightfall, toiled long hours at planting and harvesting times, took siestas in the heat of the day, and conserved water and food during droughts. Today, within Metaman, not only do climate fluctuations rarely perturb food and water supplies, but the natural rhythm of the seasons governs our activities far less than the man-made pattern of weekends[481] and holidays.[482] Even the rule of day and night over humans has weakened: involved in our indoor activities, we sometimes barely notice when daylight fades, and many people work full-time night jobs and go to bed at dawn.[483]

Metaman still bends before the blast of a hurricane or the roll of an earthquake, but for most of us such reminders of nature's irrepressible power come from the evening news rather than personal experience. We insulate ourselves ever more completely from the aspects of nature we find disagreeable. In the developed world people step inside to avoid a thunderstorm, turn up the heat when it gets cold, and switch on the air conditioning to escape a sweltering day. For many of us, the outdoors has become just another option for entertainment and recreation. Our preferred environment is indoors, where most of us eat, sleep, work and play.[484] In 1985, adults in the United States averaged two hours per week in outdoor leisure activities[485] and more than twenty hours watching television.[486]

The extent of our insulation from the outdoors is evident in our homes. They provide far more than shelter; they have become complex artificial environments where we spend much of our time.

They reflect individual tastes and generally contain so many personal possessions that changing dwellings is no small logistical task. These personal microenvironments are supplemented by enclosed shopping malls and parking structures, domed stadiums and covered walkways. During frigid Toronto winters one can walk for miles through a network of heated underground tunnels that offer shops and restaurants, and in Minneapolis the same is possible via second-story walkways. So widespread are our mini-habitats that we could actually travel between hotel rooms on two different *continents* without ever being out from under a roof!

The internal milieu of Metaman includes not only indoor environments, but an immense outdoor realm as well. Parks, farmlands, meadows, pastures and reservoirs surround us with a natural environment that is increasingly shaped and maintained. And this realm is spreading. With Metaman extending itself across the planet, one day the only remaining 'wilderness' will be the large parks, preserves and other lands explicitly set aside for recreation, science and other purposes.[487]

The evolution of Metaman is transforming humanity's relationship with 'nature' in two fundamental ways. First, we are becoming more able to control our experience of the natural environment around us – we pick and choose what suits our tastes, determine the timing and duration of the encounter, and return to the safety of our protected microenvironments when we wish. Be it a hike up a mountain peak, a stroll in the woods, or simply a pause on a park bench – except on rare occasions we are calling the tune as have no previous generations. Second, the distinction between what is 'natural' and 'man-made' is disappearing. The idea of nature as a pristine environment largely separate from and untouched by humans is becoming an abstract concept that is unrelated to the real world around us. An untamed and wild natural realm still exists in deep tropical jungle, open sea, and the Antarctic, but such places are distant and figure prominently in few people's lives. For most of us today, it is the idea of these places that is important, not our direct experience of them.

Metaman is in the process of creating a new global environment far different from that of early humans. Not only are there the many intentional changes associated with the growth and protection of the super-organism's internal milieu – the damming of rivers, the replacement of forest with cropland, and the transfer of water to arid regions – but Metaman's inadvertent influences are large as well. Human activities alter the planet's atmosphere, perturb ecological communities, and provide the means for species to hitch rides to distant continents and islands. As Metaman is becoming aware of these inadvertent influences, it is beginning to moderate many of them, but the totality of these effects none the less will always be large. Metaman is too immense and dynamic an organism for its presence not to be felt. As the workings of ecological communities are better understood however, humanity is becoming more adept at 'engineering' the environment. The clumsy squandering of valuable natural resources is gradually giving way to refinements of such present-day practices as stocking rivers with fish and planting seedlings to expand woodland.

We may feel that the newly emerging planetary environment, because it differs from our idealized conception of raw nature, is not 'natural', but this view implicitly separates humanity from 'nature'. We are a part of nature and our activities are as natural as those of any other living creatures. If wild peregrine falcons living in New York City[488] and feeding on pigeons can thrive in a man-made world, there is no need for us to scoff at this environment just because *we*, through Metaman, are its architects. Nor are humans the first life form significantly to change the planet's biosphere. The global changes of today – for example, the rise of carbon dioxide in the atmosphere from about .028 per cent to .035 per cent – are tiny compared to those some 2 billion years ago when bacteria drove the atmospheric oxygen concentration from near 0 to 20 per cent and created a veritable oxygen holocaust that obliterated much of the planet's anaerobic life.

OUR PLANET'S UNCEASING CHANGE

Many lament the present transformation of nature as the despoiling of a sacred realm – the natural environment as it was before man.[489] But it is important to realize that this idealized state exists only in our own minds. Is your image of 'nature' the temperate forests of Europe and North America? They did not exist 18,000 years ago when ice a mile thick covered much of these continents.[490] Is it the immense tropical jungles of the Amazon? Less than 50,000 years ago, these rainforests may have been less than 20 per cent of their current size.[491] Is it the drifting dunes of the Sahara? Some 8,000 years ago the region was temperate and contained numerous shallow lakes.[492] Even the icy wasteland of Antarctica has changed: drifting about a centimeter a year over the molten magma beneath it, the continent was nearer the equator and home to dinosaurs and trees a 100 million years ago.[493]

There is no unique 'natural' state to strive to retain; nature

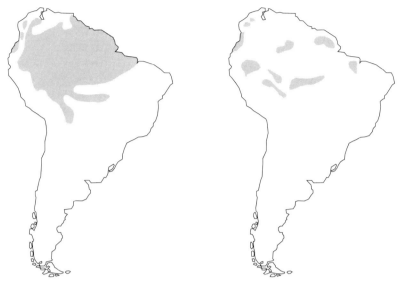

Present Day   Pleistocene Dry Periods

Several times within the past 50,000 years, dry periods have greatly diminished South America's tropical rainforests. At their maximum retreat (right), these jungles were reduced to isolated refugia that may have totalled less than 20 per cent of today's rainforest (left). Courtesy of Daniel Simberloff, University of Florida.[494]

unceasingly changes.[495] To attempt to preserve the present environment and all the species that now exist is as 'unnatural' as it is futile. Of all the species that have ever existed on this planet, some 999 of every 1000 are now extinct.[496] From our perspective, it is sad when a species dies out, because something is lost to us for ever. It is also sad that dinosaurs are no longer around and that we cannot know our ancestor *Homo erectus*. But this *is* the evolutionary process; this *is* nature.

Life's history on earth is a tale of long periods of gradual change punctuated by episodes of rapid,[497] massive extinction. The most well known is the Cretaceous extinction 65 million years ago, which marked the demise of about three quarters of the species then extant – including the dinosaurs. The Permian extinction some 245 million years ago was even more traumatic; only 4 per cent of marine species survived it. Other large extinctions occurred 208, 367 and 439 million years ago.[498] We, and all the rest of life, are the result of change. Life's complexity evolved not *despite* the earth's intermittent major

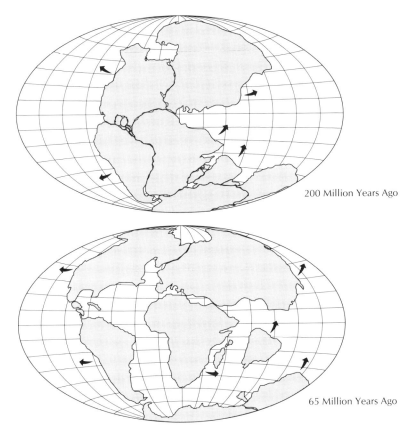

200 Million Years Ago

65 Million Years Ago

The world is continually changing; even the continents are drifting slowly. Some 200 million years ago, today's continents were clumped together to form one supercontinent, Pangaea (top), which began to fragment about 180 million years ago. By about 65 million years ago, the continents had reached the position shown at the bottom. When India, then a separate island, subsequently collided with Asia, it raised the giant Himalayas.[499] The aggregation and fragmentation of the drifting continents is cyclic, so a few hundred million years hence, there may again be only a single supercontinent.

extinctions, but *because* of them. Without the massive Cretaceous extinction, mammals might never have prospered; without the oxygen holocaust, there could be no large active animals.[500]

Some ecologists estimate that species extinctions today are occurring as rapidly as during previous massive die-offs, the world losing not the few species a *year* that perish between major extinctions,[501] but as many as a hundred a *day*.[502] Most are insects and plants endemic to

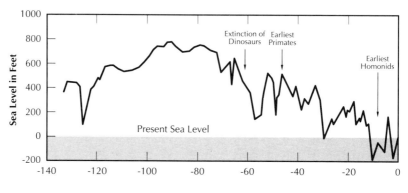

Millions of Years Before Present

The sea-level rise of a few feet that may occur in the next century is tiny compared to the large changes of previous epochs.[503] *At times the sea has been as much as 800 feet higher than its current level. Clearly, unless Metaman learns to intervene to prevent natural changes such as these, it will have to learn to adapt to them.*

the tropical rainforests,[504] but many mammals – from blue whales to mountain gorillas – are in danger of disappearing as did the woolly mammoth and giant sloth ten thousand years ago.[505] Quite conceivably half the species alive a few centuries ago will be gone a few centuries hence.

We can as yet only guess at the full extent of today's extinctions, but the earth is probably in the midst of another episode of massive extinction – this one caused not by a meteor's impact but by Metaman's birth.[506] We may feel pain and outrage at this occurrence, seeing it as an immense tragedy for both humankind and all living things, but we stand at an extraordinary juncture in the history of life. Metaman is the greatest advance in living systems in some 700 million years, and life on earth is entering a new phase in its history. In light of this reality, is it not natural for the planet's ecological systems to be undergoing wrenching change?

Targeted efforts may save various selected species, but it would be truly astonishing if the overall losses now occurring could be halted or even significantly reduced. The forces bringing these changes are too powerful and have progressed too far. A huge and growing human population is disrupting local habitats and perturbing the climate. And in much the same way that Metaman's development is mingling diverse human populations and sweeping away local cultural traditions, Metaman is joining together diverse ecological systems and thereby causing the extinction of endemic local species throughout the world.[507] The Zebra mussel, a native of the Caspian Sea, reached North America's Great Lakes in about 1985 in the ballast tanks of ships and has now devastated the region's shellfish population.[508] Or consider Hawaii, where animals and plants from mainland continents are now replacing the unique species of this once-isolated island.[509]

The probable disappearance of so many life forms is sobering, but indications are that the consequences for humankind will be far from catastrophic. The curator of entomology at the Smithsonian Institution in Washington, DC may warn about the earth becoming a 'mostly desertified environment filled with lineages of domestic weeds, flies, cockroaches and starlings,'[510] but such bleak images must be meant more to galvanize public opinion than accurately to describe the future. Even if half of the world's species were lost, enormous diversity would still remain. Most species found in highly developed regions such as Europe and North America are widely enough distributed to survive both spreading urbanization and moderate climate change, and biological diversity in the tropics will remain orders of magnitude greater than in temperate climates regardless of Metaman's actions. Immense numbers of species in tropical jungles are being and will continue to be lost, but most are beetles and other insects with very narrow distributions. Although this process may be painful for us at a conceptual level, it is hard to see how the disappearance of such insect populations, or even the loss of unique – but extremely localized – island floras and faunas, could have significant global repercussions for humankind. Metaman is not that frail.

Many issues need to be examined to evaluate the potential consequences for humanity of the large-scale loss of species now taking place. One commonly expressed concern about the destruction of the rainforests is the great economic value of the drugs that might be developed from medicinal plants growing there.[511] After all, the plant kingdom has yielded a quarter of all prescription medicines in use today,[512] and until the 1960s, screening various plant and fungal extracts was a major method for discovering new drugs. But drug development within Metaman is moving towards rational design taking place in the laboratory.[513] In 1985, the pharmaceutical industry in the US spent $4.1 billion on research and development, yet not one major company had an active research program to discover new drugs by searching for medically useful plants.[514] Today there are a few small programs, but the activity remains comparatively minor.[515] In the past, large corporations have generally been very adept at making money by overexploiting natural resources, so the lack of interest of so many profit-driven companies may not be conclusive, but it strongly suggests that no fabulous eldorado awaits the pharmaceutical industry in the rainforests.

Another concern about species extinctions is that it might cost humanity untold biological materials for basic scientific research. The availability of research materials, however, is not a limiting factor for science. There will always be far more research paths than can ever be followed. To date, only 1.4 million of as many as 30 million species thought to exist have even been named, much less studied.[516] The tremendous strides of molecular biology now taking place are being made largely on the basis of work on only a few hundred species[517] out of the many millions now alive . . . and the many *billions* long departed.[518] Research focuses on so few species not because other interesting species can't be found, but because organisms become more useful as they become better characterized. In the absence of compelling reasons to use a previously unstudied organism, biologists seek to extend knowledge by better understanding widely used ones such as mice, fruitflies or the *E. coli* bacterium. In actuality, there would be more than enough to study without looking at *any* new species at all, so a few million more or less out of the many millions of species that would survive even the most massive extinction will not have a significant influence on the larger trajectory of progress in biology.

Yet another threat from diminished biodiversity is that agriculture might become increasingly fragile. Plant ecologists, however, knowing that access to diverse strains of crops are important in maintaining agricultural resistance to pests, have created extensive seed-repository programs to ensure continuing diversity. Though receiving just 3 per cent of the public outlay directed at preserving genetic diversity, these critical programs none the less now preserve the germ plasm (seeds, cuttings, roots, etc.) of some 500,000 plant varieties including 70,000 strains of wheat, 32,000 of sorghum, 77,000 of rice.[519] Generally, about half the wild cousins of food crops have now been preserved in seed banks,[520] and the focus of such programs is shifting from collecting new strains to the task of maintaining existing ones in useful condition.

The widespread extinctions being brought by Metaman's birth will not imperil humanity's capacity to sustain medical and scientific progress or agricultural production, but there is still another consideration about this issue, that of ethics and morality. Biologists Edward Wilson and Paul Ehrlich argue that humans are the dominant species on the planet and therefore have a moral responsibility to protect the rest of the earth's species.[521] But how could this be? We humans, although endowed with consciousness, are not enthroned above the 'natural' world, studying it and protecting it from change. We are part of nature and cannot help but affect the natural realm we inhabit. Nor can we avoid the truth that life is a continuing process of endings and beginnings in a drama in which both we and Metaman are active players.[522] We can shoulder a mantle of personal responsibility for the well-being of beetles in the Amazon jungles if we wish, but this self-proclaimed custodianship does not derive from some larger cosmic obligation. Moreover, since the size of the human population will almost certainly be the major determinant in the fates of fragile local ecologies worldwide, any efforts spent to limit the growth of our own population would, besides improving the lot of humankind, probably be of more long-term benefit to the world's disappearing species than any *direct* environmental efforts.

That diminished biodiversity will probably not have serious global consequences for humanity is reassuring, but also frightening, because this conclusion together with the earlier one that neither global warming, nor ozone depletion, nor any other known environmental problem will be catastrophic for Metaman, appear to be an open invitation to those who would trample thoughtlessly upon the environment for short-term gain. But there is no such invitation. The foremost reason to respect nature is a simple and compelling one that rests neither on threat of imminent catastrophe nor lure of economic gains:[523] our desire to maintain and improve rather than degrade the quality of our surroundings. The question is not 'Can we survive?' but 'How do we choose to live?' Do we want beautiful natural landscapes filled with diverse species of wildlife, clean coastal areas that are home to water fowl, lush woodland settings, and crystal clear lakes and streams? Or do we want tar washing up on beaches, groundwater contaminated with chemical wastes, forests dying from acid rain, and topsoil eroding from denuded mountainsides?

It is neither the loss of biodiversity nor the disappearance of the natural ideal we have labeled 'nature' that has the most serious implications for our lives, but the ongoing thoughtless degradation of the ecological systems that surround us. Because some disruptions to ecological systems would cause a cascade of effects with far-reaching consequences, and others would barely be noticed by humanity, the task today is to learn to distinguish between the two. This requires a deep understanding of the broad ecological interdependencies around us.

Embracing Metaman and the changes it is bringing is entirely compatible with respecting the environment and the living things around us. Yes, it is outrageous to imperil the whale for a few tasty meals or the elephant for its ivory. There is no need to invoke ethics to rebuke such activities for their utter disregard for the immense long-term value to humankind of these unique, intelligent creatures. But, at the same time, there are scores of matters more important to humanity than the loss of the snail darter, a small perch whose threatened extinction forced a two-year delay in the construction of the Tellico dam on the Tennessee river in the late 1970s.[524] Assessments of relative 'worth' – however repugnant some may find them – need to be made. All species cannot be saved, and if significant effort is to be spent protecting an endangered species of silverspot butterfly or a rare subspecies of the seaside sparrow,[525] it is important to be clear about why these particular local variants are being selected for special attention instead of being left to their own devices in this era of environmental change.

Some creatures such as primates and dolphins have unique qualities that may tell us much about ourselves; others such as butterflies we may simply find beautiful; others have singularly interesting life cycles; and still others play key roles in maintaining important ecosystems. There are many good reasons to strive to protect the creatures around us – even the innocent pleasure we derive from their presence – but in the face of the immense transformation enveloping humanity and the biosphere itself, a dogmatic resistance to change achieves little. All change is not bad. With good reason we were happy to wave farewell to smallpox after a long battle to achieve its extinction. Would it be so terrible to live in a world without ticks, blackwidow spiders, poison ivy and a few species of mosquitos as well?

This is a very human-centered view, but is this not the most natural perspective for humans to take? Certainly, it does not in any way suggest that other life forms are not important, only that their importance *to humans* is in how they contribute to the material and emotional quality of *human* life. Indeed, we cannot escape our 'human' perspective: even our feelings of sadness over the extinction of species or the disruption of habitats are supremely human: after all, whose loss do we mourn but our own?

Most of us value porpoises, elephants and other large, impressive mammals far more than plants or insects. This is natural; we feel a kinship with these 'charismatic' mammals and value them accordingly. Such feelings, however, are only one dimension of the 'value' of other creatures to us. Even if we are only dimly aware of microscopic phytoplankton, these creatures, because they remove vast amounts of carbon dioxide from the air, are even more important to humanity than the large mammals. Ever more creatures once viewed as 'insignificant' are being found to play vital roles in key ecosystems, so our assessments of the larger impacts of ecological change need to be cautious. At the same time, however, we must remain conscious of the truth that not all creatures are important to us – there is an immense roster of species that neither affect nor interest the vast majority of humankind.

This decade's sense of impending environmental cataclysm has jolted large numbers of people into considering just how deeply Metaman is altering the environment, but has not answered the fundamental question, 'What kind of a world do we want to create for ourselves?' For the first time, humankind must confront this question on a global, not a local scale.

When a sense of impending doom drives us, the answer is easy: we don't want a barren, lifeless planet and will do anything to prevent that. But once we recognize that there is no impending disaster looming, the environmental crisis is transformed. As soon as the issue is about the 'quality' of human life, rather than our survival, we must somehow reconcile the many alternative visions of our future. Some people may favor virgin wilderness, others more economic development; some may want a rugged canyon floor, others a reservoir and hydroelectric power; some may be concerned about climate change, others about having adequate food and shelter.

There is no doubt that Metaman will reshape the biosphere, thus our challenge today is not to discover how to stop environmental change, but to learn how best to channel it along paths we consider desirable. To do this, we must comprehend the larger dynamics of Metaman, distinguish between what can and cannot be significantly influenced, and have realistic goals. These are the tasks for humanity as we move beyond this age of 'crisis' and into an age of 'creation'.

THE NATURAL ENVIRONMENT IN THE AGE OF METAMAN

One might presume that humanity's experience of 'nature' would be somehow impoverished by the broad conversion of wilderness into an environment shaped largely by human activity. This is far from the truth. Humanity's exposure to life in all its awesome diversity has never been greater.

Through modern communications, travel, botanical gardens and zoos, we can observe a range of animals and plants hitherto available only to the most intrepid explorers. Before the early 1800s, except by way of an occasional circus or a bear baiting,[526] all but a privileged few, those with access to a few special 'animal menageries', saw only farm animals and local wildlife.[527] A unicorn and rhinoceros were equally believable to most people in the Middle Ages, and yet some 1.5 million people will visit the San Diego Wild Animal Park this year and ride trams through a square mile of maintained veldt housing zebras, giraffes, black rhinos, Arabian oryxes,[528] wildebeest and other species. That some scoff at such an experience as being a far cry from traveling in Africa shows the extraordinary heights to which people's expectations have climbed. Only a few centuries ago, seeing a bear led around on a chain was a memorable exposure to wildlife. Now, at many zoos the outdoor animal enclosures have a natural feel to them, and a zoo-goer's vision is unobscured by bars. Furthermore, without leaving our living rooms, we can watch spectacular nature films ranging from the undersea life of the Great Barrier Reef to the migration of the arctic caribou. Television may be an imperfect substitute for the direct experience of nature, but it shows us aspects of the living world we would never otherwise see. And if we wish a more direct experience, that too is often possible.

In reshaping the living world we inhabit, Metaman's influences extend far beyond manipulations of local ecologies; Metaman is now at the point of using genetic engineering to alter large numbers of individual life forms.[529] Soon, the boundary between 'natural' and 'man-made' will become so blurred as to be almost meaningless. Having breached the biological barriers blocking interspecies breeding[530] and opened the door to direct manipulation of genes, molecular biology is on the verge of bringing into being a host of newly created life forms: new strains of crops, new breeds of animals, and new variants of micro-organisms.[531] Today, most genetic manipulation involves only single genes, for example adding a growth hormone gene to a carp to produce bigger fish,[532] or giving a tomato the antifreeze gene that keeps the winter flounder from freezing.[533] But this is only scratching the surface. As yet scientists are still only tinkering with the genetics of organisms; as animal and plant development is better understood, it will become possible to design entirely new organisms.

In addition to bringing new living forms into being, the techniques of modern biology are also being used to rescue selected species from extinction. For instance, embryos of endangered wild ox were transferred to a domestic cow which successfully served as a surrogate mother. It seems likely the broad application of such techniques

Attempts to engineer higher animals genetically already have been successful. When carp eggs are injected with a growth-hormone gene, adults (top) grow to be as much as 40 per cent larger than fish from untreated eggs (bottom). Courtesy of Zuoyan Zhu, University of Maryland and New York Times Photo Archive.

will become ever more common. Indeed, programs to freeze tissue and cells from endangered animals may become a routine supplement to present-day efforts to preserve particular natural habitats. Such tissue banks, together with existing programs to gather and preserve the seeds of wild plants, may eventually be the beginnings of a permanent archival reservoir of the earth's life forms. It is probable that Metaman will eventually be able to use such frozen tissue to grow entire animals, but whether or not this occurs, such material will be invaluable when distant future generations are trying to understand the details of the immense biological transition now underway on our planet.

Metaman's manipulation of the earth's living systems is playing a prominent role in shaping the natural environment, but plants and animals are only a part of the present human environment. Electronic and mechanical devices are also significant. The world around us is now populated by automobiles, traffic lights, airplanes and other

This rare Indian desert cat kitten, the first exotic cat born by interspecies embryo transfer, was born to a domestic cat surrogate mother in February 1989. Transfering in-vitro fertilized embryos between endangered species and common domestic ones is becoming an important tool for zoos.[534] Courtesy Betsy Dresser, Cincinnati Zoo.

devices. These complex, nonliving entities are a new class of element in the world, and as they proliferate and become more elaborate and diverse, they constitute an ever more integral part of the natural environment, not only for humans but for animals as well – especially domesticated ones. A dog that doesn't understand at least the rudiments of automobile behavior doesn't last very long.

Although still far simpler than biological systems, machines are evolving rapidly. As they begin to achieve the complexity of biological organisms, they will become an important component in the richness of our planetary environment. Presently, there are three kingdoms of higher organisms:[535] plants, animals and fungi. Within Metaman, advanced technological devices almost seem to constitute a fourth – one that is complex, diverse and thriving.[536]

Despite the massive extinction now underway here on earth, when those in the distant future look back on this period of history, they may well see it not as the era when the natural environment was impoverished, but as the age when a plethora of new forms – some biological, some technological, and some a combination of the two – burst on to the scene. The human environment has never been more diverse than it is today.

Homo sapiens evolved in a raw, primitive environment, and something primal and spiritual about that world so resonates within us that even if we never visit the wilderness, just knowing it is out there is important to most of us. No matter how widely human activity spreads over the earth's surface, as long as people feel this strong attachment to nature, Metaman will manifest those feelings by preserving large wilderness parks ranging from tropical jungle to arctic tundra.[537]

Humanity's primary environment, though, is now the internal milieu of Metaman, and this is gradually changing our experience of, and attitudes about, what is generally termed the 'natural' world. Today, we are able to experience the essence of what touches us about 'nature' while still holding on to the comfort and security of our very different everyday environments. To experience not only the beauty of nature but also its harshness, undiminished by our many creations, is something that few of us today would find particularly appealing except in small doses. Few of us will long endure – much less enjoy – slogging through a fetid swamp, shivering in a cold, penetrating wind, or standing in a swarm of mosquitos. And why should we?

No longer do we relate to 'nature' as our actual living environment – the source of our food, the site of our labors, a place we cannot leave no matter how inhospitable it becomes. For most of us, the experience of 'nature' is a sojourn away from our day-to-day life. And whether we take a one-hour walk in the woods, or a three-month expedition through the wilderness, we are generally in control of the experience and can adjust its intensity to suit our individual tastes. We *could* completely immerse ourselves in wild natural environments, but most of us don't. Instead, we 'visit' those locales, carrying our provisions and equipment with us rather than living off the land.[538] Even people who trek in the Himalayas, boat down the Amazon, safari through the Serengeti, or run the Colorado can make use of equipment such as light-weight tents, special clothing and footwear, dehydrated food, insect repellents and water filters, to insulate themselves from some of the difficulties inherent in these environments.

In general, what we want is not raw nature but a packaged extract of it – a hike along an alpine ridge, a swim beneath a tropical waterfall, a ski run down a powdery slope, a vibrant sunset over the ocean. And Metaman is shaping the environment to provide us with just this. For some people, that extract is to dangle on a sheer mountain wall; for others it is to park a recreational vehicle in a campground and hike along a well-travelled trail, and for still others it is to watch a wildlife show on television. Whatever the intensity of the natural experience we choose, there is a part of us that will always respond to nature: an electric heater can keep us warm but it does not affect us the way a crackling log and flickering embers do. Fireworks can be magnificent and breathtaking, but there will always be something about lightning and thunder that moves us with a deeper wonder. And who can stand in a field of wildflowers fluttering with butterflies and deny their worth, be untouched by the soft music of a brook tumbling down a fern-covered hillside, or gaze without awe at a star-filled sky on a clear desert night?

As Metaman fashions the human environment, it preserves some wild natural environments but it also transforms nature by enhancing those elements of it we value and reducing those we do not. This requires no coherent plan, it simply happens. Because so many people enjoy crisp winter air, panoramic views and the exhilaration of rapid motion, we have comfortable ski resorts where people can warm themselves before a fire after their skiing and need not dilute their experience with the strain of climbing icy hillsides. These slopes and trails are our product. Or consider the zen gardens of Kyoto, which embody the essential beauty and tranquility of nature, and have an enchanting magic. This is not 'nature' in its typical sense, but a work of art composed of elements crafted from nature. Carefully positioned stones, raked gravel, tiny walkways bridging shaped ponds, trimmed bushes: the garden exists only through the constant attention of the gardeners who pick up the leaves, trim the plants, and reset the stones and pebbles. Stop this work and the garden would soon return to the wild and lose the beauty that so moves us.

In addition to enhancing selected natural elements in the *outdoor* environment around us, we are mimicking them in the controlled microenvironments we inhabit. The waterfalls, fountains and pools common in shopping malls and other public places have become very appealing. Like the Japanese gardens, these are nature idealized – decorative art. But this is merely a hint of what lies ahead. I once sat in a living-room staring through a tall picture window at a small rock pond outside. The pond was some five feet across and surrounded by high, ivy-covered, stone walls open to the sky. A persistent rain was beating against the window. The scene was tropical, but I was not in the tropics; I was in Ohio in midwinter, and snow lay on the ground in front of the house. The entire effect was illusion: the stone walls and ivy were artificial, the rain and mist were produced by machine, the background noises were coming through speakers, the 'outside sky' was projected on to a small planetarium dome. Later, at the push of a button I watched the rain stop and the dawn slowly break to a concert of birdsong. The effect was enthralling. Even though my mind told me this was not real, my eyes and ears told me otherwise. This experimental house did not feel like some garish theme park, it felt like a wonderful little tropical retreat. The living room was only a prototype,[539] but the effects were so powerful that they are certain to be used extensively one day.

Evocations of pleasing natural elements and themes are proliferating in the internal milieu of Metaman because they touch something deep within us, but the many technological elements of Metaman that make no pretense of imitating nature figure even more prominently in our lives. The indoor microenvironments we inhabit are shaped by technology and their continuing evolution will profoundly alter the way humans view the world. As technology becomes more sophisticated and more hidden from our sight – essentially embedded in the environment – we will perceive it less and less, and one day people may even come to expect their surroundings actually to respond to their needs.

To see how technologies such as microcomputers might eventually become so pervasive as to become largely invisible to us,[540] consider the written word. Writing is everywhere, but we barely notice it. People who cannot read have difficulty today not because they lack books but because the world is filled with labels, signs, instructions, price tags, timetables and such. Electric power, too, has faded from our view. We rarely think about a house's electric wiring; we just look for an outlet.

Garage doors that open before us, lights that turn off when we leave, cars that announce when a door is ajar: these are only the beginning. Humans will soon be surrounded by far more interactive machines. What will it be like to be born into a world where objects respond meaningfully to us and even answer back when we speak to them? Imagine talking to your stove and telling it how to cook a meal to your taste, telling an alarm clock when to wake you up and start your coffee, or getting good medical, financial or legal advice from a bedside computer that patiently discusses your problems with you and knows most of the details of your life. Imagine having a refrigerator that automatically calls the grocery store to order deliveries of your favorite foods; having your daily organizer suggest good ideas for presents when reminding you about a birthday; or having a car ask you why you're driving over the speed limit, phone the police when it's stolen, or tell you you're falling asleep and should stop to rest.

We might well grow to feel a certain affection for devices that have enormous time and patience and pay more attention to us than most people do. In a psychology experiment where patients were directed in therapy by a computer program that simulated the questioning of a human therapist, some of the patients actually grew attached to their 'therapist' even though they knew it to be a computer.[541]

A key to transforming the way humans deal with computers will be language recognition. When computer chips can understand normal

---

The following is an excerpt of an actual conversation between a patient and ELIZA, one of the first computer programs to mimic human conversation. ELIZA, written in 1965 by Professor Joseph Weizenbaum of MIT, simulated a Rogerian (non-directive) therapist.[542] Though the program was relatively simple, it occasionally generated interactions that gave such an appearance of insight that people insisted it 'understood' them.[543] ELIZA's responses are capitalized; the patient's are lower-case. Courtesy of Joseph Weizenbaum, Massachusetts Institute of Technology.

– Men are all alike.
– IN WHAT WAYS?
– They're always bugging us about something or other.
– CAN YOU THINK OF A PARTICULAR EXAMPLE?
– Well, my boyfriend made me come here.
– YOUR BOYFRIEND MADE YOU COME HERE?
– He says I'm depressed much of the time.
– I AM SORRY TO HEAR THAT YOU ARE DEPRESSED.
– It's true. I'm unhappy.
– DO YOU THINK COMING HERE WILL HELP YOU NOT TO BE UNHAPPY?
– I need some help, that much seems certain.
– WHAT WOULD IT MEAN TO YOU IF YOU GOT SOME HELP?
– Perhaps I could learn to get along with my mother.
– TELL ME MORE ABOUT YOUR FAMILY.
. . .
– WHAT ELSE COMES TO MIND WHEN YOU THINK OF YOUR FATHER?
– Bullies.
– DOES THAT HAVE ANYTHING TO DO WITH THE FACT THAT YOUR BOYFRIEND MADE YOU COME HERE?

conversational speech, we will relate to them very differently. This extremely sophisticated ability, though beyond the capabilities of any existing computer systems, is well on its way. Not only is it presently relatively commonplace for computers to generate and recognize individual spoken words, but already a few systems exist that can understand conversational speech that is restricted to narrow, well-defined subject areas.[544]

How will humans relate to an environment where objects routinely talk and respond to questions and commands? Being surrounded by seemingly intelligent, yet largely incomprehensible devices might lead us to project human qualities on to our surroundings – a modern pantheism.[545] Already the natural and the man-made, the animate and the inanimate, are so merging within Metaman that we sometimes forget the distinction between them. Thus, people treat cattle like machines that should produce the most meat at the least cost, mangle animals in medical experiments as though stress testing a new manufacturing product,[546] and hope that calling a car pet names will keep it from breaking down. In Florida a few years ago, a man even went so far as to gun down an automatic teller machine that wouldn't give him money.

Although we cannot foretell what the world of Metaman will eventually become, it is evident that the natural environment will undergo profound change. Future humans will know an outdoor realm far more managed than ours, and indoor microenvironments far more pervasive and responsive to human needs. In both realms there will be an enhancement of those natural elements future humans find most appealing, but those elements may not be the ones that would appeal to *us*. For example, to many Americans born in the last few decades, artificial lemon drink tastes more 'natural' than real lemonade.[547] What humans view as 'natural' will change as the human environment is transformed, so it is virtually certain that the enhanced environment of the future will seem every bit as rich and 'natural' to future humans as today's environment seems to us. Indeed, future humans may well look back at today's world as threatening and primitive, much as we now regard the world of our prehistoric ancestors.

11

THE TRAJECTORY OF SOCIAL CHANGE
A Story of Rising Expectations

BY THE YARDSTICK OF history, we live in a uniquely privileged time. Although poverty, disease and starvation still afflict humanity, more people than ever have the luxury of pursuing more rewarding activities than providing themselves with food and shelter. In the wealthy, industrialized regions of the world, people suffer less from hunger and exposure than from the tensions and psychological distresses born of rapid change and the large disparities among us.[548] Neither social turmoil, uncertainty, nor radical extremes of affluence and poverty will disappear in the decades immediately ahead, but humanity's trajectory is towards a rich and vital future, not a bleak, dehumanized one.

To gain perspective on that future, we must see the present and the past clearly. Not surprisingly, romantic illusions about the past abound; after all, history, as we know it, is largely the tale of a privileged few living in societies successful enough to leave records. Until recent times, however, fatal childhood disease was common, poverty widespread, justice a rarity. Debtors were thrown in prison,[549] press gangs dragged men into naval service, doctors sawed off limbs without anaesthetics,[550] and small children were put to work in fields and factories. People were routinely flogged, drawn and quartered, keel-hauled, burned at the stake, and stretched on the rack. The everyday realities of most past societies would be intolerable to us today.

Our vague understanding of these realities cannot affect us like the gripping images of our present-day world continually bombarding us from near and far. We vicariously experience the ills around us as has no previous generation. Were we to scrutinize historical periods as completely, what we would see would make us shudder. In hospitals in the mid-1800s, for example, it was not unusual for a nurse to pass through a ward and 'cleanse' wounds using and reusing a sponge wrung into a bucket after each patient.[551] With such practices and no antibiotics,[552] nearly half those who suffered a traumatic injury and had a leg amputated in a large hospital did not survive.[553]

As to city life, not only was there no sewage treatment before the mid-1800s,[554] but the burning of high-sulphur coal showered inhabitants with sooty, corrosive pollution.[555] Life expectancy for a baby born to the laboring class in Manchester, England, then was only seventeen years.[556] Infant mortality was high, and tuberculosis, bronchitis and pneumonia struck down many adults. The Irish immigrants to Boston and New York in the mid-nineteenth century lived in slums so deplorable as to make today's inner-city ghettos attractive.

It is easy to forget the severity of even recent epidemics. Before the Salk vaccine was developed in 1955, polio took a terrible toll. With some 58,000 new cases in 1952, patients in iron lungs filled hospital wards throughout the US. Shown here is one such ward at the Rancho Amigos Medical Center in California in 1952. Courtesy of the March of Dimes Birth Defects Foundation.

There was no indoor plumbing, streets were ankle-deep in garbage, sewage flowed in open trenches, and the only water came from fire hydrants.[557] Cholera and smallpox took a heavy toll.[558] Whole families sometimes lived in one small windowless room, with husband, wife, brothers and sisters sharing a single bed.[559]

Britain was prosperous and powerful, but look at the social conditions there at the dawn of the Industrial Revolution. In 1833, when Parliament finally regulated child labor, it became illegal for children of ten or under to work more than forty-eight hours a week. And eleven-year-olds could work no more than sixty-nine hours a week.[560] Moreover, 200 offenses were capital crimes in Britain, including forgery, poaching and theft. A person could be transported to Australia for tampering with a steam engine in a coal mine and could be hanged for stealing or destroying linen.[561] Records of executions in London leave little doubt about the relative value of human life then. In 1748, seventeen-year-old William Stevens was hanged after being convicted of stealing a half pound of tobacco and six gallons of brandy from a shopkeeper's counter[562] – his first and last offense.

The social environment within the developed world of Metaman is far from ideal, but by historical standards it is a paradise.[563] The gap

Children in the nineteenth century often worked hours that would be considered onerous for an adult today. Eight-year-old Bill Scott from Clarksburg, West Virginia, equipped with pipe, headlight, pick axe and lunch can, is ready for a day's work in the coal mine. Courtesy Bettmann Archives.

between the relatively affluent billion people who live in the developed world and the billion in abject poverty at the fringes of Metaman is immense,[564] and yet by indices such as life expectancy, infant mortality, and literacy, even these less-developed regions are much better off than fifty years ago.[565]

Comparing humanity's present with its past throws into sharp relief just how much Metaman's emergence has given humankind. An animal's body provides its cells and tissues with a stable, healthy

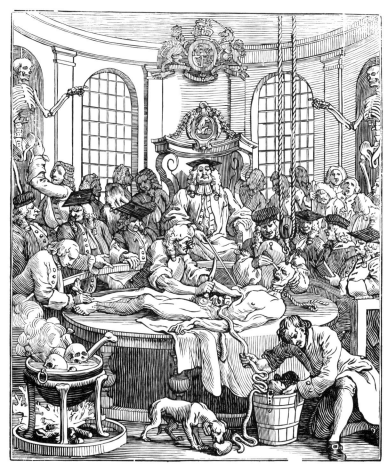

The Reward of Cruelty, *Hogarth's view of Surgeon's Hall. Executions in the eighteenth century were bawdy public spectacles, following which the victims' bodies were frequently publicly dissected by surgeons.*[566] *Courtesy British Museum.*

environment – feeding them, carrying away their wastes, protecting them from the elements. Similarly, Metaman is providing humans in the developed world with an environment increasingly tailored to our needs. Metaman shields us from the elements, provides us with medical care, brings us nourishment, and offers us diverse recreation, amusement and intellectual stimulation. Metaman gives us ever more choice in what we do, where we live, and what kind of life we lead. One sign of the affluence of humans within Metaman is the considerable amount of time now devoted to education; generally children no longer work, they attend school. Nine or more years of education are compulsory throughout the developed world,[567] and more than 95 per cent of adults in these lands can read and write. By contrast, a century and a half ago in England a third of the men getting married signed their marriage register with only a mark.[568]

We live in a world filled with marvelous recreations that are unique to our era. For instance, not only can we enjoy the world's most talented musicians, we can summon them at whim, even from beyond the grave. In her song 'Unforgettable', Natalie Cole sings us a duet

Henry Ford, who quit his job with the Edison Illuminating Company of Detroit to build a gasoline-powered vehicle, is seen in 1896 driving the first automobile he made. Only twelve years later he would be mass-producing Model-Ts. Though primitive, these early cars cost more in current dollars than some of today's vehicles.[569] Courtesy of Oil and Gas Journal *and the American Petroleum Institute.*

with the vibrant echoes of Nat King Cole, her long-dead father.[570] We can listen to the Berlin Philharmonic or Elvis Presley while hiking up a mountain or soaking in the bath. Past monarchs may have had court musicians, but could they invite a symphony orchestra into their bedroom at a moment's notice? Similarly, with videos we can watch the world's best performers in productions built from the combined talents of large technical and creative teams. Great actors wait patiently for us while we pause for a snack or chat on the phone. And if we cannot find a performance to suit our mood, we have countless other options ranging from watching sports to reading one of the millions of books and magazines that are available.

Such marvels go on and on. We cross the world in a matter of hours. We converse with friends who are far away. We wear clothing woven from diverse and colorful fabrics. We instantaneously capture a perfect image of a friend. So unbelievable would such things have been to people of previous eras that they would eagerly have paid huge sums for them; yet we receive them for a pittance. For spare change we munch on a juicy strawberry in midwinter or have an iced drink in summer; for the price of a sandwich we enjoy a film that cost tens of millions of dollars to make. So accustomed are we to these wonders that we think nothing of them. How easy it is to forget that only eighty years ago films were silent,[571] radio had not yet arrived,[572] and a 'refrigerator' was an 'ice-box'.

Furniture, clothing, shelter, food and transportation once required so much individual labor that the totality of human activity was incapable of supporting more than a narrow segment of society in affluence. Now, miraculously, mass production is so amplifying human effort that all humanity could conceivably enjoy material well-being. Since 1900, the world's output of goods and services has grown twenty-fold.[573] Today, clothing and furniture need not be the product of long hours of individual craftsmanship; a large household does not demand a brigade of servants; private transportation does not need to be fed, watered and groomed.

Some things, of course, are limited in supply: not everyone can have an ocean view or a solid mahogany table. But much is becoming less expensive and spreading to more people: the top-of-the-line products of yesterday are often surpassed by the mass-marketed ones of today.[574] The best black-and-white television of 1960 hardly compares with a cheap color television of today, and the 1920 Model-T Ford (after adjusting for inflation) was more expensive than today's far superior economy cars.[575] Being very rich now provides access to higher-quality goods but little that is functionally different: a luxury hotel, a beautiful car, and a designer watch each have a mass-market equivalent.

As Metaman enables us to easily satisfy our basic survival needs, style and appearance are becoming paramount. The man-made objects around us embody far more than the obvious functions they serve. Once a bed may have been just a place to sleep; a plate, a utensil to hold food; a car, a way to get somewhere; a chair, a place to sit. Not any more. Such devices now satisfy other human needs as well. Material things are assuming forms that offer us feelings of sexuality, freedom, power and individuality. Today, we shop for experiences and sensations. Some, like a vacation, are ephemeral; others, such as a sleek sports car or a fragrant soap, can be enjoyed again and again. Caffeine-free Diet Coke as a substitute for water is the quintessence of this trend: no calories, no caffeine, no reason to exist other than the experience it embodies.

Now we not only need technology and its products for our survival; we enjoy and desire them. So accustomed have we grown to rapid travel, changing styles and fashion, films, television and recorded music that life stripped of these stimulations would seem empty to many.

The human environment formed by Metaman is so filled with appealing images, patterns, shapes and colors that we take them for granted. Each, though, is the product of great labor. Walk into any office building: someone who studied interior design for years has devoted long hours to the choice of carpeting, light fixtures and furnishings. Look at a quirky little cornice on a building: an architect somewhere almost certainly regards it as his or her special creation. Glance at the colors, messages and designs on a box of cereal: marketing specialists and graphic artists worked hard to achieve an effect that would grab your attention. Whether it is the shape of a spoon handle, the image on a postage stamp, or the colorful pattern on a bathing suit, great labor went into it.

Our creative efforts now mingle together and propogate out into the world at large. This is the source of the broad enhancement of the human environment generated by Metaman's formation. A person may marvel at the many hours of individual energy put into a handmade quilt or a hand-knitted sweater, but even more collective care and attention go into virtually every product we use and every construction we see. Indeed, were these design efforts not paid for by a multitude of eventual users, we could not individually afford them. When we wear a piece of clothing, chuckle over a cartoon in a magazine, or listen to music, we are receiving the full benefit of enormous labor at almost no cost to us. That we must share these pleasures with others does not diminish the value of what we receive; a film does not touch us less because it is seen by millions.

This enhancement of the human environment reflects an entirely new dimension in the union of human and machine within Metaman. Our day-to-day emotional lives are becoming intimately connected with the multitude of appealing products of design and technology surrounding us.

Meaningful social change usually takes much longer than initially imagined. Society is an immense pattern of interconnections, and new developments generally take decades rather than years to penetrate it fully; but this measured pace does not reduce the enormity of the eventual changes. Consider this assessment of the fax machine:

> Newspapers have been thus sent from New York to San Francisco . . . Other uses of the same mechanism are for sending news pictures, identifications of criminals, X-ray photographs, weather maps, signed documents, chemical formulae, graphs and messages in other alphabets and symbols.[576]

It was written in 1933. Before the potentials of this technology could be realized, human activity had to accelerate to the point where rapid communication was important, and telecommunications had to progress to the point where facsimile transmissions could compete economically with mail delivery.

The effects of many of today's new technologies will have similar time lags. Despite the enthusiastic predictions of bankers in the early 1980s, we do not yet live in a world where 'home banking' is prevalent;[577] nor do we see the space colonies that so many thought were just around the corner following the 1969 lunar landing. Recall that Stanley Kubrick's 1968 film, *2001, A Space Odyssey*, is the story of a manned mission to Saturn, yet today there are not even plans for further manned landings on the moon. Or consider Fritz Lang's 1926 science-fiction classic *Metropolis*. It portrays a city in 2026 as an immense lattice of buildings towering hundreds of stories above the ground and connected by tramways so high that airplanes shuttle beneath them.

What is so revealing about *Metropolis* is not that this vast city is still beyond current technology, but that society itself is portrayed as changing so little. The city is powered by enormous heavy machines filling a cavernous underground realm of regimented workers in sweat-shop conditions. Women are shown in traditional roles, and organizations are rigidly hierarchical with government power concentrated into the hands of one man sitting at a desk filled with buttons and controls. Indeed the future is portrayed as one where amazing technologies are grafted on to a society run by a typical robber-baron of the 1920s.

But society does change profoundly in a century. In 1890 women were primarily homemakers and could not even vote,[578] travel was at the pace of a horse and wagon,[579] government bureaucracies were small,[580] far more people farmed than worked in manufacturing,[581] and talking to people meant seeing them face to face.

The immense social changes now underway are made of countless small steps augmenting and reinforcing each other from year to year. We become accustomed to the differences and sometimes even imagine them to be minor, but within a few generations their cumulative effects transform society. Consider the changing role of the family in our lives. Though not in any immediate danger of disappearing, the family is likely to be significantly redefined in the years ahead because many of its present functions are being satisfied elsewhere. The pre-eminence of the nuclear family (a husband, wife and children) is beset on many fronts: the responsibilities of child rearing (which no longer even consumes most of an adult's life) are being transferred to schools, day-care facilities and baby sitters; we are moving away from the locales where we were born; the elderly are being cared for institutionally rather than by their children.

The role of women in society is also irreversibly changing. The full effect of their participation in business and government has barely begun to be felt. Today, it is hard to believe that in 1870 in the US a man could have his wife committed to a mental institution without even getting a medical opinion.[582] In 1890, not one country allowed women to vote on equal terms with men, but within two generations, women had gained voting rights through most of the developed world, and in another generation, almost everywhere else.[583] The involvement of women at all levels of government is growing rapidly: in 1969, a mere 4 per cent of state-elected officials in the US were women; by 1975 that figure had doubled, and by 1989 doubled again to reach 16.9 per cent.[584] The participation of women in business has shown a similar trend.[585] Women's involvement in both business and government will almost certainly match that of men within a few generations. Today there are still inequalities in pay and accomplishment, but eventually these too are bound to disappear. Thus, in only a century and a half, our world will have changed from a place where men run society and women focus their lives exclusively on home and family, to one where men and women together manage society and interact routinely on professional and domestic matters. Such social changes are immense, and Metaman has many of them in store for humanity in the decades ahead.

THE IMPACTS OF TECHNOLOGY

Change that is revolutionary leads us to entirely new ways of doing things and interacting with others, and it takes society many years to shift to patterns that accommodate such changes. Thus it is the *indirect*, long-term possibilities embodied in new technologies that truly transform our lives.

Computers, for example, embodied tremendous powers but no-one could quite figure out what we could do with these devices in our everyday lives. Did we really need a device to keep track of our checkbook or organize our recipes? Even now, the direct effects of computer technology on most people's lives is small. But the indirect effects have been immense. Modern society could not exist in its present form without the information-handling capabilities of computer systems to route telephone calls automatically, schedule airline passengers and crews, process billions of check and credit-card transactions, and run giant programs such as social security.[586] The new modes of human interaction made possible by computers are now so fundamental to society that it is hard to imagine life without them. But it takes society time to change. If today's entire airline transportation system could have been plopped into the world of sixty years ago, it would have sat largely unused. Most people then had little reason to travel.

Advances in technology lay the foundation for social change, in a sense they drive that change. Thus, to understand what may lie ahead for human society requires looking where technology is heading within Metaman. Because information flow plays so central a role in Metaman's development, progress in communications has exceptionally far-reaching influences. For example, the telephone network, by enabling people to easily maintain close contact with far-flung friends and acquaintances, has greatly diminished our involvement with immediate neighbors. Individuals in the US already average 4,000 telephone calls a year.[587] With the cost of a telephone call becoming nearly independent of distance,[588] geography is becoming ever less of a factor in human interactions.

These changes, however, are just the leading edge of the social transformation that will be brought by telecommunications. Technology is now at the point where images will soon supplement voice in routine person-to-person transmissions – first for businesses and then for individuals. In 1985 video-teleconferencing equipment cost some $90,000, but by 1992 the price had fallen to only about $20,000[589] and rudimentary consumer 'videophones' were available.[590] Within a decade or two, high-quality videophones will probably be within the reach of individuals. Initially, the idea of seeing a picture during a telephone call might seem unnecessary – a mere novelty – but think about how much our everyday personal interactions are enhanced by being able to see those with whom we talk. Routine full-size, face-to-face electronic interactions would enable widely separated people to communicate nearly as well as if they were together in the same room. Being able to watch as well as listen and show as well as tell would so upgrade long-distance interactions that it would even significantly reduce people's travel needs. Imagine calling across the country and showing someone charts, graphs and pictures; including a distant grandparent in the birthday party of your child; calling a store and having them hold up a product for you to see; or simply looking into the eyes of someone you loved who was in another city. Studies suggest that building a complete fiber-optic telecommunications network in the US might reduce travel some 15 per cent[591] – enough to allow the postponement of expensive expansions to road, rail and air transportation networks. Such fiber networks are well on their way; even at *current* levels of investment in telecommunications infrastructure, the US will have such a network by 2030,[592] and Japan is pushing to achieve one a decade earlier.[593]

Another important change underway in telecommunications has to do with how calls are handled rather than what they contain. Today, phones still intrude and interrupt because they tie us into a vast world but provide no sophisticated tools to manage the link. As Metaman continues to grow, we will regain control of that link. Call-screening with answering machines and identifier-codes on incoming calls are early moves in that direction, but better solutions will come. Eventually, actual electronic secretaries will be developed, and when programmed to learn from experience, the devices will effectively handle a wide variety of calls. With rudimentary language capabilities and the capacity to take messages, alert a person to important calls, or identify callers and ask for instructions, such devices will afford us as much privacy as we desire.

As electronic communications allow interactions that are rich and easily managed, they will probably become the most common way of interacting with other people. Will people one day choose to be in the *physical* presence of strangers only on rare occasions? We cannot know. Undoubtedly, though, the technologies now evolving will transform both communication and society.

In addition to influencing *how* we communicate, technological progress also affects *what* we experience. There is an immense difference in perspective between a child on a remote farm a century ago to whom 'high technology' was the color illustration in a bible, and his or her great great grandchild who now watches films of immense intergalactic starships roaring between planets. Such differences in experience manifest themselves in society, so the profound changes in human experience in the coming century will necessarily greatly reshape the social landscape of Metaman.

A broad selection of carefully orchestrated 'experiences' is available to almost everyone within Metaman today. Dramas, concerts and sporting events were once special occurrences watched in person; now they are everyday fare sampled electronically by multitudes. Moreover, with instant-replay, stop-action, and views from multiple vantage points, a distant electronic spectator can see more than the direct onlooker who is physically present.[594] In the US, 1989 attendance at all National Football League games totalled some 17 million, yet one game – the Super Bowl – was viewed in 39 million homes by more than 100 million people.[595] Similarly, 1989 attendance at music concerts was 23 million while 750 million tapes, records and CDs were sold.[596]

The range of our choices in the experiences we receive electronically is immense, and it is getting larger. Once there were three television channels in the US, now over 60 per cent of homes receive ten or more channels.[597] Only yesterday we chose from a few films playing at cinemas, now we pick from a thousand at a video store. Soon we may have the ability to view what we want when we want it. For example, in little more than a decade, it may take only a matter of seconds to transmit an entire movie by fiber-optic cable from a film archive to the memory of a computerlike television at home.[598] This might give people direct access to any of the more than 50,000 movies ever made.[599]

Technology is also changing the substance of what we can see. By the very nature of Metaman, a pervasive layer of technology is intervening between us and the physical world, extending our senses

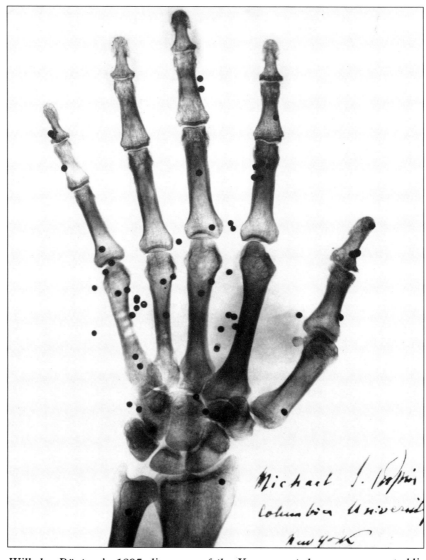

Wilhelm Röntgen's 1895 discovery of the X-ray created an enormous public sensation by allowing people to 'see' through solid materials for the first time. Viewing X-ray images of the human skull was likened by one journalist to seeing one's 'own death head'.[600] The above 1896 image by Dr Michael Pupin of Columbia University shows shotgun pellets lodged in an injured hand and is one of the earliest medical radiographs. Photo provided by the Burndy Library, Connecticut.

into realms never before penetrated by humans. We see satellite transmissions of the surface of Venus, photographs of fish a mile under

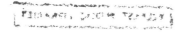

the sea,[601] images of a live human embryo or the inside of a beating heart.[602] We can even slow down what is too quick for the human eye and speed up what is too slow. Thus, we can observe the sudden blossoming of a flower, watch a bullet slowly shatter a pane of glass, or see an athlete sail gracefully through the air.

The evolving technology of Metaman, however, is on the verge of changing our experience in ways that are far more fundamental than a greater choice of entertainments, or vision that is more penetrating. Technology is beginning to allow us to participate actively in what we are viewing. Regardless how rapidly we click from channel to channel with our remote-control, our viewing experience is still a passive one. But in the future we will be able to interact with the electronic fare in front of us. Presently, this is most common with touch-screen menus that let us page through informational material, but there are already video disks that contain personalized movies that branch to alternative story lines in response to a viewer's selections. When more subtle cues such as eye movement are used to monitor our reactions and alter a film's flow, the experience might be different each time we saw it.

Technology is also allowing us to synthesize realistic experiences not rooted in *any* external reality.[603] The special effects in films are becoming ever more believable. Ghosts move through walls, strange creatures transform themselves before our eyes, people shrink to the size of ants. We may know that this is fantasy, but it none the less *looks* real and impacts us emotionally. Just as our physical environment has become largely synthetic, our experiences too are beginning to transcend the 'real' world and its constraints. No wonder the emotional links between humans and the 'natural' environment are weakening; an ever-growing fraction of human experience is in an entirely different realm.

By virtue of the computer, these two effects – active viewer participation, and the incorporation of special effects – are joining together. Full-blown 'virtual realities', powerful electronic environments so realistic and interactive as to feel almost real, are likely to exist within a few decades.[604] In today's prototypes, sensors embedded in special gloves and video goggles monitor a viewer's movements, and a computer continually modifies the stereoscopic images on the goggles to create the illusion of looking at a scene through a pair of glasses. As the viewer turns to look in a different direction the scene shifts – just as a real one would. In fact, a viewer can even reach into the illusion and move 'objects'.

Today's virtual realities, despite having objects that are grainy and motion that is jerky, are intriguing enough to have found their way into some video arcades.[605] When computers become powerful enough to display complex scenes and change them rapidly, the effects will be compelling.[606] The potential of virtual reality is evident from the immense gulf separating early silent films and modern cinema. Eventually, these virtual realms will make similar advances and look real enough to deceive our senses. At that point you may wander through a full-size duplicate of a house yet unbuilt, take a 'fantastic journey' through the human bloodstream, or fly around the surface of another planet. The possibilities are endless. These virtual worlds within Metaman will be another important step in synthesizing human experience, tailoring it to our individual preferences, and allowing it to transcend time and space.

Such effects are art, entertainment and much more. The technologies evolving within Metaman are beginning to offer us diverse experiences that are in many ways more appealing than 'real' day-to-day experiences.[607] The social impacts of these new technologies, although difficult to foresee, will be profound. At the very least, it is clear that humans will spend increasing amounts of time in comfortable indoor environments engaged in activity and communication mediated by electronics. This ever more intimate association between humans and machines is a natural consequence of Metaman's development, but it is one that easily evokes fears of loneliness and isolation in the future. Such fears are unlikely to be realized, however, because we will embrace these technologies only to the extent that they satisfy us. It is probable that advances in communications will lead to deeper not shallower interpersonal ties than are common today. Our present age is a 'transitional' one in which many of us have become geographically separated from family and friends and yet still must make use of primitive telecommunications that bring us only their voices.

Technology's transformation of human communication and experience is sometimes viewed as a pernicious social influence. The complaints are familiar: children have no attention span. We don't write letters or read books any more. We have become jaded to simple pleasures. Greater trust in the process of change and in its ultimate influence on the human condition is warranted. The benefits of a previous leap in communication technology – the development of writing – now seem self-evident, but the written word was not universally welcomed. In *Phaedrus*, Socrates, through the voice of King Thamus of Egypt, laments to the god who invented letters:[608]

This discovery of yours will create forgetfulness in the learners' souls, because they will not use their memories; . . . They will be the hearers of many things and will have learned nothing; they will appear to be omniscient and will generally know nothing; they will be tiresome company, having the show of wisdom without the reality.[609]

The challenges and opportunities brought to society by changes in communications technology can be seen in microcosm in our educational systems. The coming changes will transform the way children learn.[610] The traditional classroom environment where a single teacher stands before dozens of students and guides them through textbook exercises and class assignments is already obsolete. We now live in a fast-paced world of television, films, colorful magazines, video games and half-minute advertisements – all produced through large collaborative efforts striving to create involving, memorable experiences. In a world of sound bites and music videos, it is unrealistic to expect one overworked teacher to hold the attention of a class day after day, maintain order, *and* teach.

Already, technology is at the point where teaching materials as stimulating as the best of film and television could enhance and even replace traditional textbooks. Imagine how involving history courses would be if they were built around the presentation and discussion of documentary videos created by talented directors, writers, historians and teachers, and shown on a big screen.[611]

We have grown to expect world-class performances when we watch sports, see films, or listen to music; we will not continue to settle for less in education. When the best presentations of the best teachers are available in all classrooms, subjects will more often come alive for students. Already a few commercial ventures are beginning to offer such teaching videos,[612] and eventually the very best teachers will doubtless be as sought after – and as highly rewarded for their talents – as are the star performers in other fields.

To accommodate new methods such as these will be no easier for educational institutions than it is for society in general. For instance, the role of teachers will inevitably be significantly different: teachers will answer questions, lead discussions, help with individual problems, and orchestrate lessons, but less and less will they be the primary presenters of information. Moreover, it is quite conceivable that as communications technologies become more powerful, the 'classroom' itself will even cease to be the primary site for learning.[613]

The revolutionary educational possibilities embodied in *future* technologies emphasize the extraordinary magnitude of the social changes ahead. When computers can interact with students verbally, the devices (more patient and attentive than any human who has a dozen students clamoring for his or her attention) will be able to provide rich individualized instruction by tailoring lessons to each student's needs.[614] A foreign-language tutor could correct pronunciation, answer simple questions, and challenge each student with new vocabulary; a geography tutor could show maps, photos of monuments, and even play national anthems. Unlike textbooks, such instructional materials could guide students through large bodies of information and at any time zoom in for the detail that would satisfy a curious student or help a confused one. Further, by keeping unambiguous records of a student's day-to-day performance, exams would become largely superfluous and human teachers could be alerted promptly to individual learning problems needing special attention.

Already simple devices of this sort exist. A typing-instruction program is an interactive teaching system that tells students how their speed and accuracy are improving, identifies which specific letters are causing repeated errors, and creates individualized typing exercises that emphasize those letters. When accompanied by a human teacher who coaches students on finger positioning and such, the instruction method is very powerful.[615]

The broad social changes that result from progress in communications and other technologies do not arrive immediately, but that does not make them any less profound. Institutional inertia and individual resistance eventually are transcended as pressure for change builds year by year.

AN END TO SELF-RELIANCE

Within the developed world of Metaman, we have grown to rely on large institutions to sustain us in times of individual hardship. When we lose our job, fall ill, suffer a serious accident, or simply grow old, we turn for help not only to friends and family, but to social programs, employment benefits and private insurance.[616] How far we have traveled down this path is shown by the degree to which we hold government reponsible not only for protecting us from present wrongs but also for rectifying past abuses. The US has laws which attempt to make up for past racial discrimination in employment and education; various Native-American tribes seek redress for century-old violations of treaties; and the countries of Eastern Europe wrestle with the issue of compensating the victims of communist expropriations following the Second World War.

Using large institutions to buffer individual misfortune is a natural manifestation of Metaman's integration of human activity. This practise takes advantage of the obvious benefits of pooling resources to mitigate some of nature's unpredictableness. And it also reflects one of the fundamental realities of being part of Metaman: as our activities become more interwoven with those of others, our individual fates too are becoming more linked.

Our deepening interdependence is certain to lead to growing governmental involvement in realms now considered private and personal. Bodily injury to an individual, for example, is no longer entirely that individual's own affair: health insurance generally pays the bill. Safety regulations mandating such precautions as seat belts and motorcycle helmets are a natural by-product of this truth. Similarly, because we must now so routinely rely on the services of relative strangers and have confidence in their abilities, licensing requirements for professionals are proliferating.

An inherent quality of modern society is that our individual activities increasingly affect other people. When one person's car produces noxious exhausts, other people have to inhale them; when one person throws rubbish in the street, others have to pick it up. Zoning and construction codes, restrictions on waste disposal, and even prohibitions against disturbing the peace are all consequences of this growing human interdependence. Without a doubt, our future holds far more significant constraints on human activity. Even procreation itself is falling under the sway of governmental influence: in China, couples are fined for having more than one child.[617] In most societies, even the mention of such control provokes vehement reactions, but procreation will undoubtedly be ever more regulated within Metaman. One day having children will probably be regarded as a privilege rather than an absolute right, and government regulation of reproduction will be seen as a social necessity rather than an unwarranted interference in our lives. As society assumes more of the costs and responsibilities of raising children and feels more of the adverse social and environmental consequences of overpopulation, the pressures to regulate procreation will necessarily mount. Of all possible self-regulation by Metaman, the management of human reproduction will probably bring the largest social impacts.

Specific training is now required before someone can practice law, provide medical care, fly an airplane, teach in school, or even drive a car, but there are no requirements for being a parent. Yet child rearing is of central importance to society. The developed world spends 5 per cent of its total Gross National Product on education,[618] and the costs of dealing with crime and other problems hatched in inadequate family environments may cost even more.

Regulating that most basic of activities – human reproduction – is fraught with difficult challenges to human sensitivities, but movement in that direction has already begun. Government is involved in family life in ways that once would have seemed a grave trespass yet now seem entirely appropriate. Parents are legally bound to educate their children. Adoption proceedings and custody battles routinely grapple with issues of parental fitness.[619]

Health issues constitute the present-day frontier of government regulation of reproduction. As the fetal injuries caused by exposure to various drugs during pregnancy are becoming better understood,[620] government is beginning to intervene not only in child rearing, but in childbearing itself. Mothers have been charged with child abuse for using narcotics during pregnancy![621] When a substance is illegal, such criminal prosecutions may not differ greatly from other social efforts to prevent 'drug' abuse, but what of legal substances such as alcohol? A woman who drinks heavily during pregnancy may bear an infant suffering the mental retardation and heart defects of fetal alcohol syndrome. This realm exemplifies the difficult dilemmas that will be prominent on the public agenda in coming decades, because these personal tragedies are now social ones as well. Today, we find it quite natural for drunk driving to be illegal; the behavior is too dangerous to go uncontrolled. Tomorrow, we may find it equally natural to prohibit maternal activities known to damage a developing fetus that will be carried to term.

Such concerns are already prompting judicial and legislative efforts selectively to discourage childbearing. In 1991 a judge in California offered a mother convicted of beating her children probation if she would use a Norplant contraceptive implant,[622] and a Kansas legislator proposed paying welfare mothers $500 a year to use contraceptives.[623] As improved and less intrusive birth-control methods[624] such as vaccines begin to appear[625] the temptation for society to regulate who can have children will undoubtedly increase.

Extrapolating present movement in this direction, it is quite conceivable that parents one day will be licensed to have a child only after passing a course in parenting and demonstrating they can provide an adequate home environment. Today, society removes children from blatantly abusive environments; in the future it may attempt to eliminate such situations by going a step further and preventing births into such environments.[626]

Major social changes associated with altered human reproduction, however, need not be the product of government policy and planning; change also arrives as the automatic and inevitable consequence of technological advance. The advent of modern birth-control methods,[627] for example, gave humans some measure of control over their own reproduction and this, in and of itself, brought profound shifts in attitudes about sexuality and child bearing. Similarly, America's bitter debate over whether or not abortion should be legal is now in the process of becoming largely academic. Roussel Uclaf's 'abortion pill' (RU486) will eventually make it possible for women safely to terminate a pregnancy whether or not abortion is legal where they live.[628] The long-term social impacts of biotechnology's coming ability easily to manipulate human reproduction will be immense.[629] For example, work is now underway in Australia to control rabbit populations by infecting them with a genetically engineered virus that serves as a birth-control vaccine and spreads from rabbit to rabbit.[630] When birth-control vaccines are developed for humans, there is the obvious possibility of some contagious, flu-like infection being created and spreading widely to make large numbers of people less able to conceive children.

If infertility did one day become the normal state for humans and conceiving a child demanded a pill or some other active medical intervention – however minor – society would become very different. Attitudes about sex would change, of course, and the need for contraception would all but be eliminated. More importantly, however, unplanned pregnancies would disappear, the human population might become stabilized or even decline, and humanity might be far less willing to squander the rich potential that human life embodies.

The incursion of government into hitherto sacred realms such as childbearing may provoke fears of a bleak Orwellian future, but our individual freedom is actually expanding as Metaman develops. Through most of the developed world, not only can people worship as they choose, say and do what they want, travel where they wish, and live as they please – they have the affluence and the technology to take advantage of these freedoms.

The increasing regulation of human activity throughout Metaman is not an infringement of our freedom but a social response to its rapid expansion. For instance, there are now more bureaucratic controls over pharmaceuticals than ever, but we have access to a cornucopia of medicines unimaginable to previous generations. Similarly, in the nineteenth century, passports and visas were not generally needed for tourism, but that was because distant travel was such an arduous (and infrequent) adventure. Today we may need documents to cross borders, but we can travel effortlessly between continents. In fact, tourism has become the world's largest industry, employing 100 million people worldwide[631] and having annual receipts of some 2 trillion dollars.[632]

Metaman's birth and early development is changing our world immensely, and the adjustments are wrenching for society. Faced with oil spills,[633] inner-city poverty, ethnic strife, AIDS and other problems, we often lose sight of humanity's larger trajectory. But the vision of where humans have been and are going is an inspiring one that can renew our strength when we are facing the immediate problems of this era. Metaman is robust; humanity's distant future looks bright; and our lives today are safer, more comfortable, and filled with more opportunity than ever. The material well-being brought by technological progress and global integration does not guarantee us a 'better' life, but it offers us possibilities, freedoms and choices never before available. Whether we will take advantage of these precious gifts or squander them is our choice – both individually and collectively.

12

POWER AND CHOICE
Challenges to Human Values

METAMAN IS TRANSFORMING HUMAN existence and the changes are profoundly challenging. New medical technology forces us to make decisions about whether to extend or terminate life; greater knowledge about the global environment confronts us with choices about the costs and benefits of basic human activities; increased human interdependence generates conflicting personal loyalties and responsibilities in our lives. As Metaman continues to grow, human values will have to adjust – sometimes drastically – to the new realities of the human environment this super-organism is creating.

From the corporations that manufacture the products we use to the judicial structures that constitute our legal systems, large institutions are proliferating, and this is straining our traditional values. It is easy to relate to the human consequences of actions that *directly* affect other people, so our natural sympathies reinforce our ethical frameworks when we engage each other individually. Not so when we deal with organizations: if we collect a larger insurance settlement than we deserve or pay less taxes than we owe, we seem to be stealing from no-one because the injuries we cause are *indirect* and diffuse. Indeed, many people who would be deeply offended to hear someone say they might steal a person's wallet would feel no embarrassment describing how they had defrauded the telephone company.

This phenomenon is global. At the beginning of Poland's switch to a free-market economy, a Polish entrepreneur claimed that even though he paid high wages, he had trouble hiring enough workers because they said they didn't feel right about stealing from a 'private' employer and could do better at state-owned enterprises.[634] As Metaman becomes a creature of interacting organizations rather than individuals, more and more of human activity lies beyond the range of our natural empathies. One of the reasons for so much corruption in government and business may be that people do not see an individual victim; they are simply beating 'the system'. Unfortunately, the personal and social losses caused by 'victimless' white-collar crime can be even greater than those from armed robbery. The widespread fraud leading to the 1991 closure of the Bank of Credit and Commerce International (BCCI) had heavy costs to those around the world who lost their savings. The Savings & Loan débâcle in the US may have caused little direct loss to depositors, most of whom were insured, but the hundreds of billions of dollars[635] in losses will be felt by future taxpayers and those who are adversely affected by resultant government cutbacks.

Mechanisms to reduce such institutional losses are continually improving, but criminal methods are also growing more sophisticated.[636] Laws and guidelines to regulate key realms such as banking, insurance and government are proliferating, and modern technology is increasingly ensuring compliance, but as the commercial system grows more complex, it also becomes more difficult to monitor. Metaman need not eliminate fraud, however, only ensure that it remains a small fraction of the overall transaction volume. As long as this is done, such losses remain merely one of the many costs of commerce, akin at a functional level to the fees that merchants pay for credit-card transactions.

Improved technology, although it may never stop the most sophisticated fraud, is critical in reducing routine theft. Computerized bookkeeping and inventory controls multiply; records of financial transactions and credit histories become more easily retrievable; retail stores install electronic anti-theft tags on merchandise; electronic authorization systems for credit-cards and checks proliferate. These measures are necessary not because people are becoming less ethical,[637] but because the nature of the world is becoming such that it is far easier to ignore the larger consequences of many of our individual actions. Thus, commerce could not operate as it does today without a multitude of controls. As commercial transactions become ever more impersonal and wide-ranging within Metaman, people will have to rely on these legal and technological mechanisms rather than morality and trust. Or rather, trust will be routinely possible because it is backed by a broad array of automated measures to make fraud difficult. As the saying goes, 'To resist criminal behavior, one needs a good Christian upbringing, strength of character, and the presence of witnesses.'

THE DILEMMAS OF POWER

As, through Metaman, we become aware of the environmental impacts of various human activities, we are faced with the difficult task of balancing their relative costs and benefits. Having identified the threat of global warming, humankind must now decide how significantly to change its use of fossil fuels. Having learned the dangers of various chemical pollutants, governments must now decide which health risks to eliminate. Having discovered the dangers of high-salt and high-fat diets, we must each decide whether to adjust our eating habits. And our own individual dilemmas in these matters are not eliminated by knowing that we are part of the larger collective process by which Metaman is adjusting its behavior.

Knowledge is one source of new dilemmas for us, but an even more important one is Metaman's growing power. As humanity gains control over what was once beyond reach, we face ethical decisions never before necessary or even considered. The capacity to combat illness and even death is presenting us with some of our most difficult choices. Today, round-the-clock treatment in an intensive-care unit may save a baby born as much as sixteen weeks premature and weighing only a pound.[638] But such an intervention can cost a half-million dollars and still not prevent the brain bleeding that causes cerebral palsy, retardation, paralysis or blindness.[639] The dilemma is a painful one. Should hospitals continue to keep alive a premature baby who has already suffered crippling injuries? Even more to the point: should a society such as the US, where health-care programs leave 15 per cent of mothers without adequate prenatal care,[640] publicly fund extremely costly treatments for *any* very low birth-weight babies . . . even those who could be saved?

Choices are no easier when adults are facing death. Medical technology may add extra decades to our lives, but it forces us to decide how long to battle against infirmity and disease. No longer are we mere witnesses; we ourselves may have to balance hope, suffering and expense, to render such a decision. Society is just beginning to confront the issue of terminating medical care for the dying. As medicine continues to advance, it is becoming neither practical nor desirable always to do everything possible to hold off death. Even today, the nightmare of being trapped alive, unable to die, looms far larger for many people than the specter of death itself. Substantial adjustments in human attitudes, however, are already beginning to appear.[641] Doctor-assisted suicide by the terminally ill, though not technically legal, has been commonplace in Holland since 1984, and now is even protected from prosecution there when specific guidelines are followed. Furthermore, in a 1991 referendum, 46 per cent of voters in the state of Washington voted to actually legalize the practice.[642]

The dilemmas created by progress in medical technology would be difficult enough were they strictly personal, but they are not. Within Metaman, the costs of health care are shared. When someone is faced with imminent death, he or she may be eager to go to great lengths to try to buy a few additional years of life, but under what conditions can society as a whole afford to pay for that attempt? We have the resources to buy only so many artificial hearts, dialysis machines and intensive care units. Health care now consumes an average of 7 per cent of Gross Domestic Product in the developed world and some 12 per cent in the US,[643] how much more do we want to spend and how do we want to spend it?

As more becomes possible in medicine, societies will be forced to make choices: how will research funds be divided between afflictions of the aged, such as Alzheimer's, and those of the young, such as muscular dystrophy; or between chronic ailments such as arthritis, and acute ones such as heart attacks? Which medical procedures will be made generally available at public expense, and which will remain luxuries available to only a few? Already, the state of Oregon has designed a public-health program that explicitly faces the difficult issue of rationing health care.[644] We might, of course, hope that medical progress will somehow enable us to avoid such a troubling issue, but this is an unrealistic hope. As treatments continue to improve, deciding when, how, and on whom to use costly medical technologies will become harder not easier. It is one thing to deny someone a costly organ transplant that offers only *temporary* benefit, and quite another to withhold a nearly certain, albeit expensive cure.

It is true that nearly every *particular* procedure will become more routine and less expensive with time, but costly new technologies will continually arrive to take their place. Today, high-technology medicine is saving accident victims who, a few decades ago, would have had no hope, and the same will likely be said a few decades hence. The frontier at which medical treatment is difficult and expensive may indefinitely recede but it will never disappear. Moreover, as long as people age and life has an upper limit, each person's health must eventually fail and each person's care eventually terminate. Unlimited medical care for everyone is not a goal that is presently tenable nor will it become so in the foreseeable future – regardless of the extraordinary advances lying ahead. We will have to adjust to the idea that within the milieu of Metaman, there will always be collectively imposed priorities and constraints in medical funding. The need to make such decisions, however, is not a failure; it is a consequence of our success, and of the reality that new powers carry with them new choices.

We may not be comfortable 'playing God', but whether the issues are medical, environmental, or social, humanity will increasingly find itself in just that role. Our newfound influence over realms once beyond our control cannot be wished away; today, even *not acting* has become a deliberate act. To best expand the quality of human life in coming decades, we will have to revise the beliefs and public policies that no longer serve us.[645] Simplistic applications of traditional approaches and values generally will not be adequate in the new era of Metaman, because we are beginning to face issues that are entirely new to humankind.

The weaknesses of ignoring today's new realities are powerfully illustrated in a policy that was designed to deal with the dilemma of very low birth-weight babies. In 1985, the US passed regulations mandating medical treatment of all premature infants not inevitably dying, in a coma, or so ill that care would be futile.[646] This well-meaning, but deeply flawed policy entirely ignores the larger ethical dilemmas inherent in spending significant amounts of money to save deeply damaged, still unformed lives. Further, the policy is predicated upon two unwarranted assumptions: that human life, regardless of its quality, is invaluable, and that society has enough resources to avoid balancing difficult alternatives. We know, however, that there are limited resources for *any* endeavor, and that our individual lives, valuable as they may be to each of us, are not of unlimited importance to society as a whole. Individual loss is intrinsic to life, so our challenge is not to eliminate such loss wherever it occurs, but to mitigate it where we can do so most effectively.

Metaman exhibits a powerful dynamic towards more efficient use of resources, but this move towards efficiency is still in its infancy in the management of human risk. In the US, the EPA (Environmental Protection Agency) still sets air-quality standards without consideration of cost,[647] and the FDA (Food and Drug Administration) goes even farther. The 1958 Delaney clause of the Food, Drug and Cosmetics Act requires the FDA to ban food containing any substance that causes *any* detectable cancer in laboratory animals – regardless of cost or any other factors.[648] At first this may sound like a good policy, but it denies the reality that carcinogens (some very potent, others exceedingly weak) are all around us, in 'natural' foods just as surely as in man-made chemicals.[649] To eliminate all carcinogens is impossible, so the only meaningful goal can be to reduce our cancer risk to some 'acceptable' level.

The Delaney clause is a perfect illustration of the hazards of an inflexible approach to general goals in the age of Metaman. When the clause was written, only significant cancer threats could be detected; now, we can measure cancer risks so minuscule they are far less dangerous than the numerous other everyday risks we encounter. The chemical EDB, for example, was determined to be a mild carcinogen and the FDA banned it. But EDB was being used primarily to combat a peanut mold that harbors an extremely potent 'natural' carcinogen called aflatoxin. Thus, following this ban, the danger of cancer from eating a single peanut-butter sandwich skyrocketed to some seventy-five times the previous danger of exposure to EDB.[650] The net effect of the ban was to elevate the danger of cancer, the exact opposite of its intent.

In the past, humans faced the environmental hazards of disease, accidents, wild animals, famine, drought and cold. Today, in the milieu of Metaman, these have been largely replaced by man-made hazards such as cars, firearms, pollutants and rich foods. The doubling of human life expectancy within the developed world in the past century and a half[651] suggests that the exchange has been a good one. Humans, though, have not yet adjusted psychologically to an existence where background natural risks are low,[652] and the predominant dangers are associated with the internal milieu of Metaman. It still seems to many people that regardless of the expense, man-made risks not freely chosen must be eliminated. This is a spurious goal, however, because we are inhabiting a new and largely man-made environment that can no more be made risk-free than could a primitive forest.[653] The human environment can be made safer, of course, but to do this most effectively we will have to strive continually to minimize the greater dangers within Metaman and accept the lesser ones – in short, balance costs and benefits in such areas as health, pollution and product safety. The ethical challenges we now face in enhancing the public 'good' are less in articulating general goals, than

in designing policies that can achieve them with balanced and acceptable costs.

It may seem heartless to consider cost when the issue is human life,
but there is really no alternative. One can only ignore cost when one
has little power to intervene in life and death matters, or when one has
unlimited resources to do so. Today, we have enormous powers to
make life-saving interventions and have no choice but to ration those
interventions. Thus we cannot avoid facing the moral dilemmas
inherent in that rationing.

We already *implicitly* set a value on life when we award damages for
accidents, budget medical and social programs, or set costly pollution-
control standards. Our valuations, however, are plagued by inconsistencies, because both collectively and individually we tend to be moved
by the dramatic and the sensational rather than the commonplace. The
US, for instance, budgets billions of dollars to eliminate even the
smallest identifiable risk that nuclear-waste disposal might cause to
future generations and simultaneously balks at spending enough to
clean away the ordinary lead paint residues that are currently harming
millions of children.[654]

To enact safety programs routinely without comparing their potential costs and benefits with those of alternative programs cannot
maximize public safety. Should a society spend its resources on
additional cancer testing, air bags in cars, the removal of radium from
drinking water, or the elimination of chemicals from livestock feed?
Only with Metaman's powerful capacities for processing information
can such questions be answered. The answers are crucial, because
when such safety measures are analyzed to determine the amounts
that would be spent for each life saved, some programs are many
thousands of times cheaper than others. Additional screening tests for
rectal cancer in the US would cost some $25,000 per life saved,[655]
mandatory installation of air bags on the driver's side of new cars
$800,000 per life,[656] achieving EPA standards for radium in drinking
water $6,200,000 per life,[657] and removing DES (diethyl stilbestrol) in
cattlefeed as dictated in 1979 regulations some $160 million per life.[658]
Thus while each program seems laudable in and of itself, spending
money to remove DES from cattlefeed instead of on other safety
measures clearly takes a toll in human life. In fact, balancing alternatives so as to use resources most efficiently is becoming the most
challenging ethical domain of public-health decisions.

Costly life-saving measures, however, must not only be balanced
against one another, but against alternatives that might enhance the
quality of our lives: improved schools, public transportation, rec-

Item	$ Per Fatality Averted
Medical Screening Programs	
Rectal Cancer (Fecal Blood Tests)	25,000
Cervical Cancer (Pap Smears)	60,000
Lung Cancer (Chest X-rays)	70,000
Traffic Safety Programs	
Guard-Rail Improvements	85,000
Rescue Helicopters	160,000
Driver's Education Courses	225,000
Wheel Rim Servicing	600,000
Airbag installation (Driver Side Only)	800,000
Tire Inspection	1,000,000
Radiation Related Standards	
Inspections of Medical X-ray Equipment	9,000
Standards for Radium in Drinking Water	6,200,000
Standards Covering Uranium Mill Tailings	64,000,000
Miscellaneous Programs and Regulations	
Immunization Programs in Indonesia	250
Food for Disaster Relief	13,000
Installing Venting on Space Heaters	120,000
Installing Smoke Alarms in Homes	600,000
Fireproofing Children's Sleepwear	1,600,000
Asbestos Standards	9,000,000
Benzene Emission Regulations	20,000,000
Coke Oven Standards	75,000,000
DES Standards for Cattlefeed	160,000,000

The average cost for each fatality averted with various medical, environmental, and safety programs varies enormously.[659] *Clearly, the relative safety benefits society achieves with its resources hinges on its ability to evaluate dangers realistically and act on that information.*

reational facilities, job-training programs, health care, day care. Is it preferable to enhance a thousand lives or save one? The power to extend and protect human life coupled with the sometimes astronomical costs of doing so will soon force humanity to face such fundamental questions more explicitly.[660]

AGING AND DEATH

Increased longevity has been one of humankind's greatest triumphs, but it is greatly changing the age distribution of the population of the developed world.[661] In the US, 20 per cent of the population will be over sixty-five by 2050, nearly twice the current fraction. As the capabilities of medicine expand, we will have to grapple with the rising cost of caring for our aging population.[662]

One might hope that medical progress would let us live vital, healthy lives until immediately prior to death,[663] but the additional years of vitality and good health we now enjoy are often followed by a lengthened period of deteriorating health and high medical costs preceding death.[664] Moreover, because human life expectancy is already pushing up against the apparent limits of the 'natural' human life span, until there are basic breakthroughs in understanding aging,[665] further progress in fighting life-threatening diseases will only further expand the numbers of people who are encumbered by the various chronic health conditions brought by aging. Dealing with this demographic change and trying to balance the needs of the young and the old will be an immense challenge during the twenty-first century.

What might happen, however, were molecular biologists to uncover the proverbial fountain of youth and learn how to intervene not only to extend life, but to retain youthfulness? Such a development – as suggested earlier – is quite conceivable, and its far-reaching conse-quences serve to emphasize the extraordinary changes that human-kind may eventually face. If we did not age and could retain throughout our lives the mortality rate of a healthy twelve-year-old, we would live, on average, a thousand years.[666]

The capability of extending the human life span would generate enormous ethical challenges. On the one hand, were the process easy and inexpensive, falling death rates would so exacerbate our popu-lation problem as to compel humanity to regulate childbearing if that weren't already being done. On the other hand, were the process difficult and expensive, bitter conflict about who would have access to it would be inevitable. Hospital committees have a hard enough time choosing the transplant recipients for scarce organs; decisions about actual life-extension would be even more agonizing. On what basis would we decide whether someone deserved to have an 'extended' life?

But these challenges would be only the beginning. Although the unfolding of human life from birth through middle age, old age and death may be cut short at any time, this journey is common to us all. It orients the human psyche. The process is the basis of our symbols, our goals, our very sense of self. Were the familiar life stages that have always been with humanity to disappear, humans would be traveling in completely uncharted territory. What would be the appropriate pattern for lives lasting centuries? When would a person have children? How would family relationships change? What would be the progression for a career, or for a sequence of careers? How would society open up for the young the opportunities that are now created by retirement and death of the old? How would money be kept from concentrating in the hands of the very old – who would no longer pass their possessions on to their children?

Extending life, identifying genetic diseases, creating new plants and animals, altering the weather – the challenges to human values will be unprecedented in the centuries ahead. Changes are sweeping over humanity as Metaman evolves, and the more rapidly humanity can perceive, understand, and adjust to them, the better off we will be. Indeed, these challenges are here already: the arrival of modern medicine and the resultant widespread lowering of infant mortality came with a hidden price: the necessity of drastically reducing birth rates. Yet even now, many of us still deny this reality, believing that humanity need not or cannot respond to this challenge. The result is deep poverty and environmental destruction in many parts of the developing world.

Underlying many of today's ethical dilemmas is the question of our responsibility to future generations. Are we robbing from the future by using up planetary resources,[667] eroding valuable cropland, and creating long-persisting nuclear wastes?

In these matters, we best serve ourselves as well as future

A family planning poster in Accra, Ghana. Today, less than half the world's couples have access to birth-control devices; the UN's goal for this decade is to raise that to 75 per cent. Photo by Henning Christoph, Christoph and Mayer Photoarchive, Essen.

generations by focusing on the short-term consequences of our actions rather than vague notions about the needs of the distant future. The disposal of nuclear waste is a controversy that clearly illustrates this. Because some nuclear wastes will continue to emit dangerous levels of radiation for many thousands of years, it may seem obvious that unless we dispose of these materials with extraordinary care, we will poison our distant progeny. This widely held attitude makes us so preoccupied with finding safe 'permanent' repositories that we leave these materials for decades in 'temporary' storage sites. But the hazards of such temporary storage far outweigh any potential dangers that flawed 'permanent' storage might create for future generations. In truth, we do not know how society will view nuclear wastes a century, much less a millennium from now. If medical science develops an easy cure for cancer, these wastes will not be viewed as a significant health hazard at all. If robots can be employed to concentrate and reprocess the materials safely, they might even be valuable.

Uncertainty about the distant future makes it more sensible to dispose of nuclear wastes safely for a single century and then revisit the problem,[668] rather than spend billions of dollars today trying to guarantee that future millennia will be risk-free.[669] Not only will geology and the technology of waste-disposal be much better understood in the year 2100, but a few extra billions spent today on medical research would be virtually certain to save far more lives in coming centuries than any permanent nuclear-waste repository.

Concern about the immediate future – ten, fifty, perhaps even a hundred years ahead – is critical in setting public policies that serve humankind, but trying to look further is not useful for this purpose. Humans living far in the future may experience the effects of our present-day activities, but the nature of our distant influences cannot be gauged today because future technologies will be so much more powerful than our own. Those distant generations will be both more aware of their problems and better equipped to deal with them than we are. Current threats – ozone depletion, nuclear warfare, climate change, AIDS - were unforeseen a century ago, and try as we may, we cannot foresee, much less solve, the problems of a century from now. Fortunately, we need not do so. Metaman is not fragile, it has a vital future ahead of it.

Our knowledge of Metaman's inherent vigor and resilience gives us good reason to have confidence in the future well-being of our distant descendants, so we can turn our full attention towards the immediate traumas and pains of Metaman's birth. Our challenge is to learn how to embrace the transformation underway yet preserve our fundamental values.

A NEW VISION

No man is an iland, intire of it selfe: every man is a peece of the Continent, a part of the maine; if a Clod bee washed away by the Sea, Europe is the lesse, as well as if a Promontorie were, as well as if a Mannor of thy friends or of thine own were; any mans death diminishes me, because I am involved in Mankinde; And therefore never send to know for whom the bell tolls; It tolls for thee.

John Donne, *Devotions Upon Emergent Occasions XVII*, 1623

13

DARWIN EXTENDED
The Evolution of Evolution

As LONG AS HUMANS have existed, they have been aware of the innumerable animals and plants surrounding them. But only with the invention of the microscope did people come to learn of *micro*-organisms, living things too small to be seen with the naked eye. Now, through satellites and telecommunications, we are becoming aware of a newly emerging planetary super-organism that is, in effect, a '*macro*-organism', a living thing too large for us to see directly.

Comprehending an organism that encompasses oneself is very difficult. Imagine what we would look like to our individual cells were they conscious, intelligent, communicating creatures. To them, *we* would be the macro-organisms. And even if they somehow could dimly perceive human physiology, they could not fathom human conduct. Hope, fear, joy, and love have no meaning at the level of the individual cell because they are expressions of the ensemble. Our cells might consider us an extremely 'interesting' phenomenon, but they would not imagine us to be living creatures. On their scale, a human being isn't even enclosed by a membrane because our skin is made up of cells. Our cells would rightly maintain that the processes of 'real life' – cell division, membrane transport, carbohydrate metabolism and protein synthesis – were taking place at the cellular level, not the human one. They might readily admit that humans represent a pattern of 'social' activity that resembles 'life' and is in many ways quite relevant to their individual cellular lives, but only with great difficulty could they appreciate the larger design embracing them. For humans, the patterns of Metaman are equally elusive: only vaguely do we even perceive how resources are flowing within its 'circulatory' system or how Metaman is responding to environmental challenges. But the limitations of human understanding do not make Metaman any less real a living creature.

THE CHANGING FACE OF EVOLUTION

To appreciate fully the immense super-organism that encompasses us, we must understand the evolutionary process by which life is progressing. By seeing how Metaman is enhancing this process, we can understand how this living entity has arisen, where it fits into the larger scheme of life, and what its future may be.

No matter how well-suited an organism is to the life it leads, it must be able to respond to change. New predators appear, competition for food develops, climates shift. Darwinian evolution,[670] the process by which all animal and plant species evolve, arises from the action of natural selection on the random variation in living systems. 'Natural selection' means that organisms more adapted to the challenges they encounter tend to reproduce more successfully, and 'random variation' means that offspring differ from their parents in small, haphazard ways.

Hearing, vision, flight and other biological 'inventions' leave no doubt that natural selection – however long it may take – can generate extraordinary creations; but the evolutionary process itself seems so inefficient that it is hard not to feel a disbelieving wonder that it actually 'works'. How can all the diverse and perfect forms that surround us have grown out of random trial and error? Our puzzlement comes largely from our inability to conceive of the huge expanses of time and the immense numbers of organisms involved in the evolutionary process. If all the ants that have ever lived could line up single file, they would form a column extending to the other side of our galaxy,[671] a distance it takes light (which can reach the moon in a second) nearly 100,000 years to travel. Clearly, there has been room for a lot of trial and error.

Not only do organisms evolve, however, so too does the evolutionary process itself.[672] The planetary environment is a changing one, and species with better *ways* of evolving are better able to meet the long-term challenges and opportunities they encounter; thus evolutionary mechanisms that more effectively produce useful change tend to prevail. The evolution of sexual reproduction, for instance, was an extremely important advance of the evolutionary *process.*

Having two sexes was revolutionary because it allowed organisms to mix and recombine existing genes into useful new combinations much more effectively than was previously possible. Today's remarkable biological diversity could not exist without 'sex'. Consider random 'point-mutations' – the minute genetic changes caused by nuclear radiation and certain chemicals. Because these mutations almost always damage rather than enhance a complex organism, elaborate cellular mechanisms have evolved to minimize them.[673] Another profound evolutionary innovation is embryonic development – the process by which a single cell gives rise to an adult organism. Having a complex organism develop from one cell means that a single genetic change in that first cell – a relatively easily managed task – can significantly alter even a large creature.

With the arrival of Metaman, the evolutionary process is making yet another advance, this one so momentous that it is rendering previous Darwinian mechanisms largely irrelevant to the larger trajectory of life's evolution. Darwinian evolution still occurs in all biological systems, including humans, but it moves at a snail's pace compared to the rapid rate at which Metaman is evolving by its new methods. And as Metaman's influence on the biosphere becomes increasingly dominant, the role of Darwinian evolution in determining even the character of the planetary ecosystem will diminish sharply.

The progressive change taking place in Metaman combines the hitherto distinct biological processes of 'development' and 'evolution'. When a multicellular organism 'develops' from a single cell into its adult form, the nature of the individual organism itself is changing, which is quite distinct from biological 'evolution', where change is occurring from one generation to the next.[674] Metaman, like a *developing* organism, manifests change within itself rather than its progeny, but Metaman changes by unprogrammed adaptation that is decidedly *evolutionary* in character.[675] Indeed, just as biological evolution rests on changes in genetic information,[676] progressive change within Metaman also rests upon modifications in information – advances in scientific knowledge, technology, institutional structures, laws, economic systems.

Metaman's ability to evolve so rapidly is the result of three key enhancements of Darwinian mechanisms. First, Metaman has internalized natural selection. External competition among separate organisms has given way to *internal competition* among component elements of the super-organism. Second, *conscious design* has supplanted random variation. Because products are invented, corporate organizations planned, and machines designed, there is no need to wait for random 'happy accidents'. Third, competition among real, material entities (for example, organizations or products) has been joined by competition among *abstract representations* (concepts, ideas and plans). Thus, the military might conceive of a weapon, simulate its operation, find it inadequate, and abandon it without ever building it.

Metaman is composed of diverse, partially redundant systems that compete vigorously and thereby spur innovation. To see 'internal competition' at work, we need only look as far as Metaman's shipping methods. Distinct (though interconnected) transportation networks – highway, rail, air and water – provide slightly different but overlapping services that continually struggle to capture business from each other. Any system that cannot keep up will wither and be replaced. The displacement of rail shipments by road transport has been one such change. The migration of everyday communication from the postal service to the telephone is another.

Intense internal competition within Metaman is also evident in the non-material realm, for example among organizational and management structures. The multinational corporation is a powerful organizational form that has become globally dominant, and market economies have largely replaced centrally planned ones throughout the world.

Internal competition makes Metaman extremely adaptable, and the redundancies inherent in this competition give Metaman its resilience. With transportation, for instance, there is not only mutual overlap among different systems, but each individual system contains redundancies. The road transportation system, because it includes many freight companies, multiple fuel depots, extra vehicles, surplus drivers, and alternate routes between most locations, suffers few massive failures. Widespread redundancies also exist with communications: postal service, express overnight service, telephone, computer modem and fax are some of the choices. Not all are strictly independent because some use the same transmission paths, but few minor disruptions could long keep us from getting an important message through.

Without the two other major mechanisms of evolutionary change within Metaman – competition between ideas and the use of design – Metaman's internal competition would not be efficient enough to allow so massive a being to exist. By imagining things that are not, projecting them into an imaginary future, and observing their potential performance, Metaman is able to direct its resources towards only the most promising possibilities. Competition is becoming a fierce but bloodless struggle between rival ideas, models, proposals and plans, with the reward of success being physical existence and failure leading not to disappearance but to non-appearance.

So routine and natural does this seem that it is easy to overlook its enormous implications: not only can change now anticipate rather than respond to need, but the time and energy required to develop models and ideas is a minute fraction of that needed to build 'real' structures and systems. Metaman is not confined by the shackles that have bound previous biological evolution: the need to select from *physical* proto-types fashioned out of *randomness*. Indeed, a crucial importance of a technique like 'virtual reality' lies in its potential as a design tool; it may enhance various computer simulations enough to make them as useful as physical prototypes.

To appreciate the extraordinary power of conscious design and modeling, consider the challenge of building an aircraft carrier that handles well in high seas, supports squadrons of aircraft, and satisfies the other specialized demands of so unique and complex a vessel. Imagine what would be required for such a carrier to evolve from a battleship by a simple 'Darwinian' process. Any modification to the battleship and its progeny could occur only by incorporating random plan changes into an entirely new ship and taking it out to sea for action to see if it worked. The notion seems absurd. The world's iron resources would be exhausted without coming even close to making a working aircraft carrier. If a similar strategy were followed in an attempt to send a spacecraft to the moon, the sun would burn out long before success was achieved. Clearly, there is a degree of size and complexity that is unachievable by Darwinian mechanisms alone. Metaman could not exist were it not evolving by powerful new evolutionary mechanisms.

Just as a child moves from simple experimentation to conceptual thinking and planning as he or she develops mentally, Metaman, as it matures is further refining its power to conceive models. Computer-aided design determines the shapes of airplane wings and enables bridges and buildings to withstand peak stresses, econometric models gauge the economic effects of public policies, marketing models assist in setting production levels, population and traffic projections guide city planners, and impact studies help evaluate environmental effects. These techniques are among the fastest evolving aspects of Metaman and are continually accelerating the pace of change.[677]

The crucial role that modeling plays in Metaman's evolution empha-sizes the enormous importance of striving to refine our tools for evaluating the future consequences of policies. The ability to assess such effects is critical to formulating effective long-range strategies and is the key to remaining competitive within the new global environment.

Clearly, to understand how Metaman evolves is of more than academic interest. Such awareness is beneficial in the development of public policies and social attitudes which can keep a society vital over the long term. Metaman's reliance on internal competition, for example, emphasizes that this super-organism is a pattern of integrated activity that is resilient and stable as a result of the continual creation and destruction taking place within it. Contemporary institutions and industries will all eventually make way for more robust replacements, and such changes are a sign of health, not illness. This 'internal' change is inevitable, so it is critical to strengthen the social and economic mechanisms that facilitate it.

Metaman has been able to enhance Darwinian evolutionary mechanisms because of its ability readily to change its own behavior and form. The capacity to alter behavior has long existed in the animal kingdom, but the ability actively and substantially to adapt physical form is unique to Metaman.

Animals exhibit behaviors ranging from those that are 'programmed' to those that are 'learned'. Programmed behaviors are genetically specified, invariant responses directly embedded in an organism's neurological wiring and are particularly common among insects.[678] E. O. Wilson put it well in *On Human Nature*:

> The mosquito is an automaton. It can afford to be nothing else. There are only about one hundred thousand nerve cells in its tiny head, and each one has to pull its weight. The only way to run accurately and successfully through a life cycle in a matter of days is by instinct, a sequence of rigid behaviors programmed by the genes to unfold swiftly and unerringly from birth to the final act of oviposition.[679]

Standing in sharp contrast to such rigid programming are learned behaviors – flexible responses derived from experience. A deer must learn to avoid hunters and a sea gull does not know instinctively that picnickers mean food rather than danger. A higher animal's response to any stimulus falls between bounds set by the animal's biology: we speak of 'instinct' when the range of possible behaviors is so narrow that the response is seemingly programmed, and of 'learning' when the range is broad.[680]

Behavioral flexibility has been so powerful a competitive adaptation

in vertebrates that the central nervous system (the source of this
ability) has evolved from a mere cluster of nerve cells in primitive
worms to a mass of some ten billion neurons in humans. Our rich
behavioral repertoires are the foundation for Metaman's enormous
versatility and its organizational structures build upon our flexibility.
For instance, we can move between industries and occupations as
economic sectors grow and shrink, or social priorities change.

Modifying behavior is commonplace in animals, but reshaping
physical form is quite another story. Loose groupings of cells can
reshape themselves to some extent, but complex organisms generally
cannot, no matter how useful this would be. When a pond starts to dry
out, a fish would give anything for lungs and feet, but such large-scale
modification of form, other than in rigidly pre-specified developmental
changes, is an engineering feat never achieved by biology. A bear may
grow a winter coat and a chameleon change its color, but anything
more radical is out of the question.

Beyond genetically predetermined changes, the only way for biological systems to remodel their form significantly is through a
multi-generational process guided by natural selection. Through this
evolutionary process, living forms change over the course of many
generations in ways that are impossible for any single individual.[681]

Metaman is the first complex organism in the history of life that is
capable of adapting its form directly. It builds cities and communication
networks, forms new industries, shifts populations between continents, redraws national boundaries. The evolutionary mechanisms
previously discussed – internal rearrangement, conscious design and
model building – are the mechanisms that direct the rapid evolution of
Metaman, but its capacity for ongoing, major internal rearrangement is
what ultimately makes Metaman's evolution possible. Life, having
evolved a being that internalizes the process of natural selection, has
finally transcended that process. Through Metaman, trial and error
are giving way to conscious design. Thus, the future will be ever more
directed by the present. And the lines of causality between present
and future must also blur, because 'future possibilities' will exert a
growing influence on present occurrences and thereby shape the
present.

THE TREE OF LIFE

At the beginning of this book, I touched on how life's evolution from
simple bacteria to Metaman has produced a hierarchy of distinct

organizational levels – bacteria, eukaryotic cells, multicellular organisms and Metaman. Recall that each of these levels of organizational complexity originated as the refinement of a tightly linked group of elements from the preceding level. Bacteria arose by the enclosure of prebacterial chemical reactions in a membrane, eukaryotic cells by the symbiotic union of different bacteria,[682] animals by the organization of clusters of sister cells, and Metaman by the cooperative association of human beings and other living creatures.

Looking at the evolution not of individual species but of entire kingdoms – bacteria, protists, plants, animals and fungi – it is clear that the broad sweep of evolution is not directionless, but towards ever increasing complexity. Even the most primitive jellyfish is undeniably more complex than more ancient single-celled creatures, and the many plants and animals constituting any of today's forest communities show a complexity far beyond that of the primitive bacterial scum on a stagnant pond.[683]

Two opposing, yet interwoven, tendencies underlie all the life around us. The first is towards separation and isolation. This is evident in the biological barriers against interbreeding of species, and in the exclusive territories that animals establish. A horse and cow cannot mate; a dog defends its home turf. Without such mechanisms, variants enjoying some local advantage would not be preserved. Interbreeding would soon dilute such distinctive differences into the vast sea of living creatures around them.

The second tendency is towards integration and cooperation. This is apparent not only in diverse social groupings that range from schools of fish to corals, but also in the ubiquitous symbiotic associations between different species – the digestive bacteria in a cow's gut, flowers pollinated by bees, or humanity and its various domesticated plants and animals. All such associations arise because of the immediate mutual advantages they confer; thus any larger potentials that evolve over time are entirely fortuitous. The ensembles of organisms that lead to entirely new organisms and levels of complexity in living systems are exceedingly rare. Bees and flowers, though they have evolved a deep mutual interdependence, could never become an 'organism'. Even such tight and enduring associations as lichen, which is the union of alga and fungus, generally do not embody the potential to give rise to a diverse panoply of forms at a new level of complexity.[684]

Single-celled eukaryotes have generated rich, enduring multicellular ensembles at least *twenty* separate times,[685] but only three of these assemblages – plants, fungi and animals – succeeded in evolving large, diverse kingdoms of organisms. Animals, of course, are the most complex in both form and behavior, and they have gone on to form many close groupings: flocks of geese, colonies of ants, packs of wolves, herds of buffalo. Of such groupings, certain highly social insects and our human complex have become integrated tightly enough to be viewed as super-organisms. Thus, it is essentially humans and some species of ants, bees, wasps and termites that have reached the level of the 'meta-creature'. All are highly successful, but whereas insect super-organisms have remained essentially unchanged for 100 million years, Metaman's potential seems virtually unlimited. Metaman, by moving beyond the constraints of previous 'biological' materials and evolutionary mechanisms, is moving life into an entirely new realm.

With Metaman's emergence, biological life as a whole is taking a major step towards integration and symbiosis. In addition to spreading to encompass all of humankind and its many domesticated plants and animals, Metaman, by moving genes between different species, is merging organisms and breaching the boundaries between hitherto separate life forms. Metaman has enormous indirect influences too: by transforming the planetary environment, Metaman is creating countless biological communities that exist only by virtue of its presence. Expanding croplands, pastures, and even urban areas all have associated floras and faunas adapted to them. Metaman is creating an immense new global ecosystem that is replacing much of what has gone before.[686]

A profound evolutionary transition is underway, and it is having a large impact on humans, on the natural environment, and on society. Our immediate concern is these effects, but reflect on the influence this transition will have on the future of life over far larger time spans, time spans comparable to the millions and hundreds of millions of years that characterize the earth's fossil record.[687] One important consequence of Metaman's formation will almost certainly be life's expansion into space. With probes to the moon, Mars, and other planets, already Metaman has taken its first tentative steps in this direction. Not too far hence, Metaman will certainly extend itself (particularly its technological components) into the solar system in force. What then? Early analysis suggests that Mars might conceivably be 'terraformed' to give it an earthlike climate,[688] but such engineering would involve a sustained effort lasting perhaps 100,000 years, so the only way for humans to move beyond the earth in the foreseeable future will probably be by establishing self-contained, enclosed colonies. Such colonies, whether on asteroids, space stations, the moon, Mars, or

The 4-ton Viking I spacecraft, consisting of two modules – an orbiter and a lander (top) – reached Mars after a ten-month journey from earth. The lander touched down 20 July 1976 on Chryse Planitia and minutes later transmitted this photo (bottom) of its footpad and the Martian surface. Relayed to the earth, 220 million miles away, by the still-circling orbiter, this image was the first from the surface of another planet. Both Viking I and its Viking II cousin (a second probe that landed a month later) searched for signs of life by performing a battery of tests on samples scratched from the Martian surface. Courtesy of NASA/JPL.

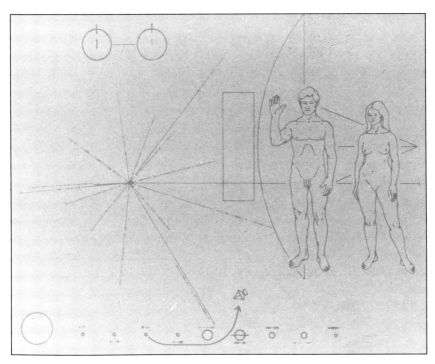

In 1973, this 6" x 9" gold-annodized aluminum plaque was carried into space aboard the Pioneer 10 spacecraft, the first construction of Metaman sent beyond our solar system. The diagram is meant to communicate when, by whom, and from where the vehicle was launched. The radiating lines on the left locate our sun by pointing to fourteen of the galaxy's giant radiowave emitters known as pulsars. To specify the time, a tiny binary number alongside each line indicates each pulsar's present frequency relative to the hydrogen atom at the plaque's upper left. Across the plaque's bottom, the path of the spacecraft from the third planet, our earth, is shown. Courtesy of NASA and the Johnson Space Center.

elsewhere, would undoubtedly remain closely linked to earth and the main body of Metaman, because within our solar system the distances are short enough to allow communication and travel that takes a tolerable amount of time.

When Metaman eventually moves out of the solar system and into the galaxy beyond, this linkage will weaken greatly; interstellar space is too vast for much meaningful two-way communication. A message traveling at the speed of light would take 4.3 years to reach the nearest star,[689] Proxima Centauri, 100,000 years to cross the galaxy, and two million years to reach Andromeda, a nearby galaxy. Thus Metaman's movement towards the stars will likely resemble a dandelion throwing off seeds that waft to distant soils. Some of Metaman's seeds will sprout and create new 'Metamen', others will perish. The nearer ones will probably stay in touch with our Metaman, the distant ones and their offspring will be too far away. This will be Metaman's 'reproduction', and with each passing millennium, it is likely that these meta-creatures will spread further into the galaxy; how quickly and how far cannot now be meaningfully guessed. As when it first emerged from the sea, terrestrial life will again be expanding into a new environment, but this time it may eventually encounter other non-terrestrial beings and meta-beings. Indeed, it is even conceivable that in this distant future, Metaman's movement beyond the solar system would include no significant 'biological' component. Intelligent technology might one day have so transcended pure biology that life as we now know it might simply be a primitive, largely planet-bound ancestor of the technological life that is our offspring and moves freely through space.

14

A NEW MYTHOLOGY

Metaman and Our Quest for Meaning

UNDERSTANDING THAT HUMAN SOCIETIES are coalescing into a powerful super-organism provides a new perspective from which to consider our significance and place. Metaman's presence, besides affirming the growing ties linking together *all* humankind, enables us to unite scientific and theological themes long considered incompatible.

The religions of the world contain great wisdom that will always have meaning to us: reflections on human strengths and weaknesses, understandings of the joys and sorrows of human experience, teachings about honor, compassion, envy and pride. Religion – a metaphorical utterance coming from the very core of human nature – is expressed in many forms because it is molded by the local landscape from which it springs. Beneath the unique cultural aspects of different religions, however, there is great similarity because the paths are all towards the same end. Only when the specifics of religious metaphors are confused for literal truth do different teachings seem at great odds with one another. Joseph Campbell puts it this way in *The Masks of God: Primitive Mythology*:

> Every student of comparative mythology knows that when the orthodox mind talks and writes of God the nations go asunder; . . . whereas, when the mystics talk, their words in a profound sense meet – and the nations, too. The names of Shiva, Allah, Buddha and Christ lose their historical force and come together as adequate pointers of a way that all must go who would transcend their time-bound, earth-bound faculties and limitations.

Sadly, religious dogma more often divides the world's peoples than brings them together. The partitioning of the Indian subcontinent into India and Pakistan following the Second World War ignited religious violence between Muslim and Hindu that still flares today;[690] the bitter struggle in the Middle East between Muslim and Jew seems never-ending. But as diverse cultures fuse within Metaman, the exclusionary elements of individual religions become increasingly untenable. The world is becoming too intertwined for philosophies to flourish that divide societies into 'us' and 'them'. We may sympathize with people whose rich traditions are wrenched by the arrival of modern technology, but denying the changes now taking place or attempting to destroy the new will not preserve those traditions. Notions of the perfidy of the infidel or the damnation of the unbeliever cannot successfully compete in a world as interdependent as ours. Societies under the sway of beliefs that inflame zealous passions and incite religious (or ethnic) strife are diminished regardless of who emerges 'victorious'. Iran's convulsion under Islamic fundamentalism extinguished the grand possibilities seemingly within that nation's grasp; battling Christians and Muslims have left once-thriving Lebanon in wreckage; and shattered Bosnia will take many decades to emerge from its nightmare.[691] It is the more placid regions that now form the vanguard of progress within Metaman, because power today comes primarily from technological advance and economic cooperation – both of which are generally throttled by religious isolationism and ethnic conflict.

Theological dogma remains a powerful global force, but its influence on everyday life in the developed world is waning. Although public opinion polls show no marked decline in church attendance,[692] and the debate about teaching evolution in American schools lingers on, from a perspective of centuries rather than decades, the trend is clear. Religions once provided the *only* cohesive views of reality and governed large aspects of most people's lives; now they are far less central to the workings of society.

Religious institutions and traditions generally respond slowly to change; yet our world is undergoing an exceedingly rapid transformation. Our children and grandchildren are *certain* to lead very different lives from our own, because they will live in vastly different worlds. To remain meaningful, traditions will have to undergo continual renewal. The orthodox Hasidic restriction against using fire (and hence, electricity) on the Sabbath, for example, is becoming ever more difficult to observe. To accomplish the underlying purpose of the practice – spiritual reflection and a pause from work and everyday concerns – requires that the interdiction be recast in a way that is more relevant to the modern world. Similarly, the strong Papal stricture against birth control is a natural extension of the advocacy of 'being fruitful and multiplying'. When human life was precarious and security was enhanced by population growth, such practices made sense, but they are an anachronism in the overpopulated world. Traditions and social conventions are meant to help us live *in* our society not separate us from it. Thus, in the rapidly changing world of Metaman we must continually revisit social practices to ensure they still serve our larger interests.

Cultures that try to preserve their cherished traditions by blocking out the rapidly changing world cannot succeed for long. Metaman will continue to evolve and these pockets of living history will either become increasingly fragile relics or be subsumed by the world's larger currents. Neither the Muslim fundamentalists of the Middle East, the endangered Yanomami of the Amazon,[693] nor the Amish of Pennsylvania can will away the modern world or indefinitely exclude it. Nevertheless, the idea of doing so is a romantic notion. In Lerner and Loewe's 1954 film, *Brigadoon*,[694] the dying pastor of an idyllic eighteenth-century Scottish village prays to God to insulate his flock from the changing world he fears will corrupt them when he is gone. His prayer is answered and each morning after his death the town awakens to find that overnight, another century has miraculously passed in the surrounding world. With any potential friendships with outsiders nipped in the bud each night, the townspeople will ostensibly be protected for ever from the world's larger influences. Such a plan might work for a few days, but by the end of the first month (3,000 years hence), the villagers would no doubt awaken to gawking throngs of sightseers. Any community that holds itself apart from the rest of the world is bound eventually to face similar problems, because humankind will move forward without them. The Amish are already a major tourist attraction, and as the gulf between them and their surroundings grows, so too will the pressure for change.

The fates of the various tribal cultures being abruptly overwhelmed by the modern world are particularly tragic, because the gulf between them and the internal milieu of Metaman is too great to allow easy adjustment. With the rapid slaughter of the American buffalo in the 1870s and 1880s,[695] the Plains Indians of North America lost their source of food, the foundation of their religion, and their very way of life. In a single generation their unique culture was doomed: the environment for which it was adapted had been swept away. When changes stretch out over many generations, the process is easier but the eventual result is largely the same – disappearance of the traditional culture except for those few vestiges incorporated into our evolving global culture. For those who are part of Metaman, however, the powerful forces of change at least are not entirely external; they are a collective expression of our own nature, accomplishments, and experiences.

Mythology speaks to our deep longing to understand the human condition: to know where we came from, why we are here, what will become of us. Every ancient mythology has its particular origin myths, almost without exception variations on the same basic theme – a powerful parental figure creates the living world and establishes or administers its laws.[696] According to the legends of the Apaches,

> In the beginning nothing was here where the world now stands: no earth – nothing but Darkness, Water, and Cyclone. There were no people. Only the Hactin [Apache gods] existed. There were no fishes, no living things. But all the Hactin were here from the beginning. They had the material out of which everything was created. They made the world first, the earth, the underworld, and then they made the sky.[697]

After this, the gods made the animals from clay, the birds from mud, the insects from seeds; then, in their own image, they made a man from pollens, clays and stones, and a female companion for him.

Buffalo Hunt under the Wolf-skin Mask, *George Catlin (1796–1872). The culture of the Plains Indians could not survive the slaughter of the buffalo in the 1870s and 1880s. In a single generation, the giant herds that were the foundation of their way of life had disappeared permanently. Courtesy of National Museum of American Art, Washington, DC and Art Resource, New York.*

Although few now regard such stories of our origins as factual histories, we none the less still can be moved by the raw, intrinsic power of their images. Imagine how such myths must have gripped those earlier peoples who not only felt the power of the stories themselves but believed them to be literal truth. In fact, many of these moving images are not so different from our own. Science has now unambiguously confirmed that the earth and sky *were* here before life, that the animals and plants *did* come from the lifeless elements of the earth, that humans *are* a recent arrival on the scene. Replace a personal and capricious deity such as the Hactin by a 'god' synonymous with the underlying laws of nature and we have in this history a powerful and poetic rendition of human origins as we understand them today. To seek literal meaning in such poetry, however, is to destroy its beauty and power.

The truths of the universe are so complex that there is no simple way of seeing them without resorting to metaphor. Even Metaman, with its vast powers, is only beginning to decipher the story's outlines, much less its details. Life is a miracle whose story is revealed all around us, and if we hope to know it we must look at the evolution of the stars and planets, the division of an amoeba, the growth of a seed, the workings of the brain, the physics of a transistor, the spirit of an individual. *This* is God's story.

Myth has long provided humans with the symbols that could guide them in their lives. Today, no framework other than science comes even close to unraveling the mysteries of the world around us or describing our origins and identity with the emotional power of early mythology. Yet, the scientific world view, though logically compelling, has not been emotionally or spiritually gripping for most of humankind. Why? Here, after all, is an explanation of our world far more comprehensive and powerful than any hitherto; it has told us the origins of the earth, cured smallpox, and let us speak to people across the globe. On another level, however, science has been barren. It has missed a critical and essential element: it has not given us a satisfying understanding of *our* place in its grand scheme. Scientifically speaking, *Homo sapiens* is just another species, one of tens of millions now alive. Science has missed a fundamental truth: the unique importance of human beings.

Religious teachings have always given humans a resonant sense of who they are, rather than what they are not. For instance, in the eighteenth century the idea of a 'great chain of being' held sway in the West. A sequence of immutable species was seen extending from the lowest organism to ever more perfect forms and finally to human beings. While our place at the foot of God may have been only the product of our own hopes, now laid to rest by an understanding of natural selection and evolution, the placement closely fits our sense of our unique cosmological importance.

The great chain of being, of course, is no more, and scientists now maintain that humans are merely one of many animal species. We cannot, however, escape the feeling that this is not the *whole* truth. Our human intuition rebels at the thought, and humans have forever tried to validate their feelings of specialness: we are created in God's image, we have self-awareness, we use tools, we have language. Our ever growing knowledge, however, has squelched these attempts to identify an essential and concrete difference between humans and the rest of the animal kingdom. Contemporary science has traced human evolution back to the simplest of creatures, discovered that chimpanzees can master a rudimentary symbolic language,[698] and found that even birds can use primitive tools.[699] The idea that evolution is even a progression stretching from lower animals up to humans has fallen into disfavor, challenged by the notion that evolution has no particular direction but is merely adaptation to local conditions.[700]

Is our feeling of uniqueness really an empty illusion, merely a manifestation of our own human pride and egocentricity? No. Though evolution is not a history of preordained progress towards the human form *per se*, it is definitely a story of the progressive development of complexity. The hierarchy from bacterium, to single-cell animal, to multicellular organism, to social super-organism reveals the nature not only of Metaman but of ourselves. Our special significance is clear. Poised at the boundary between the animal kingdom and Metaman, humans straddle two levels of organizational complexity. We are no more than animals, and yet we are *immeasurably* more: we are biological creatures with intimations of the divine. The attempt to understand and explain this duality is the essence of religion and philosophy: man has a soul, man has self-consciousness, man is aware of his own existence and mortality. Ours is an exalted place; but it is also a humble one because we each are only a tiny part of something far larger and more powerful than ourselves – a concept strikingly similar to what lies at the core of all religion.

By watching images from times long past, feeling the pain of distant others, linking our activities with those of complete strangers, we are joining together to form one immense whole that is beyond the previous constraints of space and time. Even our thoughts are not entirely our own because they are formed from countless images and ideas echoing from we know not where or when. Massive amounts of information pulse through Metaman. Once, written words moved slowly from person to person; now voice and image streak between us. No wonder we think many of the same thoughts as numerous others – we inhabit an ever more widely shared global environment. It is illusion to see ourselves as isolated individuals. Increasingly, we are each a dynamic part of an immense collective consciousness, which even after we die will retain the influences of our presence.[701]

Viewing humans as the germ of Metaman offers a powerful new image of ourselves that is in harmony with the two seemingly opposing realms we must integrate – technology and nature. Today, we live in a world of spaceships, artificial hearts and camcorders as well as wild strawberries, eagles and thunderstorms. The concept of Metaman resonates with our natural awe of the universe and gives humans a place that neither diminishes us nor contradicts humanity's understanding of the physical realm. In essence, Metaman restores to us a story of the universe that possesses the strength of the ancient myths – their ability to explain the workings of the world and our place in it. We now know the basic outlines of a history of life and the cosmos so rich that it can serve as a powerful modern mythos to orient our lives and our vision of the world.

Humanity is an important participant in a saga extending from the universe's distant past towards its far future. The story begins with the giant explosion that created everything around us,[702] tells of the formation of galaxies, the births and deaths of fiery stars, and the condensation of our own earth from the swirling gases that also bore our sun. It traces the long evolution of life from the primeval ooze: its triumphant moves into new environments, its massive die-offs, its prolific creations. Approaching our era, the saga tells of the arrival of humanity and how this led to the birth of Metaman; looking into the future it prophesies Metaman's journey out from its cradle into the larger universe awaiting it. There is no greater epic. Its scale is vast, its outline compelling, its details riveting. It is more than a story, it is *the* story, and we are privileged to know as much of it as we do.[703] No generations before us have been so fortunate.

This saga will never be fully told, because it is not a fiction that has sprouted from someone's fantasies but an ongoing rendering of the reality around us. The process of progressively unraveling nature's mysteries is never-ending because each answer invariably leads to more questions. The tale – pieced together collectively by all humankind, indeed by Metaman reaching to understand itself and its surroundings – will be recounted in an ever richer form not only to our great, great grandchildren, but to *all* future generations of humanity. This expanding knowledge does not diminish the miracle of the universe by explaining it, but deepens that miracle by revealing more of its hidden beauties. Thereby it transforms our innocent wonder into a deeper awe.

Our knowledge, vision, and power has expanded to previously unimagined levels. To the ancients, unleashing a storm, healing the sick, leveling a city, or foretelling the future would have been ample demonstration of divinity. Now, having seen equivalent powers in Metaman, we might inquire how the 'miracles' were performed rather than falling to our knees. Flight, television, a corneal transplant that restores sight, even high explosives would once have been considered godlike. Now we take them for granted. Knowing more, seeing more, having greater powers than any who have gone before, we have – through Metaman – in a sense become as gods. And yet we are 'gods' only in the limited terms of early humans, because Metaman's emergence is giving us an awareness of the true enormity and power of our universe.

Our mythic saga can do more, however, than inspire us with awe; it holds lessons for us just as the ancient mythologies did for earlier cultures. Some of the lessons are clear: ours is a world of progressive change and adaptation; human society has grown from, and is an expression of, the natural world; all humankind is joining together and can look towards a limitless future. This modern mythos offers us an expansive new vision of who we are, one that can encompass all humanity in a shared and inspiring future.

The story's affirmation that modern civilization is a part of the natural realm is particularly important to us now, when we are still uncomfortable with the new powers of Metaman and the larger influences we are exerting. Civilization is not an intrusion into the natural realm, but a harmonious extension of it. Indeed, when we reflect on all that has contributed to the creation of the familiar buildings, vehicles and other man-made devices around us, *they* can reveal the inherent beauty of life just as completely as does a wildflower sprouting in a field. Each reveals the complexity and potential of the living process. Even a simple telephone – by manifesting the networks of manufacturing, transportation and communication that crisscross our globe, the accumulated knowledge from humanity's long history, and the miracle of conscious design as a mechanism of evolutionary change – can remind us of all that life has achieved.

Human civilization is far from 'ideal'; it contains much suffering. But the same is true of life throughout the natural realm.[704] We, however, can now contemplate the prospect of one day moving beyond the 'natural' conditions of hunger, disease, and perhaps even death itself.

Metaman affirms that we are all connected – giving to and drawing from one another as we participate in a momentous step in the evolution of life. Stone tools came from Africa, writing from the Tigris–Euphrates valley, paper currency from China, the steam engine from Britain – all humankind has played a part in bringing Metaman into being. Together, we can exult in this shared accomplishment, try to solve the immediate problems at hand, and look with anticipation to the amazing future stretching before us.

GLOSSARY

Amino acids. Small organic molecules that join together to form proteins. An average protein is several hundred amino acids long.

Antibodies. Proteins produced by the body to bind and precipitate foreign molecules (antigens) detected in the blood stream.

Antigens. Molecules that trigger the body's immune system to produce antibodies.

Biodiversity. Biological diversity usually refers to the numbers of species that exist, but sometimes the term is used to refer to genetic variation within species or to the presence of broader classifications of organisms, for example families.

Biosensors. Sensing devices having both biological components and electro-mechanical ones. Because biological molecules are extremely sensitive to the presence of various chemicals and stimuli, biological molecules anchored where they can be electronically monitored can create extremely sensitive measuring devices.

Biosphere. The thin layer of atmosphere, land and water forming the earth's surface and containing all life.

Byte. see Megabyte.

Chlorofluorocarbons (CFCs). Chemical compounds that catalyze the breakdown of ozone in the earth's upper atmosphere. Their release allows increased ultraviolet radiation to reach the planet's surface.

Cretaceous. Referring to the geologic period lasting from 140 million until 65 million years ago.

DNA (Deoxyribonucleic acid). The long-chain macro-molecule that forms a double helix and contains the genetic information passed from generation to generation. Information is specified as a sequence of four different substituents – cytosine, guanine, adenine and thymine, denoted C, G, A, T. These 'bases' are arranged in triplets that code for the twenty amino acids that are the building blocks of all proteins.[705] Thus . . . AAACGACTAGCAGAA . . . would be read by the cell as . . . AAA CGA CTA GCA GAA . . . which would code for a sequence in a protein of . . . *lysine, arginine, leucine, alanine, glutamate.* . . . An average gene is several hundred triplets in length.

Enzymes. Proteins that accelerate (catalyze) specific biological reactions. Enzymes are critical to cellular metabolism, since without them many biological reactions would be too slow for living processes.

Eukaryotes. Organisms having cells with a distinct nucleus as well as a number of other features such as energy-producing mitochondria or chloroplasts. The first eukaryotic organisms were unicellular, but multicellular eukaryotic organisms later evolved from these single-celled creatures.

GDP (Gross Domestic Product). A nation's Gross National Product minus its net income from abroad.

Gene. A segment of genetic material (DNA) coding for one protein molecule.

Genetic engineering. The broad array of procedures to manipulate genes by isolating them, extracting them from cells, amplifying them, recombining them, and inserting them in new cells.

Genome. All of the genetic material of an organism.

Germ plasm. The reproductive cells, which of course contain the genetic material constituting the lineage of an organism.

GNP (Gross National Product). The value of all goods and services produced by a nation in a given year.

Hominids. The biological family containing all human species, but not gibbons, gorillas or chimpanzees. The earliest hominid was *Australopithecus africanus,* which arose some 5 million years ago; then came *Homo habilis, Homo erectus* and *Homo sapiens.*[706]

Homo erectus. 'Erect man', the immediate ancestor of *Homo sapiens. Homo erectus* emerged some 1.6 to 1.7 million years ago.

Homo habilis. 'Skillful man', which appeared some 2.5 to 2.0 million years ago. Fossils of this hominid, the immediate ancestor of *Homo erectus,* have been found in Africa and possibly Asia.

Homo sapiens. 'Wise man', the modern human species. Variants of modern humans arose some 500,000 years ago, and anatomically modern humans first appeared some 200,000 years ago.

Inorganic compounds. Chemical compounds not typical of those in living systems and generally not containing carbon.

Megabyte (Mbyte). A million bytes. A byte, which is eight bits (on/off switches) of information, encodes one alphanumeric character. Thus, a one Mbyte chip can hold some 500 typewritten pages of information.

Metazoa. Multicellular organisms made up of eukaryotic cells.

Monoclonal Antibodies. antibodies made by a cellular clone grown from a single antibody-producing cell. Monoclonal techniques can be used to produce large quantities of any particular antibody.

Nucleus. The enclosed region of a eukaryotic cell containing its genetic material.

Organic compounds. Chemical compounds typical of those in living organisms. Primarily composed of carbon and hydrogen, these molecules also often contain oxygen, nitrogen, phosphorus and traces of various minerals.

Photovoltaic power. Electrical power produced when light falls upon the surface of special semiconductor materials. Current technologies use flat plates of photovoltaic wafers or concentrators, which focus diffuse light upon smaller pieces of photovoltaic material.

Point Mutation. A mutation that alters a single base on the DNA molecule and thereby alters one triplet in a gene's code. *See* DNA.

Prokaryotes. Microbial organisms, either unicellular or colonial, with simple cells that have neither a distinct nucleus nor other features typical of eukaryotic cells.

Proteins. Versatile organic molecules formed of chains of amino acids folded into various three-dimensional shapes. Proteins generally have highly specific biological activities and play key roles in cellular metabolism.

Protists. Single-celled eukaryotic organisms.

Solar-Thermal Power. Electrical power produced by solar collectors that use sunlight to heat a fluid that runs a generator. The most promising current technology for large-scale solar-thermal power plants is the central-receiver design, which has mirrors that focus sunlight upon a central tower housing a generator.

Species. An interbreeding or potentially interbreeding population that is genetically isolated from all other populations. Animals from different species do not and generally cannot interbreed.

Super-organisms. An association of organisms so specialized and integrated that it forms an enduring entity with the characteristics of a new organism.

Transgenic organisms. Hybrid organisms produced by combining genetic material from at least two different species.

NOTES TO THE CHAPTERS

PREFACE

1.   For a good discussion of the antiquity of this idea, *see* Chapter 4, 'The World an Organism', in Carolyn Merchant's *The Death of Nature: Women, Ecology, and the Scientific Revolution* (Harper and Row, San Francisco, 1983). The idea of a deep organic commonality between humankind and nature was dominant until about the time of Francis Bacon (1561–1626), when the image of nature as an entity separate from humankind and subject to conquest and control began to displace the earlier ideas. *See* Chapter 7, 'Dominion over Nature', ibid.

2.   *See* Book I, Chapter 3 and Book VII, Chapter 9 of Aristotle's *Politics*, translated by Benjamin Jowett in *The Basic Works of Aristotle*, ed. Richard McKeon (Random House, New York, 1941).

3.   *See* John of Salisbury (Bishop of Chartres), *The Statesman's Book*, selections from the Policraticus, written in 1159, translated by John Dickinson (Knopf, New York, 1927), Book V, page 65:

> The place of the head in the body of the commonwealth is filled by the prince who is subject only to God and to those who exercise His office and represent Him on earth, even as in the human body the head is quickened and governed by the soul. The place of the heart is filled by the Senate, from which proceeds the initiation of good works and ill. The duties of eyes, ears, and tongue are claimed by the judges and the governors of provinces. Officials and soldiers correspond to the hands. Those who always attend upon the prince are likened to the sides. Financial officers and keepers may be compared with the stomach and intestines, which, if they become congested through excessive avidity, and retain too tenaciously their accumulations, generate innumerable

and incurable diseases . . . The husbandmen correspond to the feet, which always cleave to the soil, and need the more especially the care and foresight of the head, since while they walk upon the earth doing service with their bodies, they meet the more often with stones of stumbling . . . Take away the feet from the strongest body, and it cannot move forward by its own power, but must creep painfully on its hands.

4.   Herbert Spencer writes in *Principles of Sociology*, Volume 1, page 462 (Appleton and Co., New York, 1897), for example:

And the mutually-dependent parts [of society], living by and for one another, form an aggregate constituted on the same general principle as is a living organism. The analogy of a society to an organism becomes still clearer on learning that every organism of appropriate size is a society; and on further learning that in both, the lives of the units continue for some time if the life of the aggregate is suddenly arrested while if the aggregate is not destroyed by violence, its life greatly exceeds in duration the lives of its units.

See also The Evolution of Society (Selections from Herbert Spencer's *Principles of Sociology*), ed. R. Carneiro (University of Chicago Press, Chicago, 1967).

5.   Pierre Teilhard de Chardin, *The Phenomenon of Man* (Harper and Row, New York, 1959). *See also The Phenomenon of Man Revisited: A Biological Viewpoint on Teilhard de Chardin*, Edward Dobson (Columbia Univ. Press, New York, 1984).

6.   Theodosius Dobzhansky (1900–1975), *The Biology of Ultimate Concern* (New American Library, New York, 1967).

7.   Almost two decades ago, James Lovelock articulated this idea and coined the name Gaia to describe the 'planetary organism'. *Gaia: A New Look at Life on Earth*, James Lovelock (Oxford University Press, Oxford, 1979). He later updated the concept in *The Ages of Gaia: A Biography of Our Living Earth*, James Lovelock (Norton and Company, London, 1988). *See also* 'Research News', *Science* 252:379–381 (1991) for an appraisal of the concept.

The Gaia hypothesis describes a planetary equilibrium that has existed – with a few perturbations – for more than 3 billion years. In this concept, human activity is simply one of many forces in the immense, self-regulatory scheme of the planet and has no special significance. Humanity's presence or absence is inconsequential because if humankind does not significantly disturb the ecosystem its presence is hardly noticeable to Gaia, and if humankind does disrupt the environment, humanity will quickly become extinct and leave little trace.

8. *See* 'Research News', *Science* 240:395 (1988) for a discussion of the debate between enthusiasts of the Gaia Hypothesis and their critics. The early strong statements of purposeful regulation of the planetary ecosystem by Gaia have been greatly toned down since they were first suggested, but there is still much debate on how significant a role life plays in the complex processes that, for over 3 billion years, have maintained the planet at conditions that sustain life. For a discussion of various living and non-living contributions to the regulation of the planetary environment, *see* Stephen Schneider's, 'A Goddess of the Earth? The Debate on the Gaia Hypothesis – An Editorial', *Climatic Change* 8:1–4 (1986). For an excellent discussion of abiotic climate regulatory mechanisms, *see* 'Long-term stability of the Earth's climate', J. Kasting, *Palaeogeography, Palaeoclimatology, Palaeoecology* 75:83–95 (1989). For a strong critique of the Gaia hypothesis, *see* James Kirchner, *Rev. Geophysics* 278:223–235 (1989).

9. The term biosphere, though used by Edward Suess in 1875, took on its modern usage through the pioneering work of the Russian, Vladimir Vernadsky, in the early 1900s. He used the term to mean the thin envelope of life covering the surface of the earth. For more about the history of this concept, *see* pages 8–12, *The Ages of Gaia: A Biography of Our Living Earth*, James Lovelock (Norton and Company, London, 1988). *See also* 'Biosphere Models', Moisseiev et al., pages 493–510 of *Climate Impact Assessment*, ed. R. Kates et al. (John Wiley and Sons, London, 1985).

10. *See* note 7.

11. In citing statistics to illustrate global trends and developments, I would prefer using information that is worldwide in scope, but such data on all but the simplest of matters – things such as population growth and climate change – are generally both difficult to obtain and difficult to interpret because of global variation in levels of social development and methods of data compilation. Thus, I take most of my examples from individual countries, and because of easy access have mostly used US figures. Generally, of course, similar statistics from other developed countries might have been used instead.

12. Herbert Spencer, *Principles of Sociology*, Volume 1, page 463 (Appleton and Co., New York, 1897).

CHAPTER 1

13. The term super-organism was first coined in 1928 by William Wheeler in his work on ant colonies. *See* note 68.

14. In practice, the physical infrastructure of society is replaced far more rapidly than if it were simply left to decay. For example, the lifetime of

industrial plant and equipment in the US averages some twenty years. Continual turnover in the physical structures around us is what makes rapid adaptation possible for Metaman. *See* 'Does Climate still matter?', Jesse Ausubel, *Nature* 350:649–652 (1991).

15.   The oldest microfossils of bacterial cells are from 3.5 billion years ago. Stromatolites, fossil mats of bacteria from these early times, are very similar in form to present-day bacterial mats found in shallow tidal waters in such places as Baja California and Western Australia. Pages 40–9, 60 of 'The Oldest Fossils and What They Mean', J. William Schopf, Chapter 2 of *Major Events in the History of Life*, ed. J. William Schopf (Jones and Bartlett Publishers, Boston, 1992).

16.   Only in the past fifty years have scientists begun to unravel how this transition to life might have occurred. In 1953, Stanley Miller and Harold Urey, building on the ideas of Oparin, [*see The Origin of Life*, A. Oparin (Macmillan, New York, 1938)], made lightning-like electrical discharges into a flask of ammonia, water vapor, hydrogen and methane, meant to resemble the earth's early atmosphere, and produced a rich yield of amino acids and other complex organic molecules (Stanley Miller, 'Production of amino acids under possible primitive earth conditions', *Science* 117:528–529). The result was astonishing at the time: all the basic organic molecules needed by life were easily produced in the environment of the early earth. For a good general discussion of the current understanding of how life may have first formed, *see* pages 49–67 of Dorian Sagan's and Lynn Margulis's *Microcosmos: Four Billion Years of Microbial Evolution* (Summit Books, New York, 1986). *See also* 'The Prebiotic Synthesis of Organic Compounds as a Step Toward the Origin of Life', Stanley Miller, Chapter 1 of *Major Events in the History of Life*, ed. J. William Schopf (Jones and Bartlett Publishers, Boston, 1992).

17.   These single-celled creatures not only dominated the planet for some 2 billion years, they evolved all of the basic biochemistry at the heart of the more complex organisms found today. In essence, the biochemistry of living organisms – our basic metabolism, and every other creature's – is bacterial in origin. For an extensive look at bacteria and the key role they have played, and continue to play, in life on earth, *see* Dorian Sagan's and Lynn Margulis's *Micro-cosmos: Four Billion Years of Microbial Evolution* (Summit Books, New York, 1986).

18.   'The Oldest Fossils and What They Mean', J. William Schopf, page 49, Chapter 2 of *Major Events in the History of Life*, ed. J. William Schopf (Jones and Bartlett Publishers, Boston, 1992). *See* T. Han and B. Runnegar, *Science* 257:232–235 (1992) for a report of a 2.1 billion years old eukaryote.

19.   It is only recently that biologists have begun to understand how this transition occurred. Lynn Margulis's pioneering work in the 1970s was

instrumental in firmly establishing the theory of 'endosymbionts', which suggests that various components of eukaryotic cells originated as bacteria that were symbiotically linked to eukaryotic ancestors. *See*, for example, *Symbiosis in Cell Evolution*, L. Margulis (W.H. Freeman and Co., San Francisco, 1981), or 'Evolution by Endosymbiosis: The Inside Story', G. Kite, pages 50–2, *New Scientist*, 3 July 1986. *See also* note 682. There is molecular phylogenetic evidence suggesting that the ancestors of modern eukaryotic cells (possessing a nucleus but no mitochondria or chloroplasts) are very ancient and appeared near the time that the first bacteria appeared more than 3.5 billion years ago. 'The Early Evolution of Eukaryotes: A Geological Perspective', Andrew Knoll, *Science* 256:622–627 (1992).

20.   For a general discussion of prokaryotes and eukaryotes, *see* pages 10–26 of *Molecular Biology of the Cell*, Bruce Alberts et al. (Garland Publishing Inc., New York, 1989).

21.   For a good discussion of the early evolution of multicellular organisms (metazoans), *see* Bruce Runnegar's 'Evolution of the Earliest Animals', Chapter 3 of *Major Events in the History of Life*, ed. J. William Schopf (Jones and Bartlett Publishers, Boston, 1992).

22.   A recipe for the creation of the entire, complex adult must lie within the very first cell of any embryo if this cell and its offspring are to unfold into the adult form as they divide again and again. This process is called 'development' and requires precise coordination: genes must turn on and off according to schedule so that cells can divide, grow, specialize, communicate, move, and even die at the right times. Though the chemistry of the gene was uncovered thirty years ago, even today its complex regulation within the eukaryotic cell is only beginning to be understood. As it has become clear how exceedingly intricate this regulation is, it has become difficult to imagine that complex development would be possible without genetic material localized in one place (the nucleus). Thus the step to multicellularity apparently hinged on the prior evolution of the nucleus.

23.   'Creations' is used here in the broadest sense and includes not only technological, material and cultural creations, but also domesticated plants and animals produced by generations of selective breeding and symbiotic association.

24.   Page 73, *Atlas of the World Today*, N. Grant and N. Middleton (Harper and Row, New York, 1987).

25.   A girl born in France in 1900 had a life expectancy of 48.7 years; in 1850 her life expectancy would have been 39.3 years. Page 603, *QUID 1991*, Dominique and Michèle Frémy (Editions Robert Laffont, SA, Paris, 1991).

26.   Now it is known that the universe has no center and no edge: all positions in the universe are equivalent. For a discussion of our current

knowledge about cosmology, *see* Stephen Hawking's *A Brief History of Time* (Bantam Books, New York, 1988).

27. For an interesting article on this issue *see* 'Free Choice: When Too Much Is Too Much', Lena Williams, page C1 *New York Times*, August 1990.

28. J. Ausubel, 'Rat-Race Dynamics and Crazy Companies', *Technological Forecasting and Social Change* 39:11–22 (1991).

29. Cochlear Corporation, which is the world's major manufacturer of these devices, estimates that some 1300 were implanted in 1992, more than 800 of which were in the US. Personal Communication, Cochlear Corporation, Englewood, Colorado.

30. In 1944, Oswald Avery and his colleagues determined that DNA (then called 'nuclein') constituted the genetic material of the cell, but DNA's structure and the mechanism by which it could duplicate itself was unknown until the 1953 paper by James Watson and Francis Crick that brought each of them a Nobel prize. J. Watson and F. Crick, 'Molecular Structure of Nucleic Acids: A Structure for Deoxyribose Nucleic Acid', *Nature* 171:737–738 (1953).

31. The key work here was that of A. Maxam and W. Gilbert, *Proc. Natl. Acad. Sci. USA* 74:560 (1977), and of F. Sanger, S. Nicklen, and A. Coulson, *Proc. Natl. Acad. Sci., USA* 74:5463 (1977). The ability to read a gene – that is, to determine the sequence of bases making it up – opened up the field of molecular genetics.

32. A fifty-two-year-old woman, who had already been through menopause, bore a healthy child after she was treated with hormones and implanted with a donor embryo fertilized using her husband's sperm. A forty-two-year-old woman bore her own granddaughter by serving as the surrogate mother for an *in vitro* fertilized embryo from her daughter and son-in-law. The daughter was unable to bear children herself because, although she had an ovary, she was born without a uterus. *See* 'Making Babies', pages 56–62, *Time*, 30 September 1991.

33. *See* 'More and More Babies Born to be Tissue Donors', page A1, *New York Times*, 4 June 1991.

34. 'Smallest Survivors: Dilemmas of Prematurity', *New York Times*, page A1, 29 September 1991.

35. In the US, the increase in life expectancy at birth brought by eliminating all forms of cancer would be 3.17 years for females and 3.2 for males. 'In Search of Methuselah: Estimating the Upper Limits of Human Longevity', S. Olshansky, B. Carnes and C. Cassel, *Science* 250:634–638 (1990). *See also* note 665. In addition, a 1981 study for the US Congressional Office of Technology concluded that food additives accounted for less than 1 per cent of cancers, environmental exposures to carcinogens some 2 per

cent, and occupational exposures some 4 per cent. The study also concluded that 30 per cent of cancers were caused by smoking and another 35 per cent by diet. 'A review of the Record', J. Morrall, *Regulation*, pages 25–34, November 1986.

36.   In France, for example, life expectancy at birth in 1900 was 47.0; in 1989 it was 76.4. *See* note 350.

37.   *See* note 35.

38.   Some past climatic changes – a 12° shift in average temperature some 10,000 years ago in Greenland, for example – have occurred in a matter of decades. *See* note 292.

39.   Pages 47–51, *Paleoclimatology*, T. Crowley, G. North (Oxford University Press, Oxford, 1991).

40.   Throughout the developed world, population growth was under 1 per cent between 1985 and 1990, and in Sweden, Denmark, Austria, Hungary, and (West) Germany, population actually declined. *Atlas of the Environment*, Geoffrey Lean et al. (Prentice Hall, New York, 1986).

41.   *See* page 32, 'Population Images', Robert Fox et al., United Nations Fund for Population Activities (1987).

42.   For example, in India birth and death rates were balanced in 1920 at 48 per 1000 persons. By 1987, birth rates had dropped by a third – to 32 per 1000, but death rates had fallen by 75 per cent, to 11 per 1000. *Statistical Outline of India 1989–1990*, Department of Economics and Statistics, ed. D. Pendse (TATA Press Ltd, Bombay, 1989). *See also* note 261.

43.   From 1950 to 1989, international assistance for family-planning programs totalled only 10 billion dollars – just twice what the French spent on their pets in 1988 alone. *See Global Population Assistance Report 1982–1989*, United Nations Population Fund (UNFPA), New York (1990); *also* page A3, *New York Times*, 2 February 1991.

44.   For instance, the UN estimates that if merely those women who want to have no more children at all were enabled to stop bearing them, births would drop by a third in Asia, Africa, and Latin America. 'Setting a Limit', *Zero Population Growth Fact Sheet* (Zero Population Growth, Washington, DC, 1990). Because population growth is the surplus of births over deaths, reducing births by a third reduces population growth even more. In India if births dropped by a third, population growth would drop by half. In estimating a one-third decline in births, the UN considered only those women who want no more children at all; many other women, however, want to have a smaller family by spacing out their children, yet have no easy access to the contraceptives that would allow them to do so. Thus the drop in births might be even higher than the UN estimates, were easy access to birth control widespread.

45.   *See* E.O. Wilson's 'The Current State of Biological Diversity', in

Biodiversity, ed. E. Wilson (National Academy Press, Washington, DC, 1988). Some 1,400,000 species have been catalogued out of the estimated 5 to 30 million species in existence. Of the identified species, by far the largest number, some 750,000, are insects – primarily beetles. Other estimates of the number of species on the planet are as high as 80 million.

46.   Actually, much of what we now consider to be the 'natural' environment is already largely the product of human activity. The cherished hedgerows so characteristic of the British countryside are man-made, the product of deforestation and cultivation begun before Julius Caesar's arrival two thousand years ago. Large parts of Europe, North America, and Asia were once covered by thick forests. A quarter of Holland was undersea in the 1600s. For a discussion of Holland's extraordinary efforts to expand its habitable land, *see* 'Holding back the tides', Peter Tonge, *World Monitor*, May, 1990.)

47.   The previous record, passed in 1984, was the thirty-nine-year gap between the end of the Napoleonic Wars in 1815 and the beginning of the Crimean War in 1854. *See* page 1 of John Mueller's *Retreat from Doomsday* (Basic Books, New York, 1988); *also see* 'Does Murphy's Law Apply to History?', Paul Schroeder, *Wilson's Quarterly* 9(1):84–93 (1985).

48.   *See America's Energy Choices* (Union of Concerned Scientists, Boston, MA, 1991). Renewable sources could produce energy cheaply enough to replace most fossil-fuel consumption during the next century. For example, this report estimates that by the year 2030, over 60 per cent of the US's generation of electricity could be by renewable energy sources such as solar, wind, geothermal, biomass and hydroelectric, and that such changes would reduce CO_2 emissions in the US by nearly half within that period. What would be the cost of these changes? These authors may be overly optimistic, but they suggest that the 2 to 3 trillion dollars required to accomplish this during the next four decades would be more than offset by savings in energy costs.

CHAPTER 2

49.   After a star has condensed from interstellar gasses, its future course is established by the total mass it contains. A star's mass determines how long it will shine before the hydrogen fusion within it can no longer keep it from collapsing under the pull of its own gravitation. Some 10 billion years after it forms, a star the size of our sun briefly flares into a huge, cool 'red giant', then collapses into a small, hot 'white dwarf'. Recent calculations suggest that long before our sun expands into a red giant, however, life's survival might be at risk. Incresing solar radiation could cause atmospheric carbon dioxide to fall below the level required to support photosynthesis in as little as 1 to 1.5

billion years. Without technological intervention by Metaman, life on earth might disappear at that time, when life is only at its fiftieth 'story year'. *See* 'The life span of the biosphere revisited', Ken Caldeira and James Kasting, *Nature* 360:721–723 (1992) and the commentary, 'When Climate and life finally devolve', Tyler Volk, *Nature* 360:707 (1992).

50.   'The Anthropic view of nucleosynthesis', John Maddox, *Nature* 355:107 (1992).

51.   Analyses of cratering on the moon and Mars suggests that in the solar system's early years, some 3.8 to 4.5 billion years ago, collisions with immense meteors occurred every few hundred million years. Thus the earth is likely to have collided several times with meteors a hundred or more kilometers in diameter, a collision that would have generated enough heat to temporarily vaporize any oceans and obliterate all early life – essentially sterilizing the earth. *See* N. Sleep et al., *Nature* 342:139–142 (1989), and M. Waldrop, *Science* 250:1078–1079 (1990). Thus, it is quite possible that life evolved several times on the young earth before the meteor bombardments of the early solar system tapered off.

52.   At this time radiation from the sun was some 30 per cent weaker than it is now and a cycle of day and night lasted ten rather than twenty-four hours. *See The Ages of Gaia: A Biography of Our Living Earth*, James Lovelock (Norton and Company, London, 1988); *Micro-cosmos: Four Billion Years of Microbial Evolution*, L. Margulis, D. Sagan (Summit Books, New York, 1986).

53.   For a discussion of the various sources of the earth's early organic molecules, *see* the review by Christopher Chyba and Carl Sagan, 'Endogenous production, exogenous delivery and impact-shock synthesis of organic molecules: inventory for the origins of life', *Nature* 355:125–132 (1992). They estimate a concentration of organic molecules in the early oceans of about one milligram per milliliter.

54.   That life existed more than 700 million years ago, much less an extraordinary 3.5 billion years ago, was not appreciated until quite recently. Stromatolites (fossil bacterial matts) had been recognized since the mid-1800s, but these rocks were not established as biological in origin until they were compared with living stromatolites discovered in the early 1960s. *See* page 33, 'The Oldest Fossils and What They Mean', J. William Schopf, *Major Events in the History of Life*, ed. J. William Schopf (Jones and Bartlett Publishers, Boston, 1992).

Molecular biology has now provided an entirely non-geological estimate of the time since the origin of life. The technique, which calculates the time it would take for the diverse mutations seen now to have arisen if gene mutation rates have always been what they are now, also arrives at a figure of about 3.5 billion years for the time since life began on earth. *See* 'How Old is the

Genetic Code?', M. Eigen et al., *Science* 244:673–679 (1989).

55. Oxygen concentrations rose from early levels of less than one billionth per cent of current atmospheric pressure to about 1 to 2 per cent of the atmosphere some 2.8 billion years ago. The massive, banded iron-ore deposits, which are the world's primary source of iron and steel, were produced from about that time until 1.8 billion years ago, when almost all the iron in the world had been oxidized. This was when our planet rusted. *See* 'The Early Evolution of Eukaryotes: A Geological Perspective', Andrew Knoll, *Science* 256: 622–627 (1992); 'Origins of Breathable Air', H. Holland, *Nature* 347:17 (1990); pages 103–4, *Micro-cosmos: Four Billion Years of Microbial Evolution*, L. Margulis, D. Sagan (Summit Books, New York, 1986).

56. By about 1.7 million years ago, the atmospheric concentration of oxygen in the atmosphere reached modern levels of about 20 per cent. *See* page 33, 'The Oldest Fossils and What They Mean', J. William Schopf, *Major Events in the History of Life*, ed. J. William Schopf (Jones and Bartlett Publishers, Boston, 1992). At this level, oxygen will kill any organism that can neither establish itself in an oxygen-free environment nor build a protective membrane. At only a slightly higher concentration, about 25 per cent, oxygen is so dangerous that wood and other organic material may combust spontaneously in hot, dry conditions. *See* page 38, *Gaia: A New Look at Life On Earth*, James Lovelock (Oxford University Press, Oxford, 1979).

57. Aerobic metabolism extracts the energy released as heat during combustion by dividing this *uncontrolled* chemical reaction, the oxidation of Carbon ($C + O_2 \rightarrow CO_2 +$ Energy), into a linked sequence of *controlled* chemical reactions. These metabolic reactions shunt the oxygen's energy into stable, high-energy compounds such as ATP (Adenosine Triphosphate) which subsequently power the activities of the cell.

58. Some fossils thought to be of early eukaryotic cells are over 2 billion years old. *See* page 49, 'The Oldest Fossils and What They Mean', J. William Schopf, *Major Events in the History of Life*, ed. J. William Schopf (Jones and Bartlett Publishers, Boston, 1992): and *Nature* 359:13–14 (1992).

59. *See* note 21.

60. So rapidly did these new creatures diversify and proliferate that their appearance some 550 million years ago is called the Cambrian *explosion*. Prior to this time the fossil record was extremely scant because, though bones and other hard parts are preserved under a variety of geological conditions, only rare conditions will preserve a record of soft-bodied animals. For a discussion of the earliest fossils of multicellular animals, *see* 'Evolution of the Earliest Animals', Bruce Runnegar, Chapter 3 of *Major Events in the History of Life*, ed. J. William Schopf (Jones and Bartlett Publishers, Boston, 1992).

61. The notion of such a planetary collision was first suggested by Luis

Alvarez et al. in 1980 (*Science* 208:1095) to explain the fact that throughout the world, there is a high concentration of iridium – a rare element found primarily in comets and asteroids – in a narrow band of sediments deposited at the end of the Cretaceous era. Initially this hypothesis was extremely controversial, but it is now generally accepted by the scientific community because many subsequent independent observations suggest the same story. For example, deposits that contain iridium also contain the tiny glass-like particles that an impact would create. In fact, recent papers make cogent arguments that the impact was in the Yucatan Peninsula of Mexico, where it left a 100-kilometer-wide crater. *See Nature*, 357:15 (1992), *Science* 252:377 (1991), or, for an overview, 'Closing in on the Killer', *Science News* 141:56–58 (1992). For a good review of the broad evidence for this event, *see* William Glen's 'What killed the Dinosaurs?' *American Scientist* 78:354–370 (1990).

62.   The impact of a meteor 10 kilometers in diameter would not only raise a huge cloud of dust, it might also raise the concentration of atmospheric carbon dioxide several fold, cause global earthquakes a thousand times stronger than the 1960 Chilean earthquake, which at 9.5 on the Richter scale is the strongest ever recorded, some ten times the strength of the 1906 earthquake that leveled San Francisco in 1906. *See* T. Ahrens and J. O'Keefe, 'Impact of an asteroid or comet in the ocean and extinction of terrestrial life', Proceedings of the 13th Lunar and Planetary Science Conference, Part 2, *Journal of Geophysical Research* 88, pages A799–A806 (supplement).

63.   These figures are from John Ostrom's 'Osteology of Deinonychus antirrhopus, an unusual theropod from the Lower Cretaceous of Montana', *Yale Peabody Museum Bulletin* 30:1–165 (1969). *See also*, pages 129–36 of 'A History of Vertebrate Successes', John Ostrom, Chapter 5 of *Major Events in the History of Life*, ed. J. William Schopf (Jones and Bartlett Publishers, Boston, 1992): and *Nature* 359:13–14 (1992).

64.   Societies have long been growing, interacting with their environments, and using energy and materials, but only in the twentieth century – particularly its latter half – has civilization begun to take on a truly global character. The change has been rapid and profound: travel measured in hours rather than miles, fabled lands transformed into commonplace television images. During the past century, energy use has soared, population has exploded, urban growth has accelerated, trade has expanded, and communication has become largely instantaneous. In the process, Metaman has emerged as a global super-organism.

65.   For further information, *see* 'Galileo Encounter with 951 Gaspra: First Pictures of an Asteroid', M. Belton et al., *Science* 257:1647–1652 (1992).

66.   A meteor one kilometer in diameter strikes the earth every 100 to 400,000 years on average. Such an impact would have a destructive force of

some 100 million megatons of explosives and produce a crater some 10 to 20 kilometers across. *See* pages 156–65, *Extinction: Bad Genes or Bad Luck*, David Raup (Norton and Co, New York, 1991). This is some 5,000 times the *total* nuclear arsenal of all nations in the world combined – about 20 thousand megatons, *see World Military and Social Expenditures 1989*, Ruth Sivard, World Priorities, Washington, DC. (1991). Even small meteors have enormous energy; a meteor about 50 meters across exploded in the air above Siberia in 1908 with about a 12-megaton force and leveled trees over a 1,000-square-kilometer area. Such impacts probably occur somewhere in the world about once a century on average, *see* 'Our Asteroid-pelted planet', D. Steel, *Nature* 354:265–266 (1991).

67. Page 440, table 21–4, *The Insect Societies*, Edward O. Wilson (Belknap Press, Cambridge, Mass., 1971).

68. The way in which entomologists perceive the termite colony has gone through large swings in the past century. Before the turn of the century, few – if any – considered the colony to be an organism. Too little was known about insects. Then, in 1911, William Wheeler in his essay, 'The Ant Colony as an Organism' (*Journal of Morphology* 22:307–325, 1911) persuasively presented that case; later he coined the term 'super-organism' to describe such an entity. This idea – popularized by Maeterlinck and then the South African naturalist, E. Marais, in *Soul of the White Ant* (1933), remained scientifically popular through mid-century but faded in the 1960s. Now, again, it is beginning to find favor. Bert Holldöbbler and Edward Wilson describe this in their wonderful 700-page opus on Ants (page 359, *The Ants*, Belknap Press, Cambridge, Massachusetts, 1990):

> The time may have arrived for a revival of the super-organism concept. We see two reasons, both stemming from the increase of information and technical competence in its analysis since 1960. The first is the beginning of a sound developmental biology of the insect colony; and the second is the rapid improvement of optimization analysis in behavioral ecology and sociobiology. . . . There is a need now for drawing analogies at a deeper level, in which the organizational processes of [ant] societies are more precisely measured and compared with their equivalents in the growth and differentiation of tissues in organisms.

See also 'The Sociogenesis of Insect Colonies', E. Wilson, *Science* 228:1489–1495 (1985).

69. *See* page 118 and table 21–1, *The Insect Societies*, Edward O. Wilson (Belknap Press, Cambridge, Mass., 1971).

70. This particular termitary is of the termite, *Eutermes palmerstoni.*

71. *See* note 74.

72. *See* page 331, *The Discoverers: A History of Man's Search to Know His World and Himself*, Daniel Boorstin (Random House, New York, 1983).

73. *See* note 68.

74. Even the tiny bacterium, the simplest living thing, is one with large numbers of highly specialized parts. Its many ribosomes, genes, membrane receptors and flagella are minute molecular machines that are each merely a sophisticated cluster of macromolecules. A typical bacterium, such as Salmonella, has about a thousand ribosomes, two thousand genes, six flagella, and more than ten thousand membrane receptors. These molecular machines are impressive, but the product of their combination – a bacterium – is immeasurably more impressive. This 'simple' creature even has a primitive memory: as it swims it constantly compares present and past concentrations of the chemicals in its surroundings to help it find nutrients and avoid poisons. For other details on bacterial structure, *see Escherichia Coli and Salmonella Typhimurium: Cellular and Molecular Biology*, Frederick Neidhardt, American Society for Microbiology, Washington DC, (1987); R. Macnab and D.E. Koshland Jr., 'The Gradient Sensing Mechanism in Bacterial Chemotaxis', *Proc. Natl. Acad. Sci.* USA, 69:2509–2512 (1972). For a recent review of bacterial chemotaxis and other aspects of bacterial behavior, *see* 'Signal Transduction in Bacteria', Jeffry Stock, A. Stock, and J. Mottonen, *Nature* 344:395–400 (1990).

75. Actually, there is another example of a 'super-organism' of higher animals. The naked mole rat forms an eusocial colony very like insect societies in that there is only one reproductive female. For details *see* 'Naked Mole Rats', Paul Sherman et al, *Scientific American* 267(2):72–79 (1992). Moreover, among insects, not only wasps, ants, bees, and termites are eusocial, in recent years eusocial species of ambrosia beetles, aphids, and thrips also have been identified. Insect super-organisms are proving much more commonplace than was once imagined. *See* 'Social Castes Found to be Not So Rare in Nature', Carol Yoon, Page B5, *New York Times*, 16 February 1993.

76. Prior to the Second World War, human activity had become highly specialized within industrialized regions – especially large urban areas – but these regions were not yet extensively integrated with one another. The broad global integration of human activity characterized by transnational corporations and global financial markets is a phenomenon that has depended upon the postwar arrival of global telecommunications and rapid intercontinental transportation.

77. Even the *biological* capacity of humans to survive outside Metaman, however, will become greatly diminished in the future. As modern medicine makes difficulties in conception and delivery largely irrelevant to our repro-

ductive abilities, conception and pregnancy entirely free of complications will become ever more rare.

78.   Page ix, *International Energy Annual: 1989* (US Department of Energy, Washington, DC, 1989).

79.   For these consumption figures, *see* the following references: gypsum and iron – pages 355 and 422, *Mineral Facts and Problems* (US Department of the Interior, Bureau of Mines, Washington, DC, 1985); wheat – page 133, *The World Almanac and Book of Facts 1991* (St Martin's Press, New York 1991); fish – page 855, *Statistical Abstract of the United States* (US Bureau of the Census 1990).

80.   For a discussion of increasing efficiencies in energy use, *see* 'Strategies for Energy Use', J. Gibbons, P. Blair, H. Gwin, *Scientific American* 261(3):136–143 (1989).

81.   The US Department of Energy reports that known reserves of oil, natural gas, and coal are sufficient to last some 45, 50, and 300 years respectively. Pages 22, 23, 97–102, *International Energy Annual: 1989*, US Department of Energy, Washington, DC (1989). There is, however, some uncertainty about both the size of known fields and the quantities of fossil fuels remaining to be discovered. Fulkerson et al. estimate that there are 50 years of oil left, 120 of natural gas, and 1500 of coal at current rates of usage. *See* page 130, 'Energy from Fossil Fuels', W. Fulkerson, R. Judkins, M. Sanghvi, *Scientific American* 263(3):129–135 (1990). Energy forms, though, are now largely intraconvertible, so fossil fuels are unlikely to be in short supply for at least a few centuries. *See* 'Energy Sources: A Realistic Outlook', Chauncey Starr et al., *Science* 256: 981–987 (1992). Coal, which constitutes some 90 per cent of the Earth's fossil fuels, could long be used as a source of liquid fuel, but the environmental consequences of such a course are likely to be prohibitive.

82.   Currently, the best method of measuring deforestation is to assemble large mosaic images covering the rainforests and other areas, digitize the coordinates of the affected areas, and compute the deforestation totals. Cloudfree images of some 95 per cent of the Amazon rainforest are relatively easy to assemble (Personal communication, Goddard Space Center). Measurements using 167 Landsat images taken in the latter half of 1989 revealed that only 11 per cent of the Brazilian rainforest existing at the time of colonization in the sixteenth century has now been destroyed, and destruction is proceeding at a rate of about .8 per cent per year, some 30,000 square kilometers. *See Nature* 345:754 (1990).

83.   *See* note 82.

84.   To detect a change of one-half degree Centigrade in average global temperature requires the analysis of huge amounts of data collected all over the world, and the contributions of tens of thousands of scientists whose work

in many disciplines helps correlate data, interpret results, and correct inaccuracies.

85. The biggest such conference has been the Global Environmental Conference in Brazil in 1992. While the conference failed to produce any concrete plans for action and did not even discuss the sensitive issue of human population growth, it none the less attracted more than one hundred heads of state – quite an accomplishment. The conference also produced a broad accord among nations to attempt to slow the release of greenhouse gasses, retard the extinction of species, and achieve 'sustainable' economic growth. *See* 'Between Stockholm and Rio', Lord Zuckerman, *Nature* 358:273–276 (1992).

86. The 1987 Montreal Protocol called for a gradual reduction in the release of ozone-damaging chlorofluorocarbons (CFCs); as evidence of more rapid destruction than previously estimated mounted, a new accord was signed in 1990 to eliminate production entirely by the year 2000. In 1992, that target was further accelerated when eighty-seven countries agreed to eliminate all CFC production by 1 January 1996. The discharge of CFCs also accounts for some 15 per cent of the increase in the world's greenhouse capacity caused by human activities. *See*, for example, 'Ozone Hits Us Where We Live', *Science* 254:645 (1991).

87. The distances within our solar system are too small to represent anything more than growth for Metaman, but in pushing beyond the solar system Metaman would necessarily be establishing offspring largely separated from itself. The primary obstacle to such expansion is more likely to be the difficulty of establishing viable new colonies than *reaching* other stars with planets. Recent theory suggests that planets may be quite common. *See* 'Occurrence of Earth-Like Bodies in Planetary Systems', G. Wetherill, *Science* 253:535–538 (1991). In 1991, planets circling another star finally seem to have been detected. *See* 'A Planetary System around the millisecond pulsar PSR1257+12', A. Wolszczan and D. Frail, *Nature* 355:145–147 (1992); 'Evidence Grows Stronger for Planets Orbiting an Exploded Star', John Wilford, *New York Times*, page A10, 9 January 1992. Furthermore, the nearest stars could, given rocket accelerations now achievable – but not sustainable, be reached in journeys lasting only a few decades. But how is a viable 'seed' for Metaman to be created? What would be required to found a new colony that could independently spawn a vast new super-organism? What would be needed to mold a planetary habitat into a form that would support life? DNA provides such a set of instructions to propogate biological organisms, but no similar recipe for Metaman exists. To create one will be far more daunting than simply reaching the stars.

88. Some 550 million years to be more precise. *See* note 60.

89. Bones and shells are produced by the controlled deposition of the

calcium phosphate and calcium carbonate secreted by specialized cells. Such secretion is a clear evolutionary extension of the routine elimination of these same minerals by cells generally.

CHAPTER 3

90.   Page 199, *Erewhon*, Samuel Butler (Penguin Books, London, 1985). This book, a very entertaining satire set in a land where machines have been outlawed to keep them from taking over, contains a number of thought-provoking chapters about the relationship between humans and machines.

91.   'A Grandmaster Chess Machine', Feng-hsiung Hsu et al., *Scientific American* 263(4):44–50 (1990). Deep Thought, in mid-1990, compiled an 86 per cent score in fourteen games against international masters and achieved a Chess Federation rating of 2552. Average tournament players rank between 1200 and 1900, experts up to 2200, masters up to 2400, and international masters and grand masters up to about 2900. Deep Thought's designers predict that the next generation of computer chess player, one a thousand times faster, will be able to defeat *all* human players. At checkers, computers are even more competitive with the best human players. In August 1992, the champion checker-playing program, 'Chinook', narrowly lost to the world champion, Marion Tinsley, with 2 wins, 4 losses and 34 draws in a 40-game match. Previously Tinsley had lost only five games in the past forty-two years. *Science News* 142:217 (1992).

92.   For a good discussion of the challenges of developing useful computer vision, *see* 'Computer Vision', Y. Aloimonos, A. Rosenfeld, *Science* 253: 1249–1254 (1991).

93.   For a general discussion of the pace of progress in computers, *see*, for example, *Mind Children: The Future of Robot and Human Intelligence*, Hans Moravic (Harvard University Press, Cambridge, 1988).

94.   Douglas Hofstadter presents a very readable and insightful critique of computational approaches to artificial intelligence. *See* Chapter 26 of his book, *Metamagical Themas: Questing for the Essence of Mind and Pattern* (Basic Books, New York, 1986).

95.   The expression 'massively parallel' is generally applied to computer architecture and means that separate but linked calculations are occurring concurrently in different parts of the computer rather than sequentially at one place. Parallel processing allows great increases in speed. The brain is the ultimate 'parallel processor', since millions of synapses are occurring through-out it at any moment and interacting with one another in complex ways. Indeed, a major reason for believing that capacities such as intelligence,

creativity, and pattern recognition in computers will require massively parallel processing is that the only known 'device' having these capabilities, the brain, is massively parallel. *See* also note 98.

96.   The human brain provides a useful model to imitate in silicon. The so-called 'neural network' programs, which mimic some aspects of learning in our own nervous systems, show promise of eventually allowing computers to learn as we do – from raw experience. For interesting discussions of the new directions being pursued in robotic design and artificial intelligence, *see* 'New Approaches to Robotics', R. Brooks, *Science* 253:1227–1232 (1991), and 'Silicon Babies', Paul Wallich, pages 124–34, *Scientific American* (December 1991). A particularly interesting development is the construction of analog, integrated circuits that mimic the behavior of real nerve cells. These fast, low-power circuits represent one possible path to building artificial nervous systems. *See* 'A Silicon Neuron', M. Mahowald and R. Douglas, *Nature* 354:515–518 (1991). For a fascinating and readable discussion of the nature of intelligence, *see* Marvin Minsky's *The Society of Mind* (Simon & Schuster, New York, 1986).

97.   The ENIAC (Electronic Numerical Integrator and Computer) was the world's first programmable, general-purpose, electronic, digital computer. It had 18,000 vacuum tubes, occupied 300 cubic feet of space, used 140 kilowatts of electricity and was capable of 5,000 calculations per second. *See* page 182, *The Age of Intelligent Machines*, R. Kurzweil, Boston (MIT Press, 1990). Moreover, although ENIAC cost some 3 million of today's dollars, a present-day fifty-dollar calculator is more powerful. *See* page 100, *Bionomics: The Inevitability of Capitalism*, Michael Rothschild (Henry Holt and Co., New York, 1990).

98.   For example, the 1991 version of the 'Connection Machine' by Thinking Machines in Cambridge, Massachusetts, tied together 16,000 processors. *See* pages 140–1, 'Thinking of Machines', *Scientific American*, (December 1991). Most computer designs, however, now use fewer, but more powerful, processors. Parallel machines are particularly good at problems that can be fragmented into many, largely separate parts. For example, in global weather forecasting, the earth's surface is divided into a grid; and it is assumed that the conditions in each square of the grid are only influenced by those in adjacent squares. This breaks an immense problem into many smaller ones that can be worked on simultaneously.

99.   Current computer circuit elements have dimensions on the order of .6 microns. Already, the path is clear to another five to tenfold drop in cross-section, and there are several promising approaches to further substantial size reductions. By comparison, a typical neuron in the brain is some 5 or 10 microns across, although some are much larger.

100.   A major barrier to using multiple layers of computer elements on chips

is the difficulty of conducting away the heat that electronic circuitry produces. Neither optical switches nor superconducting materials, however, generate much heat when they operate, so they may prove important in overcoming this obstacle to the layering of circuitry. As to the operation of the brain itself, it is worth adding that an individual neuron, though it may have thousands of synaptic connections, operates nearly a hundred thousand times more slowly than today's fastest computer circuitry.

101.   For discussion of both sides of this issue *see* the pair of articles: 'Is the Brain's Mind a Computer Program?', John Searle, pages 26–31, *Scientific American*, January 1990 and 'Could a Machine Think?', Paul and Patricia Churchland, *Scientific American*, January 1990. Douglas Hofstadter provides a long and penetrating discussion of Artificial Intelligence in his book, *Gödel, Escher, and Bach: An Eternal Golden Braid* (Vintage Books, New York, 1980).

While computers seem likely to continue to improve their performance, and their ability to manipulate information, they are unlikely to achieve generalized intelligence until they have the ability to interpret and integrate symbolic knowledge without any direct human intervention. One step in this direction has been taken in pattern recognition by creating a neural-net program that does not have to be trained by a human. It learns by trying to achieve a common interpretation from separate images of the same scene. *See* 'Self-organizing neural network that discovers surfaces in random-dot stereograms', Suzanna Becker and Geoffrey Hinton, *Nature* 355:161–163 (1992); 'Learning from your Neighbor', *Nature* 355:112–113 (1992).

102.   For an excellent discussion of possible barriers to the construction of machine consciousness, *see* Roger Penrose's *The Emperor's New Mind: Concerning Computers, Minds, and the Laws of Physics* (Oxford University Press, Oxford, 1989). Penrose believes that intelligence depends on a subtle process (not yet understood) that cannot be mimicked by electronic circuitry. Arguments that machine intelligence will eventually be created are presented in Raymond Kurzweil's *The Age of Intelligent Machines* (MIT Press, Boston, 1990). Kurzweil provides an excellent view of the current capabilities of computer systems and what might lie ahead. His book also includes a number of stimulating essays by experts who have long considered the potentials of AI research.

103.   Already there are so-called 'expert systems', computers that make very good decisions in narrow areas such as oil exploration, medical diagnosis, or investment management by applying rules devised by human experts. These systems have no intelligence, but as they grow ever more complex and utilize ever more rules and information, there ultimately is a point at which they could be said to 'understand'.

104.   A major proponent of this point of view is the philosopher, John Searle.

See, for example, 'Minds, Brains, and Programs', John Searle, in *The Behavioral and Brain Sciences*, Volume 3 (Cambridge University Press), reprinted in *The Mind's I*, ed. D. Hofstadter and D. Dennett (Basic Books, Inc., 1981). For an excellent discussion of this debate, *see* 'Can a Computer have a Mind?', Chapter 1 of Roger Penrose's *The Emperor's New Mind: Concerning Computers, Minds, and the Laws of Physics* (Oxford University Press, Oxford, 1989).

105.   Even with today's relatively simple programs, in certain highly controlled contexts, it is surprisingly difficult for people to distinguish between a human and a computer that has been programmed to imitate human responses. In 1991, the Boston Museum of Science ran its first annual 'Limited Turing contest', named after the great British scientist Alan Turing, who in 1950 proposed that a computer could be considered intelligent if people interacting with it could not tell if they were interacting with a person or a machine. *See* 'Computing Machinery and Intelligence', Alan Turing, *Mind 59*, no. 236 (1950); reprinted in *The Mind's I*, ed. D. Hofstadter and D. Dennett (Basic Books, Inc., 1981). In the Boston contest, funded with a prize set up by the philanthropist Hugh Loebner, a group of judges without computer training interacted with ten terminals and had to determine which were linked to a computer program and which to a human operator. To give the computer programs a chance, the contestants were only given five minutes at each console and only allowed to engage in discussion about a predetermined narrow range of subject matter, such as wines or flower arrangements. One program, a 'whimsical conversationalist', fooled five of the ten judges into thinking it was human. In addition, two of the judges thought that one of the terminals linked to a person was actually tied to a computer. *See New York Times*, page A1, 9 November 1991, and page B5, 5 November 1991. For an entertaining and probing discussion of computer intelligence and the power of the full Turing test, *see* Chapter 22, 'A Coffeehouse Conversation on the Turing Test', pages 492–525, *Metamagical Themas: Questing for the Essence of Mind and Pattern*, Douglas Hofstadter (Basic Books, New York, 1985).

106.   *See* 'Matter, Minds, and Machines', Marvin Minsky, page 431 of *Semantic Information Processing*, ed. Marvin Minsky (MIT Press, Boston, 1968). The introduction of this book (pages 1–32) provides a good overview of the challenge of creating a generalized intelligence in machines.

107.   Page 147, *The Future of the Automobile, the Report of MIT's International Automobile Program*, Allan Altshuler et al. (MIT Press, Boston, 1984).

108.   This constitutes some 60 per cent of the parts of a 747. (Boeing fact sheet, Boeing Commercial Airplane Group, Seattle, Washington, January 1992.)

109.   For example, the so-called Cambrian explosion, the proliferation of

new forms at the beginning of the Cambrian period some 550 million years ago, took tens of millions of years. For a discussion of this major transition in life's history, *see* pages 86–9 of 'Evolution of the Earliest Animals', Bruce Runnegar, Chapter 3 of *Major Events in the History of Life*, ed. J. William Schopf (Jones and Bartlett Publishers, Boston, 1992). *See also* note 60.

110.   The consequences of specialization provide another good example of the similarity between machine and animal evolution. For living things, extreme specialization is perilous because adaptations that are perfect for one particular environment and lifestyle may be unsuited for any other. An insect species that feeds on only one kind of plant often leads a precarious existence because the extinction of that plant will signal the insect's demise. But the cockroach, which can live almost anywhere and eat almost anything, has been around for more than 300 million years.

Extreme specialization is equally perilous for machines. The craniometer, a descendant of the caliper, was used to measure skull dimensions in the nineteenth century when it was believed that brain size and intelligence were closely linked, but when skull measurement fell into disrepute, the device was relegated to museums. Starter cranks for Model-T cars and computer punch cards met the same fate, but the hammer, well suited for many tasks, has a future as secure as the cockroach's.

111.   For an interesting article on the habits of the warty frogfish, *see* 'Frogfishes', Theodore Pietsch and David Grobecker, pages 96–103, *Scientific American*, June 1990.

112.   *See* 'The Misnamed, Mistreated, and Misunderstood Irish Elk', pages 79–89, *Ever Since Darwin*, Stephen J. Gould (W. Norton & Co., New York, 1977).

113.   Technology, however, does more than simply 'discover' natural designs; technology is increasingly able to extend the designs and mechanisms that nature has stumbled on through long evolution. The development of pharmaceuticals provides a good example of such extensions: molecular biologists are increasingly taking naturally occurring enzymes and then modifying them to alter and enhance their properties. Now, materials science is also reaching the point where it can begin to mimic microscopic natural patterns. Ceramics can be made lighter and stronger by imitating the microscopic structure of bones. *See* 'Nature points way to tougher ceramics', *Science News* 140:150 (1991).

114.   The bat, *Taderida*, does this fifty times per second in precise synchrony with its loud ultrasound pulses. This and other aspects of the design of a bat's echo-location system are detailed by Richard Dawkins on pages 21–37 of his marvelous book on evolution, *The Blind Watchmaker: Why the evidence of evolution reveals a universe without design* (W. Norton & Co., New York, 1987).

115.   A remarkable 'non-biological' example of natural selection and evolution is discussed in 'An Approach to the Synthesis of Life', Thomas Ray *in Artificial Life II*, Santa Fe Institute Studies in the Sciences of Complexity, vol. XI, ed. J. Farmer et al. (Addison-Wesley, 1991). This work describes the spontaneous evolution of complex computer programs from small program rudiments that are allowed to mutate randomly in small ways as they compete for memory space and CPU time within a specially created computer environment functioning as a 'virtual' world.

116.   One might question the true independence of humanity's technical solutions by maintaining that engineers often solve problems by copying ideas from the natural world. This is sometimes true: humans watched birds for years, after all, before dreaming of flight. But more often, humans are able to comprehend how nature works only by drawing analogies with independently developed technical solutions. For example, the anatomical structures now known to be heart valves were not recognized as such until mining engineers developed analogous checkvalves in early pumps. The way DNA stores information was comprehended by analogies with written language – indeed the connection was made explicit by the adoption of such terms in genetics as 'translation', 'transcription', and 'genetic dictionary'. *See* pages 3 and 4 of *Cellular Energy Metabolism and its Regulation*, Daniel Atkinson (Academic Press, San Diego, California, 1977).

117.   A fascinating examination of our relationship with the dog is presented by Konrad Lorentz in *Man Meets Dog* (Methuen, London, 1954). He attributes the greater independence of cats to the fact that they have been domesticated only 10,000 to 20,000 years. By comparison, dogs have associated with humans for 40,000 to 50,000 years, enough time for selection to channel their behavior to the point where they can effortlessly inspire our deep affection. Their large success suggests they are able to satisfy some rather basic emotional needs of humans.

118.   For a stimulating discussion of the process by which animals have become domesticated, *see The Covenant of the Wild: Why Animals Chose Domestication*, Stephen Budiansky (William Morrow and Co., New York, 1992).

119.   Only about 150 of the several thousand plant species known to be edible have ever been important enough to be bought and sold in the international arena. A mere twenty plants make up the majority of the world's food today, and wheat, corn, rice and potatoes feed more people than the next twenty-six most important crops. *See* 'The Outlook for New Agricultural and Industrial Products from the Tropics', Mark Plotkin, pages 106–16 of *Biodiversity*, ed. E.O. Wilson (National Academy Press, Washington, DC, 1988).

120.   The role of crops in Metaman is closely akin to that of nitrogen-fixing

bacteria lying within the root nodules of various legumes. The root nodules provide for their bacterial symbionts, and the bacteria in turn nourish their legume hosts by breaking atmospheric nitrogen into nitrates that can be used by the plant. For a detailed discussion of this symbiotic interaction, *see* 'Rhizobium-plant signal exchange', Robert Fisher and Sharon Long, *Nature* 357:655–660 (1992) or 'Developmental Biology for a Plant–Prokaryote Symbiosis: The Legume Root Nodule', J. Nap, T. Bisseling, *Science* 250:948–954 (1990).

121.   It is estimated that even in the US, where the use of insecticide fumigants is commonplace, some 10 per cent of the wheat harvest is destroyed each year by weevils, moths, and other grain-devouring bugs. *See* 'Bugging bugs', *Science* 256:740 (1992).

122.   *See* 'News and Views', *Nature* 352: 16 (1991) for a general description of the technique. M. Tomalski and L. Miller, *Nature* 352:82–85 (1991); and L. Stewart et al., *Nature* 352:85–88 (1991) report details of the experiments. The first research group used scorpion toxin, the second, mite toxin.

123.   Of course, though the biological parasites of today may eventually be largely purged from Metaman by the rapid pace of technological progress, they may be replaced by technological parasites such as computer 'viruses'. These are small computer programs that can 'infect' a computer and copy themselves onto disks or transmit themselves over communication links to reach new machines, where they may destroy work files or cause the computers to crash.

CHAPTER 4

124.   Comparing Metaman's digestion to an animal's reveals that this super-organism's large size and discontinuous form have led to two important extensions of the physiological mechanisms found in animals. Complex industrial operations have superseded the biochemical processes of animal digestion, and a network of far-flung digestive sites has replaced the linear layout of an animal's gut, where food is broken down by successive chemicals secreted by the stomach and pancreas, and then is absorbed as it moves through the intestines. (In an animal, the resultant harvest of diverse small molecules – amino acids, sugars, fatty acids, and minerals – is passed to the liver and converted into molecules such as glucose that are circulated to the rest of the body.)

125.   A single explosive blast may free more than a million tons of iron ore from the walls of a large open-pit mine. Powerful shovels load the rock on trucks that haul it away. The crude ore is then crushed, screened, and washed to remove impurities, and shipped in cargo vessels or slurry pipes to

blast furnaces that will extract the metal. While the iron is still molten, carbon and varying traces of chromium, vanadium and other metals are added to the melt to make the different steels that will be formed into sheets, plates, ingots, bars, wires, and rods. *See* pages 390–3 and 408–12 of *Mineral Facts and Problems, Bureau of Mines*, US Department of the Interior, Washington, DC (1985). This book also provides detailed information about the production of most other minerals.

126. *New York Times*, page B1, 1 August 1990. Fish farming now extends to many species besides trout, including bass, shrimp, salmon, oysters, clams and crayfish. This industry is growing rapidly. In 1980, such farms produced only 1 per cent of all fish consumed in the US, in 1990 some 10 per cent, and the US commerce department estimates that by the year 2000 fish farming will provide 20 per cent.

127. Indeed, time-lapse cinematography at night can render the pulsing flow of vehicle headlights uncannily lifelike and seemingly transform a city into a throbbing organism. The film *Koyaanisqatsi*, produced and directed by Godfrey Reggio in 1983, uses a variety of cinematographic techniques to create wonderful renderings of modern civilization, in which society looks much like an organism.

128. By 1988 there were some 550 million cars, trucks and buses in the world. 'Energy for Motor Vehicles', D. Bleviss and P. Walzer, *Scientific American* 263(3):103–109 (1990). Moreover, there were 3.8 million miles of roadway in the US alone in 1990 (*see* page 599, *Statistical Abstract of the United States*, US Bureau of the Census, 1990), over which 184 million vehicles were driven 2.025 trillion miles. *See* page 170, *The World Almanac and Book of Facts 1991* (St Martin's Press, New York, 1991).

129. Gas main mileage in the US was 1.1 million miles in 1987. *See* page 579, *Statistical Abstract of the United States*, US Bureau of the Census (1990).

130. For example, the Colorado River, which carved out the Grand Canyon, is now reduced to a trickle by the time it crosses into Mexico. By treaty, Mexico is guaranteed a total of 1.5 million acre feet from the Colorado River's yearly flow of some 13 million acre feet. *Cadillac Dessert*, Marc Reisner (Viking, New York, 1986).

131. The closest that human circulation can come to directing materials to specific receiving sites is with such systems as hormones, where molecules are transmitted that have an impact only at a particular location. Also there are some fixed physical shunts for specific large-scale routing, for example, the portal flow carrying the products of digestion from the intestines to the liver. But such flow is not individually and flexibly addressable. Material can not be sent from any location directly to any other location as it is within Metaman.

132. Another key factor is the ability of Metaman's circulatory system to

transport finished products and component parts as well as raw materials. This enables activities to become highly specialized. For example, in addition to basic materials such as lumber and concrete, components such as toilets, heaters, bathtubs, electrical fixtures and refrigerators are used in constructing an apartment complex. All are built at different times and places in diverse, specialized factories.

133.   For a discussion of current thinking about early human evolution, *see* 'Africa: Cradle of Modern Humans', *Science* 237:1292–1295 (1987), or Philip Tobias's 'Major Events in the History of Mankind', Chapter 6 of *Major Events in the History of Life*, ed. J. William Schopf (Jones and Bartlett Publishers, Boston, 1992). The first hominids appeared some 6 million years ago; *Homo habilis* (skillful man), who appeared some 2.5 million years ago, used simple stone tools and is the ancestor of *Homo erectus* (upright man), who appeared some 1.5 million years ago. The first *Homo sapiens* (wise man) appeared some 500,000 years ago, and anatomically modern humans some 200,000 years ago.

134.   Page 828, *Columbia History of the World*, ed. J. Garraty, P. Gay (Harper and Row, New York, 1972).

135.   The first central power station was located at Holborn Viaduct in London and began operation on 12 January 1882; the second was that completed by Thomas Edison in New York City nine months later. *See* page 181, *Encyclopaedia Britannica* (Cambridge University Press, Cambridge, 1987).

136.   Although by the early twentieth century, large power grids and coal-burning power stations were routinely beginning to deliver power widely within particular regions, only since the Second World War has fuel begun to move throughout the world in the vast quantities that would be expected for an integrated biological organism. Global oil consumption has grown twenty-fold since 1940, and only a few countries now remain self-sufficient in energy. *See* 'Energy for Planet Earth', Ged Davis, *Scientific American* 263(3):55–62 (1990).

137.   Animals ingest food and extract biological materials from it, excreting both undigested food and the by-products of their metabolism. Getting rid of undigested food is straightforward: what enters at one end of our gut will, if it isn't absorbed, generally exit from the other end as fecal matter. Strictly speaking, one could correctly maintain that the unabsorbed food in the gut never even enters the body since it is always on the external side of the gut's membrane. Similarly, once urine has entered the bladder it too is external because no membrane separates it from the outside. To eliminate metabolic by-products produced throughout the body is more difficult. In humans, such wastes are collected from individual cells by the circulatory system, filtered from the blood by the kidneys and liver, and eliminated in the urine and feces.

138. The US National Aeronautics and Space Administration (NASA) estimates there are some 7000 grapefruit-sized pieces of debris, 100 to 200,000 marble-sized pieces, and billions of smaller pieces – all travelling at some 17,000 miles per hour. In the past thirty years there have been several near approaches (a mile or so) to tracked objects, and in 1983, *Challenger's* windshield was pitted by a fleck of debris the size of a grain of sand. *See* 'Encountering Junk in Space', page B8, *New York Times*, 10 December 1991.

139. *See*, for example, 'Rules Force Towns to Pick Big New Dumps or Big Costs', Keith Schneider, *New York Times*, page A1, 6 January 1992. Federal regulations enacted in the US in 1991 require new landfills to have plastic and clay liners as well as various environmental equipment such as liquid collection and treatment systems. Because the legislation raised the cost of opening a landfill to more than 10 million dollars and required town dumps to close by 1993 if they could not meet strict new requirements, a rapid consolidation of waste disposal in the US is now underway. Projections suggest that eventually the US will have only a thousand regional landfills instead of the more than 6000 local ones existing today.

For a fascinating article on the composition of solid waste in the US and misconceptions about the waste problem we face, *see* 'Rubbish', William Rathje, pages 99–109, *The Atlantic Monthly*, December 1989. For example, plastic foam, which has been the focus of much recent environmental concern, accounts for less than one-half per cent of landfill volume; the biggest contributors are paper, which constitutes some 40 per cent, and yard waste, which makes up another 18 per cent. Interestingly, because of the lack of moisture in landfills, wastes such as paper and even banana peels often do not biodegrade for many decades.

140. London's first sewer system was built in 1854. *See* page 80, H. Lancaster, *Expectations of Life: A Study in the Demography, Statistics, and History of World Mortality* (Springer-Verlag, 1989).

141. For a discussion of improving the efficiency of industry and tying industrial processes into recycling networks, *see* 'Strategies for Manufacturing', R. Frosch, N. Gallopoulos, *Scientific American* 261(3):144–153 (1989).

142. *The Lion in Winter* was an academy-award winning 1968 film directed by Anthony Harvey and starring Peter O'Toole and Katharine Hepburn.

143. *See* note 153.

144. *See* page 502, *The Discoverers: A History of Man's Search to Know His World and Himself*, Daniel Boorstin (Random House, New York, 1983).

145. The most serious shortcoming of pure barter was that both parties simultaneously had to want something the other would part with, and exchanged items had to be readily transferable and of equivalent value. Credit (the promise to pay at some time in the future) and retrading (the transfer of goods to a third party) gave barter more additional flexibility, of course, but

did not overcome the inherent shortcomings of the tool.

Barter has resurged in international trade in recent decades because it is a way for less developed countries to gain help in selling their goods on the world market. For example, Slovenia may not have the leverage to sell its shoes in the US by itself, but if it barters them as part of a deal for a power plant built by General Electric, then GE can realize their value by using its leverage to arrange for their resale and distribution. Such modern barter is not a primitive throwback, though, because it depends upon the presence of efficient secondary markets linked by global communication. Without these, bartered goods could not be quickly priced, resold, and transferred by the receiver, and they would be relatively worthless. Today's international commercial system thus overcomes the major deficiencies of ancient barter.

146. Even in recent times 'money' has assumed diverse forms; for example, tobacco, rice, cattle and whiskey each served as legal tender at one time or another in colonial America. *See* page 50 of *Money, Whence It Came, Where It Went,* John Kenneth Galbraith (Houghton Mifflin, Boston, 1975).

147. Money was the critical breakthrough that made broad exchanges between humans possible, and standardized coinage, which first appeared in about 1500 BC when the legendary King Midas cast his image on a silver piece, was an ideal monetary device because it created an easy-to-recognize piece of precious metal of known weight. By making it easy for material transfers to include intermediaries, money could organize long sequences of exchange too intricate to track individually, and this has been critical to the appearance of the many specialized activities at the core of every complex society.

148. Page 147, *Henry Varnum Poor: Business Editor, Analyst, and Reformer,* Alfred Chandler (Harvard University Press, Cambridge, Mass., 1956). *See also* page 227, *The Control Revolution: Technological and Economic Origins of the Information Society,* James Beniger (Harvard University Press, Cambridge, Mass., 1986). In 1851, the Erie Railroad was employing 112 people to run nine cars over forty-six miles of track at an average speed of 12 mph. Ten years later, 1325 people were running 1443 cars over 445 miles of track at an average speed of 25 mph.

149. This efficiency, though, carried a price – a rigid production sequence. Henry Ford nicely summed it up as follows: 'Any customer can have a car painted any color he wants, so long as it's black.' As with bureaucratic rigidity, manufacturing rigidity too has begun to disappear with the rise of the computer, which offers new ways of orchestrating complex assembly processes.

150. For example, by 1921, one grocery chain, the Great Atlantic and Pacific Tea Company (A&P), had 15,000 stores and 11 per cent of food sales in the US. *See* page 340, *The Control Revolution: Technological and Economic*

Origins of the Information Society, James Beniger (Harvard University Press, Cambridge, Mass., 1986). This book is an interesting and perceptive examination of the evolution of the modern commercial system. It is well worth reading.

151.   The idea of inventing a brand-name and using it to promote a product massively was pioneered by Quaker Oats, which ran the first national advertising campaign and reinforced it with now common gimmicks such as free samples and product testimonials. In 1882, when Henry Crowell built a large new automated oats plant that could produce twice as much oats as the market would bear, most Americans looked at oats primarily as animal fodder. Rather than sell oats in bulk, as was then common, Crowell put them in distinctive individual boxes sporting the picture of a Quaker, and called them Quaker Oats. The subsequent advertising campaign invented the idea of breakfast cereal and, more significantly, pioneered the now dominant tool for creating demand: the mass advertising of brand-name products. *See* page 265, *The Control Revolution: Technological and Economic Origins of the Information Society*, James Beniger (Harvard University Press, Cambridge, Mass., 1986).

152.   To match production effectively to sales required 'market feedback.' For manufacturers to gauge changing demand quickly enough to avoid making too much or too little of a product, sales needed to be monitored and consumers questioned. First, General Motors, under Alfred Sloan, began to gather sales data continuously and use it to set production levels. Then, others started surveying consumer preferences in order to judge *in advance* whether products would sell. The first such surveys were massive. The Curtis Publishing Company, for example, in 1924 surveyed fully 97 per cent of the households (29,000) in Watertown, New York about their buying habits. By the 1930s, however, the techniques of random sampling had, with little loss of accuracy, succeeded in greatly reducing survey sizes. The effects of polling on society have been immense. For example, it is such surveying that is responsible for the high sexual content in today's advertising. The theme was rarely used before a 1931 Gallup survey indicated that suggestions of sex attracted more attention than any other advertising approach. *See* page 387, *The Control Revolution: Technological and Economic Origins of the Information Society*, James Beniger (Harvard University Press, Cambridge, Mass., 1986).

153.   Except in the unique circumstances of wartime, when limited numbers of products are produced, central planning has not been very effective at orchestrating economic activity. Central planning worked during the Second World War because production goals were clear: military products had priority over commercial ones, and food, clothing, and shelter were produced only at the minimal levels needed to sustain military production. A wartime

economy, though, is far simpler than a vital peacetime one trying to satisfy diverse and changing individual interests. Of course, central planning has also been moderately effective in peacetime economies as long as goals have been narrowly defined and individual choices have been restricted. This is not to say that a market system is most efficient when it is entirely unregulated; but rather that basic market forces seem to be essential in effectively organizing a modern peacetime economy.

154.   Writing, first developed by the Sumerians around 3500 BC, spread to Egypt by 3,000 BC and the Indus Valley somewhat later. Early prototypes to modern Chinese reached China by about 1300 BC. *See* pages 22, 26 and 34 of *The Penguin Atlas of Ancient History,* Colin McEvedy (Viking–Penguin, New York, 1988).

155.   Gunpowder, first made in China around AD 1000, spread to Europe before 1300. *See* page 485, *Columbia History of the World,* ed. J. Garraty, P. Gay (Harper and Row, New York, 1972).

156.   The important question of the influence of the individual on the flow of history is a difficult one. The weather offers some insight on the matter. It is said that a butterfly flapping its wings over China may change the weather at some later time in New York. In chaos theory, such behavior is referred to as 'extreme sensitivity to initial conditions'. *See Chaos: Making a New Science,* James Gleik (Penguin, London, 1987). But there is more to this story. Though the butterfly may change the weather in New York, it will *not* change the climate, nor will a hydrogen bomb. The climate is untouched by such perturbations because it is the product of much larger forces. So it is with history. The details may be as sensitive to small effects – and as unpredictable – as the weather. History is a chaotic process. But, like climate, the overall character and trajectory of history is not easily perturbed, it too is governed by larger forces.

157.   Many good examples of the pervasive influence of technology on culture can be found in music. The broad impact on popular music of Leo Fender's 1948 invention of the electric guitar is a good example. The influence is discussed in the article, 'The Right Instrument at the Right Time', page H27, *New York Times,* 7 April 1991. *Also see* 'Computers are busy setting music on its ear', page D1, *Los Angeles Times,* 5 April 1992. Technology has also greatly altered the role of music in people's lives. Music can now be created and reproduced so easily that it surrounds us. Little of what most people hear today is live; in a sense the most popular 'instrument' has become the loudspeaker.

158.   Of course, the shape of society, and even technology itself, are strongly influenced by the nature of human beings and the natural world. But Alexander's presence (or absence) would have no effect on either of these.

CHAPTER 5

159.   The same occurs within any higher animal. Humans have countless sensory cells responding to light, sound, pressure, chemicals, and temperature. From a touch receptor triggered by an ant's footsteps across one's arm, to a complex assembly of photoreceptors in the retina that 'sees' a distant mountain peak, sensory structures unceasingly feed people information. Properly integrated and interpreted, these data tell a person what is going on. Frequently, the sense receptors do more than just gather raw data, they also perform a complex preliminary analysis of it. The receptors of the inner ear, for example, are intricately organized to do a great deal of local processing before sending signals to the brain.

160.   The Nielson rating service is now introducing meters that attach to a television, recognize a specific person's face and make a continual record telling when that person is watching television. These devices, because they are passive and require no active participation by the viewer, will vastly enhance the accuracy with which public viewing habits are measured. The new devices will make it possible to know whether people are leaving the room when a commercial comes on, and even the precise parts of programs that are causing people to lose interest and switch channels. Such detailed information is likely to have a powerful influence on television program content, and could lead to programming that is extremely difficult to ignore once it is on. In essence, the development is likely to tighten further the influence of viewers upon programming content. See 'Watching Americans watch TV', Erik Larson, pages 66–80, *The Atlantic Monthly*, March 1992.

161.   Page 16, *The Global Telecommunication Traffic Boom: A Quantitative Brief on Cross-Border Markets and Regulation*, Gregory Staple (International Institute of Communications, Tavistock House South, London, 1990).

162.   As technology continues to advance, the State's ability to control individuals directly is likely to diminish further. For instance, though it is very difficult to block free speech effectively in a country with a well-developed modern communications system, it is none the less possible: telephone lines can be tapped and communications monitored. But now we are at the point of having inexpensive encryption systems that are nearly unbreakable and capable of coding and decoding messages rapidly. Soon, even the government's largest computers may have difficulty deciphering the private telephone messages of anyone who wishes to prevent it. Indeed, the US government is so concerned about the prospects of being unable to engage effectively in wiretapping that it is attempting to regulate the use of encryption technology to prevent this. See 'A Public Battle over Secret Codes', *New York Times*, page C1, 7 May 1992.

These encryption systems are based on what are called trap-door algorithms. Each person has two code numbers, one public and the other private. A message encrypted using one code can only be deciphered using the other code. Thus, if people publish their public codes and keep their private codes secret, anyone can send anyone else a message but only the proper recipient can read the message. The whole process of encryption and decryption and code exchange can then be automated using computers. *See* 'The Mathematics of Public-Key Cryptography', Martin Hellman, *Scientific American*, August 1979. For a discussion of how encryption could be used to guard the privacy of all financial transactions and data-base information, *see* 'Achieving Electronic Privacy', David Chaum, *Scientific American*, pages 96–101, August 1992.

163. In the US alone, there are over 220 million phones and 1.3 billion miles of telephone lines (*1987 Statistical Abstract of the US*, US Bureau of the Census, Washington). The growth of international telephone traffic shows the speed with which Metaman is integrating globally. The 145 million international calls from the US in 1980 had grown over five-fold by 1988, to 813 million. (Statistics of Communication Common Carriers, Federal Communications Commission, Washington, DC, 1989.)

164. *See New York Times*, 13 November 1991. The estimate of 50 per cent data transmission is for 1991; within a decade an estimated 80 per cent of telephone traffic will be data transmission.

165. Already, plans for a global, satellite-based network for mobile phones is being discussed. *See* pages 14–15 and 69–71 in the 28 March 1992 issue of *The Economist*, or 'The Ultimate Portable-Phone Plan', page C1, *New York Times*, 18 March 1992 for an overview of the systems being proposed and the industrial consortia involved. A pact allocating global radio frequencies for such systems has been signed by 124 nations. *See* page C5, *New York Times*, 4 March 1992.

166. The Usenet confederation includes the members of most major networks within the 12,000 separate network domains, primarily corporations and universities, linked by Internet. Usenet traffic in July 1988 was 4.04 megabytes per day and 1,800 messages, in 1989 it was 6.6 megabytes per day and 3,000 messages, in 1990 it was 11.8 megabytes per day and 5,000 messages, and by July 1992 it had reached 35 megabytes per day and 14,000 messages. Details about Usenet are from personal communications with Brian Reed of the Digital Equipment Corporation, who since 1986 has been making detailed measurements on communication within Usenet. An attempt to examine some of the larger implications of the spread of computer networks can be found in *The Network Nation: Human Communication via Computer*, Starr Hiltz and Murray Turoff, (Addison Wesley Publishing Co. 1978).

167. Information flows electronically, and it also moves in physical packets

that stream through Metaman's circulatory system. Videotapes, compact discs, scientific journals, computer discs, and books are familiar. But a far more important and sophisticated information packet – a human being – is rarely viewed as such. People are much more than 'information packets', but this doesn't change the fact that they move immense amounts of information from place to place and sift through that knowledge with dazzling speed and efficiency to find what is needed. Someone may be able to read a manual to find how to set up a piece of new equipment, but it is so much easier to be visited by an expert who has the information in his or her head.

Time and again, immigrants with new skills arrive on foreign shores to found new industries. German immigrants brought America their brewing experience and established the beer industry in the US; Jewish immigrants did the same with the garment industry. *See Ethnic America: A History*, Thomas Sowell (Basic Books, New York, 1981). Human movement – to and from meetings, conferences, remote offices and educational facilities – is a powerful way of carrying information. But as advances in telecommunications enable people to project an increasingly realistic presence from afar, travel will undoubtedly become less important and will constitute an ever diminishing fraction of overall communication within Metaman.

168. A unique monument may last several thousand years; a building, a few hundred years; tools and other devices, far less. The durability of these objects saves time and energy because their utility – and their cost – can be spread over several generations, but eventually they are gone. *See also* note 14.

169. Language, the foundation of people's ability to preserve and communicate what they know and experience, is believed to have arisen some two million years ago. *See* page 154, 'Major Events in the History of Mankind', Phillip Tobias, chapter 6 of *Major Events in the History of Life*, ed. J. William Schopf (Jones and Bartlett Publishers, Boston, 1992). Language made possible the complex social exchanges needed in any large human grouping and greatly expanded people's ability to teach others. Enormous amounts of knowledge were preserved using only language and memory. Today, in an age when people barely use their memories, some of us are happy just to remember the names of the people we meet. Long epic poems such as the 250,000-word *Iliad*, however, were originally exclusively oral, and Peter of Ravenna, author of a 1491 text on systems of memory, boasted of being able to recite verbatim two hundred speeches of Cicero and 20,000 points of law. For an excellent examination of the use of memory systems in ancient times, *see* chapter 60 of *The Discoverers: A History of Man's Search to Know His World and Himself*, Daniel Boorstin, (Random House, New York, 1983).

170. Writing's origins seem to lie in a simple need: to retain counts of things. This need, which arose only after agriculture increased population enough to create larger communities, was solved by using a pictorial

representation followed by a tally. From these rudimentary beginnings, the Sumerians developed pictographs (by 4000 BC), which later led to Egyptian hieroglyphs, and Sumerian cuneiform. By about 2500 BC, there were three literate civilizations in the world: those of the Nile Valley, the Indus Valley, and the basin of the Tigris-Euphrates. *See* pages 22–8, *The Penguin Atlas of Ancient History*, Colin McEvedy (Viking-Penguin, New York, 1988).

171.   A fascinating discussion of the transition to printing and its diverse influences on society is presented in Daniel Boorstin's 'Widening the Communities of Knowledge', pages 480–556 of *The Discoverers: A History of Man's Search to Know His World and Himself*, Daniel Boorstin (Random House, New York, 1983).

172.   The profound impact of the arrival of printing is shown by its effect on language. Printing enabled the vernacular tongues – French, German, English, Spanish, Italian, Portuguese – to eclipse Latin (previously the language of all educated Europeans) and opened science and literature to a wider community. This brought an intellectual renaissance that saw the creation of true national languages. France, for example, in 1200 still had five major dialects, so a student from Brittany could not understand a fellow student from Marseilles; but with printing centered in Paris, that regional dialect displaced the others and in 1539 was proclaimed 'official' French by King Francis I. A mere 500 years ago, many thousands of local dialects dominated small geographical regions; today over half the world's population uses one of eight written languages.

  The ensuing flowering of France's national literature through the works of Rabelais (1483–1553), Ronsard (1524–85) and Montaigne (1533–92) was repeated elsewhere in Europe as true national languages came into being. *See* chapter 65 of *The Discoverers: A History of Man's Search to Know His World and Himself*, Daniel Boorstin (Random House, New York, 1983).

173.   Block printing appeared in China around AD 700 and reached Europe 600 years later, but in neither East nor West was its influence far-reaching. Movable type also was first developed in China, but the use of some 30,000 different characters instead of an alphabet kept it from achieving much importance there. The story was different in Europe. There, the combination of movable type, which Gutenberg also developed, and Western alphabets finally created a mechanism for efficiently duplicating written text. Its impact was tremendous. See chapter 62, 'Widening the Communities of Knowledge', pages 480–556 of *The Discoverers*, Daniel Boorstin.

174.   Page 533, *The Discoverers*, Daniel Boorstin. Moreover, only after printing arrived did 'books' began to assume their modern form with numbered pages, an index, a table of contents, and a title page. Each of these innovations was enormously significant. Without page numbers, material could not readily be cited; without an index and table of contents, information

could not readily be located. Before printing, in fact, there was only infrequent indication of the author of a manuscript. It was printing and the use of title pages that created the modern author. *See* Chapter 65 of *The Discoverers*, Daniel Boorstin.

175.   For example, work is now underway on small computer programs called 'knowbots' that could migrate through computer networks to seek information for their originator. These programs would shuttle around getting information and directions from other like programs until they finally found the information they were seeking. Then they would collect the information and return to the sender with it. *See* 'Learning to Drink from a Fire Hose', M. Waldrop, *Science* 248: 674–675 (1990).

176.   The potential for learning about human genetics through widespread genetic screening and observation of humans is discussed in 'The Human as an Experimental System in Molecular Genetics', R. White, C. Caskey, *Science* 240: 1483–1488 (1988).

177.   Smoking is responsible for about 350,000 annual deaths in the US each year, including about a third of all cancer deaths. *See* 'Health and Economic Implications of a Tobacco-Free Society', K. Warner, *Journal of the American Medical Association* (JAHA) 258(15): 2080–2086 (1987), and *Banishing Tobacco*, William Chandler, Worldwatch Paper No. 68, Worldwatch Institute (1986).

178.   See, for example, 'Statistics of chronic disease control', Richard Peto, *Nature* 557: 557–558 (1992), a commentary illustrating some of the kinds of treatment information to be obtained from broad clinical trials.

179.   The development of a global brain is also suggested by the amount of effort our modern society devotes to information handling. In 1800 in the US, agricultural production occupied 87 per cent of the civilian labor force, by 1880 it accounted for only 44 per cent of the labor force, manufacturing 25 per cent, and information processing 6 per cent, but by 1980 information processing had grown to 48 per cent of employment, while manufacturing was only 28 per cent and agriculture less than 2 per cent. *See* pages 23, 24 of *The Control Revolution: Technological and Economic Origins of the Information Society*, James Beniger (Harvard University Press, Cambridge, Mass., 1986.)

Calculating the fraction of Metaman's energy involved in information processing would be difficult, but the demands this activity will make on Metaman's metabolism will eventually be very high. After all, our own brains use about a quarter of the total calories we consume!

180.   It is easy to recognize that Metaman is able to process information, but it is not easy to label this 'thinking'. One reason is that Metaman's large-scale integration of information is so slow compared to our own thoughts and activities that we barely perceive it; another is that we credit ourselves with Metaman's information processing. But not only does our collective activity

within Metaman transcend the individual, Metaman's pace of information processing and action is entirely appropriate to its scale. Metaman does 'think', and furthermore its thoughts are becoming increasingly complex. It is intriguing to consider whether one day this giant super-organism will also have a consciousness of its own.

181.   It took the arrival of computers, satellites, and telecommunications to enable large clusters of humans and machines scattered throughout the world to begin to integrate detailed data about society and the environment into an increasingly clear global picture of population, natural resources, trade, disease, or even weather. For example, we now take weather maps for granted, but no storm system had been seen in its entirety before 1947, when a V-2 rocket took the first weather photographs. See *Watching the World's Weather*, W. Burroughs (Oxford University Press, Oxford, 1991). Such developments are giving Metaman an increasingly clear 'vision' not only of its environment, but of itself. And these are the rudiments of large-scale self-awareness, and perhaps even the early stages of eventual consciousness.

182.   *1987 Statistical Abstract of the US*. US Bureau of the Census, Washington, DC (1987).

183.   'The complete DNA sequence of yeast chromosome III', S. Oliver et al., *Nature* 357: 38–46 (1992). *See also* 'Ever-longer sequences in prospect', John Maddox, *Nature* 357: 13 (1992). For a discussion of the results now being achieved by bringing robotics and industrial techniques to gene sequencing efforts, *see* 'New French genome centre aims to prove that bigger really is better', *Nature* 357: 526–527 (1992).

184.   In some realms, the human component of Metaman's 'thinking' is far less apparent than in science. In guiding a spaceship, a human may choose the ultimate destination, but a computer determines the best trajectory and how to achieve it. In routing a call through the telephone network, no human hand is necessary. In designing a computer chip, a computer determines large portions of the physical layout of the circuit.

185.   Another example of this phenomenon is the enormous attention the world immediately gave the civil war in Yugoslavia and the many years it took for awareness of, and concern about, the far bloodier strife in Somalia to build. *See New Yorker*, page 23, 6 January 1992.

186.   People who long inhabit any locale become attuned to their environment and often are aware of subtle climate changes extending over decades, but these are local or regional, not global. For every person claiming to have been aware of climatic warming long before the 'scientists', there is another person somewhere else who professes to have seen no such change . . . or even cooling. Moreover, newspaper commentaries that a record heat wave heralds global warming are no closer to the truth than those denying the effect because the last few summers have been cold. Significant warming has

occurred in specific areas, but warming as a global effect is still nearly negligible – less than one degree Centigrade during the past century. *See also* note 285.

187. *See* note 283.

188. *The Future of Man*, Teilhard de Chardin (Harper and Row, New York, 1964). Written in 1920 and published some 40 years later.

CHAPTER 6

189. According to a recent poll, half of Scots favor outright independence, and another quarter favor home rule. 'Scots' Sentiments Surge Towards Independence', page H3, *Los Angeles Times*, 25 February 1992.

190. For example, merchant fleets have now largely migrated to international registries where they are not tightly controlled; in 1990 more international shipping was under the Panamanian flag than any other. As of 1 January 1990, the size (in billions of gross tons) of the largest merchant fleets in the world were: Panama 3.2, USSR 2.4, Liberia 1.4, China 1.3, Cyprus 1.1, Japan 1.0, Greece .9. Together these countries represent 50 per cent of the world's 23 billion tons of merchant shipping. *The World Almanac and Book of Facts 1991* (St Martin's Press, New York, 1991).

191. 'Germany's Gene Law Begins to Bite', Patricia Kahn, *Science* 255:524–527 (1992).

192. 'Change: Microchips and Transnational Companies Lead', *Los Angeles Times*, 26 November 1989.

193. Page C1, *New York Times*, 21 November 1991.

194. Honda exported 12,000 cars from the US to Japan in 1990 and expects to be exporting 25,000 to Japan by 1994. *See* 'Honda to Export', *New York Times*, page C4, 20 December 1991. For more information, *see* 'Honda's New Wagon: A US Auto, Almost', *New York Times*, 14 March 1990. Significantly, US trade officials have maintained to European negotiators that Honda cars made in the US should be treated as American cars when tariffs are assessed. *See* page C1, *New York Times*, 16 September 1991.

195. *See*, for example, 'Does "Buy American" Mean Buying Trouble', page A1, *New York Times*, 27 January 1992, or 'An American Dilemma', page D1, *Los Angeles Times*, 30 July 1992.

196. For a quick overview *see* 'The Stateless Corporation', *Business Week*, 14 May 1990.

197. The December 1991 agreement in Maastricht in The Netherlands committed the EEC to the creation of a single currency and a regional central bank by 1999. It also specified the framing of a common defense policy, and governments pledged to coordinate their policies on police, judicial, and

immigration matters. For details of the agreement, *see* page A5, *New York Times*, 9 December 1991. This extension of the EEC integration already underway has, however, met with a decidedly mixed reaction from the populations of its member countries and may need to be renegotiated. In 1992, Ireland overwhelmingly confirmed it, Denmark narrowly rejected it, and France narrowly approved it. The step towards *political* union is an immensely symbolic one that elicits serious misgivings among many people. Economic union, however, is moving forward powerfully regardless of any hesitations on the political front, and will compel ever closer ties.

198.   In October 1991 the EEC reached agreement with the European Free Trade Association of Sweden, Finland, Norway, Iceland, Switzerland, Austria and Liechtenstein to form a nineteen-nation free-trading zone. In December 1992, Swiss voters decided by a margin of 50.3 to 49.7 per cent not to ratify the agreement, but Sweden, Norway, Finland and Austria are likely to join the EEC itself. And several Eastern European countries are also likely to seek and eventually gain admission to the community.

199.   *See* note 197.

200.   Moreover, global corporations will increasingly become not just 'transnational', but 'multidomestic'. That is, having such breadth that they can appear to be a domestic company wherever they are operating. A good example of this is Asea (Asea Brown Boveri Group) which runs a global matrix of companies containing some 1300 legal entities scattered throughout the world. *See* 'The Very Model of Efficiency', Roger Cohen, *New York Times*, page C1, 1992.

201.   Page C1, *New York Times*, 5 July 1991. 'Chip Deal Ties IBM to Siemens'. Moreover, in 1992 IBM, Siemens and Toshiba agreed jointly to develop a 256-megabyte memory chip (enough to hold 10,000 pages of typed text), which is some sixteen times more powerful than the 16-megabyte chip, the highest capacity chip in production in 1992. This 256-megabyte chip is estimated to cost more than a billion dollars to develop and is likely to be available before the turn of the century. The research will take place at the IBM facility in New York. *See New York Times*, page C1, 13 and 14 July 1992. *See also note 400.*

202.   *See* 'Technology Transcends Borders', page A1, *New York Times*, 1 January 1992. Between 1980 and 1984, there were 345 alliances between the US and Europe, 101 between Europe and Japan, and 274 between Japan and the US. Between 1985 and 1989, there were 593 alliances between the US and Europe, 150 between Europe and Japan, and 309 between the US and Japan. Thus the decade totals are 1772 alliances: 938 between the US and Europe, 251 between Europe and Japan, and 583 between Japan and the US. Information supplied by the Maastricht Economic Research Institute on Innovation and Technology, Maastricht, Holland.

203.   It is not true that trade imbalances will necessarily bring currency devaluations that correct those imbalances, because there are far larger flows of capital not associated with trade. The daily transfers of funds to and from stock, bond and currency markets and between other financial instruments dwarf those that result from trade. In 1988, trade among Japan, the US and Europe amounted to some 600 billion dollars *annually*, which is less than the current *daily* volume of foreign exchange transactions in the world's currency markets. *See* Chapter 10, 'The FX Empire', of Kenichi Ohmae's excellent book, *The Borderless World: Power and Strategy in the Interlinked Economy* (Harper Business, 1990). It is now beyond the capacity of national governments to manage currency exchange rates by direct currency transactions; governments don't have enough resources. In 1992, the total foreign currency reserves held by all of the world's governments totalled some one trillion dollars, a single day's trading volume in the world's currency markets. *See* page A1, *New York Times*, 25 September 1992.

204.   For example, between 1980 and 1989, US imports from Japan increased from 30 to 93 billion, and Japanese imports from the US increased from 21 to 44 billion dollars. Moreover, joint ventures between US and Japanese companies have become routine; even the US space station program involves Japanese and European participation.

205.   European countries, of course, have had numerous joint ventures and shared scientific facilities for years. Some specific ventures are: CERN (Conseil Européen de Recherches Nucléaires), ESRF (European Synchrotron Radiation Facility), JET (Joint European Torus), and ESA (European Space Agency). These are very successful projects. For example, on 9 November 1991, the JET, using a mixture of deuterium and tritium, produced the first controlled fusion to release significant power (about a megawatt). This put the European program ahead of efforts in the US, Japan and Russia, and now all four programs have agreed to proceed jointly with a more advanced reactor, ITER (International Thermonuclear Experimental Reactor). *See New York Times*, page 88, 28 July 1992, and page A1, 11 November 1991.

Space exploration, however, is the quintessential example of a realm that will demand ever more cooperation. Estimates of the cost of a manned mission to Mars run so high – some 500 billion dollars – that any such enterprise is nearly certain to be international when it takes place. *See* 'A New Order in Space', page 46, *World Press Review*, January 1992. This article also discusses the growing international competition in the commercial exploitation of space.

206.   For instance, India is now seeing television broadcasting such as CNN and MTV from satellites. The programs are distributed by small neighborhood cable companies. By 1991 Bombay alone had 100,000 homes wired for

cable. *See* 'TV comes in on a dish', page A4, *New York Times*, 29 October 1991.

207. Bridges, airports, train stations, movie theaters, and office buildings today are quite similar the world over because their forms embody their functions. Many buildings and homes, of course, are traditional in style, but they are often older constructions. The origin of the modern architectural style emphasizing the primacy of function lies in the work of the German architect Walter Gropius and the Bauhaus movement. The Am Horn House exhibited in 1923 marked the beginning of the international style, which spread rapidly after the Second World War to transform skylines with the modern styles so commonplace today. A fascinating examination of this architectural transition can be found in O.B. Hardison's *Disappearing Through the Skylight* (Viking Penguin, New York, 1989).

Not only do cities have an increasingly similar look, they also are becoming increasingly similar in the way they operate. Entering a distant city for the first time, a visitor who does not know its layout is already familiar with most of its basic workings. Buses, taxis and subways provide public transportation. Hotels provide lodging. And, of course, there are airports, train stations, movie theaters, restaurants, traffic lights, stores, and phone booths. All big cities work in essentially the same way. Small differences can be frustrating: unable to understand the language in a foreign country, a tourist might never figure out how to use a public phone. But if everyone had the same native language, most cities in the world would feel uncannily similar.

208. One reason the clothing of Navajo Indians, Hawaiian islanders, or Chinese farmers was so distinctive is that it reflected the materials, lifestyle and climate of a specific locale. No longer; within Metaman the same dyes and cloths are available everywhere, people are ever more insulated from the weather in micro-environments, and regional variations in human activities are diminishing.

209. For a broad discussion of the influences of the early voyages of discovery on modern cuisine, *see Why We Eat What We Eat, How the Encounter Between the New World and the Old Changed the Way Everyone on the Planet Eats*, Raymond Sokolov (Summit Books, New York, 1991).

210. Films have also become internationalized, as can be seen by the foreign profits of Hollywood films. *Terminator II*, for example, had 490 million dollars in total receipts, and only 205 million dollars of that was in the US. In 1986, foreign receipts comprised 40 per cent of the earnings of US studios; in 1991, the figure was 46 per cent, and by the year 2000 it is expected to be as high as 70 per cent.

211. *New York Times*, 12 August 1991. By comparison, only 35 per cent of the fiction programs were French. Among the most popular American shows were *Twin Peaks, The Cosby Show, Santa Barbara, Miami Vice* and *LA Law*.

The prevalence of English in France is further discussed on page B1, *New York Times*, 3 March 1992.

212.   This increasing development of standards is natural in an evolving super-organism because living things characteristically have parts that operate by the same mechanisms as one another. Our bodies, for example, store energy not in a host of different molecules, each particular to its own specific organ or tissue, but as glycogen and fat throughout. Similarly, we employ the same neurotransmitters in brain, heart and foot. Such 'standards', facilitate the cooperation between parts and make an organism more efficient and adaptable than one whose parts all work in fundamentally different ways.

213.   English is even being taught in rural China. *See* page A7, *New York Times*, 6 May 1991.

214.   The French journal *Comptes Rendus*, for example, now publishes in English, and so does *Toyo Gakuho* (Japan), *Al-Katib* (Egypt), *Acta Crystallographica* (Sweden), *Clavileno* (Spain), *Kogo Misul* (S. Korea), *Kutsch* (Switerland), to name only a few. *See also* 'Publish in English, or perish?', *Nature* 648:356 (1992).

215.   *See* 'Endangered Languages', *Science* 251:159 (1991). Of the world's 6000 existing languages, about half will probably die outduring the next century because few, if any, children speak them. In fact, only about half of the world's languages now have more than 5000 speakers. Some 300 languages are considered safe from extinction, but even seemingly unthreatened languages can die out very rapidly. Breton, for example, had some 1 million speakers in living memory and now has very few children who speak the language, and the same is true of Navajo, which had 100,000 speakers only a generation ago. *See* 'On Endangered Languages and the Safeguarding of Diversity', Ken Hale, The 65th Annual Meeting of the Linguistics Society of America, Chicago, 3 January 1992.

216.   Page 128, *Atlas of the World Today*, N. Grant and N. Middleton (Harper and Row, New York, 1987). Some 100,000 books a year are published in English and nearly as many in several other languages, but only a few hundred are published in Swahili. For example, in 1983, 75,000 books were published in the US alone, 80,000 in the Soviet Union, 60,000 in West Germany, 40,000 in Japan, and 40,000 in France. The same year, however, saw only 200 published in Kenya, and some of these were in English rather than the official Swahili.

217.   When the global store of written information is computerized and becomes broadly available through computer networks, the incentives to learn a major language will be even greater. One day, computers may be able to translate written materials cheaply, but this is unlikely to happen soon enough to save the vast majority of minor languages.

For a discussion of some current approaches to automating language translation, *see* 'The Education of the Silicon Linguists', *Science* 253:854–855 (1991). To be applied broadly, any computerized language translator will have to be both competent and *economical*. Thus, developing any specific translator (and each will have to overcome many problems unique to it alone) will require strong economic incentives that are lacking for many languages. An English–German translator will long precede an English–Swahili one, because the incentives to develop the latter would not be sufficient until translation technology became very routine.

218.   *See*, for example, 'Iran can't stem the tide of Western Culture', Chris Hedges, *New York Times*, page A12, 28 March 1992; also 'Jihad Vs. McWorld', Benjamin Barber, pages 53–63, *The Atlantic Monthly*, March 1992.

219.   For example, in Rome, individual slaves might be freed, slaves might even revolt, but no-one questioned the justness of the institution of slavery itself . . . even the slaves themselves. *See* pages 64–5, *A History of Private Life: From Pagan Rome to Byzantium*, ed. P. Aries and G. Duby (Harvard University Press, Cambridge, Mass., 1987).

220.   *The Merchant of Prato*, Iris Origo (Penguin Books, London, 1963). The quoted merchant lived in Prato, a small town outside Florence. *See also* page 4 of *Is Science Necessary?*, Max Perutz (Dutton, New York, 1989).

221.   In 1794, following the French Revolution, slavery was abolished in France, the first European country to do so. Then, at the Congress of Vienna in 1807, the trading in slaves was banned. Slavery was abolished in Britain in 1833, in the US in 1864, and in Brazil in 1888.

222.   Page 57, *A History of Private Life: From Pagan Rome to Byzantium*, ed. P. Aries and G. Duby (Harvard University Press, Cambridge, Mass., 1987). An interesting discussion of the Roman institution of slavery and the lot of slaves in this period can be found on pages 51–94. About a quarter of the agricultural workers were slaves. *See also* 'Industrial Slavery in Roman Italy', W.L. Westermann, *Journal of Economic History* 2:149–163 (1942).

223.   In 1848 Karl Marx wrote in *The Communist Manifesto*, 'The proletariat have nothing to lose but their chains. They have the world to win. Working men of all countries unite!' Early industrialists were able to extract enormous work from laborers at very low cost because workers had little leverage to balance the power of owners. Thus, such images likening early labor practices to slavery were not so far from the mark. *See* Karl Marx and Frederick Engels, *The Communist Manifesto* (Labor News Company, New York, 1948).

224.   Page 27, *Ethnic America: A History*, Thomas Sowell (Basic Books, New York, 1981).

225.   John of Salisbury's discussion of the natural hierarchy of human society

illustrates clearly how ludicrous universal equality would have seemed in that era. *See* note 3.

226. The division of the developed world into Eastern and Western blocs limited the growth of connections between these two regions as Metaman emerged. The division was deep enough to create serious dangers of conflict, but it was hardly deep enough to cause a real split into two separate super-organisms. There was too much communication, trade, and even travel, and the division of less than fifty years was too short for development to diverge significantly. Broad interaction between the populations may have been greatly diminished, but each bloc was constantly gathering intelligence and information on the other.

227. The reunification of Germany provides a compelling illustration of the power of economic forces: the political reunification process was overwhelmingly driven by the economic forces unleashed by the lifting of the iron curtain.

228. In 1992 in Barcelona, Abram Rhwala, a welterweight boxer from Soweto, became the first black South African ever to compete in the Olympics. South Africa, barred from the Olympics since 1960, fielded a team of ninety-five athletes including eight blacks. *See* page A1, *Los Angeles Times*, 27 July 1992.

229. The US provides a revealing illustration of the need for an educated work force, because without attracting large numbers of educated foreigners to work and study in America, it would be unable to remain competitive. In effect, the US utilizes foreign educational facilities to supplement its own internal labor needs. Because of this dependency, any significant tightening of US immigration policy towards skilled workers and students would almost certainly imperil the long-term health of the American economy, which may well experience significant shortages of trained scientists and engineers anyway. *See* 'Supply and Demand for Scientists and Engineers: A National Crisis in the Making', R. Atkinson, *Science* 248:425–432 (1990).

CHAPTER 7

230. In 1988, the hottest year in a century, heat and drought reduced the US grain harvest by 27 per cent from its 1987 level. *See* page 63, 'Feeding the World in the Nineties', Lester Brown and John Young, *State of the World – 1990* (W.W. Norton & Company, New York, 1990).

231. In the winter of 1992, chlorine monoxide concentrations above the Arctic rose to the highest values ever recorded in those regions. *See Science* 255:798–799 (1992); page B7, *New York Times*, 4 February 1992.

232. The Maldive's UN petition was prompted by severe flooding caused by

tidal waves in 1987 (*see* United Nations Agenda Item 86, 12 October 1988). In 1990 the country had a population of 219,000, and consisted of 1,087 islands with a total area of 115 square miles, much of which was less than 6 feet above sea level. Recent projections of sea-level rise are only about half of the .9 meters projected in 1987. As of 1992, the best estimate for the rise of sea level by the year 2100 was some .5 meters. *See* 'Implications for climate and sea level of revised IPCC emissions scenarios', T. Wigley and S. Raper, *Nature* 357:293–300 (1992). While still far from inconsequential, the world-wide problems of coastal inundation, river-delta flooding, and water-table salination that rising sea levels would bring now seem unlikely to be as significant as many other environmental and social problems. For a discussion of the damages that would be caused by a rise in sea level, *see* 'Holding Back the Sea', Jodi Jacobson, pages 79–97 of *State of the World – 1990*. (W.W. Norton & Company, New York, 1990). It is worth noting that some studies now suggest that while sea levels would eventually rise as a result of global warming, the immediate result would be a fall in sea level. *See* 'Will greenhouse warming lead to Northern Hemisphere ice-sheet growth?', Gifford Miller, Anne de Vernal, *Nature* 355: 244–246 (1992). For a critique of this conclusion, *see* 'Will sea level rise or fall?', Stephen Schneider, *Nature* 356:11–12 (1992).

233.   Though not accepted by all, the idea that human hunting caused these extinctions seems more likely than the other major theory – that the extinctions were the result of global climate change. A powerful argument for human causation is that such extinctions occurred in different places at different times, each roughly coincident with the arrival of large numbers of humans. In North and South America 78 of the 102 species of large mammals (those weighing more than 100 pounds) became extinct 10,000 to 12,000 years ago. In Australia, 19 of 22 such animals disappeared around 15,000 years ago. On many of the islands in the Pacific, Mediterranean and Caribbean the extinctions occurred between 1,000 and 6,000 years ago and were even more severe because they included many small animals as well. *See* 'Twilight of the Hawaiian Birds', Jared Diamond, *Nature* 353:505–506 (1991). If the extinctions had been in response to any large-scale climatic change it seems likely they would have all occurred simultaneously. Paul Martin presents other weaknesses in the arguments for climate as the source of these extinctions in 'Refuting Late Pleistocene Extinction Models', pages 107–30 of *Dynamics of Extinction*, ed. D. Elliot (John Wiley & Sons, New York, 1986). Arguments for a climatic source for these extinctions is presented by Russell Graham in 'Plant-Animal Interactions and Pleistocene Extinctions', pages 131–54 of the same book.

234.   Moreover, these changes arrive silently and almost unnoticed, a

by-product of the everyday activity of billions of humans setting fires, raising cattle, planting crops and driving cars.

235. The US, Russia, Britain, France and China all have large nuclear arsenals and seem likely to continue to maintain them. In addition, India has tested nuclear weapons, and both Israel and Pakistan are believed to possess limited nuclear capabilities. North Korea and Iran may or may not be developing such capabilities. At this time there are no other nuclear powers and no immediate prospects for others to appear. All states of the former Soviet Union have agreed to transfer their weapons to Russia. South Africa, Brazil and Argentina have recently foresworn nuclear weapons and signed the 1968 Non-Proliferation Treaty. Iraq's budding nuclear potential has been dismembered. *See* 'Nuclear Non-proliferation Policy Issues in the 102nd Congress', Zachary Davis, Environmental and Natural Resources Policy Division, US Government Printing Office, Washington, DC, 1992. *See also* 'Finally France will Sign Nuclear Pact', *New York Times*, 4 June 1991.

236. Page 1 of *Retreat from Doomsday*, John Mueller (Basic Books, New York, 1988) also Paul Schroeder, *Wilson's Quarterly* 9:84–93 (1985).

237. As it turned out, the Gulf War was probably an economic windfall for the US. America's estimated costs of 61.1 billion dollars for the war were almost completely compensated by substantial payments – totalling 53.8 billion by mid-1992 – from Japan, Germany, Kuwait, Saudia Arabia and other nations. And US 'expenses' may have been overstated in various ways; for example, military armaments were used that will probably never be replaced and would have otherwise become obsolete, and various personnel costs would undoubtedly have been incurred even without the war. For detailed cost analysis, *see* 'Persian Gulf War: US Costs and Allied Financial Contributions', Stephen Daggett and Gary Pagliano, May 1992, Order Code IB91019, Congressional Research Service, Washington, DC.

238. In 1984, for example, Japan spent 1 per cent of GNP on its military, Germany 3.3 per cent, the USSR 11.5 per cent, the US 6.4 per cent, the United Kingdom 5.4 per cent, and France 4.1 per cent. *See World Military and Social Expenditures 1987–88*, World Priorities, Washington DC, 1987.

239. France and the Austro-Hungarian empire were at war during the periods 1792–4, 1801–2, 1805–6, and 1813–14. The creation of the German nation by Bismarck in the 1860s brought no end to such struggles. There was the Franco-Prussian War (1870–1), the First World War (1914–18) and the Second World War (1939–45). *See The Penguin Atlas of Recent History*, and *The Penguin Atlas of Modern History*, Colin McEvedy (Viking-Penguin, New York, 1988).

240. The Mexican-American War lasted from 1845 to 1847. With the defeat of Mexico, the US seized the present states of New Mexico, Arizona, California, Nevada, Utah and Colorado. *See* pages 811 and 902, *Columbia*

History of the World, ed. J. Garraty, P. Gay (Harper and Row, New York, 1972).

241.   The reporting of the 1991 war in the Persian Gulf demonstrated how completely the experience of war has changed for those who stay at home. Hourly satellite news reports transformed the struggle into a sort of grisly international sporting event complete with instant replays, sideline commentary, cheering supporters, and hissing critics. The juxtaposition of images of American soldiers in desert tents watching the Super Bowl, interviews with residents of bombed neighborhoods in Tel Aviv, live eyewitness accounts of air raids on Baghdad, military news conferences in Washington, and oil-covered cormorants in the Persian Gulf created a surreal immediacy to the struggle.

242.   For example, though the Iraqi government was reviled in Western news reports, never were the people themselves represented as other than victims. In contrast, during the Second World War, before the age of mass communications, public hostility towards the 'enemy' was fanned by war propaganda and embraced vicious ethnic and racial slurs. This allowed a sharp line to be drawn between 'us' and 'them', between 'good' and 'evil'.

243.   The advances in military technology since Vietnam have been dramatic but have none the less not overshadowed the growing disincentives for war. Modern technology now enables a major power to take harsh punitive action against a less-developed country, but not much more. The US wreaked havoc on Iraq's military while suffering few casualties and injuring relatively small numbers of civilians – less than 5,000 by some estimates – but any US attempt to conquer and administer Iraq might well have turned into a bloody quagmire. Not only do the broadcast media make it politically costly for developed countries to repress civilian populations harshly, but technology also enables even relatively backward countries to inflict heavy terrorist if not battlefield casualties. The loss of 240 American Marines and 40 French paratroopers in two terrorist attacks in Lebanon in October 1983 are stark reminders of the dangers of military occupations. The days of knife-wielding natives charging Gatling guns are gone for ever.

As to casualties during the Gulf War, Greenpeace estimates that 110,000 to 150,000 Iraqi troops and 5,000 to 15,000 civilians died in the Gulf War, and that the brief but bloody disorder immediately following the armistice was responsible for all but a few thousand of the civilian deaths. *See New York Times,* page 15, 12 June 1991. The US Census Bureau estimates that 40,000 Iraqi soldiers and 5,000 civilians died during the war, that 30,000 people died in the Shiite and Kurdish rebellions immediately after the war, and that 70,000 died from health problems brought by the loss of power and water facilities. *See New York Times,* page A5, 7 March 1992.

244.   The diminishing chances of intentional war between major powers

does not address the important matter of accidental conflict in our nuclear age. An accidental nuclear exchange remains a possibility, but whatever its horror, it would not be Armageddon. When 50,000 nuclear weapons were stockpiled in the arsenals of five nuclear powers against a backdrop of severe global tension, it was easy to imagine an accident triggering global holocaust. But now that the Cold War is over, such a scenario seems improbable. Without deep political tension worldwide, an accidental nuclear discharge – or even an intentional nuclear exchange in some bitter regional conflict – would stand little chance of triggering a global nuclear war. Moreover, with economic and cultural integration drawing nations ever closer, humanity is unlikely to see again the extremely high level of global military tension characteristic of recent decades. For information about nuclear proliferation, *see* note 235.

245. Immediately following the First World War, the world was full of bold prophesies about an end to war. For example, in 1914 H.G. Wells said of the First World War, 'This, the greatest of all wars, is not just another war – it is the last war!' That they were greatly premature does not mean that they weren't essentially on the right track. *See* page 56, *Retreat from Doomsday*, John Mueller (Basic Books, New York, 1988).

246. Some world leaders maintain that there is not yet a crisis, that there is enough to feed the world and that the only problem is one of distribution. This may have been true in 1960 when world population was only 3 billion, but today it is true only when harvests are good, and soon it will be patently false. (*See* note 255.) Moreover, who would seriously maintain that keeping a population from starving is enough in this day and age?

247. The current average growth rate of the world's population is 1.8 per cent per year, which would bring a doubling of population in only forty years. Moreover, some 90 per cent of the planet's population increase is outside of the developed world. An excellent discussion of the dimensions of the population problem can be found in *The Population Explosion*, Paul and Anne Ehrlick (Simon & Schuster, New York, 1990).

248. Recent studies have shown, however, that the image of steadily expanding deserts caused by overgrazing is greatly oversimplified. The boundaries of the Sahara, for example, have shifted unpredictably in the past few decades. From 1980 to 1990 the Sahara grew some 7 per cent, but this growth includes a 15 per cent expansion from 1980 to 1984 and an 8 per cent contraction during the rest of the decade. *See* 'The Ebb and Flow of the Sahara,' page B9, *New York Times*, 9 July 1991

249. For an excellent discussion of the global problem of depleted or overused water resources, *see Water: Rethinking Management in an Age of Scarcity*, Sandra Postel, Worldwatch paper 62, Worldwatch Institute, Washington, DC, 1984.

250.   A 1992 UN study indicated that some 10 per cent of the world's productive soil, about 3 billion acres, has been badly damaged by human activity. The worst damage is in Asia and Africa. According to the study, 35 per cent of the damage is the result of overgrazing, 30 per cent results from deforestation, and 28 per cent is the product of poor agricultural practises. *See New York Times*, Page A1, 25 March 1992.

251.   *The Population Bomb*, Paul Ehrlich (Ballantine, New York, 1968).

252.   *See* page 771 of *The 1991 World Almanac and Book of Facts*, ed. M. Hoffman (Pharos, New York, 1991). Hong Kong's 1991 population density of 247,000 people per square mile was the largest of any city in the world; New York's in the same year was 11,500.

253.   Page 40, *The Population Explosion*, Paul and Anne Ehrlich (Simon & Schuster, New York, 1990).

254.   Sometimes notions such as sending our excess population to colonize space are bandied about, but they are obviously absurd. If humankind could fill every large commercial passenger jet with people and send the 10,000-plane armada to the moon each year, population growth would slow from 95 million a year to 92 million a year – hardly enough to be noticed.

255.   In the 1960s and 1970s food production more than kept pace with population growth because more land was put into production, more fertilizers were used, and better strains of grain were introduced. In the past few years, however, this has not been the case. Agricultural production has actually fallen slightly. Not only is erosion, desertification, salination, and encroaching urban growth now removing land from agricultural production, but crop yields have stabilized and so much fertilizer is used that farm production now gains little from using more. For an excellent discussion of these issues, *see The Changing World Food Prospect: The Nineties and Beyond*, Lester Brown, Worldwatch Paper 85, Worldwatch Institute, Washington, DC, 1988

256.   Genetic engineering has been applied already to over fifty plant species and hundreds of field tests have been performed, but large-scale commercial application of genetic techniques to the enhancement of crop strains is still only in its infancy. For a general discussion of this field, *see* 'Transgenic Crops', Charles Gasser and Robert Fraley, pages 62–9 of *Scientific American*, June 1992. *See also* note 255.

257.   For a discussion of the ecological consequences of eating meat, *see* note 374.

258.   Modern efforts to curb population have been aggressive in some countries, almost non-existent in others. China's two-decades-old family planning program has been one of the most successful. In 1970, China's population was 800 million and growing at an annual rate of 2.6 per cent which, if unchecked, would have led to a population of 1.8 billion by the year

2000, far more than the 700 million long-term carrying capacity of China estimated by the Chinese environmental agency. Thus, in 1971, the Chinese leadership launched the *wan-xi-shao* ('later-longer-fewer') program to control its population. It was extraordinarily successful, and in 1990 the population stood at 1.1 billion and the growth rate at about 1.4 per cent. At this rate of growth, China's population in the year 2000 will be 1.3 billion, some 500 million less than might have occurred without the program. *See* pages 205–7 of *The Population Explosion*, Paul and Anne Ehrlick (Simon & Schuster, New York, 1990). Also 'An Uncompromising Position', *ZPG Backgrounder*, Zero Population Growth, Washington, D.C..

India has made much less progress and is moving down a path that will make it more populous than China early in the next century. In India in the 1970s, an aggressive and successful birth-control program offered cash inducements to men who would voluntarily be sterilized. Unfortunately, the program, by also offering large bonuses to local administrators, generated a variety of abuses and coercive methods that created a large public backlash and brought the effort to an abrupt end in 1980 following the death of its architect, Sanjay Gandhi. This fiasco has blocked effective family-planning efforts in India until very recently. Some other democratic societies have been much more successful. Thailand, for example, halved its fertility rate in only eight years. *See* page 8, *The State of World Population 1991*, United Nations Population Fund, New York.

Africa has had the least success controlling its population growth. Indeed growth there seems more likely to be curbed by famine and disease than family planning, and some demographers even calculate that African population growth will cease early in the next century because of the AIDS epidemic. For a discussion of Africa's many problems, *see* Blaine Harden's *Africa: Dispatches from a Fragile Continent* (Norton and Co., New York, 1990). *Also see* 'Reversing Africa's Decline', Worldwatch Paper 65, June 1985; and 'The spread of HIV-1 in Africa: sexual contact patterns and the predicted demographic impact of AIDS', R. Anderson et al, *Science* 352:581–588 (1991). *See also* note 387.

259. *See* page 3 of 'Denial in the Decisive Decade', Sandra Postel, pages 3–8, *State of the World 1992*, Lester Brown et al (W.W. Norton and Company, New York, 1992). Moreover, the average woman bears seven children in the Middle East and Africa, and only two in developed lands; Kenya's population is growing by more than 4 per cent each year, while Germany's, Sweden's, and Austria's are decreasing. Page 17, *Atlas of the Environment*, Geoffrey Lean et al (Prentice Hall, New York, 1986).

260. *See* page 32, *Population Images*, Robert Fox et al, United Nations Fund for Population Activities, 1987.

261. In the decade 1911–20, the death and birth rates in India were in

balance, 48.6 and 48.1 per 1,000 respectively; by the decade 1951–60 the death rate had fallen to nearly half the birth rate, 22.8 compared to 41.7; by the 1981 to 1986 period, the death rate tumbled further, to about a third of the 1986 birth rate, 12.2 versus 33.2. Thus, though birth rates declined significantly during the period, death rates dropped far more rapidly and a surge of population growth resulted. In less than seventy years, from 1921 to 1988, the population of India rose from 251 to 796 million. The cause of the change is clear: it is the dramatic change of life expectancy at birth, which rose from 20.1 years (1911–20) to 41.2 (1951–60) to 56.0 (1981–86). *Statistical Outline of India 1989–90*, Department of Economics and Statistics, ed. D. Pendse (TATA Press Ltd, Bombay, 1989).

262.   The lack of focus on family-planning issues in the past few decades has slowed basic contraceptive research to the point where dramatic new developments may not occur for a decade or more, but such technologies as end-of-the-month contraceptive pills, reversible male contraceptives, or contraceptive vaccines would be likely to have major impacts.

An excellent discussion of the reasons for the relative dearth of research on birth control, particularly in the US, is provided in Carl Djerassi's excellent article, The Bitter Pill, *Science* 245:356–361 (1989). One of the major impediments in the US is the immense potential product-liability costs. Until legislation curbs such litigation, it is unlikely that the American pharmaceutical industry will develop any significant new birth-control products. Indeed Depo-Provera – a long-acting injectable contraceptive first produced in the early 1970s and currently marketed in some ninety countries worldwide by the American company Upjohn – was recommended for approval in the United States by the Food and Drug Administration only in 1992. *Science* 256:1754 (1992).

263.   Contraceptive vaccines work either because they block fertilization by creating antibodies to sperm, or because they contain antigens from the surface of the egg and thus cause the body to produce antibodies that destroy its own eggs. Primate testing on such vaccines has already begun, and they might well eventually lead to a procedure that, with a single vaccination (possibly oral), would provide several years of safe, reliable, and reversible birth-control to humans. Such vaccines might be administered orally or even with infectious bacteria. For a good overview of this work, *see* 'New animal vaccines spread like diseases', page B5, *New York Times*, 26 November 1991, and 'Contraceptive vaccines: possibilities with a sperm surface egg-binding protein', Jen-yuc Tsai and Lee Silver, from 1992 National Institutes of Health conference, *Opportunities in Contraception: Research and Development*, in press.

Besides direct work on developing a human contraceptive vaccine, progress in this realm is moving ahead on two other fronts: First, there is work underway to develop vaccines to sterilize pets without surgery. Second, genetically engineered viruses have been used to immunize populations of wild foxes in Belgium against rabies, and researchers are trying to use similar techniques to cause infertility to control rabbit populations in Australia. These vaccines can be administered orally using bait, but attempts also are underway to deliver them using infectious viruses. *See* 'Large-scale eradication of rabies using recombinant vaccinia-rabies vaccine', B. Brochier et al, *Nature* 354:520–522 (1991); Immunization in the field, R. Anderson, News and Views, *Nature* 354:502–503 (1991); 'Control of Rabies in Wildlife', William Winkler and Konrad Bogel, *Scientific American*, June 1992.

264.   *See* note 263.

265.   The potential for population growth to be halted in the less-developed world by AIDS and other diseases is also a distinct possibility. The immense burst of population growth at the margins of Metaman during the past century could bring a temporary return in these regions to times when disease ravaged populations to hold them in check. One way or another, human population growth will cease. *See* note 383 and 387.

266.   *Global Population Assistance Report 1982–1989*, United Nations Population Fund (UNFPA), NY, 1990.

267.   'Setting a Limit', *Zero Population Growth Fact Sheet*, Zero Population Growth, Washington, D.C., 1990. Nor are less-developed regions generally reluctant to implement family planning measures, they spend some 2.6 billion dollars of their own money (four times as much as the international assistance they receive) on such programs. *1990 Report on Progress Towards Population Stabilization*, Population Crisis Committee, Washington, D.C. 1991.

268.   *Global Population Assistance Report 1982–1989*, United Nations Population Fund (UNFPA), New York, 1990; *1990 Report on Progress Towards Population Stabilization*, Population Crisis Committee, Washington, DC 1991. International family-planning assistance in 1990 came from the following sources: government assistance $534 million, private philanthropy $40 million, multilateral development banks $85 million. To reach the year 2000 target of $5.5 billion in assistance from the developed world, the UN projects that these sources would need to contribute respectively $4 billion, $500 million, and $1 billion annually.

269.   In 1988, global military spending totaled some 900 billion dollars. *World Military and Social Expenditures*, R. Sivard, World Priorities, Washington, DC, 1989.

270.   'The Role of Induced Abortion in the Fertility Transition of Latin America', Seminar on the Fertility Transition, Buenos Aires, Argentina, 3 April 1990. *See also* page 29, *The Global Politics of Abortion*, Jodi Jacobson, Worldwatch Paper 97, Worldwatch Institute, Washington DC, 1990.

271.   'Setting a Limit', *Zero Population Growth Fact Sheet*, Zero Population

Growth, Washington, DC, 1990. As a specific example of the potential for progress, consider Kenya, where current rates of population growth would increase population from the 22 million it is today to 37 million by the turn of the century. In 1990 only 27 per cent of women in Kenya were using contraceptives, but 75 per cent said they wanted to limit family size. *See* 'Kenya Fights its Baby Boom', page 67, *World Press Review*, July 1990.

272.   For example, with IUDs in Kenya in 1990 costing 14 per cent of per capita GNP, birth-control pills 37 per cent, condoms 7 per cent, and sterilization 88 per cent, is it any wonder that only a quarter of women there were using contraceptives? For a country-by-country analysis of the cost of contraception, *see Access to Affordable Contraception: 1991 Report on World Progress Towards Population Stabilization*, Population Crisis Committee, Washington DC, 1991.

273.   See page 25, *The Global Politics of Abortion*, Jodi Jacobson, World-watch Paper 97, Worldwatch Institute, Washington DC, 1990. This book is an excellent discussion of the abortion issue and its relationship to family planning. Of particular interest is the clear reduction in abortion rates when contraceptives and family planning services are readily available, and the sharp rise in abortion rates when such services are unavailable.

274.   In Argentina, the abortion rate for women with five or more children is over twice that for women with a single child or without children. In Kenya, 75 per cent of abortions are provided to women who already have children. *The Global Politics of Abortion*, Jodi Jacobson, Worldwatch Paper 97, Worldwatch Institute, Washington DC, 1990.

The experience of Romania illustrates that the best way to halt population growth *and* to reduce the number of abortions is to increase spending on family planning significantly. In an unpopular attempt to increase Romania's population, President Ceausescu outlawed contraceptives in the early 1980s and made abortions a criminal offense, in some cases punishable by death. During this repressive period, Romania had one of the highest abortion rates in the world, ten times that in the Netherlands, where abortion laws are very liberal.

The annual abortion rate in Romania was 9 per 100 women of childbearing age. *See* page 1, 26 of *The Global Politics of Abortion*, Jodi Jacobson, Worldwatch Paper 97, Worldwatch Institute, Washington DC, 1990. With the demise of European communism, the birth rate has fallen significantly throughout Eastern Europe, some 25 per cent in Romania between 1987 and 1990, for example. 'Birth Rates Plummeting in Some Ex-Communist Regions of Eastern Europe', *New York Times*, page A3, 31 December 1991. *See also*, 'The Abortion Fight – Again', page 30, *World Press Review*, June 1991.

275.   The history of the abortion debate in the US is an interesting one. In 1800, no state had laws on abortion and a woman could terminate a pregnancy

up until the time she felt fetal movement. Throughout the 1800s, various restrictions on abortions were passed, but abortions early in a pregnancy were considered a misdemeanor and depended on a woman's own testimony that she had felt 'quickening', that is fetal movement. By 1900, most abortions were illegal. *See* 'Editorial: The Contraception/Abortion Issue: Should We Get Involved?' *Endocrinology* 127(4):1559–1560 (1990).

Before modern methods of contraception, many women used abortion as their exclusive form of birth control (more than 10 per cent of women in Britain in the 1920s and '30s, for example). Estimates of other forms of birth control in Britain during this period are: vaginal cap 30 per cent, coitus interruptus 15 per cent, total abstinence 12 per cent, condoms 10 per cent, douche 9 per cent. It seems likely that in earlier times, before even these birth-control devices, the use of abortants was significantly higher. For an interesting discussion of birth control methods in this period, *see* 'Birth Control in Britain During the Interwar Years', C. Davey, *Journal of Family History* 13(3):329–345 (1988).

276.   In 1985 and 1986, President Reagan withdrew US funding from the International Planned Parenthood Federation and the United Nations Population Fund on the grounds that these organizations were funding abortions. *See* 'Exporting Misery', pages 16–17, *Scientific American*, August 1991. Continuing the Reagan policies, in 1989, President Bush vetoed a bill to restore US support to Population assistance programs. *The Population Explosion*, Paul and Anne Ehrlich, Simon & Schuster, 1990. One of President Clinton's first acts in 1993, however, was to restore these funds.

277.   After avoiding the population issue for more than a decade, many environmental groups in the US have become active in this area again. In 1991, the National Wildlife Federation, the Sierra Club, the Audubon Society, the World Wildlife Fund, and some 100 other groups resolved to make reducing population growth a top priority. 'News and Comment', *Science* 252:1247 (1991). *See also*, 'Economists start to Fret Again About Population', *New York Times*, 18 December 1990.

278.   See William McNeill's *Plagues and Peoples* (Anchor Books, New York, 1989) for an interesting and thought-provoking examination of the serious impact of disease upon the course of history.

279.   Page 180, William McNeill, *Plagues and Peoples* (Anchor Books, New York, 1989). McNeill estimates the Amerindian population of Mexico to have been between 25 and 30 million at the time of Cortez's arrival in 1519, only 3 million by 1568, and a mere 1.6 million by 1620.

280.   See Chapter 2, 'War Advocacy Before World War I', *Retreat from Doomsday*, John Mueller (Basic Books, New York, 1988).

Before the First World War, war was variously considered natural, manly, noble, and even glorious. It was not generally viewed even as a necessary evil. For example, the German poet Friedrich Schiller (1759–1805) wrote.

> Man is stunted by peaceful ways,
> In idle repose his courage decays. . .
> But in war man's strength is seen,
> War ennobles all that is mean.

In a similar vein, John Ruskin wrote in 1866 that 'All healthy men like fighting, and like the sense of danger; all brave women like to hear of their fighting, and of their facing danger.' In 1900, Winston Churchill commented that on the field of battle life is 'at its best and healthiest' as one 'awaits the caprice of the bullet.' In 1910, even the pacifist William James commented that 'military feelings are too deeply grounded to abdicate their place among our ideals until better substitutes are offered.' *See* pages 39, 41, 43 of *Retreat from Doomsday.*

281.   *See* page 603, *QUID 1991*, Dominique and Michèle Frémy (Editions Robert Laffont, SA, Paris. 1991).

282.   *See* for example 'The Global Warming Panic', W. Brookes, Forbes, December 1989. *See also* the article, 'Haze Clouds the Greenhouse', Richard Monastersky, *Science News* 141: 232-233 (1992), which discusses how sulfur pollution may be temporarily balancing some of the warming brought by increased concentrations of atmospheric carbon dioxide.

283.   Almost no serious scientists dispute that the concentration of greenhouse gases – carbon dioxide, methane, and CFCs (Chlorofluorocarbons) – have risen in recent decades because of human activity, or that the 'greenhouse' trapping of heat by these gases will *eventually* raise the earth's surface temperature, or that the temperature of the globe has risen about one degree Fahrenheit in the past century. Today's scientific debate is only about how much global warming will occur and how long it will take to happen. Present climatic models are not sophisticated enough to answer these questions conclusively, but they are none the less suggestive. *see*, for example, 'Global Warming Trends', P. Jones and T. Wigley, *Scientific American*, August 1990, or the ice-core record: climate sensitivity and future greenhouse warming, C. Lorius et al, *Nature* 347: 139–145 (1990) *See also* note 286.

284.   Since record-keeping of the average world temperature began in 1951, the warmest year on record was 1990, and the second warmest was 1991. In fact, all six years from 1986 to 1991 have been among the warmest nine years of this period. Cooler temperatures (and increased ozone depletion) caused by the 30 million tons of sulphur dioxide hurled into the atmosphere by the June 1991 volcanic eruption of Mount Pinatubo in the Philippines, however, are now being felt and will persist as long as 3 years. 'Mount Pinatubo Aerosols, Chlorofluorcarbons, and Ozone Depletion', Guy Brasseur and

Claire Granier, *Science* 257:1239–1242 (1992), and *Science* 251:274 (1991). *See also, New York Times*, page A15, 9 January 1992.

285.   There has been an increase of about three-quarters of a degree centigrade in global temperature during the past century, which seems to correlate with the increase in carbon dioxide that has been occurring. It has been suggested that this temperature increase may have resulted from changes in solar radiation during the period 'Length of the Solar Cycle: An Indicator of Solar Activity Closely Associated with Climate', E. Friis-Christensen, K. Lassen, *Science* 254:698–700, 1991), but more recent work indicates that rising greenhouse gasses have probably been the dominant force in this temperature rise. *See* 'Keeping the sun in proportion', Andrew Lacis and Barbara Carlson, *Nature* 360:297–298 (1992) and 'Solar cycle length, greenhouse forcing and global climate', P. Kelly and T. Wigley, *Nature* 360:328–330 (1992).

286.   *See* 'Next steps on Global Warming', *Nature* 348:181–182 (1991), or *Science News* 141:365 (1992). For a discussion of different assumptions about population growth, economic growth, and technological development *see* 'Implications for climate and sea level of revised IPCC emissions scenarios', T. Wigley and S. Raper, *Nature* 357:293–300 (1992).

There is still little understanding of how local weather and precipitation would change in response to global warming. Computer modeling suggests that the higher latitudes, such as Europe and North America, will show more dramatic warming: more than twice as much as equatorial regions. These models, however, are too crude and the influence of the oceans and clouds too poorly understood to make confident predictions about such details concerning global warming. *See*, for example, *Modelling the hydrological cycle in assessments of climate change*, D. Rind et al, *Nature* 358:119–123 (1992).

287.   Pages 193, 208–210, 252–254 of *Paleoclimatology*, T. Crowley, G. North (Oxford University Press, Oxford, 1991).

288.   For a brief general discussion of past ice-ages, *see New York Times*, page 85, 16 January 1990.

289.   The last glacial maximum extended from 22,000 to 14,000 years ago. During this period, glaciers 3,500 to 4,000 meters (2 to 2.5 miles) thick covered large parts of northern North America and Europe, and the sea level was roughly 120 meters lower than it is today. During the subsequent 4,000 years, the ice receded and in the past 10,000 years we have enjoyed an interglacial. Pages 47–54 of *Paleoclimatology*, T. Crowley, G. North (Oxford University Press, Oxford, 1991). This book is a readable, comprehensive treatment of the earth's climatic history, and also discusses global warming in some detail. For maps of the maximum ice-age glaciation in North America and a general history of our growing understanding of the origins of ice-ages,

see Ice Ages: Solving the Mystery, J. Imbrie, K. Imbrie (Enslow Publishers, New Jersey, 1979).

290.   The patterns of glaciation and deglaciation that have existed during significant periods of the earth's history are driven by orbital variations of the earth. The planet's orbit around the sun shifts every 100,000 years between a nearly circular and a more elliptic path; the tilt of the earth oscillates with a period of 41,000 years, and the elliptical orbit of the earth precesses around the sun with a period of some 20,000 years. Together these produce the Milankovitch effect – cyclic changes in solar radiation with a period of roughly 100,000 years. Pages 132–137, *Paleoclimatology*, T. Crowley, G. North (Oxford University Press, Oxford, 1991). Pages 141–175, *Ice Ages: Solving the Mystery*, J. Imbrie, K. Imbrie (Enslow Publishers, New Jersey, 1979).

291.   The current interglacial has now lasted between 10,000 and 13,000 years, and no interglacial in the last half-million years has lasted for longer than 12,000 years. Modelling suggests that, in the absence of greenhouse-induced global warming, the earth would within a few thousand years begin to move towards a period of glaciation, and probably with various fluctuations reach maximal glaciation within some 50,000 years. *See* pages 177–187 *Ice Ages: Solving the Mystery*, J. Imbrie, K. Imbrie (Enslow Publishers, New Jersey, 1979); pages 256–258, *Paleoclimatology*, T. Crowley, G. North (Oxford University Press, Oxford, 1991).

292.   For example, studies on Greenland's ice cap indicate that the North Atlantic took less than fifty years to shift from glacial to warmer conditions at the end of the last ice-age, when a cold period, known as the Younger Dryas (11,000 to 10,000 years ago) ended. Greenland warmed by some 12 degrees Fahrenheit during these few decades. *Science News* 135:374 (1991) and 142:199 (1992). Such things are possible because shifting ocean currents can bring sudden and dramatic climate changes. If the Atlantic Gulf Stream were to stop for instance, Northern Europe would become *very* cold, *very* rapidly. At the end of the Younger Dryas, a warming in the surface temperatures of the North Atlantic of approximately 8 degrees Fahrenheit occurred within about forty years. *See* 'Sudden changes in North Atlantic circulation during the last deglaciation', Scott Lehjman and Lloyd Keigwin, *Nature* 356:757–762 (1992). Although a 12-degree temperature shift in fifty years is much more rapid than was thought possible in 1990, a recent report makes even this change seem gradual. A detailed analysis of Greenland ice cores suggests that this shift actually took place in only two or three years. *Science News* 142:404 (1992).

293.   For example, during the 1987 El Nino, rising sea-level temperatures led to the formation of large anvil clouds that then cooled the oceans by reflecting solar radiation. This cloud-formation mechanism is thought to limit maximum sea-level temperatures from global warming to about 87 degrees

Fahrenheit. 'Thermodynamic Regulation of Ocean Warming by Cirrus Clouds deduced from Observations of the 1987 El Nino', V. Ramanathan, W. Collins, *Nature* 351:27–32 (1991); 'Limits to greenhouse warming?', Andrew Heymsfield and Larry Miloshevich, *Nature* 351:14–15 (1991).

294.   Currently, the cheapest 'power source' in the developed world is conservation. Improving energy efficiency and reducing the demand for energy is effectively the same as adding more generating capacity.

295.   Biomass fuels are those derived directly from plant matter. Burning them does not add to atmospheric carbon dioxide, because the carbon in the fuel was taken from the air by the plant during its growth and if not burned would still eventually return to the atmosphere when the plant died and decayed. Ethanol and methanol are the most common biomass fuels, but it is their source rather than their nature that makes them biomass fuels. Methanol derived from coal would, just as gasoline, add previously buried carbon to the atmosphere when it burned. For an assessment of progress at producing such fuels at competitive prices, *see Science* 232:1469 (1991).

296.   *See* notes 289 and 291.

297.   Photovoltaics (the generation of electricity directly from sunlight) and solar-thermal generation (the use of sunlight to heat water or other fluids and use them to generate electricity) are already competitive at sites not connected to existing power grids – for example, in isolated geographical regions or underdeveloped countries. These solar technologies are also becoming competitive for generating the additional power needed by utilities at times of peak load.

In mass production, photovoltaic technologies would be capable of generating power today for somewhere around 15 cents per kilowatt hour, some three times the 5 or 6 cents per kilowatt hour figure for coal. But photovoltaic cells, when used in concentrating systems that focus large areas of sunlight on to each photovoltaic cell, will be capable of generating power for about 12 cents per kilowatt hour by 1995, 8.5 cents by 2000, and 5.3 cents by 2010. *See* pages E1–10, *Technology Characterization*, State of California Energy Resources Conservation and Development Commission, Alec Jenkins et al, November 1991. Solar-thermal generation, already technologically capable of generating electricity at about 7 cents per kilowatt hour, holds even greater immediate potential. *See* note 330.

The fossil-fuel costs of 5 to 6 cents per kilowatt hour, of course, include no allowance for the indirect social costs of pollution, mining and greenhouse warming – estimated to be a cent or more per kilowatt hour. Solar power has a large role to play in electrical power generation in the future, and whenever the transition to solar power becomes economically feasible or environmentally necessary, the shift may be rapid because new solar power plants can be brought into operation in only one to two years. 'Photovoltaics Today and

Tomorrow'. H.M. Hubbard. *Science*, 244: 297–304. 1989. *Also see* pages 27–45 *Cool Energy: The Renewable Solution to Global Warming, A report by the Union of Concerned Scientists* Michael Brower (Cambridge, Massachusetts, 1991), and 'Chemical Fuels from the Sun', I. Dostrovsky, pages 102–107, *Scientific American*, December 1991, for a discussion of ways of generating storable fuels using solar energy.

298.　In 1991, wind power was generating 1,600 Megawatts of electricity in California, some 1.5 per cent of the electrical power in that state. Further, new turbines in windy areas could generate power at a cost of about 5 cents per kilowatt hour, cheaper than oil or gas and about the same cost as coal. *See Nature* 354:344–345 (1991). *Also see* pages 45–52, *Cool Energy* Michael Brower.

299.　Page 23, *Cool Energy* Michael Brower. *Also see* page 27, 'Designing a Sustainable Energy System', C. Flavin and N. Lenssen, pages 21–38, *State of the World 1991*, ed. Lester Brown (Norton and Co., New York, 1991). This article presents a good overview of the bright prospects for renewable energy sources in the near future and also provides an excellent discussion of the way the general mix of energy sources will likely shift as the world moves away from fossil fuels. Generally, though, significant shifts in the mix of global energy supplies take at least fifty years to occur. *See* 'Energy Sources: A Realistic Outlook', Chauncey Starr et al, *Science* 256:981–987 (1992).

300.　Page H4, *Los Angeles Times*, 7 April 1992. For a discussion of the great potential of wind power, *see* 'Energy from the Sun' Carl Weinberg and Robert Williams, *Scientific American* 263:146–155 (1990). The author estimates that wind power might supply more than ten per cent of US electricity capacity by 2010 at a cost under four cents per kilowatt hour.

301.　'Windfarms may energize the future', *Wall Street Journal*, 6 September 1991; 'Power to the Wind', page H1, *Washington Post*, 17 November 1991.

302.　*See Scientific American*, 'Energy for the Developing World', A. N. Reddy, J. Goldemberg. 263(3):111–118. 1990.

303.　In 1989, the US department of energy reported China's coal reserves as between 30 and 50 per cent of world reserves. Page 100, *International Energy Annual: 1989*, US Department of Energy, Washington, DC. 1989. For additional information on China's future energy needs and capacities, *see* 'Energy for the Soviet Union, Eastern Europe, and China', W. Chandler, A. Mararov, Z. Dadi, *Scientific American* 263:120–127 (1990).

304.　For example, *see* 'Difficult Algebra for China: Coal=Growth= Pollution', Sheryl WuDunn, Page A1, *New York Times*, 25 May 1991.

305.　'Energy for the Developing World', A.N. Reddy, J. Goldemberg, *Scientific American* 263(3):111–118, 1990.

306.　Page A1, *New York Times*, 26 November 1992.

307. Page B7, *New York Times*, 9 April 1991, and page A6, 16 November 1991.

308. *See* note 85.

309. The general approaches that might be taken in trying to slow global warming are discussed in 'How to Slow Global Warming', D. Victor, *Nature* 349:451–456 (1991) and 'Realistic Mitigation Options for Global Warming', Edward Rubin et al, *Nature* 257:148–149, 262–266 (1992). Indications are that US emissions, for example, could likely be reduced from 10 to 40 per cent at relatively low cost.

310. *See* note 299.

311. Ice cores in Greenland suggest that 10,500 years ago the North Atlantic region warmed some 12 degrees Fahrenheit in less than 50 years. Page 374, *Science News*, 17 June 1989. For a discussion of climate data from ice cores, *see* 'Tales from Ice Time', *Science News* 140(11):168–172 (1991) and 'Irregular glacial interstadials recorded in a new Greenland ice core', S.J. Johnson et al, *Science* 359:311–313 (1992). *See also* note 292.

312. 'Does Climate still matter?', Jesse Ausubel, *Nature* 350:649–652 (1991). This is an extremely interesting article about humanity's growing independence from the effects of climate change.

313. 'Does Climate still matter?', Jesse Ausubel, *Nature* 350:649–652 (1991).

314. Page 9, 132 of *The Future of the Automobile: The Report of MIT's International Automobile Program*, Alan Altshuler et al (MIT Press, Cambridge, Massachusetts, 1985).

315. 'Does Climate still matter?', Jesse Ausubel, *Nature* 350:649–652 (1991).

316. 'Does Climate still matter'?, Jesse Ausubel, *Nature* 350:649–652 (1991).

317. For an examination of the possible effects of climate change on agricultural production, *see* 'Global climate change and US Agriculture', R. Adams et al, *Nature* 345:219–224 (1990). Regional shifts in agriculture might temporarily disrupt agricultural production, but the details of such disruptions are very difficult to estimate. A major obstacle to developing good estimates is that even the regional climate changes themselves, much less their effects, are extremely sensitive to the specific climate models used to predict them.

318. Today, the major agricultural: cushions in the world are the idled cropland in the US (which could add several per cent to the world's total agricultural production) and the one third of total grain production being used to raise poultry and livestock. This third could theoretically be routed to human beings in the event of shortages. Raising meat is relatively inefficient in that it takes some nine pounds of grain to produce one pound of beef. *See* note 374.

By 1988, two years of drought had brought the amount of carryover grain stocks in storage worldwide to their lowest level in more than a decade, little more than what is required to maintain a steady flow from producers to consumers. Stocks have since rebounded, but any widespread climatic disruptions of harvests would almost certainly bring global food shortages. In fact, some environmentalists maintain that a few years of North American crop failures like those of 1988, when US corn production fell 35 per cent, would cause worldwide famine. *See*, for example, *The Changing World Food Prospect: The Nineties and Beyond*, Lester Brown, Worldwatch Paper 85, Worldwatch Institute, Washington DC, 1988; 'Feeding the World in the Nineties', L. Brown and J. Young, pages 59–78 of *State of the World 1990* (Worldwatch Institute, Washington DC, 1990, or Norton and Company, New York).

319. 'Blue Planet', produced by Graeme Ferguson. Large color photographs of some of the images appearing in the film also can be found in the book, *Blue Planet: A Portrait of the Earth*, Lydia Dotto (H. Abrams, Inc, New York, 1991).

320. Imax, a wide-angle cinematic technique developed in Toronto and introduced in 1970 at the Osaka World Fair, projects a four-story image that virtually fills a viewer's field. Its effects can be so realistic that a scene through the window of a moving airplane can actually bring on motion sickness. In 1990, there were some sixty-five Imax theaters scattered in fifteen countries. The process has now been enhanced to create a wrap-around, three-dimensional image that requires goggles for viewing. Page B3, *New York Times*, 20 March 1990.

321. It is even more impressive that despite a rise in the sun's intensity of a full 25 per cent since life began, the earth's surface has remained in the narrow temperature range capable of supporting life. James Lovelock in his *The Ages of Gaia*, (W. Norton & Co, New York, 1988) presents a lucid description of this planetary regulation.

322. The energy of such a meteor is equal to 100 million megatons of explosives, and this immense power is still only one thousandth the energy of the meteor that caused the Cretacious extinction. *See* pages 156–165, *Extinction: Bad Genes or Bad Luck*, David Raup (Norton and Co, New York, 1991); *World Military and Social Expenditures 1989*, Ruth Sivard. World Priorities, Washington, DC (1991); *and also* footnote 66.

A collision with a planetary asteroid is a rare example of a serious danger to Metaman that hardly threatens us individually. There will always be more worrisome day-to-day dangers than this to preoccupy humans, but Metaman's time horizon is different. The situation is akin to the one your body's cells face with respect to car accidents: even if your individual cells were conscious, they could not concern themselves about being hit by a speeding car, but *you* do need to watch for cars. As to asteroids, scientists are already seriously proposing to track them and develop ways of deflecting any that might strike the earth, and it appears that a system for this purpose will be feasible within the next century. Tracking asteroids? Deflecting them? Such nascent concern and effort is not that of individuals protecting *themselves*, but of Metaman beginning to perceive and respond to a threat. *See* 'Asteroid Defense: Planners Envision Real Possibility of Collision with Earth', *New York Times*, page B5, 7 April 1992; 'A Rocky Watch for Earthbound Asteroids', *Science* 255:1204–1205 (1992).

Once this technology is in place, no further destructive impacts with large meteors will occur. Besides protecting Metaman, this will have the intriguing secondary effect of making the earth's environment much more stable; no longer will there be the periodic massive extinctions that have in previous times challenged biological life and brought significant evolutionary change. That phase of life's evolution on earth now seems to have drawn to a close!

323. 'Ironing away a greenhouse wrinkle', *Science News*, 139(4):63 (1991).

324. For a commentary suggesting that environmental engineering proposals to mitigate global ozone depletion should be more seriously considered, *see* 'Global Environmental Engineering', Ralph Cicerone et al, *Nature* 356: 472 (1992).

325. Sustainable growth is growth that can persist indefinitely because it is not dependent upon resources that are irreplaceable and will eventually be used up: fossil fuels, concentrated mineral deposits, and such.

326. *See* page 1 of *The Other Energy Crisis: Firewood*, Erik Eckholm, Worldwatch Paper 1, Worldwatch Institute, Washington, DC.

327. *See* 'Energy Sources: A Realistic Outlook', Chauncey Starr et al, *Science* 256:981–987 (1992). This article foresees no significant energy shortages even with substantial population and economic growth. Such growth is estimated – despite increased efficiency and conservation by users – to more than double total energy use by 2060. An important consideration in this analysis is the intraconvertibility of energy forms so that coal, which constitutes 90 per cent of the earth's fossil fuels, could be extensively used.

328. If funding to develop alternative energy sources had continued at the high levels of the late 1970s, when the world was reacting to the shock of OPEC's 1973 quadrupling of oil prices, Metaman would likely already be moving rapidly towards energy alternatives. None the less, that crisis spurred rapid progress in generating energy from new sources and in using it more efficiently. By forcing changes in energy use well before permanent critical shortages became a reality, the sharp price increases of the 1970s may, in the long term, have greatly smoothed Metaman's weaning from fossil fuels.

The oil price rise in 1973 was extremely abrupt. The posted price of a barrel of oil rose from $1.80 in 1970, to $2.18 in 1971, to $2.90 in mid-1973, to $5.12 in October 1973, to $11.65 in December 1973. Moreover, the spot price of oil in September 1973 was over $17. (Page 625, *The Prize: The Epic Quest for Oil, Money, and Power*, Daniel Yergin (Simon & Schuster, New York, 1990). The response to this lagged by several years, but it was substantial. In the US, Department of Energy funding for renewable-energy research peaked in 1980 at some $700 million annually. With the departure of Jimmy Carter from the Presidency, priorities changed and two years later funding had fallen to $250 million; by 1989 it stood at only $150 million. Page 77, *Cool Energy: The Renewable Solution to Global Warming. A report by the Union of Concerned Scientists* (Cambridge, Massachusetts, 1991). For a discussion of wind, photovoltaics, biomass, solar thermal, and other renewable resources, *see* notes 295, 297, 298, and 299.

329.   The success of energy technologies such as wind power and solar-thermal power has undercut the justification for heavy expenditures to develop fusion energy, which once seemed the most likely candidate to replace fossil fuels. (The generation of wind power is already cheaper than that from the construction of new coal-burning plants, and solar-thermal power is competitive for generating power for peak periods – about a factor of two higher than base line power costs.) Even fusion advocates now admit that commercial production in less than a century is unlikely, and meanwhile, other technologies are racing ahead. The largest obstacle to the use of energy technologies such as solar and wind power is the need for economic storage facilities to compensate for their intermittent nature. Chauncey Starr and Milton Searl estimate that until this problem is overcome, their contribution will be limited to some 12 per cent of total electric power usage. *See Energy Syst. Policy* 14:53, 1990. Hydrogen may eventually serve as the storage reservoir for the intermittent energy derived from these various renewable sources. *See* pages 41–45 of 'Building a Bridge to Sustainable Energy', Christopher Flavin, pages 27–45, *State of the World 1991*, ed. Lester Brown (Norton and Co., New York, 1991).

330.   *See Technology Characterization*, State of California Energy Resources Conservation and Development Commission, Alec Jenkins et al, November 1991. According to this report (Pages E1-9), a 200-megawatt power plant using the technology of Solar II could produce electricity for just 6.7 cents per kilowatt hour, and the next generation of central-collector power plant – which might be built by around 2005 – would be capable of producing power for about 5.1 cents. (All dollar figures are in 1989 dollars). *See also* note 297.

331.   Solar power generation would be particularly responsive to any demand fluctuations because a new solar generating plant could be built in only a year or two, far less than is required for a coal-burning plant.

'Photovoltaics Today and Tomorrow'. H.M. Hubbard. *Science*, 244: 297–304, 1989.

332.   In the Middle East, oil can be brought to the surface for such a low cost that a long-term market price of 5 dollars per barrel would be quite possible without a cartel, *see* 'The Competitive Floor', Morris Adelman, *The Energy Journal* 7(4):9–31 (1986). Or *see* the short piece, 'Cheap Oil, Expensive Cartel', page C2, *New York Times*, 20 March 1991.

333.   Oil as a fraction of world energy use has declined from 47 per cent in 1973 to 39 per cent in 1989. Page A14, *The Wall Street Journal*, 30 November 1990.

334.   High prices hasten the switch from fossil fuels and spur greater conservation, so it makes perfect economic sense for countries such as Saudi Arabia, with huge oil reserves likely to last a century, to try to moderate world oil prices as they have. Although Saudi Arabian oil reserves are estimated to be able to last some 110 years at current production levels, known reserves in other countries might be depleted in fifty years. Page 23, 'Designing a Sustainable Energy System', C. Flavin and N. Lenssen, pages 21–38, *State of the World 1991*, ed. Lester Brown (Norton and Co., New York, 1991). New discoveries might push these figures back a few years, but it seems unlikely that fifty years from now the world will be using as much oil as it does today.

335.   Cost figures have been assembled from the following sources: table 1–1, *Technology Characterization*, State of California Energy Resources Conservation and Development Commission, Alec Jenkins et al, November 1991; figure 8, *Cool Energy: The Renewable Solution to Global Warming, A report by the Union of Concerned Scientists*, Michael Brower, Cambridge, Mass., (1991); exhibit 1, *Barriers to commercialization of large-scale solar electricity: Lessons learned from the Luz experience*, Michael Lotker, Sandia Laboratories (SAND91–7014) 1991; 'Energy from the Sun', Carl Weinberg and Robert Williams, *Scientific American* 263:146–155 (1990); Table 2–3, 'Designing a Sustainable Energy System', C. Flavin and N. Lenssen, pages 21–38, *State of the World 1991*, ed. Lester Brown (Norton and Co., New York, 1991; 'Windfarms may energize the future', *Wall Street Journal*, 6 September 1991; 'Power to the Wind', page H1, *Washington Post*, 17 November 1991. The baseline price of coal-generated electrical power varies from region to region and fluctuates somewhat with coal price changes, but it generally remains between 4.2 and 6 cents per kilowatt hour. As various clean-air regulations are enacted, the price of this generating method is gradually rising. *Also see* notes 297 and 330.

336.   For example, the nitrogen used in fertilizers is a resource that is essentially unlimited since it can be extracted from the air to make ammonia (NH_4), but this requires significant energy. In 1983, over 70 per cent of

production costs for ammonia in the US were spent on the natural gas needed in the process. Another example is aluminum, which requires some 6 to 9 kilowatt hours of electrical energy per pound for a reduction step in its production (some 25 to 35 cents at current energy prices). Aluminium was sold in 1992 for $.50 per pound, energy costs are clearly the major component of its cost. For a full discussion of world supply and demand, as well as costs and reserves of all key minerals, *see Mineral Facts and Problems,* Bureau of Mines, US Department of the Interior, Washington, DC, 1985. More than 20 per cent of the energy used in the developed world is used to convert ores and feedstocks into basic commodities. 'Energy for Industry', M. Ross and D. Steinmeyer, *Scientific American* 263(3):89–98 (1990).

337.   John Young's article 'Mining the Earth' (Pages 100–118 in *State of the World 1992,* ed. Lester Brown, Norton and Co., New York, 1992) presents a strong argument that the most serious problem associated with humanity's voracious use of mineral resources is not their potential exhaustion, but the immense environmental destruction associated with their extraction. He sees this as the primary reason that the appetite of the developed world for such materials needs to be moderated.

338.   *See* note 392.

339.   For example, American cars were an average of 400 lbs lighter in 1986 than in 1978. 'Hydrogen and the Green Wave', Jesse Ausubel *The Bridge, Technology and the Environment* 20(1):17–22 (1990). Even some engine parts such as intake manifolds are now being made of strong, heat-resistant plastics. Page C7, *New York Times,* 20 March 1991.

340.   For example in 1989 the US population, consuming an average of 2,000 calories per day (2.2 kilowatt hours), used roughly .6 quadrillion British thermal units of energy. Meanwhile, the entire US economy used some 81 quadrillion British thermal units during the same period.

341.   'Does Climate still matter?', Jesse Ausubel, *Nature* 350:649–652 (1991).

342.   Page 74, 'Efficient Use of Electricity', A. Fickett, C, Gettlings, A. Lovins, *Scientific American* 263(3):64–75 (1990). The average new refrigerator in 1972 required some 1,726 kilowatt hours per year to run, that in 1990 needed only 930. This paper discusses the enormous potential – variously estimated between 30 and 75 per cent – still remaining for increasing the efficiency of energy use.

343.   *How to Make the World a Better Place: A Guide to Doing Good,* Jeffrey Hollender (William Morrow, New York, 1990).

344.   Some tribal peoples have been very careful in their use of materials, but the habit is a relatively new direction for most of the modern industrialized world. Anxieties about environmental destruction had begun to grow signifi-

cantly by the mid-nineteenth century, but widespread public concern about the environment has only existed in the last few decades. *See* 'The origins of environmentalism', Richard Grove. *Nature* 345:11–14 (1990).

345.   Moreover, more than nine out of ten girls born today will reach the age of sixty-two. *See* page 603 *QUID 1991*, Dominique and Michèle Frémy (Editions Robert Laffont, SA, Paris, 1991).

346.   *See* note 663.

347.   *See* note 35.

348.   Smoking is responsible for nearly a third of all cancer deaths in the US and contributes strongly to other health problems such as heart disease and emphysema. 'Toward the Primary Prevention of Cancer', B. Henderson, R. Ross, M. Pike, *Science* 254:1131–1138.

349.   *See* note 35.

350.   In 1900, life expectancy in France was 45.4 for men and 48.7 for women; by 1989 the respective figures were 72.3 and 80.5. It is worth noting that when life expectancy was this short, cancer would have been much less of a health problem for society since people generally didn't live long enough to be affected, page 603 *QUID 1991*, Dominique and Michèle Frémy (Editions Robert Laffont, SA, Paris, 1991). Even in 1920 in the US, life expectancy was only 53.6 for men and 54.6 for women, whereas by 1988 the figure were 71.4 and 78.3. Page 852 *The 1991 World Almanac and Book of Facts*, ed. M. Hoffman (Pharos, New York, 1991).

351.   Of course, practices such as wearing sunscreen and sunglasses when spending long hours in bright sunlight could significantly reduce such numbers. Moreover, two medical developments have the potential to diminish the cancer danger from ultraviolet light. There has recently been progress both in using monoclonal antibodies to treat skin melanoma and in developing vaccines to boost the body's defenses against this cancer. (Science News, 140:388 (1991); 'A Gene Encoding an Antigen Recognized by Cytolytic T Lympohocytes on a Human Melanoma', P. van der Bruggen et al, *Science* 254:1643–1647 (1991).

352.   The ozone layer is diminishing by some 4 per cent each decade according to measurements made in 1991 using the orbitting Total Ozone Mapping Spectrometer (TOMS). *Science*, News and Comment, 254:645 (1991).

353.   Estimate of Select Committee on Hunger, Washington, DC.

354.   Another potential hazard from depleting atmospheric ozone is the indirect effect on other plant and animal life. A study indicates that the 50 per cent fall in ozone levels above the Antarctic reduces phytoplankton growth in the waters below by some 10 per cent. At present this would account for an inconsequential .1 per cent of global phytoplankton growth, but the consequences of substantial global ozone depletion remain uncertain. 'Ozone

Depletion: Ultraviolet Radiation and Phytoplankton Biology in Antarctic Waters', R.C. Smith et al, *Science* 255:952–958 (1992); *see also New York Times*, page B7, 7 January 1992.

355. The production of CFCs is scheduled to end by 1996, and their atmospheric concentration will gradually begin to decline about a decade later. The ozone layer itself is likely to return to 1990 levels by about 2050 if current international agreements in eliminating CFCs (Chlorofluorocarbons) are followed. A detailed discussion of the long-term ozone depletion caused by the different CFCs is presented by Susan Solomon and Daniel Albritton in 'Time-dependent ozone depletion potentials for short- and long-term forecasts'. *Nature* 357:33–37 (1992). *See also* 'The CFC–Ozone Issue: Progress on the development of Alternatives to CFCs', L. Manzer, *Science* 249:31–35 (1990) and 'Help is on the way for the ozone shield', *Science* 259:28–29 (1993).

356. The murder rate in the US in 1990 was 9 per 100,000, ten times that of Japan and Ireland, the worlds two safest nations, but less than twice that of Sweden and Denmark, which report rates of 5 per 100,000. 'Comparing Lives', page 52, *World Press Review*, October 1991.

357. Pages 849 and 838, *The 1991 World Almanac and Book of Facts*, ed. M. Hoffman (Pharos, New York, 1991).

358. Page 838, *The 1991 World Almanac and Book of Facts*, ed. M. Hoffman (Pharos, New York, 1991).

359. The suicide rate in Hungary in 1990 was 46 per 100,000, while that in the US was 12.5. 'Comparing Lives', page 52, *World Press Review*, October 1991. In Germany the rate was 20, in Belgium 23, in Switzerland 24.5. *New York Times* page A11, 3 April 1992.

360. For example, John Montgomery (1771–1854) wrote in his poem *The Issues of Life and Death:*

> Beyond this vale of tears
> There is a life above,
> Unmeasured by the flight of years;
> And all that life is love.

CHAPTER 8

361. Pages 147 to 150, William McNeill, *Plagues and Peoples* (Anchor Books, New York, 1989), provides an account of the bubonic plague's sweep through Europe between 1347 and 1350. Ibid, pages 143–146, and 264 describes the progress of the plague in China. Ibid, page 144 alludes to the plague's presence in the Middle East and India.

362.   For an examination of the effects of the Plague on Europe, *see* Barbara Tuchman's *A Distant Mirror: The Calamitous 14th Century* (Knopf, New York, 1978).

363.   Moreover, there have been dozens of bloody regional and civil wars that have together taken over 21 million deaths in wars between 1945 and 1989. *World Military and Social Expenditures*, R. Sivard, World Priorities, Washington DC, 1989.

364.   Wolfgang Amadeus Mozart lived from 1756 to 1791. *Mozart*, Marcia Davenport (Scribner's, New York, 1932).

365.   To succeed in the long term, conservation strategies must allow for possible future climate changes. For example, global warming might shift the southern limits of a planet's range beyond the northern edge of a preserve meant to protect it. With fragmented habitats separated by populated regions, it will be more difficult for species to migrate to new locations on their own, so Metaman may routinely have to assist them actively.

366.   The 'New-Age' idea that widespread spontaneous shifts in individual consciousness will somehow bring about a society with a sharply reduced appetite for consumption of material goods is wishful thinking. If a large-scale decrease in such consumption does arise, it will almost certainly come from constraints such as taxes, or from new technologies that provide more alluring alternatives. For instance, easy video-based telecommunications might decrease travel.

367.   Moreover, it is not feasible for each individual even to do the research required to identify what the consequences are of each of his or her actions. Consider the simple choice which confronts shoppers in grocery stores in the US daily: whether to use plastic grocery bags or 'biodegradable' paper bags. What is an 'environmentally conscious' citizen to do? Interestingly, the answer is that it doesn't make much difference. The paper may be biodegradable, but neither it nor the plastic will degrade in the sealed landfill they both eventually reach. Further, if resources are the issue, the amount of oil used in each plastic bag is equivalent to the gasoline a car uses in driving some 100 yards, so giving up one 25-mile car trip would conserve more petrochemical resources than a year's worth of plastic bags.

368.   Although Metaman's total consumption is the sum of all individual consumption, reducing Metaman's appetite for fuel does not hinge upon altering individual attitudes about waste and thereby 'persuading' people to use less gasoline. Reducing consumption hinges upon reshaping the social environment that is largely determining individual behavior. As long as highways are plentiful, gasoline cheap, and mass transit inconvenient, people will use cars routinely; only as these conditions change will they look seriously for alternatives. Of course, some people, solely out of concern

about pollution or global warming, might greatly reduce the mileage they put on their cars, but most will not.

369.   Assuming a random age distribution, the effect would be to remove some 5 to 10 per cent of couples from the actively reproducing population, depending on how many of these people's partners or potential partners sought other mates. The UN projects 133 million births in the year 2000 and 55 million deaths. Thus, the extraordinary commitment by over 250 million people to try to stop population growth would eliminate at most some 7 to 13 million births. (Of course, such committed people would actually be more likely to have small families anyway, so the effect would not even be this large.) The net result of this effort would thus be to reduce the world's population growth in the year 2000 from about 80 million to 70 million a year.

370.   *See* note 268.

371.   Water is provided to farms for prices as low as $2.50 an acre foot in some forty-year, fixed-rate contracts in the San Joaquin Valley of California. Were subsidized users to pay the full cost of the water they are using, they might pay ten times what they pay now – more than $30 per acre foot. The US government's use of fixed-rate water contracts was, however, discontinued in the 1960s, so most of the most dramatic rate imbalances will disappear by the first decade of the next century. More significant than the cost of the water, though, is its availability. With long-term contracts, water resources can be shifted between various competing uses only very slowly. Thus, it is difficult to meet the rising water needs brought by rapid urban growth even though cities such as Los Angeles, which are already paying some 250 dollars an acre foot for their water because of transportation costs (nearly $200 an acre foot), could easily pay much more for water. Ultimately, in an area of high population density and scarce water, agriculture must be moved elsewhere if it is not to be heavily subsidized. Information provided in various communications with the US Bureau of Reclamation and the California Department of Water Resources.

372.   An excellent discussion of this approach to regulation is provided in *Bionomics: The Inevitability of Capitalism*, Michael Rothschild (Henry Holt and Co., New York, 1990).

373.   The data in the chart is for the fourth quarter of 1991. The highest gasoline prices in the developed world were in Italy, and the lowest were in the US. *See* tables 1 and 2 of *Energy Prices and Taxes*, International Energy Agency Organization for Economic Co-operation and Development. *Also see* 'Energy for Motor Vehicles', D. Bleviss, P. Walzer, *Scientific American* 263(3):102–109 (1990).

374.   For an examination of the ecological consequences of the global livestock industry, *see* 'Reforming the Livestock Economy', Alan Durning and Holly Brough, pages 66–82, *State of the World – 1992*, ed. Lester Brown

(Norton and Co., New York, 1992). There are currently some 11 billion fowl and 4 billion cattle, horses, pigs, goats and other herbivores in the world. Some 70 per cent of grain produced in the US is used to feed livestock (ibid, page 69). Durning estimates that if public costs such as the overgrazing of public land or the $2.3 billion dollar annual federal subsidy to Western water projects in the US were included in livestock production costs, meat prices would double or triple in the US (ibid, page 80). *See also*, 'The Beef Against Beef' Madeleine Nash, pages 76–77, *Time*, 20 April 1992. Each pound of beef produced requires 9 pounds of grain and 2500 gallons of water.

375.   *See* for example, 'Controlling Urban Air Pollution: A Benefit-Cost Assessment', A. Krupnick and P. Portney, *Science* 252:522–528 (1991). This attempt to quantify the real-world tradeoffs inherent in improving Los Angeles's air quality considers various specific policy options that have been proposed. It is a worthwhile illustration of the complexity of such decisions and the difficulties of balancing costs and benefits. Another effort to quantify the health costs of air pollution in the Los Angeles basin is presented in 'Valuing the Health Benefits of Clean Air', Jane Hall et al, *Science* 255:812–816 (1992).

376.   This program allows companies to buy and sell pollution credits so that overall reductions in pollution can be brought about more cheaply. Theoretically, such an approach will allow more aggressive overall reductions in pollution to be mandated by government because companies that can reduce pollution at little expense will go beyond mandated levels and then sell whatever extra credits they earn to companies for whom direct reductions would be very costly. *See* 'Trying a Market Approach to Smog' Richard Stevenson, *New York Times*, page C1, 25 March 1992, and 'Pacific Stock Mart close to "smog credits' trading pact', *Los Angeles Business Journal* 14(27):1 (1992).

377.   Were global growth to continue even at a modest 2 per cent annual rate – about half India's pace in the past quarter century – the global economy would in five centuries be an absurd 20,000 times its present size. The amount of solar radiation striking the earth's surface each year is some 15,000 times the world's current energy consumption. 'Energy for the Planet Earth', Ged Davis, *Scientific American*, 263(3):55–62, (1991). Such a projection of future energy consumption assumes that each unit of GNP is generated with the same amount of energy, which would not be true because efficiency has been improving. The energy to produce equivalent amounts of GNP has approximately halved since the early 1900s. Ongoing efficiency gains of this magnitude would mean that energy consumption would take some 750 rather than 500 years to reach that level. Page 112, 'Energy for the Developing World', A.N. Reddy, J. Goldemberg, *Scientific American* 263(3): 111–118, (1990).

378.   In fact, GNP does not provide even a good measure of a nation's *total* production, because GNP doesn't include all goods and services produced by an economy, only those bought and sold. Activities such as the rearing of children, volunteer work, home maintenance and personal recreation, are not mediated by money and are not counted. Shift these into the money economy, and GNP will rise but not necessarily individual well-being; nothing new is being done. For example, when a person must go to work and leave a child in daycare instead of caring for him or her at home, GNP goes up, but is society better off?

379.   If the depletion of resources were considered, Indonesia's 1989 growth rate would drop from 7 per cent to only 4 per cent according to the World Resources Institute. *See Science* 254:1724 (1991).

380.   James Tobin, William Nordhaus, those at the United Nations Environment Program, and others have pioneered new indices of economic well-being. For a discussion of one such index, called the Index for Sustainable Economic Welfare (ISEW), *see For the Common Good: Redirecting the Economy Toward Community, the Environment, and a Sustainable Future*, H. Daly and J. Cobb (Beacon Press, Boston, 1989).

381.   Hazel Henderson, *The Politics of the Solar Age: Alternatives to Economics*, (Knowledge Systems Inc. Indianapolis, 1988). This is a very good discussion of the many flaws of traditional economic thinking. She discusses a number of such indices, one being the Physical Quality of Life Indicator (PQLI) developed by the Overseas Development Council. *See also* pages 9–11, *State of the World – 1991*, ed. Lester Brown (Norton and Co., New York, 1991).

382.   For example, the US had non-government assets of some 14.4 trillion dollars in 1988. Page 537, *1990 Statistical Abstract of the United States*, US Bureau of the Census, Washington, DC.

383.   In 1991 the deterioration of water supplies brought the first significant outbreak of cholera in South America in a hundred years. There were some 320,000 cases of the disease and nearly 4,000 deaths in Peru, the worst affected country. Efforts to stop the spread of the disease failed, but at least the associated mortality was greatly reduced from historical levels of about 20 per cent to little more than one per cent. *See* 'Epidemic Cholera in the Americas', R. Glass, M. Label and A. Brandling-Bennett, *Science* 256:1524–1525 (1992).

384.   Moreover, with the end of the Cold War, the third world will no longer be able to count on strategically motivated largesse from the major powers. The power of global communications to portray their ills, and the growing understanding of the global nature of environmental problems will probably keep them from being forgotten by the developed world, but it is unclear how much assistance they will receive.

385.   For example, the annual per capita costs of floods in Sri Lanka are much lower in overall dollar amounts than in the US, but they amount to some 2 per cent of Sri Lanka's GNP, whereas in the US they account for some .1 per cent of GNP. 'A Second Look at the Impacts of Climate Change', Jesse Ausubel, *American Scientist* 79:210–221 (1991)

386.   One of the most successful paths to development has been that of the Asian rim of the Pacific. Following the example of Japan in the 1950s and 1960s, Hong Kong, Taiwan, South Korea and Singapore in the 1970s and 1980s took advantage of low labor costs to swell exports and build modern societies. Now, as these nations grow richer, another Pacific group – Thailand, Malaysia, and Indonesia is following successfully in their footsteps. Unfortunately, however, it is unlikely that low-cost production and large exports can continue to fuel the development of further generations of developing countries – much less a billion people in China. Not only is automation steadily reducing the labor content in manufacturing, but earlier waves of development have created aggressive global and regional corporations that are strong competitors. Lower overhead costs, cheaper labor and looser control over operating practices may still be important lures for business, but other factors such as modern infrastructure, an educated labor force, easy access to markets and a political environment stable enough to protect investments are becoming even more important.

An entirely different path to development has been the sale of natural resources, but except for those few countries with large reserves of petrochemicals or various strategic minerals, natural resources generally cannot provide adequate funds to develop a country.

387.   For insights into the tremendous problems facing Africa, *see* Blaine Harden's, *Africa: Dispatches from a Fragile Continent* (Norton and Co., New York, 1990). Not least among them is AIDS, which could be so destructive as to halt even population growth in some regions. 'The spread of HIV-1 in Africa: sexual contact patterns and the predicted demographic impact of AIDS', R. Anderson et al, *Science* 352:581–588 (1991). The appearance of drug-resistant strains of many infectious microbes also has serious implications for the less-developed world. As more expensive drugs and treatment regimes become the only way to combat various diseases successfully, their treatment may well move beyond the reach of public-health programs in many parts of the world. For example, treating a case of tuberculosis that is multidrug resistant costs some $180,000 as opposed to $12,000 for a drug-susceptible strain. 'Epidemiology of Drug Resistance: Implications for a Post-Anti Microbial Era', Mitchell Cohen, *Science* 257:1050–1055 (1992). An excellent overview of this general topic is provided in the six articles in *Science* 257:1050–1082 (1992).

388.   Such a rate is quite reasonable. In India, for example, GNP growth has

averaged between 3.4 and 5.5 per cent during each five-year period since 1965. Unfortunately, population growth has averaged some 2 per cent throughout the period and washed away about half of India's per-capita economic growth. *Statistical Outline of India 1989–1990* (TATA Services Limited, Department of Economics and Statistics, Bombay, (1989).

Growth without population increase is possible because technology has now decoupled productivity from overall labor content. No longer are more people needed to increase output. A small percentage of the population of the developed world can produce enough food for all. Even fewer people are involved in manufacturing; a giant telephone communications network is operated by a relative handful of people.

389. Page 39, *Cool Energy: The Renewable Solution to Global Warming, A report by the Union of Concerned Scientists*, Michael Bower (Cambridge, Mass., 1991).

390. For example, as of 1990, over 6,000 outlying villages in India depended on photovoltaics for their power. Page 28, 'Designing a Sustainable Energy System', C. Flavin and N. Lenssen, pages 21–38, *State of the World 1991*, ed. Lester Brown (Norton and Co., New York, 1991).

391. 'Optical Communication for the Public Network', Paul Shumate, The Second International Conference on Optoelectronics, November 1990, Kobe, Japan. Contributing to the drop in cost for long-distance cable transmission has been a fiftyfold increase in fiber transmission rates, a tenfold decrease in the cost of fiber cable, and a more than tenfold decrease in fiber transmission losses. *Personal communication*, Paul Shumate, Bellcore, 1993.

392. The first transatlantic telephone cable, called TAT-1, stretched from Scotland to Newfoundland and could handle only twelve calls at a time. By 1968, TAT-4 was handling 850 calls at a time, and by 1982, TAT-6 was handling 4,000. With the shift to fiber-optic cable (TAT-8) in 1988, capacity rose to 40,000, and by 1991, TAT-9 was handling 80,000 simultaneous calls. *See* volume 7 of *History of Engineering and Science in the Bell System*, ed. E.F. O'Neill, AT&T, 1985, and AT&T press releases. Capacity continues to increase; AT&T and KDD (Kokusai Denshin Denwa) plan in the mid-1990s to complete a cable between Japan and the US that can handle 500,000 simultaneous telephone calls. 'Lightwave Communications: The Fifth Generation', E. Desurvire, *Scientific American* 226(1): 114–121 (1992).

393. Long-distance fiber links have already become much cheaper than older technologies, and the same will eventually be true for residential installations. The costs of fiber hookups to homes in the US will be about half the price of copper wire by the year 2000, even without considering its greater capacity, lower maintenance costs, and longer useful lifetime. *See* Evolution of Fiber in the Residential Loop Plant', Paul Shumate and Richard Snelling. *IEEE Communications Magazine*. Pages 68–74, March 1991.

394.   Not only is a box of discs immeasurably cheaper and more portable than a library, with computer-guided instruction it will be easy for trained aides to help alleviate shortages of teachers. Educational software is progressing rapidly as hardware capabilities expand: even today, portable computers costing only a few thousand dollars offer individualized instruction making use of text, graphics, pictures and sound. These advanced tools are only now beginning to appear in the developed world, but like other technologies, they will eventually make their way to developing lands.

395.   For a discussion of the growing gap between the developed and underdeveloped world, *see Our Demographically Divided World*, L. Brown, J. Jacobson, Worldwatch Paper 74, Worldwatch Institute, Washington, DC, 1986.

396.   For example, work on the Yucca Flats nuclear disposal site in Nevada was strongly challenged on the grounds that an earthquake might at some point raise water tables high enough to flood the disposal caverns and allow radioactivity to escape. The challenge was based on theories – since rejected by the regulatory commission – that the deep water table in this desert area might have risen briefly 10,000 years ago. *See also* note 668.

397.   From 'The Times They Are A-Changin'. Copyright © 1963, 1964 by Special Rider Music; copyright renewed 1991 by Special Rider Music, All rights reserved. International copyright secured. Reprinted by permission.

CHAPTER 9

398.   *See*, for example, 'Atom by Atom', page B5, *New York Times*, 26 November 1991. For a detailed discussion of microscopic machinery and molecular manufacturing and an aggressive assessment of their potential, *see* Eric Drexler's book on 'nanotechnology', *Engines of Creation* (Doubleday, New York, 1986). *See also* 'Micron Machinations', Gary Stix, pages 113–117 *Scientific American*, November 1992.

399.   Improving communication within Metaman not only speeds the rate at which progress on a problem propagates to others doing similar work, it also carries developments from one field to another. When exciting discoveries are made they immediately attract attention and resources and spur great efforts to extend them.

400.   In 1992, the standard memory chips were 1 and 4 MBytes (million characters of information), 16 MBytes chips were in production, 64 MBytes in development and targeted for release in 1995, 256 MBytes in research with prototypes already developed, and 1,000 to 4,000 MBytes – enough to hold some 100,000 pages of text – in preliminary research. (*See also* note 201). For more than two decades, memory densities have been roughly

doubling every three years and they show no sign of slowing. Moreover, some processing chips now have several layers so they are becoming three-dimensional. When this happens, it will be like the breakthrough from clay tablets to books with many pages. Using three dimensions, storage expands immensely even if written elements remain the same size. But of course, the dimensions of the writing – the etched circuits on the chips – is not staying the same size; it is growing ever smaller. An optical storage system that stores data at a density of some 5,000 Mbytes per square inch, has already been demonstrated in the laboratory. For an exuberant discussion of the possible implications of progress in computers, *see Microcosm: The quantum revolution in economics and technology*, George Gilder (Simon & Schuster, New York, 1989).

401.   For a discussion of the likely ten to a hundredfold increase in peak computing speeds for massively parallel computers in the next five years, *see* 'Ultracomputers: A Teraflop Before Its Time', Gordon Bell, *Science* 256:64 (1992). *Also see*, 'Massively Parallel Machines Usher in Next Level of Computing Power', *Science* 256: 50–51 (1992).

402.   Humans have evolved gradually, biological change taking place over hundreds of thousands of years. It has even been maintained, though results are now disputed by some, that all humanity can be traced back to a common ancestor in Africa some 200,000 years ago. 'African Populations and the Evolution of Human Mitochondrial DNA', L. Vigilant et al, *Science* 253: 1503–1507 (1991). Although human skeletal remains from at least 125,000 years ago are indistinguishable from those of modern humans, but this does not rule out more subtle changes during the intervening period. But in any case biological species tend to remain largely static except for brief incidents of rapid change when speciation occurs. *See also* note 133.

403.   'Fabrication and testing of the planar magnetic micromotor', H. Guckel et al, *Journal of Micromechanics and Microengineering*, 1: 135–138 (1991).

404.   The nutrients, hormones and sensory stimulation needed by a developing fetus are very complex, so the development of an artificial womb would be extremely challenging. Moreover, little incentive to work on such a system now exists, though it might be gradually developed as a useful research tool for studying embryonic development in animal systems. None the less, human embryos fertilized in a test tube and immediately implanted into the uterus develop normally, and premature deliveries at twenty-four to twenty-six weeks can be kept alive in an incubator now. *See* note 639.

To keep a prematurely delivered infant alive at an earlier stage is much more difficult because an infant's lungs and other organs have not progressed far enough to support life. Thus, any incubator for an embryo would have to be more like a tissue culture device – actually an artificial placenta – than a mechanical incubator, it would have to supply hormones, filter blood, and do all the basic things that the mother's body now does. Just how complex the interactions between mother and fetus are is only now becoming understood, but Metaman's progress is very rapid. Such a task as this is a bit reminiscent of early efforts to create machine intelligence. In this case, early hopes for success grew out of an ignorance of the enormous complexity of the human mind. Challenges such as language recognition were far too complex for the early machines or approaches used, but now, only a few decades later, language recognition is beginning to arrive. Thus, that we are only now beginning to understand the extraordinary complexity of the interactions of our individual organs and bodily systems may mean that the creation of an artificial womb is not close at hand, but eventually it will come. We are rapidly learning how to influence embryological development, and it is unlikely to be beyond us to one day create biological environments that can support a developing embryo or fetus.

405.   Such an organ trade already exists. In India, for example, people can sell one of their corneas or kidneys to someone needing a transplant. Some 2,000 such kidney transplants a year are performed there, and the going rate in 1992 was 6,000 to 12,000 dollars. *See* 'India Debates Ethics of Buying Transplant Kidneys', *New York Times*, page A14, 17 August 1992; and 'Egypt's Desperate Trade', *New York Times*, page A1, 23 September 1991.

406.   In 1991 a law was passed in India to allow prenatal diagnostic testing only with a physician's advice and only to determine genetic diseases. This was done because female fetuses were being selectively aborted at special clinics so that couples could have sons; before the law, some 2,300 such abortions were estimated to occur every year in Bombay, *Nature* 353:594 (1991). Laws to keep people from using abortions for gender selection are unlikely to succeed in the long term. Moreover, what will happen when medical technology allows parents to choose in advance the gender of the child they will conceive?

The ethical issues surrounding broad genetic testing are immense. At the same time that a bitter struggle over the legality of abortion is occurring in the US, there have already been over a hundred suits over 'wrongful birth'. These are suits brought by parents in cases where genetic tests were improperly performed, birth defects went undetected, and births that *would have been* aborted had the tests been done properly proceeded to term. Page A1, *San Diego Union*, 30 November 1991.

407.   The development of clothing may well have been a much more important breakthrough for humanity than is generally recognized. Together with fire, clothing is what probably allowed primitive humans to leave tropical regions for more temperate zones. William McNeill argues in his *Plagues and Peoples* (Anchor Books, New York, 1989) that the migration of primitive humans into the temperate regions is what allowed them to escape the many

diseases and parasites that had long kept population in check. Most of the micro-organisms adapted to the tropics and to their human hosts could not survive in more northern climates. Thus, as human health improved, and human population expanded, additional human energies became available for social development. McNeill maintains that the burden of tropical disease is largely responsible for the absence of powerful civilizations in the tropics, as well as for the difficulty empires from temperate climates have had in conquering these regions.

408.   Actually, some cellular phones for luxury cars already can respond to voice commands to dial a list of frequently used phone numbers. They will 'call home' when so commanded. Also, Nynex (New York and New England Telephone Co.) has announced it will offer a similar voice-dialing system in 1994 to its regular customers. Page A1, *New York Times*, 11 February 1993.

409.   The oldest known book on dentistry, the anonymous *Artzney Buchlein* published in Germany in 1530, describes the use by Moslem physicians of gold foil in fillings in AD 857. It is interesting in light of today's understanding of the toxicity of lead, that in the seventeeth century in France, it was widely used for fillings. *Encyclopedia Britannica*, Eleventh Edition (Cambridge University Press, Cambridge, 1910).

410.   *Biomaterials, Science, and Engineering*, Joan B. Park (Plenum Press, New York, 1984). Wires and pins were probably used as early as the late nineteeth century, but not until 1893 were steel plates and screws used medically. The first total hip replacement was in 1938.

411.   A cataract operation to improve vision by implanting a synthetic lens in the eye is now so common that 10 per cent of those over seventy-five in the US has lens implants.

412.   Nearly one in twenty people in the US (4.6 per cent) now have medical implants, and over 2 million new devices are implanted each year. *The Johns Hopkins Medical Letter: Health after Fifty* 3(8):1. As of 1988, some 4.4 million people had one or more fixation devices (pins, wires, screws and such), 2.5 million had artificial lenses, 1.3 million had artificial joints, 900,000 had ear vent tubes, 550,000 had breast implants, 460,000 had pacemakers, 253,000 had artificial heart valves. *Use of Selected Medical Device Implants in the United States, 1988*. Advance Data No.191 (February 1991). US Department of Health and Human Services, Hyattsville, Maryland.

413.   There are several different technologies under development to produce a human blood substitute for use in surgery. One technology uses genetically engineered bacteria to produce human hemoglobin; another uses genetically engineered pigs to accomplish that task, and the third uses a non-biological oxygen-binding chemical as a hemoglobin substitute. Page C5, *New York Times*, 8 July 1992. Furthermore, Metaman's immense system for storing human plasma and blood for medical purposes is an external blood

reservoir for humans within the super-organism.

414. Surprisingly, as few as four independent electrodes can yield good results. The maximum number of electrodes used today is twenty-two, but most of them are not functionally independent because several stimulate the same nerve bundles. 'A multipeak feature extraction coding strategy for a multichannel cochlear implant,' D. Koch et al, *Hearing Instruments* 41(3) (1990).

415. 'Better Speech Recognition with Cochlear Implants', B.S. Wilson et al. *Nature* 352:236–237 (1991).

416. Moreover, children who have been deaf from birth and receive implants in early childhood also can develop hearing skills, although none have yet achieved the remarkable levels of some of the adults who were verbal before losing their hearing. It is much more difficult to learn language from scratch than to learn to recognize speech that is already familiar. 'Consonant Production in Children Receiving A Multichannel Cochlear Implant', E. Tobley et al, *Ear and Hearing* 12(1):23–31 (1991).

417. The cochlear nerve fibers are splayed out along a spiral canal, and different sound frequencies stimulate nerve fibers situated at different positions along the canal. Thus, it is relatively easy to mount electrodes where they will stimulate fibers that would normally be activated by particular sound frequencies.

418. 'Visual Sensations Produced by Intracortical Microstimulation of the Human Occipital Cortex'. M. Bak et al, *Medical and Biological Engineering and Computing* 28:257–259, 1990.

419. Another approach to artificial vision is to stimulate the optic nerve directly, but little has so far been done in this area because the optic nerve is not an easy implantation site. Placing microelectrodes in the brain or optic nerve is far more difficult than in the cochlea, which is a convenient and stable bony platform for electrodes.

420. For a more complete overview of the state of prosthetics, *see* 'Applied Neural Control in the 1990s', W. Heetderks and F. Hambrecht, *Proceedings of the IEEE* 76(9):1115–1121 (1988).

421. 'Functional Electrical Stimulation: Current status and future prospects of applications to the neuromuscular system in spinal cord injury', P. Peckham, *Paraplegia* 25:279–288 (1987).

422. Moreover, any such 'creature' would probably soon be out of date, replaced by next year's model. Using our hands and legs to control a variety of machines makes more sense, because machines can then be replaced as they wear out or become obsolete.

423. 'A High-Yield IC-Compatible Multichannel Recording Array', Khalil Najafi, Densall Wise, and Tohru Mochizuki, *IEEE Transactions on Electron Devices*, 32(7)1206–1211 (1985).

424.   For example, it might not be possible to generate patterns of stimulation that the brain can interpret, or microelectrodes might not remain stationary enough.

425.   The most familiar case of this is insulin for diabetics; their pancreases can no longer produce the natural insulin needed to regulate their blood sugar levels so it must be supplied by Metaman. In this case, an implantable device to regulate insulin is now being developed.

426.   For example, toxic compounds can be hooked to monoclonal antibodies which bind only to cancerous cells. When antibodies carry these toxins to the cancer cells, the cells are selectively destroyed. Without the antibodies, the toxins would not be useful because at high enough concentrations to harm cancer cells they would also destroy healthy cells.

427.   'Ethnobotany and the identification of therapeutic agents from the rainforest', M. Balick. in *Bioactive Compounds from Plants*, ed. D. Chadwick and J. Marsh (J. Wiley and Sons, New York, 1990).

428.   This is in no way meant to suggest that the body is like a simple machine and can be easily fixed. There is an extraordinary and complex interdependence among all of the body's systems. But being able to alter specific internal subsystems selectively is an extraordinary leap, and simple interventions can be extremely effective: The use of thyroxin can compensate for the loss of the thyroid gland. Scopolamine can quiet the vestibular apparatus of the inner ear and reduce motion sickness. Lithium can manage manic-depressive behavior.

429.   Roughly 1,000 chemicals are examined to produce one that is suitable for clinical trials. And only one in ten that reach clinical trials ever gains FDA approval in the US. *See* 'Are Prescription Drug Prices High?'. P. Vagelos, *Science* 252:1080–1084.

430.   Primaxin was derived from the compound Thienamycin from Streptomyces cattlaya. Private communication, Merck Corporation.

431.   Here I use the term 'genetic engineering' very generally to refer to the broad array of techniques to manipulate genes by isolating them, extracting them from cells, copying them, recombining them, inserting them in new cells, producing proteins from them, and so forth.

432.   For this reason, the diverse species of *all* habitats will in the years ahead be valuable sources of prototypes for potential new drugs. *See*, for instance, 'Drug Industry Going Back to Nature,' *New York Times*, Page C1, 5 March 1992. Over the longer term, however, this value will diminish as drugs designed from scratch begin to steer pharmaceutical progress.

433.   This anticoagulant is called Bat Plasminogen Activator (BPA) and in 1991 was undergoing animal tests by Merck. *Science* 253:621 (1991).

434.   This very problem is occurring with taxol, the promising anticancer drug found in the bark of the Pacific yew tree of America's Pacific Northwest.

Thousands of trees are being killed to produce the drug but it takes 60 pounds·
of bark (about three very old trees) to make enough of the drug to treat one
patient for a year, (page A1, 'Trees That Yield a Drug for Cancer are Being
Wasted', Timothy Egan, *New York Times*, 29 January 1992). Synthesis is the
only way of relieving shortages. Taxol is an unusually complex molecule, but
the efforts to produce it using plant tissue culture are progressing rapidly.
Moreover efforts to synthesize taxol by modifying related – and more
common – molecules, (*see* page 121, *Scientific American*, October 1991) are
proving a success. In 1992, scientists synthesized taxol analogs from
compounds in the more common European Yew.

435.   'New enzyme synthesized from scratch', *Science News* 137:388
(1990). Some contemplate going much further than designing particular
drugs, though, and imagine actually altering the cells' basic metabolic
pathways themselves. *See*, for example, 'Toward a Science of Metabolic
Engineering', James Bailey, *Science* 252:1668–1674 (1991).

436.   This drug, Cimetidine, was developed by James Lack's group at
Smithkline Beecham over a fourteen-year period and first released commercially in Britain in 1974. For the history of this project, *see The Discovery of the
Histamine H2-Receptors and Their Antagonists* (SmithKline & French International Company, 1982).

437.   *Science News* 137(25): 137 (1990).

438.   Progress in x-ray crystallography has been so rapid in the past decade
that if a chemical can be crystallized, chemists now can generally determine
the arrangement of its atoms by taking the crystals to a crystallography lab.
Learning molecular structures not only enables chemists to understand
chemicals better, it allows them to choose the best compounds to modify and
combine in synthesizing chemicals.

Even taxol (*see* note 434), which is an extremely complex molecule,
appears likely soon to be synthesized. *See* 'Beyond Yew: Chemists Boost
Taxol Yield', *Science News* 141:244 (1992), and 'Chemists Vie to Make a
Better Taxol', *Science* 256:311 (1992).

439.   As an example of how willing people are to modify their bodies to gain
a special edge in competition, some runners now 'boost' their red blood cell
levels for special races by drawing blood weeks before an event, extracting
the red blood cells, then reinjecting the cells just before the race. Such an
auto-transfusion temporarily raises red blood cell count and, therefore,
stamina. Now, the same effect can be achieved with the growth factor,
erythropoetin.

In the future, it is quite possible that athletes will become like the biological
equivalent of a race car. Race-car competition depends on the most
up-to-date technological innovations and a team of mechanics and designers.
Maybe retinues of trainers and physicians will do the same sort of priming and

design on human competitors. The pretense of 'amateur' athletics is already disappearing; amateurs simply cannot compete. Training regimes are of utmost importance, and though drugs on the whole can still be eliminated from competition, how long until they become too diverse and subtle to be readily detectable?

440.   Preventable is used here to mean premature. About a million of the two million deaths in the US each year are so classified: some 500,000 of them are attributed to smoking and another 100,000 to alcohol. *See* Elizabeth Whelan's 'Alarm Clocks Can Kill You. Have a Smoke', page A21, *New York Times*, 8 September 1992.

441.   It feels natural to speak of Metaman's accomplishments and choices as though they are our own, and I sometimes do so. But keep in mind that using 'us' or 'we' to refer to Metaman's global activity is a little like a stomach cell happily twittering to its epithelial buddies that 'we cells' should all go out and find a juicy peach this afternoon. It may be true, but it misses the point of how much more than just a group of cells the body is. The real actor here is Metaman, not 'us'.

442.   For an overview of how far genetic engineering has now come, *see* A. Miller's review, 'Human gene therapy comes of age', *Nature* 357:455–460 (1992). Also, there is a special biotechnology section in *Science* 256:766–812 (1992).

443.   The twelfth-century Rubáiyát written by Omar Khayyám was translated into English by Edward Fitzgerald in 1859.

444.   Using mice, researchers have added new genes to muscle cells and have had these cells release gene products such as human growth factor. Thus, muscle cells might one day serve as a delivery system for gene therapy on adults. 'Putting New Muscle Into Gene Therapy', *Science* 254:1455–1456 (1991) and 'Systemic Delivery of Human Growth Hormone by Injection of Genetically Engineered Myoblasts', J. Dhawan et al, *Science* 254:1509–1523 (1991).

445.   This work brings only a temporary 'cure' for ADA deficiency because all white blood cells eventually die and are replaced by new cells produced by the bone marrow. Thus the blood-cell inoculation must be periodically repeated. *See* Beusechem et al, 'Somatic cell gene therapy: the model of adenosine deaminase deficiency'. *Bone Marrow Transplantation* 4(Suppl.4): 133–135 (1989). More recently, however, Italian scientists have placed the ADA gene into stem cells (the bone-marrow cells that produce white blood cells) and thereby hope to effect a permanent cure. 'Gene Therapy News', *Nature*, 356:465 (1992). For a sketch of the rapid progress being made in Gene Therapy, *see* 'At Age 2, Gene Therapy Enters a Growth Phase', *Science* 258:744–745 (1992).

446.   A major step in human genetic manipulation is to read the genetic

constitution of a human embryo at an early stage in its development without damaging it. And this has already been accomplished during *in vitro* fertilization. In 1992, it was reported that a single cell could be removed from an embryo at the eight-cell stage and tested for the presence of the cystic fibrosis gene. Because removal of a cell at this stage of development does not effect the development of the embryo, the results of the test could be used to ensure that a child conceived by *in vitro* techniques did not suffer from cystic fibrosis – a 25 per cent chance for certain parents. Indeed, a healthy baby girl from an embryo on which such a test was performed has now been born. (Page A1, *New York Times*, 24 September 1992.)

This technique is critical for two reasons: First it suggests that when inexpensive genetic testing of embryos is possible *in vitro* fertilization may become a routine way of avoiding genetic diseases. Perhaps one day it will be considered as foolhardy to conceive a child through 'normal' sexual means as it would be considered today to forego prenatal care. When a simple medical procedure can virtually guarantee a child free from major genetic diseases the procedure will become routine. Secondly, this technology offers an easy path to human genetic design. There is a blurry line between screening for diseases, and screening to select for gender, hair color and other traits that will soon be revealed by sophisticated genetic tests. And once broad screening is done, is it really much different to go further and engineer desirable genetic traits directly into the genome of the embryo before implanation occurs?

447. In 1991, papers describing three independent transgenic systems to study Alzheimer's were presented and seemed to hold out the hope for rapid progress on the disease. *See New York Times* page A15, 12 December 1991. Unfortunately, two of the three papers were later retracted. For a discussion of these systems and the controversy surrounding the early reports, *see* pages 20–21 of 'The Mice That Missed', *Scientific American*, June 1992.

448. 'Transgenic Models of Tumor Development', J. Adams, S. Cory, *Science*, 254:1161–1166 (1991).

449. For example, *see* 'NIT-1 a Pancreatic beta-cell line established from a transgenic NOD/Lt mouse', K. Hamaguchi, H. Gaskins, E. Leiter, *Diabetes* 40:842–848 (1991).

450. In 'Medline', a computerized index of several thousand journal publications relevant to medicine, there were 956 papers with 'transgenic' in the title between 1986 and 1991.

451. The toxins are from the bacterium, Bacillus thuringiensis, and are called 'Bt toxins'. In field tests, genetically altered cotton fared as well as cotton that was protected by conventional insecticides. *Science* 252:211–212 (1991). For an overview of recent work in creating plants that can be used for producing a variety of proteins and other chemicals, *see* 'High-Tech Plants

Promise a Bumper Crop of New Products', Anne Moffat, *Science* 256:770–771 (1992).

452.   For example, hibernating bears are inactive for five months yet suffer no bone loss. Evidently the bear releases a hormone into its blood that promotes bone growth using the calcium released by the breakdown of bones also occurring. If the genetics of this system could be transferred to selected human cells, osteoporosis (the loss of bone mass common in aged and bedridden people as well as astronauts) might be halted or even reversed. *See* 'Hibernating Bears Emerge with Hints About Human Ills', Elisabeth Rosenthal, *New York Times*, page B7, 21 April 1992. *See also* note 446.

453.   The first successful transplant of tissue between fetuses was performed in 1990 to cure a child of a fatal condition known as Hurler's syndrome, where cells do not produce an enzyme critical in breaking down sugar. Cells with the enzyme were transplanted from an aborted fetus. *See* 'Fetal transplant said to block defect', *New York Times*, 21 November 1991.

454.   A good discussion of relative brain weights in different species, particularly in primates is presented on pages 38 to 53 of *The Evolution of Culture in Animals*, John Bonner (Princeton University Press, Princeton, New Jersey, 1989).

455.   This has been shown by comparing various performance factors between identical twins and fraternal twins. Identical twins are genetically identical whereas fraternal twins are genetically no closer than any other siblings. Such studies show strong genetic components in memory, language development, perceptual skills, and other mental capacities. 'Sources of Human Psychological Differences: The Minnesota Study of Twins Reared Apart', T. Bouchard, D. Lykken, M. McGue, N. Segal, A. Tellegen, *Science* 250:223–228 (1990). *See also*, 'The Role of Inheritance in Behavior', Robert Plomin, *Science* 248:183–188.

456.   The brain's size relative to the body's overall weight is identical during the early growth and development of a rhesus monkey, a chimpanzee and a human. The increase in adult brain size from rhesus to chimpanzee to human results from the progressive lengthening of the early growth period. *See* figure 11, *The Evolution of Culture in Animals*, John Bonner (Princeton University Press, Princeton, New Jersey, 1989).

457.   Stephen J. Gould mentions the idea that human head size was limited by its ability to pass through the birth canal. Thus to increase the size of the brain, more development had to occur *after* birth, during an extended infancy. 'The Child is Man's Real Father', pages 63–69, *Ever Since Darwin*, Stephen J. Gould (Norton, New York, 1977).

458.   John Bonner has an excellent discussion not only of the developmental differences between *Homo sapiens* and other primates, but of how natural selection might have brought increased brain size to humans. Pages 46–53,

The Evolution of Culture in Animals, John Bonner (Princeton University Press, Princeton, New Jersey, 1989).

459.   For example, an early study of mortality in Wroclaw (Poland) around 1690 found that 43 per cent of all babies died before the end of their fifth year of life, which is probably typical for the period and not very different than in earlier times throughout the world. Page 25, *Expectations of Life: A Study in the Demography, Statistics, and History of World Mortality*, H.O. Lancaster (Springer-Verlag, New York, 1989).

460.   Nowadays, childhood is so safe that a baby in the developed world who survives the first year of life has about a 98 per cent chance of reaching the age of thirty-five. Page 30, *Expectations of Life: A Study in the Demography, Statistics, and History of World Mortality*, H.O. Lancaster (Springer-Verlag, New York, 1989).

461.   Moreover, once the various human genes involved in brain growth are identified, they could possibly be spliced into a chimp's genome to recapitulate evolution by creating a chimpanzee with something akin to human intelligence.

462.   For an overview of the purpose and significance of the Human Genome Project, *see* 'The Human Genome Project: Past Present, and Future', James Watson, *Science* 248:44–48 (1990). The Human Genome Project is also joined by smaller projects to map the genomes of several experimental animals including the mouse, round worm (nematode), fruit fly (Drosophila), yeast (Saccharomyces cerevisiae) and E. Coli bacterium.

463.   *See* note 446.

464.   For example, children of parents who live beyond the age of eighty live an average of six years longer than children of parents who die by the age of sixty. Page 340 of *Longevity, Senescence, and the Genome*, Caleb Finch (University of Chicago Press, Chicago, 1990). Moreover, in the nematode (*Caenorhabditis elegans*) it has been possible to select mutations that increase or shorten lifespans. Ibid, pages 300–304. The largest known genetic influences on lifespan are the five to thirtyfold differences in insect lifespans between queens and worker castes. Ibid, page 354.

465.   *See* 'Annual internal growth banding and life history of the ocean quahog Artica islandica', I. Thompson, D. Jones, D. Dreibelbis, (Mollusca: Bivalvia) *Marine Biology* 57: 25–34 (1980). For a full discussion of senescence *see* chapter 4, 'Negligible Senescence', in *Longevity, Senescence, and the Genome*, Caleb Finch (University of Chicago Press, Chicago, 1990). This gives many examples of animals and plants that are very long lived, from 5,000-year-old bristlecone pines, to rockfish and tortoises that survive more than 120 years; further, it provides a very interesting discussion of the enormous diversity of aging patterns that exist in nature.

466.   It is unlikely that there is a single cluster of genes serving as a general

pacemaker for senescence (the gradual increase in mortality and loss of function with age), but rather that there is a scatter of genes that each affect various organ systems of the body. Page 354, *Longevity, Senescence, and the Genome*, Caleb Finch, University of Chicago Press, Chicago, 1990.

467. *See* 'Evolution at two levels in humans and chimpanzees', M. King and A. Wilson, *Science* 188: 107–116 (1975).

468. The life expectancy of various primates in captivity are 23 to 31 years for the White-headed Gibbon, 11 to 39 for the Brown Lemur, 45 to 50 for the Mountain Gorilla, 35 to 50 for the Orangutan, and 30 to 60 for the Chimpanzee – man's closest living primate relative. *See Biological Values for Selected Mammals*, Larry Brainard (The American Association of Zookeepers, Topeka, Kansas, 1985); *see also* 'Primates', F. King et al, *Science* 240: 1475–1482 (1988).

469. 'Growth Hormone, Body Composition, and Aging', D. Rudman. *Journal of American Geriatric Society*, 33:800–807 (1985).

470. 'Effects of Human Growth Hormone in Men over 60 Years Old', D. Rudman et al, *New England Journal of Medicine*, 323(1):1–6 (1990). In this experiment, men undergoing triweekly injections of growth hormone over a period of six months showed a 9 per cent increase in lean body mass, a 14 per cent reduction in adipose-tissue mass, and a 7 per cent increase in skin thickness.

471. Another example of such an experiment is one on some 1,100 mice. In this case, cutting calories by some 40 per cent lengthened life spans by 29 per cent and led to significant reductions in most kinds of tumors and other signs of aging. *Science* 254:373 (1991)

472. This bank, started in 1977, contains sperm primarily from scientists of 'superior' intellectual ability including a few Nobel laureates. No comprehensive follow-ups of the children seem to have been performed. *See* 'The 139 Children of Dr Graham', pages 46–53, *California Magazine*, September 1991.

473. Reproductive policies differ sharply througout the world. In Rumania, birth control devices were illegal before the overthrow of Ceausescu, in Scandinavia they are supplied by the government. In the USSR, the average number of abortions during a woman's reproductive lifetime is four, whereas throughout Latin America abortion is generally illegal. In China, large families are illegal; in Singapore they are encouraged. The response to new capabilities is likely to be equally diverse.

474. The concept of enhancing human capacities over time is an appealing one for most people, but it brings up appalling images of controlled human 'breeding' or ethnic 'purification'. This is hardly surprising, in the past, so little was known about human biology that the theories behind such genetic manipulations could hardly be anything but racist or supremacist charades;

moreover, their implementation could only be abusive and repressive, because the only way to intervene in human reproduction was to seize and hold control over people's private lives. Today, modern biology is beginning to provide both the techniques and the knowledge to alter both the theory and practise of manipulations of human genetics. The regular medical use of genetic engineering to treat various diseases is likely to change the widespread negative perceptions of the idea of eugenics, (*See,* for example, 'Choosing a Demographic Future', R. Herrnstein, in *Evolutionary Theory and Human Values,* ed. P. Williams, in press.) and various new technologies including birth control vaccines and implantible birth control devices are making it possible to regulate the conception of children without violent repression.

475.   Keep in mind that the techniques of genetic engineering can be performed by any motivated biologist with access to the equipment in many university biology laboratories.

476.   If a salamander loses one of its limbs, a small nodule of tissue forms over the wound and grows into a new limb over a period of a few months. Generally, the new limb is equivalent to the original one being replaced. *See* 'Studies of digit regeneration and their implications for theories of development and evolution of vertebrate limbs', Gregory Stock, Susan Bryant, *Journal of Experimental Zoology* 216: 423–433 (1981).

477.   Today we already select and enhance the physiques of people through arduous training regimes. As a result, professional athletes in many sports now have physiques very distant from the average. If a professional weight lifter or basketball player came to your door, you would not be confused as to their profession. Only a few decades ago this might not have been the case.

478.   Only a decade ago bone-marrow cells could not be grown and maintained outside the body, now this is routinely done using nutrient fluid that is entirely synthetic. The same is true of skin cells. *See* 'Cultured Cells for the Treatment of Disease', Howard Green, pages 96-102, *Scientific American,* November 1991. Until scientists understand precisely what growth factors and other chemicals a specific type of cell needs to stay healthy, the cells must be sustained on a preparation of nutrients called serum, which is made by drawing the blood from fetal calves, clotting it, and extracting the clear plasma that remains. But eventually, all the essential requirements of the cells being cultured are identified and manufacturers can synthesize a 'serum-free' culture medium. Such a nutrient medium, because it is very clearly defined, is more desirable than serum for research use.

479.   The developments that would make possible so profound a human transformation as this are likely to flow quite naturally from today's mainstream medical research. A speech synthesizer tied directly to electrodes in the vocal nerves is an obvious enhancement of the speech-generating

computers used by the handicapped today, and both organ culture techniques and sensory prostheses are already the focus of large research efforts.

480. To most people the whole concept of a bodiless brain is repugnant, but it is hard to know how it would be viewed in the future, or even what such an existence would be like. After all, most people find dreaming a very enjoyable state, and quadriplegics, despite limited mobility and no sensory input from most of their body, find existence quite meaningful. Moreover, people who think of spirits or ghosts roaming after death frequently think in terms of some sort of disembodied entity that sees, hears, sometimes even talks, but has no sensations of the flesh. Is this so different from a 'brain-in-a-bottle'?

If this were the only way of staying alive, many people would no doubt be eager for it (at least on a trial basis). After all, a few people go so far in trying to escape death as to have themselves frozen, and others willingly suffer great pain in futile attempts to live.

CHAPTER 10

481. The seven-day week, which is strictly man-made and takes no notice of seasons or lunar cycles, became firmly established in the Western calendar in the second century AD in Rome, but the weekend itself is a modern invention. In the late nineteenth century it became common in Britain to have a half-day holiday on Saturday afternoon, which, coupled with Sunday, was first coined the 'weekend' by the *English Magazine,* 'Notes and Queries', in 1879. It was the shortened work weeks of the depression of the 1930s, however, that firmly established the modern two-day weekend. The 104 weekend days in the year, by dwarfing all other holiday time, have installed the line between 'weekend' and 'weekday' as the primary division between work and leisure in the developed world. 'Waiting for the Weekend', Witold Rybczynski, *The Atlantic Monthly,* 35–52. August 1991.

482. Of course many holidays have origins rooted in seasonal festivals and activities. For example, summer holidays from school were originally necessary so that children could help with the harvests. 'Does Climate Still Matter', Jesse Ausubel, *Nature,* 350: 649–652 (1991).

483. There are some seven million people in the US with full-time night jobs. *Wellness Letter* (University of California Press, Berkeley, California, February 1991).

484. For example, fewer than 10 per cent of the US work force is now employed in outdoor occupations such as farming and construction. *1990 Statistical Abstract of the United States* (US Bureau of the Census, Washington, DC).

485. Page 25, *The Futurist,* September 1991.

486.   In 1991, television sets were on for an average of forty-seven hours per week in American homes, and people in most age groups averaged from twenty to twenty-five hours of weekly television viewing time. People over fifty-five, the heaviest viewers, average some thirty-five hours a week. 'TV or not TV', Patrick Cooks, *In Health*, pages 33–43, January 1992.

487.   For example, Kruger Park in South Africa has an area about the size of Israel and began to be enclosed in 1959 in an effort to prevent the spread of hoof and mouth disease. In 1988, it was self-supporting, received 625,000 visitors (mainly domestic tourists), and had a budget of 20 million dollars (page B5, *New York Times*, 23 January 1990). There are sixteen wild-animal parks in Kenya, and about 600,000 overseas tourists each year visit them. For instance, some 200,000 foreign tourists a year visit the Amboseli National Park to see elephants, lions and other game of the Serengeti. One reason the Serengeti plains will likely be preserved is that it is far more valuable as a tourist attraction than anything else (page F4, *New York Times*, 26 May 1991). Such 'eco-tourism' is growing at a rate of about 30 per cent a year and is providing an increasingly powerful incentive for countries to preserve any rich natural environments they possess (*World Press Review*, page 45, January 1992).

488.   *Urban Roosts: Where birds nest in the city,* Barbara Bash (Little Brown, New York, 1990).

489.   For an eloquent eulogy for the dying concept of nature as an entity independent of man, *see The End of Nature*, Bill McKibben (Anchor Books, New York, 1989).

490.   Moreover, in the next few thousand years such cold temperatures may well return. In the depths of the last ice age, the earth was an average of about six degrees Centigrade cooler than it is now. The current interglacial, the period between ice ages, is now 10,000 to 13,000 years long, and no interglacial in the last half million years has lasted for longer than 12,000 years. Thus, scientists who study glaciers predict that the earth will move into another ice age within the next few thousand years. Whether it will be delayed by the increase in greenhouse gases caused by burning fossil fuels is unclear. One theory for the initiation of an ice age is that it would be triggered by the shifting of warm northward ocean currents such as the Atlantic Gulf stream that keeps Europe mild. For a general discussion of past ice ages, *see New York Times*, page B5, 16 January 1990. *See also* note 289.

491.   During the past 50,000 years, there have been several periods in which the climate of equatorial South America and Africa were cooler and drier than they are now, and during these periods the rain forests were almost certainly considerably smaller than today. 'Are we on the verge of mass extinctions in tropical rain forests?', D. Simberloff, pages 165–180 of *Dynamics of Extinction*, ed. D. Elliott (Wiley, New York, 1986). Moreover,

tropical rainforests may not have existed at all for roughly three quarters of the past 350 million years. *See* pages 134–137, *Extinction: Bad Genes or Bad Luck?*, David Raup (Norton and Co, New York, 1991).

492. The Sahara was temperate between 6,000 and 10,000 years ago, and also between 35,000 and 40,000 years ago. Pages 31, 82, *The Sahara, Ecological Change and Early Economic History*, Ed. J. Allen (Middle East and North African Studies Press Ltd, England, 1981).

493. Pages 43–46, *Evolution, Mammals, and Southern Continents*, ed. A. Keast, F. Erk, and B. Glass (State University of New York Press, Albany, 1972). Amphibian and reptile fossils (therapsids) were first found in Antarctica in 1970; they date from the Triassic period, which lasted from 200 million years ago until the end of the Cretacious, 65 million years ago. Moreover, forests containing pine and other trees existed there much more recently.

494. This figure is redrawn from figure 1 in 'Are we on the verge of mass extinctions in tropical rain forests?', D. Simberloff, pages 165–180 of *Dynamics of Extinction* ed. D. Elliott (Wiley, New York, 1986). Simberloff in turn has used a figure from 'Speciation in Amazonian forest birds', *Science*, 165: 131–137 (1969).

495. For a discussion of the idea that nature is not in equilibrium but rather in constant flux, *see* the *New York Times*, 31 July 1990, 'New Eye on Nature: The Real Constant is Eternal Turmoil'.

496. Page 4, *Extinction: Bad Genes or Bad Luck?*, David Raup (Norton & Co., New York, 1991).

497. The time course of the large extinctions of the past cannot be seen with a precision of centuries or even millennia because of the imperfect nature of the world's fossil record. None the less, these massive extinctions were almost certainly the product of cascades of secondary extinctions brought by greatly disrupted ecological systems. Even the 65-million-year-old Cretacious extinction, caused by the impact of a comet or meteor, seems to be the product of tens of thousands of years of global ecological turmoil following the collision. 'Extinctions: A Paleontological Perspective', David Jablonski, *Science*, 253:754–757 (1991).

498. Each of these five massive extinctions is thought to have caused over three quarters of then existing species to become extinct. In addition, there have been during the past 200 million years other lesser mass-extinctions of more than one-third of existing species. 'Extinctions: A Paleontological Perspective', David Jablonski, *Science*, 253:754–757 (1991), or 'Phanerozoic Overview of Mass Extinction', J. Sepkoski, pages 277–95, *Patterns and Processes in the History of Life*, eds. D. Raup, D. Jablonsky (Springer-Verlag, Berlin, 1986).

Interestingly, meteoritic impacts may have brought not only the Cretacious extinction, but others as well. In particular, recent evidence suggests that the

Devonian extinction some 367 million years ago may also have coincided with a large meteor impact. *See* 'Another Impact Extinction?' *Science*, 256:1280 (1992).

499.   These figures are primarily based on drawings and information in 'The Breakup of Pangaea', Robert Dietz and John Molden, *Scientific American*, October 1970.

500.   Without oxygen metabolism, animals could not generate the power they need to carry on their energetic lifestyles. Photosynthesis provides enough energy for a vegetative existence, not for movement and activity. It is no quirk of nature that there are neither plants running around in the world, nor green animals living directly off the sunlight.

501.   The rate of extinction at times other than during massive extinction events is estimated at roughly one species per year for every 10,000,000 species. *See* the article by D.M. Raup, pages 51–57, *Biodiversity*, ed. E.O. Wilson (National Academy Press, Washington, DC, 1988).

502.   There is significant controversy about how rapidly species are going extinct. The rate of extinction cited here is derived from modeling by E.O. Wilson that indicates that a 90 per cent reduction in the size of a habitat will eventually eliminate half the species there. E. Wilson. *Scientific American* 261:108 (1989). Higher estimates can be found in *Keeping Options Alive: The Scientific Basis for Conserving Diversity* (World Resources Institute, Washington, DC, 1989). Criticisms of such high estimates are discussed in 'Extinction: Are Ecologists Crying Wolf?', Charles Wolf, *Science* 253:736–737 (1991).

503.   The data in this graph was taken from 'Chronology of fluctuating sea levels since the Triassic', Haq, B.U., J. Hardenbol, P. Vail, *Science* 235:1156–1167 (1987). *See also* page 186, *Paleoclimatology*, T. Crowley and G. North (Oxford Univ. Press, Oxford, 1991).

504.   For example, in a three-acre jungle area in Peru, 300 species of trees were found, nearly half as many as all the native species of trees in North America. *New York Times*, page B5, 20 August 1991. It is probable that the extent of tropical jungle has fluctuated significantly during the last few hundred thousand years. If so, this suggests that the total biodiversity of the planet has probably also fluctuated significantly in recent times. Page 136, *Extinction: Bad Genes or Bad Luck?*, David Raup (Norton and Co., New York, 1991). *See* note 492.

505.   Pages 90–93, *Pleistocene Extinctions: The Search for a Cause*, eds P. Martin, H. Wright (Yale University Press, New Haven, 1967).

506.   Though there are debates about the current rate of species extinction, there is general agreement that it is large. To be in the midst of a so-called massive extinction, however, does not mean that half of today's species must die in the next few centuries (though that could well occur), it requires only

that such levels of extinction will occur during the coming *millennia* or *tens of millennia*. Given the rate of environmental change now occurring, this is very likely, whether or not radical environmental action is taken. Global warming seems to be bringing significant climate change, extensive destruction of tropical jungle is continuing, human numbers and activity continue to grow, and the mixing of plant and animal species from different locales is increasing. Indeed, the major remaining uncertainty about the full extent of current extinctions is the sea; there is simply not very much information about how severe the disruption of oceanic ecosystems is. An excellent collection of short papers on many diverse aspects of the topic of biodiversity can be found in *Biodiversity*, ed. E.O. Wilson (National Academy Press, Washington, DC, 1988). *See also* Michael Soule's paper, 'Conservation: Tactics for a Constant Crisis', *Science* 253:744–750 (1991).

507. For a general discussion of how the spread of species into new habitats is bringing extinctions, *see* 'Biological Immigrants Under Fire', E. Culotta, *Nature* 254:1444–1447 (1991), or *Science News* 142:56.58 (1992).

508. *Science News* 139:282–284 (1991).

509. *Local* diversity may increase with the arrival of new species, but because the new species are cosmopolitan ones with wide distributions while those that disappear are endemic species found nowhere else, total *global* diversity continues to fall. In Hawaii there were some sixty-eight species of passerines (the largest order of birds, which includes almost all perching songbirds) present 2,000 years ago and almost all were endemic. Some thirty disappeared around the time of Polynesian colonization, another eleven with the arrival of Europeans, and today several more are threatened. But since 1780, fifty new species of alien passerines have become established. Thus Hawaii now has more bird species than it did before human settlement, but the world has fewer 'Diversity and Biological Invasions of Oceanic Islands,' Peter Vitousek, pages 181–189 of *Biodiversity*, ed. E.O. Wilson (National Academy Press. Washington, DC, 1988).

510. 'An Evolutionary Basis for Conservation Strategies', Terry Erwin, *Science* 253:750–752 (1991).

511. For example, *see* 'Screening Plants for New Medicines', Norman Farnsworth, pages 83–97, in *Biodiversity*, ed. E.O. Wilson (National Academy Press, Washington, DC, 1988).

512. 'Ethnobotany and the identification of therapeutic agents from the rainforest', M. Balick in *Bioactive Compounds from Plants*, eds. D. Chadwick and J. Marsh (J. Wiley and Sons, New York, 1990).

513. The advent of modern robotic screening methods provides a powerful alternative to trying to trace individual traditional herbal remedies. In addition, many of the potent herbal remedies that might lead to valuable modern drugs have already been examined, and the tribal communities whose

knowledge might lead to new medicines are rapidly disappearing. A few important drugs undoubtedly still remain to be found in the rainforests, but modern pharmacology is moving beyond this phase in its development.

514.   'Screening Plants for New Medicines', Norman Farnsworth, pages 83–97, in *Biodiversity*, ed. E.O. Wilson (National Academy Press, Washington, DC, 1988).

515.   In 1991, for example, Merck, with the largest effort, had only about thirty scientists involved with research on all natural products combined; which includes efforts on marine organisms, fungi, and microorganisms, as well as plants. *Natural Products Research and the Potential Role of the Pharmaceutical Industry in Tropical Forest Conservation*, Christina Findeisen and Sarah Laird (The Periwinkle Project of the Rainforest Alliance, New York, 1991).

516.   Estimates of the total number of species vary widely and range from about 10 million to 80 million species. *See* for example, Robert May's 'A fondness for fungi', *Nature* 352:475–476 (1991). Slightly more than 50 per cent (740,000) of the 1.4 million species so far identified are insects and another 15 per cent (220,000) are flowering plants. 'Biodiversity Studies: Science and Policy', Paul Ehrlich and Edward Wilson, *Science* 253:758–762 (1991).

517.   In *Medline*, a computerized index of publications in several thousand journals relevant to medicine, some 93 per cent (278,000 papers) of the 300,000 papers written between 1988 and 1992 about non human vertebrates were written about only a dozen animals: rats (93,000), mice (39,000), rabbits (27,000), cattle (25,000), dogs (25,000), pigs (14,000), guinea pigs (13,000), cats (10,000), sheep (9,000), hamsters (9,000), chickens (8,000), and macaque monkeys (6,000).

518.   It is estimated that somewhere between 5 and 50 billion species have existed on the earth at one time or another. *See* note 497.

519.   'Ex Situ Conservation of Plant Genetic Resources: Global Development and Environmental Concerns'. Joel Cohen et al, *Science* 253:866–872 (1991); 'Utilization and Conservation of Genetic Resources: International Projects For Sustainable Agriculture', J. Cohen, J. Alcorn, C. Potter *Economic Botany* 45(2):190–199 (1990).

520.   The fraction of the total wild species so far preserved varies widely from crop to crop, ranging from some 90 per cent of barley and sorghum to 20 per cent of Cassava. *See* pages 130, 131 of *Atlas of the Environment*, Geoffrey Lean et al (Prentice Hall, New York, 1986).

521.   'Biodiversity Studies: Science and Policy', Paul Ehrlich and Edward Wilson, *Science* 253:758–762 (1991).

522.   An interesting question to consider is how long it might take for species diversity to increase to its previous levels. One might argue that the

loss of species occurring today will reduce the planet's diversity for some 5 to 10 million years, since this is how long it has taken natural biological processes to restore levels of plant and animal diversity to pre-existing levels after each previous massive extinction. This prediction explicitly assumes that the patterns of the past will obtain in the future, which in this case is very unlikely. The earth's level of biodiversity even thousands of years from now will almost certainly depend more on what Metaman does than on any of the more gradual processes that would predominate in Metaman's absence. In the coming millennia Metaman will employ biotechnology and other methods to create any level of planetary species diversity it chooses. But, of course, a more interconnected global environment may mean that species diversity will never again approach the historic levels when the earth's local environments were all isolated from one another. For a discussion of the aftermaths of past extinctions, *see* 'Extinctions: A Paleontological Perspective', David Jablonsky, *Science* 253:754–757 (1991).

523.   Basing environmental action on prophesies of doom is a very risky strategy because, if the threat is found to be exaggerated (as is often the case), the justification for *any* action fades. Similarly, invoking economic arguments encourages decisions about the environment to be made largely on the economic grounds that are bringing about destructive current activities. Neither businesses nor individuals are fools about money; they are very good at understanding and furthering their *immediate* economic interests. Whether we like it or not, the existing economic system favors short-term over long-term gains, and that generally is a force for exploiting the environment. To change our economic system is a far more difficult task even than protecting the environment.

The truth is that if humans do not feel a sufficient resonance with, and aesthetic attachment to, the biological environment around them to want to preserve it, that 'natural' environment is likely to pass away.

524.   *The Academic American Encyclopedia*, Electronic Version (Grolier Electronic Publishing, Danbury, Connecticut, 1991).

525.   Despite long efforts and several million dollars spent to prevent the extinction of the dusty seaside sparrow (*Ammodramus maritima nigrescens*) – one of nine subspecies of the seaside sparrow – the last living dusty sparrow died in 1987, 115 years after the subspecies was first identified in the mosquito-infested marshes in Florida that were its habitat. For a discussion of the efforts to save the dusty sparrow, and those directed towards the silverspot butterfly (S.z. hippolyta), *see* 'The Butterfly Problem', Charles Mann and Mark Plummer, *The Atlantic Monthly*, pages 47–70, January 1992. This article is an examination of the inadequacy of policies, such as the 1973 Endangered Species Act in the US, that despite limited budgets seek to prevent species extinctions without regard for relative costs and benefits.

526.   Bear baiting, a death struggle between dogs and bears generally taking place in an arena, was outlawed in Britain in 1835. Until then bears were raised expressly for this popular spectacle. For a short overview, *see* the *Encyclopedia Britannica*, 11th Edition, volume 3, page 575 (Cambridge University Press, Cambridge, UK, 1910).

527.   The first modern zoo was the London zoo, founded in 1828 by Stamford Raffles. Page A15, *Los Angeles Times*, 18 June 1992.

528.   The last wild Arabian oryx was killed in 1972, but in 1982 animals from captive breeding colonies in zoos were reintroduced successfully into large preserves in Oman. Page 45, *World Press Review*, October 1991.

529.   The potential of these techniques is evident from the powerful impact of simple selective breeding: corn, tomatoes, potatoes, cattle, dogs, cats, horses, roses: all have been radically transformed. Indeed they have taken on their present forms largely as a result of selective breeding. For a wonderful discussion of selective breeding, *see* chapter 1, 'Variation under domestication' of *The Origin of Species*, Charles Darwin (Mentor, 1958).

530.   The recent proliferation of gene transfers between species can be seen by looking at reported research using 'transgenic' techniques. A computer search of the *Medline* index revealed that in the period from 1983 to 1985, there were only twenty-one research papers dealing with transgenes listed in life-science journals; from 1986 to 1988 there were 273; and from 1989 to 1991 there were 683. *See also* note 450.

531.   For instance, genetically engineered bacteria are central to the industrial 'bioreactors' that produce drugs such as tissue plasminogen activator (TPA), which dissolves blood clots. Transgenic goats and sheep have also been engineered to secrete this human enzyme – TPA – in their milk. *Science News* 140(10):148 (1991), and 'Research news', *Science* 254:35–36 (1991). Moreover, pigs have been genetically transformed to produce human hemoglobin, *Science* 253:32–33 (1991).

532.   'A feast of gene-splicing down on the fish farm', *Science* 253:512–513 (1991), or *New York Times*, page B7, 27 November 1990.

533.   *Science* 253:33 (1991). In the US in 1992, the Food and Drug Administration embraced the principle that there would be no extra regulatory hurdles applied to new food products simply because they were developed using genetic engineering instead of traditional plant breeding. *See* 'The Safety of Foods Developed by Biotechnology', David Kessler et al, *Science* 256:1747–1749 (1992); 'Genetically engineered foods get green light,' *Nature* 357:352 (1992).

534.   *Newsletter, Center for Reproduction of Endangered Wildlife*, volume 5, No. 2, November 1987 and volume 7, No. 1, July 1989.

535.   In this context, 'higher' organisms refer to all complex, differentiated, multicellular organisms. The creatures called eukaryotic protists have cells as

complex as those of the multicellular creatures, but being single-celled have not been included.

536.   Of course, boundaries are blurring and machines may not remain strictly nonbiological for ever. Just as mechanical and electronic components are surgically incorporated into living creatures, biological components are also being added to machines. For instance, cell receptors, enzymes and even living cells are being linked to microelectrodes to create sophisticated 'biosensors' that detect minute concentrations of compounds ranging from glucose to nerve gas. 'Biosensors', J. Schultz. *Scientific American*, pages 64–69, August 1991. For a comprehensive survey *see Biosensors: Fundamentals and Applications*, eds A. Turner, I. Karube, G. Wilson (Oxford University Press, Oxford, England, 1987).

537.   Today, some 3 per cent of the earth's land surface is now protected as national parks, wildlife preserves, nature preserves, or other such areas. *See* pages 137–140 *Atlas of the Environment*, Geoffrey Lean et al (Prentice Hall, New York, 1986).

538.   Our relatively easy access to 'nature' can be seen in the numbers of visitors to National Parks in the US. Beautiful Yosemite National Park in California already handles some 3.5 million visitors a year, and over 8 million visit Smokey Mountain National Park each year.

539.   The prototype was constructed by the Michael Braunstein Group Inc. of Columbus, Ohio.

540.   An interesting article on how computers will begin to fade into our environment is Mark Weiser's 'The Computer for the 21st Century'. *Scientific American* 265(3):94–105 (1991).

541.   'ELIZA – A Computer Program for the study of Natural Language Communication between Man and Machine', Joseph Weizenbaum, *Communications of the Association for Computing Machinery* 9:36–45 (1966).

542.   *See* page 204 of Raymond Kurzweil's, *The Age of Intelligent Machines* (MIT Press, Boston, 1990). More recently, in a 1990 study on the effectiveness of treating mild to moderate depression using an interactive computer program to mimic a psychoanalytic approach called cognitive-behavioral therapy, a computer proved to be as effective as a therapist and was even described by some patients as showing 'therapist understanding.' *Science News* 137:37 (1990), *Newsweek* 115:61 (1990).

Cognitive-behavioral therapy attempts to teach patients how to 'unlearn' negative patterns of perceiving their experiences and replace them with more positive thoughts and responses. For example a cognitive-behavioral therapist (or computer) might ask a patient feeling rejected because of a someone's rudeness whether the rudeness might possibly have not been directed at them personally but only interpreted in that way. In the reported experiment, a pilot study involving only thirty-six patients, some two thirds in each group showed improvement over the six weeks of therapy.

If this rapport is possible with the systems of today, there can be little question that people would become deeply attached to a speaking computer that really did know them intimately. The effects such attachments ultimately might have on human relationships is hard to gauge. *See also* note 105.

543. Page 600, *Gödel, Escher, and Bach: An Eternal Golden Braid*, Douglas Hofstadter (Vintage Books, New York, 1980). *Also see* note 105.

544. One prototype developed for the US Department of Defense responds to verbal queries about flight schedules. Ask it to list all the flights from Los Angeles to Karachi by way of Berlin on a certain day, and the computer will do so regardless how the question is phrased. 'Computers that Hear and Respond', page C1, *New York Times*, 14 August 1991.

There are many applications – getting directory information from the phone company, controlling an electronic appliance, making hotel reservations – that are equally narrow, so this technology may soon begin to find its way into our lives. For example, AT&T announced in 1992 that it was beginning a program to replace a third of its operators in the next few years with voice recognition software. (Page D1, *Los Angeles Times*, 4 March 1992.) Progress is also being made in using computers to read human handwriting, and the US Post Office hopes by 1995 to machine-read half of the handwritten envelopes received. 'Moving Scribbled Mail Along', Tim Race, page C1, *New York Times*, 27 May 1992.

545. Another interesting effect may be a continuing rise in the general acceptance of various parapsychological effects. Even today, people sometimes use garbled references to quantum theory or 'electronic vibrations' to justify their beliefs in telepathy, clairvoyance, psychic surgery, or the power of crystals and pyramids. To many people such ideas seem as plausible as the black holes, quarks, charm numbers or gravity waves of theoretical physics.

546. This is not to say that animal experimentation is not of value; it is absolutely essential to progress in medicine and biology. At times, however, animals are handled so callously in experiments that it is hard to believe they are being viewed as living creatures, but this takes place in only a small minority of the animal research done today. In 1988 the Department of Agriculture estimated that 94 per cent of animals used for research in the US are not subjected to painful procedures. Animal Welfare Environmental Report, US Department of Agriculture, Washington, DC, 1988.

547. Page 13, *Health*, February 1992. As another example, Americans born in the early 1900s associate the smell of pine with the outdoors and find it pleasant, while many people born since the Second World War associate the same smell with disinfectants and find it disagreeable; they like the smell of Play-Doh or Lego plastic.

CHAPTER 11

548.   In the US there are now a million and a half millionaires, and yet in 1988 there were 31,745,000 people in poverty, which was defined as an annual household income of under $12,092 for a family of four. Page 561, *The 1991 World Almanac and Book of Facts*, ed. M. Hoffman (Pharos, New York). 'Asking How Much is Enough', Alan Durning, page 155, *State of the World 1991*, A Worldwatch Report, Lester Brown et al (Norton and Co, New York). *See also* note 564.

549.   Imprisonment of debtors did not disappear from Europe until the 1870s. It was abolished in England by the Debtors Act of 1869, in Ireland by the Debtor's Act of 1872; in France in 1867, in Sweden and Norway in 1874, and in Italy in 1877. *The Encyclopedia Britannica*, Eleventh Edition, Volume VII (Cambridge University Press, Cambridge, 1910).

550.   The first anaesthesia, ether, was introduced in 1846. Page 454, *Expectations of Life: A Study in the Demography, Statistics, and History of World Mortality*, H.O. Lancaster (Springer-Verlag, New York, 1989).

551.   Page 117, *Expectations of Life*, H.O. Lancaster (Springer-Verlag, New York, 1989).

552.   Before the first clinical trials of penicillin in 1941, there were no antibiotics. Pages 454, 460, *Expectations of Life*, H.O. Lancaster (Springer-Verlag, New York, 1989).

553.   Because of decreased infection, a patient's chances of survival increased in smaller hospitals. Thus in British hospitals in 1868, the mortality rate for an amputation at the thigh was 46 per cent in a hospital with more than 300 beds but only 20 per cent in one with less than 25 beds. Conditions in crowded wartime hospitals were even worse, so much so that death from disease was much more common than from combat injuries. In the Crimean War (1852–4), there were 1,724 British deaths from wounds and 14,792 from diarrhea, dysentery, scurvy and other diseases. Pages 119, 321 *Expectations of Life*, H.O. Lancaster (Springer-Verlag, New York, 1989).

554.   For example, the first sewage treatment in London was in 1854, page 80, *Expectations of Life*, H.O. Lancaster (Springer-Verlag, New York, 1989). For more information about the early history of waste disposal and the development of modern sewage treatment, *see* the brief book review 'Signature of Deadly Water', Eric Ashby, *Science* 348:495–496 (1990), and the book, *A Science of Impurity*, Christopher Hamlin (American Institute of Physics, New York, 1990).

555.   *The Big Smoke: A History of Air Pollution in London since Medieval Times*, Peter Brimblecombe (Methuen, New York, 1987).

556.   Page 8, 'City Limits: Emerging Constraints on Urban Growth', Kathleen Newland, Worldwatch paper 38, August 1980. Also look at Barbara

Ward's 'The Home of Man' and Piers Norton's 'Can we save Britain's Ailing Sewers?' *New Scientist*, June 1980.

557.   Page 29, *Ethnic America: A History*, Thomas Sowell (Basic Books, New York, 1981). This book provides a penetrating and stimulating examination of the history of the Irish and other ethnic groups in the US and is well worth reading.

558.   Page 114, *Boston's Immigrants*, Oscar Handlin (Atheneum, New York, 1970); page 29, *Ethnic America: A History*, Thomas Sowell (Basic Books, New York, 1981).

559.   Page 27, *The Irish in America*, Carl Wittke (Russell and Russell, New York, 1970); page 29, *Ethnic America, A History*, Thomas Sowell (Basic Books, New York, 1981).

560.   Page 35, *Bionomics: The Inevitability of Capitalism*, Michael Rothschild (Henry Holt and Co., New York, 1990); pages 41–49 *History of Factory Legislation*, B. Hutchins and A. Harrison (Frank Cass and Co., London, 1926). It now seems reprehensible to have eleven-year-olds work 70 hours a week, but in the eighteenth century the practise was not so shocking; after all most families were farmers for whom working from dawn until dusk was the rule not the exception.

561.   Pages 18–22, *Albion's Fatal Tree: Crime and Society in Eighteenth-Century England*, Douglas Hay (Pantheon Books, New York, 1975). The US one of the few Western nations that still has capital punishment, executed some 128 people between 1976 and 1990. Interestingly, the cost of an execution and the various appeals leading up to it is estimated to exceed that of 100 years of imprisonment. 'The Death Penalty', pages 17–18, *Scientific American*, July 1990. *See also* note 566.

562.   Page 108, *Albion's Fatal Tree: Crime and Society in Eighteenth Century England*, Douglas Hay (Pantheon Books, New York, 1975).

563.   The harsh reality of some residual practices in the developing world serve as a reminder of what was accepted in earlier times. For example, two Americans convicted in 1991 of robbing $3,365 from a bank in Pakistan were sentenced to have one hand and one foot amputated in addition to five years in jail. Page 13A, *St Petersburg Times*, 26 September 1991. *See also* note 566.

564.   The poor within Metaman may stand out starkly from the affluent around them, but they can generally obtain food, shelter, clean water and medical care. In the US, for example, some 32 million people (13 per cent of the population) were living below the poverty level in 1988. *The 1991 World Almanac and Book of Facts*, ed. M. Hoffman (Pharos, New York). The poverty level however is $6,024 for a single person, which would be considered affluent in much of the world, and is adequate to avoid bodily privation. We tend to gauge welfare in relative terms rather than historical ones, so such things as not having indoor plumbing or decent heating, living

with many others in one room, or surviving on rice and beans seem intolerable; but a few centuries ago they would have been acceptable.

For estimates of the relative affluence of different population segments, *see* page 153 of 'Asking How Much is Enough', Alan Durning, pages 153–169, *State of the World 1991*, A Worldwatch Report, Lester Brown et al (Norton and Co. New York).

565.   For example, infant mortality in less-developed countries fell from 180 to 70 deaths per 1,000 live births between 1950 and 1990. By comparison, throughout the developed world this mortality figure is now under 10. During these four decades, life expectancy in Africa, the lowest on any continent, has increased from about 38 to 55. *See* charts 4, 14, *World Military and Social Expenditures 1989*, Ruth Sivard (World Priorities, Washington, DC, 1989).

566.   For descriptions of public executions during this period, *see Albion's Fatal Tree: Crime and Society in Eighteenth-Century England*, Douglas Hay (Pantheon Books, New York, 1975). A fascinating and comprehensive exploration of the changing nature of punishment is presented in *Discipline and Punish: The Birth of the Prison*, Michael Foucault (Vintage Books, New York, 1979). Regarding punishment for capital offenses, the idea of a 'painless' death is a very recent one born in the late eighteenth century. Previously, torture was the rule rather than the exception, and the duration and pain of the execution were meant to match the severity of the crime.

567.   In 1983, 9 years of education were compulsory in 33 countries, 10 years in 35 countries, 11 years in 5 countries, and 12 years in 4 countries. Further, in virtually all countries outside Africa, more than 80 per cent of children under twelve were attending school. Page 129, *Atlas of the World Today*, N. Grant and N. Middleton (Harper and Row, New York, 1987).

568.   The use of a mark instead of a signature to sign marriage registers has been tabulated by county for England in 1840 and ranged from 55 per cent in Bedford to 17 per cent in Middlesex. *See* diagram 27 in *Industry and Empire: An Economic History of Britain since 1750*, E. J. Hobsbawm (Weidenfeld and Nicolson, London, 1968).

569.   Page 80, *The Prize: The Epic Quest for Oil, Money, and Power*, Daniel Yergin (Simon & Schuster, New York, 1990). *Also see* note 575.

570.   'Unforgettable' is on Natalie Cole's album, *With Love* (Elektra, 1991). Nat King Cole died in 1965.

571.   The first talking movie was in 1924; the first silent movies in the 1890s. *The 1991 World Almanac and Book of Facts*, ed. M. Hoffman (Pharos, New York).

572.   The first crystal-oscillator radio was built in 1918, *The 1991 World Almanac and Book of Facts*, ed. M. Hoffman (Pharos, New York).

573.   Alan Durning, 'Ending Poverty', pages 135–253 in *State of the World 1990* (Norton and Co., New York).

574. Those who buy the very first models of such new devices as lap-top computers, CD players, or videocameras pay a premium to have them before others. But these early purchases are crucial to the development of a new technology because they fund the development of the new product and allow it to reach the point of mass production. Essentially, the people who buy these early models are playing a critical role in technological advance by funding research and development for new products.

575. The model-T sold for 600 dollars in 1920, which is about 5,000 current dollars. Page 188, *Bionomics: The Inevitability of Capitalism*, Michael Rothschild (Henry Holt and Co., New York, 1990).

576. The quote is from W. Ogburn and S. Gilfillan, 'The Influence of Invention and Discovery', Report of the President's Research Committee on Social Trends, in *Recent Social Trends in the US* (McGraw-Hill, New York, 1933), pages 122–165. *See also*, page 21, Jesse Ausubel, 'Rat-Race Dynamics and Crazy Companies', *Technological Forecasting and Social Change* 39:11–22 (1991). The facsimile machine was discovered in 1842 by Alexander Bain, a Scotsman, and the first transmission of a wire photo was in 1924, between Cleveland and New York.

577. In the early 1980s, industry analysts predicted 3 million home-banking terminals in the US by 1990 but only 100,000 were actually installed by that date. Many other predictions also proved to be inflated; for example analysts predicted that 10 per cent of homes would have fiber-optic cable by 1990 but only 1 per cent did, and that annual sales of teleconferencing equipment would be threefold higher by 1990 than the actual sales of 450 million dollars.

These delays do not mean that the eventual impacts of such technologies will be less profound than early analysts suggested, just that society takes decades rather than years to make such immense changes. Pages 44–46, 'What New Age?', T. McCarroll, *Time* magazine, 12 August 1991.

578. New Zealand, in 1893, was the first country in the world to enfranchise women on an equal footing with men. Page 7, *Women in Politics: A Global Review*. Kathleen Newland (Worldwatch Institute, Washington DC, 1975). *See* note 583.

579. In the US, the shift from horses to automobiles occurred between 1900 and 1930; in 1915 there were approximately an equal number of cars and horses being used in transportation. We may complain about automobile pollution, but in this regard the automobile, which produces some 5 grams of pollutants per mile, is a vast improvement over the horse, which produces an average of some 940 grams of solid and liquid wastes per mile. At the current density of cars, horses would be an impossible environmental problem. *See* Table 1 and Figure 6 of J. Ausubel's 'Regularities in Technological Development: An Environmental View', *Technology and Environment* (National Academy Press, Washington, DC, 1989).

580. The expansion of government has been immense in the past 150 years and was already well underway by 1890 in the US. Under President Jackson in 1831, all three branches of the US Federal government were run by only 666 people. Fifty years later, after the industrialization accompanying the Civil War, this number had grown to 13,000, and in 1990 the number was almost 3,000,000. The fraction of the population employed by the federal government rose from 1 in 20,000 people to 1 in 75 during this 150-year period. *See* page 14 of *The Control Revolution: Technological and Economic Origins of the Information Society*, James Beniger (Harvard University Press, Cambridge, 1986) and *1991 Statistical Abstract of the US*, US Bureau of the Census, Washington, DC.

581. In the US in 1890, the agricultural, manufacturing, service and information sectors of the economy respectively constituted 37, 28, 22, and 12 per cent of the civilian labor force. In 1980, the distribution of these same sectors had shifted to 2, 22, 28 and 46 per cent respectively. Page 24, *The Control Revolution*, James Beniger (Harvard University Press, Cambridge, 1986).

582. *The Private War of Mrs. Packard*, Barbara Sapinsley (Paragon House, New York, 1991).

583. The first country in the world to enfranchise women on equal terms with men was New Zealand, in 1893; Australia was the next in 1902. The first country in Asia was Burma in 1922; the first in South America was Equador in 1929; the US allowed women's suffrage in 1920; France didn't do so until 1945. Women enjoyed full voting rights in only one country in 1900, in 15 by 1920, in 30 by 1940, in 92 by 1960, and virtually everywhere by 1970. Pages 6–10, *Women in Politics: A Global Review*, Kathleen Newland (Worldwatch Institute, Washington, DC, 1975).

584. *See 1990 Statistical Abstract of the US*, US Bureau of the Census, Washington, DC, and for a general discussion *see Women in Politics: A Global Review*, Kathleen Newland (Worldwatch Institute, Washington, DC, 1975).

585. For example, some 11 per cent of lawyers in the US were women in 1974, but in 1988 the figure had risen to 19.5 per cent. *1990 Statistical Abstract of the US*, US Bureau of the Census, Washington, DC.

586. Imagine what the cost would be of servicing – without computers – the 44 million social security beneficiaries who received payments each month from the US government in 1992. Today, there are some 63,000 social security employees, one for each 700 beneficiaries; in 1940 there were 9,000 employees, one for every 25 of the 222,000 beneficiaries. Moreover, during the past twenty-five years, the processing time for a new application has gone from about three months to about a week. (Information provided by the Social Security Administration, US Department of Health and Human Services.)

587. In 1988, there were 398 billion local calls and 48 billion long distance

calls in the US, nearly 4,000 calls that year for every person able to speak. Statistics of Communication Common Carriers, Federal Communications Commission, Washington, DC, 1989.

588.   Compare for example the relative costs of two calls from New York: one to Philadelphia, which is some 100 miles away, and one to San Francisco, nearly 3,000 miles distant. In 1920, the longer call cost 30 times more than the shorter one; in 1940, 9 times as much; in 1960, 4.5 times as much; and in 1992 *only 10 per cent more*. The New York to Philadelphia call has dropped more than sixfold in real dollars since 1920, and the New York to San Francisco call some 200 fold. Page 784, *Historical Statistics of the US: From Colonial Times to 1975*, US Bureau of the Census (Government Printing Office, 1975).

589.   In addition, the hourly phone rates for teleconferencing have dropped from $96 per hour to as little as $30 during these half-dozen years. *See New York Times*, page C1, 21 February 1991; and page C5, 5 February 1992.

590.   In early 1992, AT&T announced a mass-market videophone that works over standard telephone lines. The videophone, priced at $1,500, has a tiny, three-inch flip-up screen showing a ten-frames-per-second image. (*New York Times*, page B5, 7 January 1992.) Later the same year, MCI Communications Corporation announced a similar phone for only $750. (Page C4, *New York Times*, 24 September 1992.) While these devices are too primitive to be very widely used, they are harbingers of the move towards widespread video telecommunications that is virtually certain to parallel the conversion to fiber-optic telephone communication lines in the first few decades of the twenty-first century.

591.   *New York Times*, page C2, 10 April 1991.

592.   'Cost Projections for Fiber in the Loop', P. Shumate, *IEE LCS Magazine* 1(1):73–76 (1990).

593.   New York Times, page C31, November 1991.

594.   The new experiences offered by technology continue to multiply: cameras mounted on race cars at the Indianapolis 500, for instance, can bring television spectators the visceral excitement of the driver's view of a high-speed race. 'Technology Turning Spectators into Participants', page B9, *New York Times*, 24 May 1990.

595.   *The 1991 World Almanac and Book of Facts*, ed. M. Hoffman (Pharos, New York). Total attendance at *all* professional sporting events in the US was some 200 million in 1991, whereas movie attendance was over 1 billion.

596.   *The 1991 World Almanac and Book of Facts*, ed M. Hoffman (Pharos, New York).

597.   This figure is for 1990. Page 318, *The 1991 World Almanac and Book of Facts*, ed. M. Hoffman (Pharos, New York). Moreover, two thirds of American homes had two or more television sets.

598.   Some estimates suggest that storing an entire movie on five one-gigabyte chips (1,000,000 Megabytes of information) will be possible within a decade. 'Products and Services for Computer Networks', Nicholas Negroponte, *Scientific American* 265(3):106–113 (1991). Experimental fiber-optic systems, for example the Synchronous Optical Network (SONET) support transmission speeds as high as 2.4 gigabits per second, so a movie could be transmitted in only a few seconds. 'Networks', Vinton Cerf, *Scientific American* 265(3):72–81 (1991). And the potential exists for eventually transmitting information a thousand times as rapidly as the newly evolving fiber technologies are refined. 'Lightwave Communications: The Fifth Generation', E. Desurvire, *Scientific American* 226(1):114–121 (1992).

599.   'Products and Services for Computer Networks', Nicholas Negroponte, *Scientific American* 265(3):106–113 (1991). Given such a wide offering of films; it would be essential to have ways of identifying the ones a person wanted to see. Computer systems would be of great assistance. For example, it is quite probable that systems could be developed even today that would do a good job of searching a library for films that would appeal to us. We would merely have to indicate which actors or directors we liked, which critics we trusted, what mood we were in, or even what other films we had previously enjoyed. As such a system learned our specific tastes, it could become very adept at pleasing us.

600.   Page 25, *The New Rays of Professor Röntgen*, Bern Dibner (Burndy Library, Norwalk, Connecticut, 1963).

601.   'Symbiosis in the Deep Sea',. J. Childress et al, pages 114–120, *Scientific American*, May 1987.

602.   Lennart Nilsson's, *A Child Is Born* (Dell Publishing, New York, 1977) contains a series of extraordinary photos of the developing human embryo. And, of course, we are moving beyond images that rely on *visible* light. We use heat detectors to see in pitch darkness, X-rays to look at our own skeletons, radar to watch a storm and frequency converters to hear a bat's sonar.

603.   The simplest example is the animated cartoon. No longer is there even a sharp line between animated and real characters; onscreen they can be equally 'real' and interact with each other accordingly. A good demonstration of this is the animation in the 1988 film *Who Framed Roger Rabbit?*, directed by Robert Zemerckis, Amblin Entertainment and Walt Disney.

604.   Some interactive artificial environments are already in use. Flight simulators complete with sound, vibration, and moving images of the earth, for instance, create realistic training exercises for pilots. But the full 'virtual realities' will be far more flexible and eventually, more powerful. For discussions of these possibilities, *see* Glenn Emery's 'Virtual Reality's Radical Vision'. *Insight Magazine*, pages 21–25, 6 May 1991; 'Grand Illusion', S.

Ditlea, *New York Magazine*, pages 28–34, 6 August 1990; 'Looking-Glass Worlds', Ivars Peterson, *Science News* 141:8–10 (1992).

605.   Representing objects and scenes so that they look realistic is not particularly difficult, nor is altering the images as a viewer manipulates them or changes position. What remains beyond the capacity of present computers is to do this rapidly enough to create the illusion of reality. In today's systems, computers eliminate the fine detail of the objects represented and only refresh their images a half-dozen times a second, which makes moving images grainy and jerky. As these shortcomings disappear, the illusions of virtual reality will become extremely impressive.

606.   Progress should be rapid because virtual reality effects are very suited to parallel-processing techniques, an area of computer development evolving rapidly. For example, the visual field can be broken into separate regions computed simultaneously by different processors. Enhanced realism in 'virtual reality' will eventually be gained by including sensory input other than vision. Already, scientists are developing ways of creating 'virtual acoustics'. In this work, computers are used to alter the sounds that arrive at each of a person's ears as his or her head changes position. This makes a sound seem to originate from a particular place in the surrounding environment rather than from the right or left side of one's head, which is what current stereo earphones do. Realistic effects have been produced by not only delaying sounds and changing their strength, but by modifying them in the same way the external ear does when sound reaches us from different directions. *See* 'Virtual Acoustics Puts Sound in its Place', Gordon Graf, *Science* 256: 616–617 (1992).

607.   Today many people favor television over numerous other activities and prefer music from a 'Walkman' to the natural sounds around them. Video games are very popular, and virtual realities will be many times more alluring. In 1991 more than 70 per cent of all homes with children between the ages of eight and twelve had one of some 30 million Nintendo game machines in the US. 'Products and Services for Computer Networks', Nicholas Negroponte, *Scientific American* 265(3):106–113 (1991).

As to people's interest in fabricating their own realities, an intriguing 'product' sold in Japan – 'artificial realities' without technology – suggests that we have a great appetite for such fare. The Japan Efficiency Corporation uses actors to create synthetic experiences for people. For example, for a fee a family (played by actors) will visit an older couple who no longer have contact with their own children. Page H2, *Los Angeles Times*, 12 May 1992.

608.   Ironically, writing is what preserved Greek philosophy, and reading and writing have become so embedded in society that we loudly bemoan any decline in these skills. Now, advancing communication technology is again raising the importance of the *spoken* word. Writing has long preserved

information and enabled it to be sent great distances, but people now can increasingly achieve this with voice and image. Already many watch the news rather than read the paper, see a movie rather than read a book, and telephone a friend rather than write a letter. Locating information in an electronic database of an encyclopedia is becoming much easier than using an actual encyclopedia, and there are now even computerized children's 'books' (for example, Broderbund Software's CD-ROM 'Living Books' series) where characters and objects on each 'page' speak and move when they are pointed to electronically and 'clicked' to life. How completely traditional books will be overtaken by these evolving technologies is unclear, but there can be little doubt that voice-recognition technology and video telecommunication will thoroughly transform the way we communicate.

609.   Page 485, *The Discoverers: A History of Man's Search to Know His World and Himself*, Daniel Boorstin (Random House, New Work, 1983). This book contains an examination of the use of memory systems in ancient times.

610.   Significant improvements in telecommunications will change the face of adult education too. For example, the University of Maine began a program in 1991 that offers thirty-five 'interactive television' courses. Some 4,000 students at 77 locations throughout the state watch video lectures and interact with remote instructors over the phone. Such a cross between teleconferencing and talk radio offers high-quality instruction to a widely dispersed population. 'On-Line-Teaching', *Wall Street Journal*, 24 September 1991.

In fact, the rapid expansion of adult education is *per se* a product of Metaman's evolution. Education is now by necessity a lifelong process; life cannot be divided into two phases, one for learning, and another for applying that knowledge.

611.   One might wonder why technological change in education is not more advanced. Not only is there an inertia to educational bureaucracies, but large cost reductions and technical improvements in video equipment have been very recent. Only one in ten homes in the US had a video cassette recorder in 1984, yet a mere five years later (in 1989) two thirds did. Another important factor is that a market to support the creation of quality educational materials is only now developing. As this market expands, the creation of powerful teaching materials will come rapidly. In 1990 in the US, $4,500 per student was spent on primary and secondary education. A one-year, 10 per cent increase in that budget would provide nearly $10,000 for each class of twenty students, enough to buy video tapes, a VCR, a large-screen television and even a few computers today. Tomorrow it will buy even more. *The 1991 World Almanac and Book of Facts*, ed. M. Hoffman (Pharos, New York), and *1990 Statistical Abstract of the US*, US Bureau of the Census, Washington, DC, 1990.

612. The Teaching Company in Washington, DC, for example, offers various video lecture courses by college professors whose teaching has been rated highly in student evaluations.

613. Although education will become dependent upon high-technology tools, the large component of it that has little to do with mastering knowledge will never be taught by video programs or computers. Children will continue to learn social skills, personal values and the ability to live responsibly among others from their interactions with people. As our schools change, the sports teams, clubs and social activities peripheral to intellectual development but critical for individual growth may become the most important 'learning' experiences that take place in the social setting we now call 'school'.

614. The eventual possibilities of computer instruction go far beyond these interactive programs. When computer systems powerful enough to understand casual speech – not just recognize a few words – arrive, the possibilities will explode. Computer 'companions', perhaps small enough to be carried around, may one day be used even by young children. And if you had long interacted with a high-technology tutor and had routinely relied on its knowledge since early childhood, would you not seek its advice in other matters too? Such a device would be like a friend who not only knew you well enough to anticipate your behavior, but – if periodically copied to back-up storage – would remain 'faithful' to you for life.

An electronic companion of this caliber would not need to 'think' or 'understand' in order to be of use; merely being able to interpret the information from its previous interactions with us would be enough. For example, by knowing a person's interests, attention span, medical history and habits, such a device might offer very useful insights. Interacting with a machine as though it were a friend might seem outlandish now, but would this really be so strange? Recall ELIZA, the computer therapist mentioned earlier. *See also* note 541.

615. For an overview of current applications of computers in education *see* Alan Kay's, 'Computers, Networks, and Education', *Scientific American* 265(3):138–148 (1991). Computers will do much more than present traditional material in new ways; by allowing students to model reality, this technology will carry education into realms hitherto out of reach. Students could simulate a biological ecosystem and manipulate that simulation to further their understanding of our natural environment; they could explore a climate model to look at the potential effects of global warming on rainfall patterns; they could try different transportation networks for a city and figure out how to relieve congestion.

616. For example, in the US, total government expenditures on social welfare programs grew from 10.3 to 18.5 per cent of GNP between 1960 and

1980, and despite all the Reagan-era efforts to cut such spending, it was as high when Reagan left office in 1988 (18.4 per cent) as when he was elected in 1980. In Western Europe and Japan, the figures are even higher. Throughout the developed world most people obtain health care through government programs or private insurance, receive institutional support as they grow older, and obtain unemployment assistance if they lose their jobs. Page 352, *1990 Statistical Abstract of the US*, US Bureau of the Census, Washington, DC, 1990.

617.   The most common form of birth control in China is the IUD, but in 1983 there were some 16 million sterilizations and 11 million abortions; page 71, *World Press Review*, November 1990. None the less, China's population is still growing at a rate of about 1.4 per cent each year, roughly 13 million people annually; page 19, *Atlas of the Environment* (Prentice Hall, New York, 1986).

618.   Page 46, *World Military and Social Expenditures 1989*, Ruth Sivard (World Priorities, Washington, DC, 1989).

619.   What once would have been viewed as unthinkable intrusions into family life may soon become commonplace. In 1992, for instance, a juvenile-court judge in Florida ruled that an eleven-year-old child, though a minor, had the right to sue to sever all legal ties with his natural parents. The boy, who wanted to be adopted by his foster parents, charged his natural parents with abandonment and neglect as he sought the 'termination of the parent/child relationship'. *New York Times*, page A12, 10 July 1992. And he won his case.

620.   For a discussion of the effects of cocaine during pregnancy, *see* 'Innocent Victims', pages 56–60, *Time* magazine, 13 May 1991.

621.   Even more dramatically, in California in 1991 authorities, judging that a woman had given birth to a stillborn child as a result of cocaine and alcohol abuse, charged the woman with murder. They determined that a 1970 law against fetal murder could be applied not only to outside assailants, but to parents as well. Page A1, *Los Angeles Times*, 17 June 1992. Moreover, in October 1992, a woman was sentenced to six years in prison for 'child endangerment' when her infant died as a result of the drug methamphetamine the mother passed to her child through her breast milk. Page A1, *New York Times*, 28 October 1992.

622.   Page A14, *New York Times*, 10 January 1991.

623.   Page A11, *New York Times*, 29 November 1991.

624.   Before 1960, there were few safe, reliable and convenient methods of birth control available. People had to make do with condoms, diaphragms, rhythm, antispermicidal foams and jellies. The decade of the 1960s brought a number of new techniques – the birth control pill and IUD in particular. Until recently, however, with the arrival of implantable hormones (Norplants), and hormonal abortants (RU486), no new methods have appeared. Now such

techniques as birth-control vaccines, and end-of-the-month pills may finally render family planning simple and easy. *See also* notes 262 and 263.

625.　An overview of new directions in contraception research is provided in 'Fertility studies for the benefit of animals and human beings: Development of improved sterilization and contraception methods', B. Dunbar and E. Schwoebel, *Journal of the American Medical Association* 193(9):1165–1170 (1988). The many political problems that have and are likely during the immediate future to continue to slow both the pace of research and the development of new contraceptive options is described in Carl Djerassi's excellent article, 'The Bitter Pill', *Science* 245: 356–360 (1989). *See also* footnote 262.

626.　Children may succeed in overcoming horrible early environments but the emotional and physical damage of those early years is often permanently disabling. It stands to reason that, as society increasingly suffers the consequences of such abuse, it will strive to minimize it.

627.　*See* note 624.

628.　The worldwide traffic in illegal narcotics tells us that RU486 will soon become broadly available regardless of local government policy. And this pill is just one early step. Aborting pregnancies is bound to become progressively easier as molecular biology advances.

629.　Social changes that are a consequence of Metaman's technological advance are impossible to hold back. It is hard enough to stop the spread of nuclear weapons, which demand sizable engineering programs as well as highly regulated materials. Government could never block molecular biology advances that any number of small research groups anywhere in the world will one day accomplish with ease.

630.　In 1981, the Australian government announced a major grant for work on 'immunocontraceptive' vaccines. Researchers hope to release into the wild an infective rabbit virus, myxoma, that contains antigens to rabbit sperm. By impeding conception, the virus might control rabbit populations. 'New Animal Vaccines Spread Like Diseases', *New York Times*, page B5, 26 November 1991. *See also* note 263.

631.　According to Wharton Economic Forecasting Associates, in 1989 the tourist industry, which includes lodging, transportation and restaurants, employed 112 million people. Furthermore, in that year there were more than 425 million *international* tourist visits as compared to some 60 million in 1960. *New York Times*, page F4, 26 May 1991.

632.　*Financial Times*, 17 April 1989.

633.　Oil spills are very dramatic and destructive, but the amount of oil dumped by car owners changing their own motor oil in the US totals some 400 million gallons a year, nearly *40 times* the 10 million gallons spilled by Exxon in Alaska in 1989.

CHAPTER 12

634. 'Zlotys Cannot Buy Happiness', page 46, *World Press Review*, October 1991.

635. In 1991, estimates of the eventual cost of the scandal had reached 500 billion dollars. *The Greatest Ever Bank Robbery*, Martin Mayer (Macmillan, 1992).

636. For an examination of various measures and countermeasures taken in the ongoing battle between credit-card companies and card counterfeiters, *see* page A1, *Los Angeles Times*, 23 June 1992.

637. An interesting confirmation of the basic honesty of people in their interactions with other individuals is shown by the results of the following experiment I performed. Eleven wallets, each containing $25 plus credit cards and a few scribbled notes, were dropped at scattered locations in the city of Boston. All of them were returned by those who found them, and 7 of them were returned with the cash untouched. If people are this honest in a large impersonal city, why is there such a lack of faith today in human integrity? One reason is that we hear so much negative news, but there is another reason. We come into contact with so many people today, that it just takes a few dishonest ones to bias our impressions. If you park a car on the street and leave a wallet on the seat, hundreds of people will see it so it probably will be stolen. But pick a single random individual, as occurred in my experiment, and he or she is probably honest.

638. 'Parents of Tiny Infants Find Their Care Choices Are Not Theirs', *New York Times*, page A12, 30 September 1991.

639. For a quick overview of the problems of 'very low birth-weight babies' see the three-part series of articles, 'Smallest Survivors: Dilemmas of Prematurity', *New York Times*, page A1, 29 September–1 October 1991. Very low birth-weight babies are those under 1,500 grams (3.3 lbs) and account for less than 1 per cent of live births. Of those who survive, some 17 per cent have cerebral palsy or are mentally retarded. Babies weighing less than 750 grams (1.6 lbs) account for about 1 in 500 births and are called 'extremely low birth-weight babies'. Of those that survive, some 30 per cent are mentally impaired, but that figure rises to about 50 per cent for the very smallest babies, those weighing about 500 grams (1.1 lbs).

640. 'Prenatal Care in the US: Reports Call for Improvements in Quality and Accessibility', *Family Planning Perspectives* 22(1):31–35 (1990). Between 1984 and 1986, 67 per cent of women in the US were judged to receive 'adequate' prenatal care, 18 per cent 'intermediate' care, and 16 per cent 'inadequate' care. Care was considered 'inadequate' when it begins after the fourth month of pregnancy or involves fewer than half the visits recommended by the American College of Obstetricians and Gynecologists.

641.   For instance, there is a growing 'Right to Die' movement in the US that asserts the individual's right to terminate his or her life. Derek Humphry's 1991 best-seller, *Final Exit* (The Hemlock Society, Eugene, Oregon, 1991), by giving detailed instructions about how to use relatively accessible drugs to end one's life, took a large step towards making rational suicide an entirely personal choice. The dissemination of such information, though it does not make government policy on euthanasia irrelevant, does make circumventing that policy increasingly easy for individuals.

642.   The 1991 ballot measure in Washington State, initiative 119, would have allowed a doctor to assist a patient in committing suicide if two people with no family or financial ties to the patient witnessed the patient's written request, and two doctors concluded that the patient had less than six months left to live. (Page A1, *New York Times*, 14 October 1991.) In November 1991, 46.4 per cent voted to pass the initiative; efforts are underway to put similar measures on the ballot in California and Oregon. (*New York Times*, 7 November 1991.)

In reality, physicians in the US already assist in such procedures, even though they are not yet legal. Currently it is not rare for doctors to terminate care for terminally ill patients or otherwise bring about death. A 1991 survey of 500 physicians reported that 58 per cent had ordered removal of life-sustaining technology at some time, 45 per cent had taken clinical action that would indirectly cause death, and 9 per cent had taken actions that would directly bring death. *Nature* 353:788 (1991). *See also, New England Journal of Medicine* 324(20):1434–1436 (1991). Physician assistance in ending life has been commonplace in Holland since 1984, and a new euthanasia law, which was passed there in 1993, set specific procedures to follow which would protect a doctor from any danger of prosecution for such an act. *See* page A1, *New York Times*, 9 February 1993.

643.   In 1960, expenditures on health care ranged from Italy's 3.3 per cent of GNP to 5.9 per cent in Iceland; in 1986 the range was from 6.1 per cent in Denmark to 11.1 per cent in the US. Table 2, page 269, *What Kind of Life: The Limits of Medical Progress*, Daniel Callahan (Simon & Schuster, New York, 1990). This book is a thoughtful and stimulating examination of the necessity of setting limits in medical care.

644.   Oregon's innovative system of health care ranks medical procedures in terms of their costs and benefits and uses available public-health resources to maximize benefits. Thus, only procedures above an established cost-benefit threshold are covered by public funding, and the specific threshold is determined by the amount of health-care funds that are available. For a detailed look at this effort, *see 'Prioritization of Health Services: A Report to the Governor and Legislature'*, Oregon Health Services Commission, Portland, Oregon, 1991. A short article on Oregon's efforts is 'Too Bitter Medicine',

page A8, *New York Times*, 5 August 1992. For a discussion of how the benefits of different medical procedures are estimated and compared *see* 'Ethicists struggle with judgment of the value of life', page 85, *New York Times*, 24 November 1992.

645. To explore some of the diverse ethical dilemmas surrounding present-day public policy decisions, *see The Book of Questions: Business, Politics, and Ethics*, Gregory Stock (Workman Press, New York, 1991).

646. *See* 'Parents of Tiny Infants, Care Choices Are Not Theirs', *New York Times*, page A1, 30 September 1991.

647. 'Risk Within Reason', R. Zeckhauser and W. Viscusi, *Nature* 248:559–564. This paper presents an excellent discussion of risk perception and the need for balancing gains and losses when regulating activities and products.

648. *Regulatory Aspects of Carcinogenesis and Food Additives: The Delaney Clause*, ed. F. Coulston, (Academic Press, New York, 1979). In 1992 a US Federal Court ruled that the Environmental Protection Agency must strictly abide by this law. *See* 'Delaney's Revenge', *Science* 358:181 (1992).

649. For example, some 99.99 per cent (by weight) of the pesticides humans ingest are chemicals that occur naturally, not ones that are man-made. *See* 'Rodent Carcinogens: Setting Priorities', Lois S. Gold et al, *Science* 258:261–265 (1992).

650. 'Hazards of risk assessment', C. Anderson, *Nature* 351:176 (1991). Some good insights into the problems of regulating health hazards are presented in this brief note.

651. 'In Search of Methuselah: Estimating the Upper Limits of Human Longevity', S. Olshansky, B. Carnes and C. Cassel, *Science*, 250:634–638 (1991).

652. 'Facts to guide thinking about life-threatening risks', Ralph Keeney, *Man and Cybernetics*, IEEE Symposium Proceedings (1988), provides an excellent general discussion of risk in society.

653. Because ever more of what surrounds us is part of Metaman, when accidents befall us they will increasingly involve people and institutions. If we lived in the forest and tripped over a tree trunk we would not expect compensation from anyone, so why should we when we trip over a rough place on a public pavement? Why should the families of the 500 unlucky victims of major airline crashes each year receive any more compensation for their tragedies than the families of the equally unlucky 500 killed by lightning in the developed world each year? Assigning blame and responsibility for largely accidental occurrences within Metaman will become increasingly difficult as human activity grows ever more integrated.

As to the relative danger of these accidents, on average, major airline crashes killed more than 400 people a year in the late 1980s and a similar number died each year from lightning in the developed world. *World Almanac and Book of Facts 1991*, ed. M. Hoffman (Pharos Books New York, 1991), and 'A Review of the Record', John Morrall, *Regulation* 10:25–34 (1986).

654.   In October 1991, the US lowered the threshold at which it considers children to be at risk of lead poisoning from 2.5 to 1.0 micrograms per milliliter of blood. This increased the number of children in the US with possible lead poisoning from several hundred thousand to some 4 million. At the same time, the federal government proposed a $15 million testing program, but no federal funds to clean up lead paints. Page B6, *New York Times*, 8 October 1991.

655.   'Society's Valuation of Life Saving in Radiation Protection and Other Contexts', Bernard Cohen, *Journal of Health Physics* 38:33–51 (1980). The dollar values taken from this and the next three examples are quoted in 1990 dollars for comparative purposes.

656.   Ibid.

657.   Ibid.

658.   'Risk Within Reason', R. Zeckhauser and W. Viscusi, *Nature* 248:559–564; and page 30, 'A Review of the Record', J. F. Morrall, *Regulation* 10:25–34 (1986). *See also* note 655.

659.   Maintaining that human life is 'invaluable' is all very well, but anyone who sought funding to build an intensive-care hospital for premature infants in overpopulated Bangladesh would be thought crazy. There are too many ways of achieving a broader good using such funds.

Various attempts have been made to try to quantify the value that people place on their lives. One way of probing the value we individually place on our own life is to decide the maximum we would pay for a one-year *guarantee* that we would not die in any accident – car, fire, drowning, poisoning, even lightning or bee stings. Because our annual risk of a fatal accident is some 1 in 2,000 ('A Review of the Record', John Morrall, *Regulation* 10:25–34, 1986) each $50 we are willing to pay for such protection adds an additional $100,000 to the valuation we place on our lives. Various studies in the US trying to estimate what average value people place on their lives come up with figures ranging from $400,000 to $10 million, well below the costs of many safety programs. 'A Review of the Record', John Morrall, *Regulation* 10:25–34 (1986).

660.   The data for this chart is taken from 'Society's Valuation of Life Saving in Radiation Protection and other Contexts', Bernard Cohen, *Journal of Health Physics* 38:33–51 (1980), and 'A review of the Record', J.F. Morrall, *Regulation* 10:25–34 (1986). Costs are quoted in 1990 dollars, but are based on technologies and social conditions that existed at the various times when each particular study was performed. The cost of any specific item would be different (perhaps significantly) with the newer technologies of today, but the

range of potential costs for various life-saving activities would be just as broad now as it was a decade ago.

661. This problem, and different approaches to it, are discussed in 'Population Aging Policies in East Asia and the United States', L. Martins, *Science* 251:527–531 (1991).

662. 'Some of the Tough Decisions Required by a National Health Plan', L. Russell, *Science* 246:892–896. This is an excellent discussion of the choices that need to be made in national healthcare services. It is not only a matter of deciding what services to provide, but how much of them. For example a program of pap smears every three years will save one year of life expectancy for each $13,000 (roughly $500,000 per life saved), but expanding the program to provide *yearly* smears would cost some $1 million per additional year of life saved ($40 million per additional life saved). The large difference in cost effectiveness occurs because pap smears every three years already catch 19 out of 20 cervical cancers while they are still treatable.

663. *Setting Limits: Medical Goals in an Aging Society*, Daniel Callahan (Simon & Schuster, New York 1987) is an excellent book that explores how an aging society must inevitably face difficult dilemmas about whether to try to cure or merely care for the aged as they approach the end of life. In 1985 those over sixty-five made up 11 per cent of the US population and consumed 31 per cent of health-care expenditures. What portion of health-care costs will older people use when in 2050 they make up 21 per cent of the population, especially considering that the fraction of older people over eighty-five will rise from a tenth to a quarter of those older people? Ibid pages 119, 120 and 226.

664. 'In Search of Methuselah: Estimating the Upper Limits of Human Longevity', S. Olshansky, B. Carnes and C. Cassel, *Science* 250:634–638 (1991).

665. For a general discussion of the limits of human life expectancy, *see* 'How Long is the Human Life-Span?', *Science* 254:936–938 (1991). For example, in the US, the life-expectancy increase brought by eliminating all forms of cancer would be 3.17 years for females and 3.2 for males. Eliminating ischemic heart disease would bring increases of 3.0 years for females and 3.55 for males. To raise life expectancy at birth to eighty-five years would require a reduction in mortality from all causes of 43 per cent for females and 65 per cent for males. 'In Search of Methuselah: Estimating the Upper Limits of Human Longevity', S. Olshansky, B. Carnes and C. Cassel, *Science* 250:634–638 (1991). Some researchers, however, argue that there are no limits to the human life span and that life expectancy will continue to increase gradually as medical progress continues. This would have enormous demographic consequences. *See New York Times*, page A1, 16 November 1992. Some support for this comes from the recent finding that (at least in

certain flies) mortality rates rise with advancing age but then plateau instead of continuing to increase. *See* 'Demography of Genotypes: Failure of the Limited Life-Span Paradigm in *Drosophila melanogaster*', James Curtsinger et al, *Science* 258:461–463 (1992) and 'Slowing of Mortality Rates at Older Ages in Large Medfly Cohorts', James R. Carey et al, *Science* 258:457–460 (1992).

666.   The minimum mortality rate in humans occurs between the ages of ten and fifteen, and is as low as one death per year per 2,000 people in some populations. If this mortality rate were maintained throughout life, then half of the population would die by the age of 1,200. Page 29 of *Longevity, Senescence, and the Genome*, Caleb Finch (University of Chicago Press, Chicago, 1990). For a good general discussion of aging, *see* 'On Growing Old', R. Sapolsky and C. Finch, pages 30–38, *The Sciences*, March 1991.

667.   As to cutting material consumption to preserve critical resources for future generations, such cuts might buy a few additional decades or even centuries of undisrupted supply but would not prevent eventual depletion. Ultimately, the key to Metaman's future lies in shifting towards recycling and the use of plentiful resources such as plastics, ceramics, glass and silicon. Movement in this direction, governed as it is by technological advances generally driven by economics, will probably be stimulated – not retarded – by whatever specific shortages occur. There is no need to interfere with this process, because it is a continuing and automatic one in which an unending sequence of specific shortages lead to compensating adjustments by Metaman. Indeed, Metaman's capacity to engage in this process is a critical attribute that makes this super-organism so robust. As a perfect example of this, at the turn of the last century, the US faced so critical a crisis in wood supplies that in 1905 President Theodore Roosevelt said,

> Commercial disaster, that means disaster to the whole country, is inevitable. The railroads must have ties . . . If the present rate of forest destruction is allowed to continue, with nothing to offset it, a timber famine in the future is inevitable.

Of course, the crisis was soon forgotten because a technological break-through – the use of chemical preservatives – kept the ties from rotting, and then the automobile arrived. Page 20, 'Hydrogen and the Green Wave', Jesse H. Ausubel, *The Bridge: Technology and the Environment* 20(1):17–23 (1990).

668.   A further, even stronger argument for temporary disposal of nuclear wastes is today's extreme public concern about them. Although the *technical* difficulties of safe disposal might be easy to overcome, the political difficulties of implementing any solutions seem insurmountable at present. This is perhaps not surprising considering the freshness of humanity's images of Hiroshima and Chernobyl, and the seriousness of the recent threat of global

nuclear war. *See,* for example, 'Another Panel Rejects Nevada Disaster Theory', *Science* 256:434–435 (1992), which discusses some of the obstacles being encountered in trying to move ahead on a 4 billion dollar project to build a permanent storage site in Nevada.

Fortunately, temporary on-site disposal of nuclear wastes for a century could be nearly as safe as that at a permanent nuclear repository, and public attitudes may be quite different a century hence. For an excellent discussion of the political realities of nuclear waste disposal, *see* 'Perceived Risk, Trust, and the Politics of Nuclear Waste', Paul Slovic, James Flynn and Mark Layman, *Science* 254:1603–1607 (1991).

669.   For example, in 1980 the US Department of Energy proposed setting up a permanent trust of 500 million dollars to fund the operation of the nuclear waste disposal facility at the Savannah River Plant in the Southern US indefinitely. The alternative was to build a permanent disposal facility in a deep underground repository at a cost of 2.7 billion dollars. 'Society's Valuation of Life Saving in Radiation Protection and other Contexts', Bernard Cohen, *Journal of Health Physics* 38:33–51 (1980). This article is an interesting examination of the magnitude of the risks involved with various low-level radiation sources and the costs society pays to reduce them. For a recent discussion of efforts to site a disposal facility in the US, *see* 'Grants Stir Interest in Nuclear Waste Site', Keith Schneider, *New York Times,* page A10, 9 January 1992.

CHAPTER 13

670.   For a lucid discussion of the evolutionary process, *see* Richard Dawkins', *The Blind Watchmaker* (W.W. Norton & Company, New York, 1987).

671.   E. O. Wilson estimates that there are 10^{15} ants alive at any one time. *The Insect Societies* (Belknap Press of Harvard University Press, Cambridge, 1971). Estimating an average ant life span of one year, and a distribution of ants equivalent to today's during the last 400 million years would mean there have been some 4×10^{23} ants on the earth. A column of 5×10^{18} ants averaging some 2 millimeters in length would stretch a distance of one light year, so all the ants that have lived since the first ant some 400 million years ago could form a column that would extend to the other side of our galaxy, nearly 100,000 light years away. Light travels 186,000 miles in one second.

672.   *See,* for example, 'The New Gene and its Evolution', John Campbell in *Rates of Evolution,* ed. K. Campbell and M. Day (Allen and Unwin, London, 1987).

673.   Point mutations (those occurring at a single site on the DNA) are some

300 times less frequent in fruit flies than in viruses. 'Spontaneous Mutation', J. Drake et al, *Nature* 221:1128–1132 (1969).

674.   Actually, in biological systems, four distinct types of change occur. In addition to 'development' and 'evolution', there are 'turnover' (renewal of existing structure without modification) and 'growth' (size increase without change in form). Turnover and growth, of course, have clear counterparts in Metaman. The super-organism continually replaces aging roadways, buildings and other structures, and it also extends itself by duplicating existing patterns. Cities spread, underdeveloped lands are 'Westernized', businesses construct new branches and facilities.

675.   Metaman also changes through the replacement of its internal parts and through simple growth. *See* footnote 674.

676.   'Development' of an egg into an adult involves no information change, but rather the unfolding of the developmental program stored in the DNA of the first cell.

677.   Not only are the models themselves improving, however, so too are the *mechanisms* for generating the models. For instance, models can not only process more information, automated tools now assist with the design and refinement of the models themselves.

678.   Behavioral rigidity is no stranger to higher animals, though. For example, a salmon's migration is genetically programmed, and so is a bird's nest-building.

679.   Page 56, *On Human Nature*, E.O. Wilson (Harvard University Press, Boston, 1978).

680.   For example, speaking a language is clearly a learned behavior, yet linguists such as Noam Chomsky maintain that to be comprehensible to us, language must assume certain patterns of syntax that are a consequence of the way the human brain is organized. Language is learned, but its form may well be bounded by our genetics and physiology. For instance, there are brain lesions that can cause a person to be unable to write vowels, but be fully capable of using consonants. 'Nvrthlss, ndrstndng wtht vwls s nt tht dffclt,' quite a lot of the information is communicated. 'News and views', J. Marshall, *Science* 353:209–210; *also* 'A selective deficit for writing vowels in acquired dysgraphia', R. Cubelli, *Nature* 353:258–260 (1991).

681.   The process of development in multicellular organisms is what precludes the flexible, large-scale remolding of form in animals. Large and intricate cellular assemblages are formed by sequences of precisely timed and executed cellular interactions that start with the embryo's first division. At critical junctures even tiny disruptions will cascade into severe birth defects. Thus, there is no possibility of dramatically remolding the adult in a flexible manner.

As a consequence, an animal's 'developmental program' is replayed again and again in its offspring, and changes are saved or discarded depending on their usefulness. Only through reproduction and death guided by natural selection – Darwinian evolution – can multicellular organisms remold themselves into new physical forms. Reproduction and death are not an inherent biological necessity, they are a means to an end: large-scale change. If change could be achieved directly, these two evolutionary tools would no longer be necessary.

682.   In the 1970s, Lynn Margulis helped show that the mitochondria of cells were bacterial in origin. The concept is now widely accepted, but the precise nature of the series of transitions that generated the eukaryotic cell remains the focus of much debate. It seems likely that two of the bacteria involved are eubacteria, which became the chloroplasts and mitochondria of eukaryotic cells, and eocytes, which became the nucleus. *See* 'Origin of the eukaryotic nucleus: eukaryotes and eocytes are genetically related', James Lake, *Canadian Journal of Microbiology* 35:109–118 (1989) and 'Origin of the Metazoa', James Lake, *Proc. Natl. Acad. of Sci. USA* 87:763–766 (1990). *See also Symbiosis in Cell Evolution*, Lynn Margulis (Freeman, San Francisco, 1981).

683.   Moreover, there has been an increase in the number and diversity not only of organisms making up ecological communities, but of cells within multicellular organisms. The maximum size and intricacy of multicellular organisms has grown over time. *See* for example, Table 1, page 122, and figure 5, page 27, *The Evolution of Complexity*, John Bonner (Princeton University Press, Princeton, New Jersey, 1988).

684.   The symbiotic union of bacteria that formed eukaryotic cells formed just such a new level, but Myxobacteria, a complex cluster of bacteria with a life cycle similar to the slime mold, never created a distinctly more potent level of organization. For the life cycle of the Myxobacteria, *see* page 64 of *Five Kingdoms*, Lynn Margulis (W. H. Freeman, New York, 1988).

685.   Lynn Margulis, *Five Kingdoms* (W. H. Freeman, New York, 1988).

686.   Estimates of the size of Metaman's direct and indirect influences on the biosphere are quite high. Raymond Coppinger and Charles Smith estimate that domesticated animals and plants constituted 5 per cent of the terrestrial biomass in 1860, constitute 20 per cent now, and will constitute 40 per cent by 2020. 'The Domestication of Evolution', *Environmental Conservation* 10:283–292 (1983). Paul Ehrlich estimates that humanity presently uses either directly or indirectly some 30 per cent of the net energy captured globally through photosynthesis by terrestrial green plants. This, together with the ocean plankton, is the supporting foundation for all animals. *See* 'The Loss of Diversity: Causes and Consequences', Paul Ehrlich, Chapter 2 in *Biodiversity*, ed. E.O. Wilson (National Academy Press, Washington, DC, 1988).

687. The average life span of a species in the fossil record is some 4 million years. (Page 108, *Extinction: Bad Genes or Bad Luck*, David Raup, Norton and Co., New York, 1991). Thus, to consider what Metaman might be doing several million years from now does not even require the assumption that Metaman is more resilient than a typical animal species. Yet, Metaman is almost certainly far more resilient. It is already global in extent, and thus not threatened by any 'local' catastrophes; indeed when Metaman reaches other planets, it will not even be threatened with extinction by a *global* catastrophe like a giant meteor. Metaman is not highly specialized, and thus is not dependent on unique environmental conditions. Metaman is increasingly insulated from external influences. The only obvious danger to Metaman is itself, and within a century or so, this danger too will probably have faded. In short, to consider a future of hundreds of millions of years for Metaman is reasonable.

688. 'Making Mars Habitable', C. McKay, O. Toon and J. Kasting, *Nature* 352:489–496 (1991), is an excellent review of the difficulties that would face any effort at planetary-scale engineering to make Mars habitable for plants or humans. Such 'terraforming' would depend upon forming a Martian atmosphere that could create a greenhouse effect capable of keeping the planet above freezing, and the atmosphere would have to come from the minerals or ice-caps already on Mars' surface because bringing enough materials from off the planet would be out of the question. It would require some 40 billion tons – one *billion* space shuttle loads – of even a trace gas like Chlorofluorocarbons (CFCs) to create such a greenhouse effect. The feasibility of terraforming thus hinges on the composition of the Martian surface, which, though poorly understood, seems likely to hold enough carbon dioxide either in polar 'dry ice' caps or sequestered under the planet's surface. Mckay concluded that creating a Martian atmosphere to sustain human life might require a sustained effort lasting 100,000 years.

689. If a spaceship could continuously accelerate at the rate of gravitational acceleration at the earth's surface, it would reach one-half the speed of light in about six months and could make the journey to the nearest star in less than a decade.

CHAPTER 14

690. Britain's failure to find an acceptable formula for creating a single independent state on the Indian subcontinent led in August 1946 to the onset of rioting and strife between Muslims and Hindus. The culmination came in July 1947 with the partitioning of the region into the separate states of India and Pakistan and a massive exodus of fleeing refugees. An estimated 10

million people attempted to change lands that summer, and a million died in the process. Pages 341–349, *A New History of India*, Stanley Wolpert (Oxford University Press, New York, 1989).

691.   Regions where widespread unrest reigns cannot become, or perhaps even remain, actively integrated into Metaman. Cambodia, Ethiopia, Sri Lanka and Angola have been racked by slaughter and the world has barely noticed. The major exception is the Middle East, where local struggles threaten more global consequences because of the oil there.

692.   In the US, for example, those adults who indicate they have attended some form of worship service within the previous week, have remained steady at roughly 40 per cent throughout the 1980s. *World Almanac and Book of Facts 1991*, ed. M. Hoffman (Pharos Books, New York, 1991).

693.   For a discussion of the plight of the Yanomami *see The Canopy: A publication of the Rainforest Alliance*, Summer 1991.

694.   The 1947 Broadway musical, *Brigadoon*, was released as a film by MGM in 1954. The screenplay was by Alan Lerner and the music by Frederick Loewe.

695.   In the 1850s, some 20 million buffalo still roamed the Great Plains, but as railroads pushed into this territory, the huge herds were slaughtered for their hides. Finally, in 1889, when some 550 of the animals remained, legislation was passed to protect them. For more details, *see The Book of the American West*, ed. J. Monoghan (Bosnian Books, New York, 1963).

696.   Page 84, *Primitive Mythology: The Masks of God*, Joseph Campbell (Penguin, New York, 1968).

697.   Page 232, *Primitive Mythology: The Masks of God*, Joseph Campbell (Penguin, New York, 1968).

698.   For a discussion of the language capacity of animals and a good description of early language experiments with chimpanzees, *see The Dragons of Eden*, Carl Sagan, pages 113–131 (Ballantine, New York 1977).

699.   A Galapagos woodpecker finch will grasp a long cactus spine in its beak and poke it into crevices to flush out insects, and an Egyptian vulture breaks open ostrich eggs by flinging stones at them. *See* 'Tool-using bird, the Egyptian vulture', *National Geographic Magazine* 133(5):630–641; and volume 7, pages 55, 330, and 331, *Grzimek's Animal Life Encyclopedia*, ed. Bernhard Grzimek (Van Nostrand Reinhold Press, 1972).

700.   This idea is articulated by Stephen J. Gould in his book, *Wonderful Life* (W.W. Norton & Co., New York, 1989).

701.   Increasingly, our images and our histories live on. We can think of the human story as taking place in three phases: prehistory, history and 'recorded' history. Prehistory was the time before writing and will always remain a period of which we can glean only the most meager knowledge. History, the time of written records, is much less obscure, but even diligent

study may still bring us little understanding of it. But recorded history, the time of electronically archived information such as films, records and pictures, is very different. As technology advances, the masses of information from this period will keep it almost as fresh and accessible as the present. Thus Metaman's ongoing evolution is extending the effects of our actions and our lives through not only space but time. An old letter or photograph can touch us deeply, but how much more powerful are voices and animated images. How amazing it is to watch a video of ourselves as infants, to see our parents as they were before we were born, to watch soldiers fighting in wars long past, to see an old musical and realize that those who are entertaining us are dead.

702.   The Big Bang theory – the concept that the universe as it now exists had its origins in an immense explosive discontinuity some 15 billion years ago and has been expanding ever since – is broadly accepted because of its remarkable consistency with virtually all known cosmological data. For instance, the Big Bang theory explains the existence of a background cosmic radiation left over from that original explosion. Slight variations recently detected in that background radiation pervading the universe provide insights into the nature of the early universe. *See* 'The case for the relativistic hot Big Bang cosmology', P. Peebles et al, *Science* 352:769–776 (1991) and 'The Seeds of Cosmic Structure', R. Partridge, *Science* 257:178–179 (1992).

703.   But though we hear this story, it is beyond us to appreciate it fully. We see the immensity and power of the universe only indirectly, through analogies that translate it into realms we can understand. How are *we* to visualize the Big Bang when the entire universe was supposedly compressed to the size of a pinhead? To conceive of as many stars as there are grains of sand on the beach? To imagine whole continents slowly colliding and thrusting mountain chains miles into the sky? To have a real sense of a duration a million times longer than that since the pharaohs built their pyramids?

704.   Moreover, through the immense sensory apparatus of Metaman, our individual awareness has so expanded that we vicariously experience many ills that are far from our personal lives. If we are to live with this almost 'godlike' awareness of the ills around us, we will have to learn to accept that life, by its very nature, has its dangers and tragedies.

GLOSSARY

705.   The DNA message also includes various punctuation and control operations, such as 'start' (promoter sequences), 'stop' (termination sequences), and 'delete' (splicing junctions). For further details, *see Molecu-*

lar Biology of the Gene – Volume 1, James Watson et al (Benjamin/Cummings, Menlo Park, California, 1987).

The number of DNA bases in the entire nucleus varies greatly from organism to organism: an E.Coli bacterium has 4 million, a yeast cell 13.5 million, a fruit fly 165 million and a human 2,900 million. As to the physical dimensions of the DNA molecule, there are about 2,500 genes per millimeter. Thus the 2.9 billion bases in the human genome form a strand of DNA about 1 meter long folded into a bundle within the cell that is less than a hundredth of a millimeter . . . and yet this package can none the less be unraveled and read. *See Molecular Cell Biology,* James Darnell, Harvey Lodish and David Baltimore (Scientific American Books, New York, 1986).

706.   *See* note 133.

INDEX

Numbers in italic represent pages on which there are illustrations.